GREGORY THAUMATURGOS'
PARAPHRASE OF ECCLESIASTES

SOCIETY OF BIBLICAL LITERATURE
SEPTUAGINT AND COGNATE STUDIES SERIES

Series Editors
Claude E. Cox
William Adler

Number 29

GREGORY THAUMATURGOS'
PARAPHRASE OF ECCLESIASTES

John Jarick

GREGORY THAUMATURGOS'
PARAPHRASE OF ECCLESIASTES

John Jarick

Scholars Press
Atlanta, Georgia

GREGORY THAUMATURGOS' PARAPHRASE OF ECCLESIASTES

John Jarick

© 1990
Society of Biblical Literature

Library of Congress Cataloging-in-Publication Data

Gregory, Thaumaturgos, Saint, ca. 213-ca. 270.
  [Metaphrasis of Ecclesiastes. English]
  Gregory Thaumaturgos' paraphrase of Ecclesiastes / John Jarick.
  p. cm. -- (Septuagint and cognate studies series ; no. 29)
  Translated from classical Greek.
  Includes bibliographical references and index.
  ISBN 1-55540-484-7. -- ISBN 1-55540-485-5 (pbk.)
  1. Bible. O.T. Ecclesiastes--Paraphrases, Greek. 2. Bible.
O.T. Ecclesiastes--Paraphrases, Greek--Translations from Hebrew.
3. Bible. O.T. Ecclesiastes--Paraphrases, Greek--Translations into
English. 4. Bible. O.T. Ecclesiastes--Paraphrases, English-
-Translations from Greek. 5. Bible. O.T. Ecclesiastes-
-Parahrases, Greek--History and criticism. I. Jarick, John.
II. Title. III. Title: Paraphrase of Ecclesiastes. IV. Series.
BS1476.G7413 1990
223'.8048--dc20   90-39125
                                            CIP

Printed in the United States of America
on acid-free paper

CONTENTS

Preface — vii

Introduction
The Treatment of Ecclesiastes before Gregory — 1
Gregory and his Paraphrase — 4

Text, Translation, and Commentary
Chapter One — 7
Chapter Two — 27
Chapter Three — 55
Chapter Four — 81
Chapter Five — 109
Chapter Six — 137
Chapter Seven — 155
Chapter Eight — 195
Chapter Nine — 223
Chapter Ten — 249
Chapter Eleven — 277
Chapter Twelve — 289

Conclusion
The Linguistic Transformation — 309
The Theological Transformation — 311

Notes — 317
Bibliography — 361
Index — 369

PREFACE

Rabbi Judah said: "The one who translates a verse literally is a liar, and the one who adds anything is a blasphemer" (*Tosephta Megillah* 3:41). If this is so, then it must be frankly admitted that the earlier Greek translator of Ecclesiastes — the interpreter whose work now forms part of the Septuagint — is a liar, and the man who later sought to improve upon his work — "our holy father Gregory Thaumaturgos", as he is styled in the superscription to his paraphrase — is a blasphemer. What that makes the present writer, who has attempted to explain in English what these two Greek writers wrote, and how their words relate to what was written by the original Hebrew writer (as well as to the other classical versions of his words), I am not sure. I can only plead, as no doubt my two Greek predecessors would also plead in their own cases, that it was not my intention either to lie or to blaspheme.

If any untruths or impieties can nevertheless be detected in the following study, they are not the fault of Professor Taka-mitsu Muraoka, for whose guidance of the project I am most grateful. The original work, a dissertation submitted to the University of Melbourne in June 1988, was supported by a Commonwealth Postgraduate Research Award; its modification for the present series was supported by a Golda Meir Postdoctoral Fellowship at the Hebrew University of Jerusalem. In addition, my thanks are due to all the colleagues and friends who have assisted in various ways and have made these years of wrestling with the words of Koheleth and his interpreters seem — ironically, in view of Ecclesiastes 7:4 — like time spent more in the בית שמחה than in the בית אבל.

John Jarick
Jerusalem
January 1990

INTRODUCTION

The Treatment of Ecclesiastes before Gregory

When the Christian Church appropriated the Hebrew Bible, christening it "the Old Testament", they received as part of the collection of sacred Jewish writings "the words of Koheleth" — the little book of Ecclesiastes.

This book had not taken an unquestioned place in the canonical Scriptures. Indeed, it was a matter of rabbinic discussion at the time when the Christian Church was just beginning as to whether it should be employed in public reading and exposition or even in private reading and study.[1] The rabbinic literature preserves a tradition that "the Sages wished to withdraw the book of Ecclesiastes because its words are self-contradictory" (or "because they found in it matters which smacked of heresy"),[2] but that they did not withdraw it because upon closer examination they found "a reconciliation", namely that the book "begins with words of Torah and it ends with words of Torah". Also recorded is "a dispute concerning Ecclesiastes" as to whether or not this book, like "all the Holy Scriptures", "defiles the hands";[3] apparently Ecclesiastes was "among the lenient decisions of the School of Shammai and among the stringent decisions of the School of Hillel" (in other words, if the School of Shammai had had its way Ecclesiastes would not be in the Hebrew Bible), and "a tradition from the seventy-two elders on the day that Rabbi Eleazar ben Azariah was appointed head of the academy" said that Ecclesiastes did indeed "defile the hands" (which suggests that the rabbinical academy in Jamnia around the end of the first Christian century made a formal decision to accept Ecclesiastes as canonical).

No precise historical information can be gleaned from these traditions as to when and how Ecclesiastes was "canonised". The rabbinical discussions have the character of a scholarly controversy which in the end had to confirm a *fait accompli*, that the Jewish community had already accepted the book of Ecclesiastes as part of the collection of sacred Hebrew writings.[4] But the traditions do demonstrate just how serious and persistent were the doubts about the correctness of Ecclesiastes' inclusion in the Bible. Quite a number of the pious must have concluded, along with Rabbi Simeon ben Menasia in the second century, that it was not "composed under divine inspiration" but was "only the wisdom of Solomon",[5] and in his fourth-century commentary Jerome gives the impression that there were still Jews who were saying that the book ought not to be circulating because it asserts false teachings.[6]

But the authority of Solomon ultimately overpowered the many and strong reservations among the Jewish sages concerning the sacred character of Ecclesiastes. This scroll contained "the words of Koheleth, the son of David, king in Jerusalem" (1:1), and no-one doubted that the work was Solomon's; had it been thought that it had been composed by some ordinary, uninspired mortal — particularly after the time when the Immortal had ceased to inspire any prophets — there would hardly have been any support for its inclusion or retention in the collection of inspired writings.[7] Once it had taken its place in that collection, however, its context demanded that Solomon be seen to be speaking with an orthodox tongue, and so the problematic nature of the plain sense of the words was overcome by midrashic and allegorical expositions,[8] and the true meaning was shown to be in perfect harmony with Scripture as a whole.[9]

Thus "the words of Koheleth" gained and maintained a place in the Hebrew Bible, and consequently, under the Greek title of "Ecclesiastes", came to be part of the Christian Old Testament. But there is a great silence about this particular biblical book in the early Christian community. Not one of the New Testament writers ever quotes from Ecclesiastes with an impressive "It is written..." — indeed, none of them ever betrays any familiarity with Ecclesiastes at all, with the possible exception of Paul's statement to the Romans (8:20) that "creation was subjected to futility ($\mu\alpha\tau\alpha\iota\acute{o}\tau\eta\varsigma$)", which may be an allusion to Koheleth's dominant theme. There are a number of Old Testament books which are never cited in the New Testament writings,[10] and it is readily understandable why Ecclesiastes would be one of them. Its unique character would hardly commend it for prominent use by those who were overwhelmingly concerned with the gospel message, and it evidently did not affect the style or influence the thought of those who had searched the Scriptures for christological material.

Similarly, Ecclesiastes does not seem to have been in great favour with the Apostolic Fathers, for the only trace of it in their writings is in the seventh mandate of the *Shepherd of Hermas*,[11] where the shepherd instructs the visionary to "fear the Lord and keep his commandments" (φοβήθητι τὸν κύριον καὶ φύλασσε τὰς ἐντολὰς αὐτοῦ), in words closely resembling the "conclusion" of Ecclesiastes (12:13, τὸν θεὸν φοβοῦ καὶ τὰς ἐντολὰς αὐτοῦ φύλασσε).

In the third century the Fathers of the Church were beginning to use isolated verses of Ecclesiastes as proof texts,[12] so the book was gradually being appropriated by Christianity. Hippolytus of Rome and the great biblical scholar Origen wrote the first Christian commentaries on the book, but these highly significant works have been preserved only in a few fragments. Origen also made use of particular verses from Ecclesiastes in other of his voluminous writings,[13] and it is evident that he did not reject the study of this book in his academy — in contrast to the way in which the earlier Christians seem to have treated it.

Two of the men who studied under Origen[14] — Dionysius of Alexandria and Gregory Thaumaturgos — produced interpretive works on Ecclesiastes. Dionysius wrote a commentary, but only on the opening chapters of the book, and only fragments have survived.[15] Gregory, however, penned a complete paraphrase, and his work is still extant. As such, it is the earliest systematic Christian treatment of Ecclesiastes which has come down to us, and accordingly it invites investigation as a document offering first-hand insights into the way in which the Church sought to come to terms with this peculiar biblical book, the cause of so much puzzlement for Rabbis and Fathers alike.[16]

Gregory and his Paraphrase

The man who produced the first Christian version of
Ecclesiastes had been born in Neocaesarea in Pontus about the
year 213. The son of pagan parents, Gregory had travelled in his
youth to various cities in order to pursue studies aimed at
preparing him for a career in law, until at Caesarea in Palestine
he came under the influence of Origen, who had recently
opened a school there after leaving Alexandria. Converted to
Christianity and imbued with a love for the great teacher and his
philosophy, Gregory returned to Neocaesarea, where he became
that city's first bishop — an office in which he was so successful
that many legends grew up concerning miraculous powers on
his part, such that Christian tradition has given him the
surname Θαυματουργός, "wonder-worker". After an earnest
and faithful ministry of many years, he died about the year 270.[17]

Some time during his years as Bishop of Neocaesarea, or
perhaps already as a student in Caesarea, Gregory set about
paraphrasing the book of Ecclesiastes. It may be that some of his
flock were having difficulties with this book — perhaps Gregory
had heard it said by those under his spiritual care that
Ecclesiastes was not a Christian book, or perhaps some had
interpreted the book in ways with which their bishop could not
agree. On the other hand, it may be that Gregory himself was
particularly fascinated by "the words of Koheleth", and wished to
render them in a form which would make them readily
accessible to a people who had been overlooking them.

It is not difficult to see why Gregory should have set
himself the task of re-expressing in readily-understandable form
a book which would have appeared to many to be the most
difficult to understand in all of the Scriptures. In his *Panegyric
to Origen*, delivered when he "graduated" from his beloved
teacher's academy, Gregory had confessed his admiration for
Origen's ability to

> interpret and make clear whatever was dark and enigmatical, such as are
> many utterances of the sacred voices, whether because it is God's wont to
> speak thus to man, that the Divine word may not enter in bare and
> unveiled to some soul unworthy, as most are; or else, although every
> oracle of God is naturally most clear and simple, yet by reason of time and

antiquity it has come to seem indistinct and dark to us who have revolted
from God and have unlearned how to hear;[18]

and he had expressed the hope that in the future he might bear
"the fruits and the sheaves of these seeds" which he had received from Origen.[19] In interpreting and making clear the dark
and enigmatical utterances of Koheleth, Gregory is fulfilling his
hope; he is following in his mentor's footsteps,[20] enabling
people to hear a sacred voice they had been unable to hear aright.

The voice in which Koheleth had been speaking to the early
Christians was that of the Septuagint, the authoritative Old
Testament of the Church and certainly the principal, if not the
only, text in front of Gregory as he laboured on his own version.
In the case of Ecclesiastes, the Septuagint is a particularly literal
translation of the Hebrew text — so literal that it looks suspiciously like the work of Aquila, who had aimed at a faithful and
consistent representation of the Hebrew original in opposition to
the widely divergent Septuagint. "Septuagint" Ecclesiastes
betrays prominent Aquilan characteristics, notably the representation of אח by σύν even when the former is merely functioning
as the sign of the accusative, the representation of the prepositional *beth* by ἐν regardless of the sense of the passage, and the
absence of the particles δέ and γάρ (which are so common in
Greek literature and in the Septuagint).[21] It may not be Aquila's
final version of Ecclesiastes, as it does not tally exactly with
extracts of that work which are known to us,[22] but it does seem as
though the earlier Septuagint translators had neglected to translate a book which in their time and place may not have been in
favour, and so a translation made by a later hand had to be incorporated into the collection[23] — or that the translation which
they had made fell out of favour itself and was replaced by one
which was felt to be preferable to it.[24] But whoever is responsible
for what came to be transmitted as the Septuagint text of
Ecclesiastes, the fact is that it is written in a style quite foreign to
Greek literature, and for that reason, too — in addition to the
strangeness of its ideas in a biblical context — it was an eminent
candidate for re-expression in readily-understandable Greek.

It might be expected that Gregory would have consulted the
Hebrew or other versions of Ecclesiastes. He had studied for five

years under the scholar who produced the Hexapla and who was not afraid to emend the authoritative Septuagint where it was inaccurate when compared both with the Hebrew text and with other Greek translations.[25] In Gregory's *Panegyric to Origen*, in which he gives interesting particulars of what and how the master taught his disciples, he makes no mention of receiving any instruction in the Hebrew language — in fact, he claims to have had difficulty with the Greek and Latin languages,[26] but this smacks of rhetorical modesty. It is evident that Gregory had quite a flair for Greek composition, but he may well have remained completely ignorant of the Jewish tongue.[27] Nevertheless, if he had access to the Hexapla of Ecclesiastes,[28] then more than just the Septuagintal understanding of a given verse was open to him. At the very least, we might anticipate that he was aware of Symmachus' efforts at producing an acceptable Greek rendering.[29] But, as we shall see, it appears that Gregory had only the Septuagint in front of him when he undertook his task.

The Greek composition which Gregory produced bears the title Μετάφρασις εἰς τὸν Ἐκκλησιαστὴν τοῦ Σολομῶντος,[30] "A Paraphrase of Solomon's 'Ecclesiastes'". Actually, most of the manuscripts assign the work to Gregory of Nazianzus rather than to Gregory Thaumaturgos, but both Jerome (*Famous Men*, 65) and Rufinus (*Ecclesiastical History*, book 7, ch. 25) are sure that it is an authentic work of the latter Gregory.[31] The edition used for the following study is that printed in Jacques-Paul Migne's *Patrologia Graeca*, vol. 10 (Turnholt: Brepols, 1978 [a reprint of the Paris edition of 1857]), cols. 987-1018, where the title includes the words τοῦ ἐν ἁγίοις πατρὸς ἡμῶν Γρηγορίου τοῦ Θαυματουργοῦ, "by our holy father Gregory Thaumaturgos".

The following study will examine this paraphrase in detail, giving a verse-by-verse[32] translation and commentary — with particular comparative attention to the Septuagint (hereafter LXX), and to the Hebrew text (hereafter MT) when this differs from or sheds particular light upon its Greek translation,[33] but also taking due note of the other early interpreters of Koheleth's words[34] — before drawing conclusions on Gregory's paraphrastic enterprise and the place of his version in the history of the Church's appropriation and interpretation of Ecclesiastes.

TEXT, TRANSLATION, and COMMENTARY

Chapter One

(1) Τάδε λέγει Σαλομών,[1] ὁ τοῦ Δαβὶδ βασιλέως καὶ προφήτου παῖς ἁπάσῃ τῇ τοῦ Θεοῦ Ἐκκλησίᾳ, παρὰ πάντας ἀνθρώπους βασιλεὺς ἐντιμότατος, καὶ προφήτης σοφώτατος.

Solomon (the son of the king and prophet David), a king more honoured and a prophet wiser than anyone else, speaks to the whole assembly of God:

The introductory verse of Ecclesiastes has its mysteries removed by Gregory Thaumaturgos. The original sage's anonymity had been preserved behind the somewhat puzzling title קֹהֶלֶת, but LXX translated this as ἐκκλησιαστής (a derivative of ἐκκλησία, on the postulation of קֹהֶלֶת being a derivative of קהל) and accordingly Gregory understands the writer to have been "one who speaks to the ἐκκλησία"; moreover, he identifies this speaker as none other than the great Solomon, an identification in keeping with the then unquestioned view that the royal patron of Wisdom in Israel was the author of the book of Ecclesiastes. For Gregory there was no question that the person of Solomon might be merely a literary disguise adopted for the early section of the book but soon dropped once its purpose had been served; the paraphrase has it that all which is to follow came from the very lips of Solomon himself.

Lest any reader should doubt Solomon's right to a hearing, we are told that he and his father David were both kings and prophets; moreover, the two superlatives (of ἔντιμος and of σοφός) make it clear that the son far outshone the father — and all other mortals — with respect to honour and wisdom. The text before Gregory was content with one simple βασιλεύς which could ambiguously refer either to Δαυίδ or to his υἱός, or to both. Gregory takes it to refer to both men, and makes it unambiguously do so by using the word βασιλεύς twice, adding the reference προφήτης twice in order to record the wider role which he believes these two servants of God to have played. The additional title of προφήτης also adds a more religiously valid authority to what is to be said than that which the words of a merely secular βασιλεύς might otherwise possess, and it allows for a prophetic interpretation of certain passages in the book, culminating in the great "allegory of old age" of 12:1-7.[2]

Gregory's formulation here recalls 1 Kings 8:14,15, where Solomon is also recorded as speaking to the whole ἐκκλησία. It is of course quite specifically the "assembly of Israel" which is there addressed, and here too the biblical text locates ἐκκλησιαστής in Jerusalem (LXX includes a reference to Israel as well). But in Gregory's paraphrase these Jewish national references have given way to the phrase "ἐκκλησία of God", which can include — or even exclusively denote — the Church.[3] Also noteworthy is the use of the present tense: Gregory has λέγει, as opposed to LXX's εἶπεν (in the next verse).

The combined effect of all these elements in the introductory verse of the paraphrase is to give to the reader the impression that the book of Ecclesiastes, far from being merely the thoughts once expressed by some unknown Hebrew sage or even an address once given by a well-known Israelite king, is a sermon being preached to God's congregation by the wisest of his chosen prophets. Each Christian reader, as part of "the whole ἐκκλησία of God", is assured that Solomon's words are also directed to him.

(2) Ὡς κενὰ καὶ ἀνόνητα τὰ τῶν ἀνθρώπων πράγματά τε καὶ σπουδάσματα, ὅσα ἀνθρώπινα.

How empty and useless human activites and all human pursuits are!

At the very beginning of his sermon, Solomon announces his theme. The Hebrew text had employed the word הבל, which has a concrete meaning of "breath" or "vapour" and thus also carries the abstract nuances of transitoriness and unsubstantiality. LXX captured this figurative sense with ματαιότης, "emptiness, foolishness",[4] but in mimicking the Hebrew means of expressing the superlative degree (ματαιότης ματαιοτήτων for הבל הבלים) did not express the sense of the Hebrew in good Greek. Gregory's paraphrastic enterprise frees him from the Semitic

forms to which the LXX translator had felt himself bound, and
prompts him to use various synonyms of ματαιότης — κενός
and ἀνόνητος in this verse, and others to appear later in the book
(on occasion he does employ a derivative of ματαιότης, but he is
quite uninfluenced by the more literal rendering of ἀτμός,
"vapour" on the part of Symmachus, Theodotion, and Aquila).
With such variations, Gregory avoids the repetitiveness of the
earlier version, which presented ματαιότης no less than five
times in this single verse alone and over thirty times elsewhere
in the book.
      He also avoids the all-embracing scope of this opening
pronouncement. "All is ματαιότης" embraced not only human
labour (v. 3) but also the ceaseless cycles of nature (vv. 4 ff.), but
Gregory limits it to the first of these by introducing two nouns to
govern his judgmental adjectives: human πράγματα, "things
done" and σπουδάσματα, "things eagerly pursued" are what are
to be pronounced κενός and ἀνόνητος. The futility of human
strivings was indeed a major preoccupation of Koheleth, so
Gregory is not doing him a great injustice by specifying it here,
but it does seem that he is concerned to remove the possibility of
having ματαιότης attributed to the work of the Creator — an
impression strengthened by his rounding off of the verse with ὅ
σα ἀνθρώπινα, emphasising that it is human matters which are
in view.[5]

      (3) Οὐδὲ γὰρ ἔχει τις εἰπεῖν ὄφελός τι τούτοις προσηρτημένον,
ἅπερ ἄνθρωποι περὶ[6] γῆν ἕρποντες, καὶ σώμασι καὶ ψυχαῖς
ἐκτελέσαι σπεύδουσι, τῶν μὲν προσκαίρων ἡττημένοι, ἀνωτέρω δὲ
τῶν ἄστρων τῷ γενναίῳ τῆς ψυχῆς ὄμματι, οὐδ᾽ ὁτιοῦν κατιδεῖν
βουλόμενοι.

      **Nor can anyone say that there is any use connected with the
things which human beings, crawling on the earth, are striving
to achieve by physical and mental effort. They have given
themselves over to transitory things, not wanting to look —
with the soul's noble eye — at anything higher than the stars.**

      Koheleth here posed a rhetorical question, expecting a
negative answer. Gregory agrees that no-one can give an

affirmative answer, and adds the reason why this should be so. The question was: Is there any use (LXX περισσεία, "surplus, abundance") in human striving (LXX μοχθέω, "to be weary with toil")? Gregory's Kohelethine answer is: No, there is no use (ὄφελος, "advantage, profit") in human striving (σπεύδω, "to be eager/anxious, to press on")! His non-Kohelethine reason follows immediately: humans are striving for the transitory (πρόσκαιρος, "lasting but for a time") rather than for the heavenly (ἀνωτέρω τῶν ἄστρων, "above the stars"); for the one who has eyes to see, there is more than ματαιότης.

One of Koheleth's favourite expressions, "under the sun" (LXX ὑπὸ τὸν ἥλιον) receives a new formulation in the paraphrase: "upon the earth" (περὶ γῆν), which is essentially the same thing (cf. LXX ἐπὶ τῆς γῆς, 8:14) — unless we take it to mean "in the dust", in which case Gregory may be intending a moralistic nuance not present in Koheleth's expression. In any case Gregory supplies a contrary expression not present in the original book — namely the phrase ἀνωτέρω τῶν ἄστρων mentioned above — and thus introduces a perspective quite unknown to the original author. Koheleth's keen observations of life had led him to his proclamation of futility and his belief that human beings were incapable of discovering truth, but Gregory makes him say that there is another method of observation (the eye of the ψυχή) and that it is actually a matter of human beings being unwilling to lift themselves above futility and to discover truth.[7]

(4) Καὶ κατατρίβεται ὁ τῶν ἀνθρώπων βίος ἡμέραν ἐξ ἡμέρας, καὶ ὡρῶν καὶ ἐνιαυτῶν περιόδους, ἡλίου τε δρόμους περιωρισμένους, τῶν μὲν παραγινομένων, τῶν δὲ ὑπαπαιρόντων. Ἔοικε δὲ τὸ πρᾶγμα, χειμάρρων παρόδῳ, ἀμετρήτῳ θαλάσσης ἐμπιπτόντων βυθῷ σὺν ταράχῳ πολλῷ. Καὶ τὰ μὲν δι' ἀνθρώπους ὑπὸ Θεοῦ γεγονότα, μένει τὰ αὐτά, οἷον, τὸ ἀπὸ γῆς γεννᾶσθαι, τὸ εἰς γῆν ἀπιέναι, τὸ αὐτὴν ἑστάναι τὴν γῆν, ...

Human life is worn down day by day, and in the cycles of seasons and years, and the defined courses of the sun — there are people coming and people passing away. It is like the movement of torrents rushing with great commotion into the im-

mense depths of the sea. The things created by God for the sake of the human race remain unchanged. For example, we come from dust and return to dust, while the earth itself goes on.

Gregory seems to offer two alternative paraphrases of Koheleth's little poem on the ceaseless cycles of nature. The first alternative consists of the first two sentences above, and sees the realms of humanity and nature in comparative terms. The second, beginning with the third sentence above and continuing on in the verses to follow below, sees those two realms in contrastive terms.

At first Gregory draws together the pictures of the generations coming and going (from v. 4), the sun running its course (from v. 5), and the rivers running into the sea (from v. 7) to draw a comparison between the continual procession of human beings and the continuous processes of nature. The blowing of the wind (from v. 6) is missing, and the order of the processing (in v. 4) is reversed: LXX πορεύομαι followed by ἔρχομαι, but Gregory παραγίγνομαι followed by ὑπαπαίρω[8] (to be echoed by γεννάομαι followed by ἄπειμι later in the verse). But Gregory is true to the picture which had been painted before him: δρόμος, "race-course, running" is employed for the place where the sun is feverishly engaged in its rounds (in v. 5 LXX pictured the sun's activities by means of the verb ἕλκω, "drag, pull" [MT's imagery is שאף, "gasp, pant"], but Gregory may have an eye on δραμεῖν, "run" in the analogous passage of LXX Psalm 18:6,7 [English 19:5,6]); χείμαρρος, "a torrent swollen by winter rain" does service for the streams which run into the sea (cf. LXX χείμαρρος, v. 7, where Gregory opts for ποταμός); ἀμέτρητος βυθός, "the immeasurable depths of the sea" gets across the idea of the sea not being filled (LXX οὐκ ἐμπιμπλάμενος); and κατατρίβω, "wear out, exhaust" is a very appropriate word to introduce to this context. Gregory thus approaches Koheleth's meaning: the procession of generations and the processes of nature are part of a ceaseless, goalless cycle.[9]

But then Gregory backs away from this unsettling formulation, and begins again. This time he will make it clear that there is a distinction between what God does on the one hand (τὰ μὲν... ὑπὸ Θεοῦ γεγονότα, in this verse) and what human beings do on the other hand (τὰ δ' ὑπ' ἀνθρώπων ἐπιτεχνώμενα, in v. 8). He will not allow Solomon to suggest that the works of the Creator are also characterised by ματαιότης — rather, they are characterised by permanence and reliability, as the verbs μένω and ἵστημι indicate.

And far be it from Solomon to suggest that God acts against human interests (as Koheleth's complaint seems to have been in 1:13 and 3:11, for example); in fact God has acted δι' ἀνθρώπους, Gregory's Solomon assures us.

He also reminds us of our creatureliness by clearly employing the two senses of the word γῆ, which LXX used in this verse for ארץ and in 3:20 (and in Genesis 3:19, to which that verse alludes) for עפר. Combining the thoughts of Koheleth in those two verses, Gregory creates a hybrid thought: the creature is brought forth from γῆ, and dissolves back into γῆ, but the γῆ itself remains.

(5) ... τὸ τὸν ἥλιον ἅπασαν αὐτὴν ἐκπεριϊόντα, πάλιν εἰς τὸν αὐτὸν περιτρέχειν ὅρον, ...

The sun does a complete circle, running around to the same place again.

For the first time, Gregory makes no significant changes or additions to a verse. He merely summarises the sun's "rising up" (LXX ἀνατέλλω) and its "going down" (LXX δύνω) by speaking simply of its "going round" (ἐκπερίειμι), and he uses ὅρος, "limit, landmark" (already reflected in the περιωρισμένος, "defined, marked out by boundaries" of v. 4) for LXX's τόπος, "place".

(6) ... καὶ τὰ πνεύματα ὡσαύτως, ...

It is the same with the winds, ...

Koheleth now itemised the incessant movements of the wind, blowing to the south and then to the north, ceaselessly moving around and around in circuits comparable to the sun's continual rotation (in fact LXX translated the first half of this verse as still referring to the sun's movements). Gregory does not want to bore his readers by being so repetitive, so he opts for a short, sharp ὡσαύτως, "in like manner, just so". But through such brevity the impression conveyed by Koheleth's repetitiveness — namely the monotony of nature's cycles, going around and around without achieving anything meaningful — is lost.[10]

It has been proposed that Gregory's text should read ῥεύματα, "streams" instead of πνεύματα, "winds".[11] True, he mentions winds (ἄνεμοι) again later in the sentence, but it is there the sea-winds which he has in mind. To mention the πνεύματα in general here, immediately after referring to the ἥλιος (v. 5) and immediately before referring to the ποταμοί (v. 7), is quite in keeping with the order of reference in the biblical text (LXX ἥλιος, πνεῦμα, χείμαρροι).

(7) ... τούς τε ποταμοὺς τοσούτους εἰς θάλασσαν ἐκδιδόντας, καὶ τοὺς ἀνέμους ἐμπίπτοντας, μὴ ἀναγκάζειν αὐτὴν ὑπερβαίνειν τὰ αὐτῆς μέτρα, μηδὲ αὐτοὺς παρανομεῖν. Καὶ τὰ μὲν ὡς εἰς τουτονὶ συντελοῦντα ἡμῖν τὸν βίον, οὕτως ἄραρε.

... and the mighty rivers which empty into the sea, and the winds which blow hard against it. They do not force an overstepping of the mark, nor do they break the natural laws. It is only right that such things, which affect our lives, should be that way.

Once again Koheleth spelt out the fact that the processes of nature — in this case the movement of water — are cyclical and never achieve any meaningful goal, and once again Gregory's brevity means that this impression is lost. He was truer to Koheleth's picture in his first depiction of the streams moving to the sea, as we noted in v. 4. For variation, he now uses ποταμός, "river" (the word chosen by Symmachus, but a natural enough synonym for Gregory to have hit upon it unaided) for v. 4's χείμαρρος (which LXX had here in v. 7) and ἐκδίδωμι, "give up, empty" for ἐμπίπτω, "fall upon, burst in" (LXX had used the more prosaic πορεύομαι, "go"), but is content to leave θάλασσα, "sea" unvaried. The close proximity of reference to wind (v. 6) and sea (v. 7) prompts Gregory to add a phrase concerning the sea-winds, perhaps because of the distrustful attitude the ancient Hebrews had had towards the sea (or because of an unpleasant

experience Gregory himself had had with the sea?). The use of
ἄνεμος provides more variation (he had just used πνεῦμα in v.
6) and the use once again of ἐμπίπτω provides an analogy
between the movements of the two elements of water (v. 4) and
air (v. 7), which are thus both pictured as beating against the sea.
Gregory concludes the brief inventory of natural processes
by offering a positive appraisal of what has been pictured.
Koheleth's evident appraisal, though not explicitly stated, seems
to have been: Nature, like human beings, never gets anywhere.
Gregory's evident appraisal, explicitly stated, is: Nature, unlike
human beings, never gets out of line. The contrasting human
situation will be in focus in v. 8; here we are told that the verbs
ὑπερβαίνω, "overstep, transgress" and παρανομέω, "transgress
the law" do not hold true of the natural situation. (The
feminine entity referred to in the phrase μὴ ἀναγκάζειν αὐτὴν
ὑπερβαίνειν τὰ αὐτῆς μέτρα, literally "they do not force her to
overstep her mark", is presumably "the earth" mentioned
earlier in the sentence — γῆ, v. 4 — or, we might say, "Mother
Nature".)   According to Genesis, God had pronounced his
creation to be "good" (LXX καλός);   accordingly, Gregory's
Solomon now pronounces it to be "fitting" (ἄραρε). Μέν here
quickly recaps the μέν at the beginning of the long sentence just
completed, before the δέ to follow immediately in v. 8; εἰς
τουτονὶ συντελοῦντα ἡμῖν τὸν βίον echoes δι' ἀνθρώπους in v. 4.

     (8) Τὰ δ' ὑπ' ἀνθρώπων ἐπιτεχνώμενα ῥήματά τε καὶ
πράγματα, μέτρον οὐκ ἔχει. Καὶ λόγων πολὺς μὲν ὅμιλος, ὄνησις
δὲ οὐδεμία ἀπὸ τῆς πεπλανημένης φλυαρίας· ἀλλ' ἄπληστόν ἐστι
τὸ τῶν ἀνθρώπων φῦλον, πρός τε τὸ λέγειν, πρός τε τὸ ἑτέρου
λέγοντος ἀκούειν· ἔτι δὲ καὶ τὸ ὄμμασιν εἰκαίοις ἕκαστα τῶν
παραπιπτόντων ὁρᾶν γλίχεσθαι.

     **But the things which human beings contrive — both words
and actions — have no limit. There is a great multitude of
words, but there is no use in rambling, foolish talk. Yet the
human race is never satisfied, as regards talking and listening to
what others are saying, and wanting to look — with indis-
criminate eyes — at everything that is going on.**

The conclusion which Koheleth made to his little poem on the ceaseless cycles of nature is considerably amended by Gregory. The Hebrew sage remarked that the processes of nature are so wearisome (LXX ἔγκοπος) in their monotony and pointlessness that the matter cannot adequately be put into words, but the Christian paraphrast feels that too many improper matters **are** put into words by people, who do not behave as nature behaves — in accordance with the correct "rule, standard" (μέτρον, echoing the μέτρα to which nature adheres [in the previous verse]). Where Koheleth had indicated the human response to nature's behaviour, Gregory depicts human behaviour in contradistinction to nature's behaviour.

Despite this revision of meaning, and a reversal of the order of "seeing" and "hearing" (LXX ὁράω before ἀκρόασις, but Gregory ἀκούω before ὁράω), Gregory's rounding-off of this section (vv. 3-8) is well composed: ὄνησις (v. 8) recalls ὄφελος (v.3), γλίχομαι recalls σπεύδω, ῥήματα καὶ πράγματα — which take into account the possible ambiguity of λόγοι (דברים) — are the respective products of σῶμα καὶ ψυχή (though again in the reverse order), and what people are looking at with their natural ὄμμα in v. 8 recalls the lament about what they are not looking at with their spiritual ὄμμα in v. 3. For Gregory, then, the way in which nature functions should be an example to humankind, to live as God intends; for Koheleth, it had been an example of ματαιότης.

(9) Τί[12] ἂν γένοιτο ὕστερον, ὅπερ οὐκ ἤδη τετέλεσται, ἢ πραχθείη πρὸς ἀνθρώπων; Τί καινὸν τὸ μηδέπω εἰς πεῖραν ἐλθόν, ὅτου καὶ μνησθῆναι ἄξιον;

What can happen in the future, or what can be done by human beings, that has not been done already? What new thing is there that has not been tried yet, that is worth mentioning?

Koheleth now stated that "what has been, will be". LXX interpreted this sentence, on the basis of its form with מה and הוא, as an interrogative clause with τίς and an answering clause with αὐτός: "What has been? The same as what will be!"[13] In both versions this was paralleled by a second sentence concerning "what has been done". Gregory, taking his cue from LXX, phrases his paraphrase as a rhetorical question, combining the two concepts of happening (γίγνομαι, as in LXX) and doing (πράσσω for LXX's ποιέω) into one sentence.

Koheleth followed up with the statement that "there is nothing new under the sun". LXX did not interpret this sentence as an interrogative clause, but Gregory again expresses it in the form of a question, perhaps because he was influenced by the form of the opening of the next verse. He employs the straightforward καινός here and then πρόσφατος, "fresh-slaughtered, late" in v. 10, whereas LXX had used πρόσφατος here and καινός in v. 10 (Symmachus has καινός in both places, just as MT has שׁדח in both places; Gregory repeats καινός in the latter place). His equivalent to ὑπὸ τὸν ἥλιον comes in the first part of the verse instead of at the end: πρὸς ἀνθρώπων, which does not at all carry an equivalent meaning. For Koheleth, it was the works of God in this world no less than the activities of human beings which he meant to depict as repetitive; he saw nothing καινός in all creation. Not surprisingly for someone who believed that the Creator had instituted a διαθήκη καινή,[14] Gregory is concerned to restrict the frame of reference here to the works of the creature.

(10) Ἐγὼ μὲν γὰρ οἶμαι οὐδέν, ὅ τι δ' ἂν εἴπῃ[15] πρόσφατον, ἢ καινὸν ἀναλογιζόμενος εὑρήσει, μηδὲ τοῖς πάλαι ἄγνωστον.

I believe that there is nothing that you can call "fresh", or that you will find, after thinking it over, to be new or unknown to people in the past.

There was no mention in Ecclesiastes that what was written here was merely personal opinion; the impression was rather that straight facts were being presented.[16] Gregory may begin v. 10 with ἐγὼ οἶμαι (= οἴομαι), "I suppose, think, believe" for stylistic reasons — to introduce Solomon's answer to the questions he had posed in v. 9 — or for theological reasons — to imply that although Solomon in his day would reasonably have held this view, it is not necessarily a view which has to be shared by those who live in the last days.

Τοῖς πάλαι is most probably a reference to those who lived in olden days. If it were a neuter form, referring simply to "the past", we would expect the singular rather than the plural article, although the latter is conceivable.[17] It is also conceivable that LXX's αἰῶνες is to be understood, such that the expression refers to "past ages", but we would expect that meaning to be made evident if it was intended. The most straightforward interpretation of οἱ πάλαι is that ἄνθρωποι is to be understood and the meaning is to be taken as "the ancients", an alternative expression (employing the adverb πάλαι rather than the adjective παλαιός) to οἱ παλαιοί. The expression is paralleled by οἱ μετέπειτα in the next verse, which supports the interpretation of οἱ πάλαι as "the people of old" (see comments under v. 11). It seems that Gregory is seeking to improve on the literary structure of his predecessor by placing at the end of v. 10, not a precise parallel to the ending of v. 10 (LXX αἰῶνες... ἀπὸ ἔμπροσθεν ἡμῶν, the "ages before us"), but a precise antithetical parallel to the ending of v. 11 ("the people of the future").

(11) Ὥσπερ δὲ τὰ πρότερα λήθῃ κέκρυπται, οὕτω καὶ τὰ ἐνεστῶτα, εἰς τοὺς μετέπειτα χρόνῳ ἀμαυρωθήσεται.

Just as earlier things have been consigned to oblivion, so current things will in time become dim to people in the future.

LXX's τοῖς πρώτοις and τοῖς ἐσχάτοις could be either masculine or neuter, and so could mean either "the first, and last, people" or "the first, and last, things", whereas MT's ראשנים and אחרנים are masculine, and so probably mean "earlier people" and "later people" respectively (since "earlier things" and "later things" would most likely have been expressed by the feminine). In paraphrasing these expressions as τὰ πρότερα and τὰ ἐνεστῶτα, clearly neuter and so undoubtedly meaning "earlier things" and "things at hand", Gregory has taken his cue from a possibility more evident in LXX than MT; even so, in spite of LXX's narrowly-literal translations of ראשון by πρῶτος and אחרון by ἔσχατος, Gregory's rendering is actually more in keeping with the evident meanings of the Hebrew words in this context: πρότερος and ὕστερος.

Ὕστερος itself is not actually used by Gregory, but rather two alternatives to it. The reason for this is no doubt to avoid the somewhat confusing formulation of the biblical text, which repeated the equivalent words: "there is no remembrance of those who have been[18] τοῖς ἐσχάτοις by those who will be εἰς τὴν ἐσχάτην." Gregory reformulates this as, in effect: "there is no remembrance of τὰ ἐνεστῶτα (things just beginning or just about to happen) by οἱ μετέπειτα (those who come later)." The latter expression is evidently a masculine form, unlike its opposite number οἱ (or τὰ) πάλαι in the previous verse, and it paraphrases Kohelethine phrases which appear to have been referring to people — further justification for the translation "the people of the past" at the end of v.10 and "the people of the future" at the end of v.11.

It is interesting that Gregory makes no use of LXX's ἔσχατος, even though — particularly in its second occurrence (εἰς τὴν ἐσχάτην, "until the last") — it seems to invite a Christian interpreter to give an eschatological meaning to this verse, such that the pattern which Koheleth had described of generation passing after generation, with no remembrance of what has happened or been done in the past, will not go on forever.[19] Gregory ignores this possibility, however, and retains Koheleth's less prophetic meaning. But he does not feel constrained to retain Koheleth's negative construction; instead of saying that "there is no μνήμη (remembrance)", he says in effect that "there is λήθη (forgetfulness)".[20]

(12) Καὶ οὐκ αὐτοσχεδιάζω ταῦτα νῦν ἐκκλησιάζων· ἀλλά μοι βασιλείαν Ἑβραίων ἐν Ἱεροσολύμοις πεπιστευμένῳ, ἱκανῶς ἅπαντα πεφρόντισται.

Now in addressing the assembly, I am not saying these things thoughtlessly, but — since I have been entrusted with the kingdom of the Hebrews in Jerusalem — it has all been fully considered by me.

The reappearance of the title ἐκκλησιαστής in the text before Gregory prompts him to use the verb ἐκκλησιάζω, "attend or address an ἐκκλησία", for the Christian reader carrying the idea of preaching in a church service. This treatment of the writer's *nom de plume* was already established in v. 1 of the paraphrase, where Gregory had named the speaker as Solomon but omitted any national references. Here he does not add the name again, but neither does he dispense with the Jewish identification: being entrusted with the βασιλεία Ἐβραίων parallels LXX's being βασιλεὺς ἐπὶ Ἰσραήλ, and Ἰεροσόλυμα is an alternative form for LXX's Ἰερουσαλήμ. These identifications here serve to reinforce the idea that such a speaker would not speak unadvisedly or in an off-handed way (αὐτοσχεδιάζω), but only after sufficient reflection (ἱκανῶς πεφρόντισται).

LXX's aorist formulation ἐγενόμην (even more strongly than MT's perfect formulation הייתי) gives the impression that the writer is not the βασιλεύς at the time of writing. In reality, of course, the writer (Koheleth) never was king, and was simply looking back to the time when the historical personage whose role he was now assuming (Solomon) was king. But for an interpreter who believed that Solomon was the actual writer, the formulation "was king" would present difficulties.[21] Gregory solves the problem by taking the meaning as "became king". Thus he offers in paraphrase the perfect passive participle of πιστεύω, "believe", here in the sense of "entrust" — having Solomon recall that he has been entrusted with the kingdom removes the implication that he is no longer exercising kingly office at the time of delivering his address to the assembly, and at the same time adds the implication that he recognises that his office has been granted to him by God, an appropriate implication for one who preaches (ἐκκλησιάζω).

(13) Ζητήσας δὲ μεμελημένος, καὶ σοφῶς κατανοήσας τὴν περὶ γῆν φύσιν ἅπασαν, ποικιλωτάτην ἔγνων, ὡς ἀνθρώπῳ δέδοται πονεῖν ἐπὶ γῆς, ἄλλοτε ἀλλοίᾳ καμάτου προφάσει ἐγκαλινδουμένῳ εἰς τὸ μηδέν.

I thoughtfully examined and wisely learnt the nature of everything on earth. I discovered that it was all very complex, because human beings are allowed to toil away on earth, wallowing about uselessly in various kinds of pretentious effort at various times.

Gregory begins this verse by sticking fairly closely to the basic pattern established by the text before him, particularly if we take μεμελημένος, "giving care or thought to" as a parallel to "I applied my heart" (i.e., "I put my mind to": LXX ἔδωκα τὴν καρδίαν μου).

Thus he has ζητέω, "seek" for LXX's ἐκζητέω, "seek out"; κατανοέω, "observe" for κατασκέπτομαι, "view closely"; σοφῶς, "wisely" for ἐν τῇ σοφίᾳ, "by wisdom"; ἅπας, "all" for πᾶς, "all"; and περὶ γῆν, "relating to earth" for ὑπὸ τὸν οὐρανόν, "under heaven". Gregory offered περὶ γῆν also in v. 3 for ὑπὸ τὸν ἥλιον, "under the sun", so it may be that the manuscript in front of him had ἥλιος here too,[22] but this need not be presupposed since all these expressions mean essentially the same thing. Gregory's "everything on earth" is a simplified version of LXX's "everything that happens (γίγνομαι) under heaven" — MT's "everything that is done (עשׂה niphal) under heaven", which could be taken as limiting "Solomon's" investigation to human toil, would probably have suited Gregory better. But even if the Hebrew text was closed to him, we might nevertheless expect, in the light of his πρὸς ἀνθρώπων in v. 9, that Gregory would make a similar explicit delimitation here (and especially in the next verse, where both MT and LXX seem to have done so), but perhaps he thinks the use of ἄνθρωπος in the second part of this verse and in v. 15 does this well enough, or perhaps he deliberately intends not to limit his range of investigation (see comments on v. 14).

In the second part of this verse Gregory departs from the basic pattern before him when Koheleth stated that "God has burdened human beings with an evil task" (LXX περισπασμός, signifying something which distracts or disturbs a person). This simple statement that the Creator is responsible for the human plight would not sit well with a pious reader. Gregory's approach is to remark on the exceedingly complex (ποικίλος, "many-coloured, elaborate, ambiguous") nature of things, implying that no-one should jump to the kind of conclusion to which Koheleth had in fact jumped, and to remove the word θεός in favour of the impersonal construction δίδοται, "it is given, granted, permitted", opening the possible implication of human responsibility for the things they choose to do (ἄλλοτε ἀλλοίᾳ καμάτου, "various kinds of effort at various times"). The two expressions πρόφασις, "pretence" and ἐγκαλινδούμενος, "wallowing or rolling about in" strengthen the impression that human beings have chosen their distress (κάματος) rather than had it determined for them by a hard God.

(14) Πνεύματος δὲ ἀλλοκότου καὶ μυσαροῦ τὰ κάτω ἄπαντα πλήθει, ...

Everything down here is full of a strange, foul spirit.

רעות/רעיון רוח was a favourite expression of Koheleth, occurring nine times in his work (seven times paralleled by הבל) but nowhere else in the Hebrew Bible. Quite likely it should be rendered "desire of wind", denoting an aimless and futile striving after something transitory and unattainable.[23] LXX's rendering in all instances was προαίρεσις πνεύματος, "choice of wind", which might similarly denote the empty pursuit of the unsubstantial. But there is always an ambiguity about רוח and πνεῦμα, such that the expression might be taken as "desire or choice of spirit". This latter interpretation seems particularly facilitated by LXX, with its coupling of προαίρεσις, "deliberate choice, purpose" and πνεῦμα, "wind, spirit", for just as προαίρεσις βίου is "a plan of life" and προαίρεσις πολιτείας is "a governmental policy", so προαίρεσις πνεύματος sounds like "a spiritual plan or policy". Thus LXX's formulation could promote the idea that what is done under the sun is in accordance with a spiritual choice or purpose (and in the context it must be an evil one rather than a good one), which can be read either from above or from below — that is, either the "plan of [an evil] spirit" results in everything being ματαιότης, or else the "choice of [the individual human] spirit", which continually makes "choice of [an evil] spirit", produces the same result.

Gregory indeed takes the Kohelethine expression as a reference to the designs of a "spirit" rather than a desire for "wind". Moreover, he makes it clear that the spirit in question is an evil one by the use of ἀλλόκοτος, "strange, monstrous" and μυσαρός, "foul, abominable". But he does not make it clear, by

the use of a simple ἅπας, that what is in focus here is
"everything that is done" (LXX πάντα τὰ ποιήματα), presumably
a reference to human activity.

Gregory keeps things general
here, as he did with ἅπας in the previous verse; it may be that
he has in mind a thought similar to that in Romans 8:20, that all
of creation has been subjected to ματαιότης, and does not wish to
restrict the observation just to what human beings do. This
"strange, foul spirit" permeates "everything κάτω", that is
"everything down below" — presumably a parallel to LXX's ὑπὸ
τὸν ἥλιον and thus to Gregory's περὶ γῆν of vv. 3 and 13 rather
than a reference to the netherworld where such a spirit might be
thought to reign (perhaps both "on the earth" and "under the
earth", in contrast to the heavenly realm of the good spirit, are
intended to be encompassed).

The Gregorian interpretation of προαίρεσις πνεύματος owes
nothing to any of the other ancient versions. Aquila and
Theodotion (νομὴ ἀνέμου) and Symmachus (βόσκησις ἀνέμου)
were convinced that the correct meaning of the Hebrew phrase
רעות רוח is "feeding on wind", but Gregory is certain that a "spirit"
is intended here. In the Targum (רוחא תבירות) and in the Peshitta
(ܪܘܚܐ ܬܒܝܪܘ) the talk is of the "breaking down" or "vexation
of the [human] spirit" in the face of the observable futility of
things, an understanding which is also later reflected in the
Vulgate's adflictio spiritus, but for Gregory the focus is on the
machinations of a superhuman spirit.[24] As for the futility itself,
Gregory has no parallel to ματαιότης here, but the thought is
covered by ποικίλος in the previous verse and ἀτοπία in the
following verse.

(15) ... ὥστε μὴ εἶναι αὐτὰ ἀνακτήσασθαι, ἀλλὰ μηδὲ
ἀναθυμηθῆναι τὸ παράπαν ὅση τὰ κατὰ ἀνθρώπους πράγματα
κατείληφεν ἀτοπία.

So it is not possible to put things right again, nor to make
an offering of the utter absurdity which has taken control of
human affairs.

Following on from his spiritualisation of v. 14, Gregory
takes v. 15's "what is twisted" (LXX διεστραμμένος) in the sense

of spiritual corruption and "what is lacking" (LXX ὑστέρημα) in the sense of a dearth of spiritual merit.

So when "Solomon" said that the former "cannot be straightened" (LXX οὐ δυνήσεται τοῦ ἐπικοσμηθῆναι), Gregory takes him to have meant that "things cannot be put right" (μὴ εἶναι αὐτὰ ἀνακτήσασθαι — ἀνακτάομαι is used by the Church Fathers of moral and spiritual recovery and restoration, the regaining of sinners by means of the cross).[25] And when "Solomon" said that the latter "cannot be counted" (LXX οὐ δυνήσεται τοῦ ἀριθμηθῆναι) Gregory takes him to have meant that no humanly-performed sacrifices (ἀναθυμιάω, "to send up incense or smoke, offer up") can count for anything, since all human activity is under the sway of "a strange, foul spirit" (v. 14) and hence of ἀτοπία, "strangeness, unnaturalness, absurdity".

Koheleth's point here seems to have been that people should accept the conditions of life as they are, rather than "chase the wind" by trying to straighten what cannot be straightened or count what cannot be counted. Gregory's point seems to be that people should recognise their fallen condition and their consequent need for a Saviour, since they are under the power of an evil spirit and cannot straighten themselves out or perform any sufficiently meritorious activity.

(16) Λογισάμενος γάρ ποτε ἐγὼ κατ᾽ ἐμαυτόν, καὶ οἰηθεὶς ὡς ἀπάντων εἴην τότε τῶν πρὸ ἐμαυτοῦ γεγονότων ἐνταυθοῖ σοφώτερος·

At one time I thought things over by myself, and I believed that at that time I was wiser than everyone who had been here before me.

The Semitic idiom "I said in my heart (LXX ἐλάλησα ἐγὼ ἐν καρδίᾳ μου)[26] can often be adequately translated by a verb of thinking, such that Gregory's λογισάμενος ἐγώ, "I reckoned, calculated, reasoned" might be regarded as sufficient. But the phrase can be taken as meaning "I argued with myself", in which case ἐν καρδίᾳ μου would require some parallel when this expression is translated, or the strictly-speaking unnecessary pronoun ἐγώ can be taken as emphasising the individuality of the thought to be expressed[27] — that is, that it was Solomon's own personal opinion. Thus Gregory has κατ' ἐμαυτόν, "by myself", and he strengthens the idea of it being a personal opinion by his use of οἴομαι, "suppose, believe". Moreoever, it was an opinion held only at a particular time, as ποτέ, "at one time" and τότε, "at that time" indicate.

So Solomon had thought that he was wiser than everybody else. But Gregory had said in v. 1 that Solomon was indeed wiser than everybody else. The meaning here must therefore be: when Solomon thought he was wise, he was not, because he was relying on his own resources (κατ' ἐμαυτόν); he was only wise when he gave himself over to divine wisdom, whereafter he could speak as a prophet (cf. v. 1) and look back with scorn on his human "wisdom". The story of 1 Kings 3:4-15 may have given rise to this idea of a disjunction between false opinions entertained during a misspent youth and true opinions adopted under divine guidance. It will prove to be a useful device in Gregory's paraphrase, for it will enable him to preface seemingly heterodox statements with "I once thought that..." and seemingly orthodox statements with "but now I know that...."

MT depicts "Solomon" as being wiser than "all who were before me over (על) Jerusalem", a phrase which betrays knowledge of a long line of kings ruling in David's city. Solomonic authorship of Ecclesiastes might be preserved by taking this as a reference to the Jebusite kings who ruled the city before David made it his capital, but LXX overcame the problem by offering the translation "all who were before me in (ἐν) Jerusalem".[28] Accordingly, Gregory speaks of "all who were before me here" (ἐνταυθοῖ, literally "to here, hither"). Thus there is no difficulty in either Greek text concerning the number of kings who reigned in Jerusalem before Koheleth arrived on the scene. Indeed, in Gregory's version there is no reference at all to Jerusalem, which has the effect of universalising the expression into the foolish boast of every brash youth, "I'm wiser than everybody who's been before me." Gregory may intend, by removing the particular reference, that everyone who relies on human wisdom should see his own reflection here and realise that to "think things over by oneself" (as opposed to accepting what the Church has revealed as divine wisdom?) is folly.

(17) ἔγνων παραβολάς τε συνεῖναι καὶ πραγμάτων φύσεις. Ὠήθην δὲ τηνάλλως ἐπὶ τούτῳ φέρεσθαι, ...

I gained knowledge, becoming familiar both with parables and with the nature of things. But I believed that there was no use in my gaining of this knowledge, ...

The Hebrew text which has come down to us pictures "Solomon" as having applied himself to gain knowledge of wisdom (חכמה) and of senselessness (הוללות) and folly (שכלות), and concluding that this too is a "chasing of wind" (רעיון רוח). This could mean that he attempted to distinguish what is wise and what is unwise, but found this to be an impossible task. LXX, however, found it impossible to make sense of the reference to "senselessness and folly", and so substituted "parables (παραβολαί) and understanding (ἐπιστήμη)". The former is conceivable as a Greek scribal error for παραφοραί,[29] "madnesses" (cf. περιφορά and περιφέρεια for הוללות elsewhere in Ecclesiastes),[30] while the latter shows an eager acceptance of the Hebrew scribal variation of שכלות with *sin* (elsewhere it is spelt with *samek* and rendered ἀφροσύνη, "foolishness")[31] as suggesting the root שכל, "to understand" rather than סכל, "to be foolish". Clearly it was felt that better sense, or at least a more comfortable sense, was made here by linking Solomon with a knowledge of "parables and understanding" rather than of "senselessness and folly".[32]

The appearance of παραβολαί in Gregory's paraphrase demonstrates his dependence on LXX. The Hebrew text might have offered him a chance to make a further comment on Solomon's former condition of folly (see discussion under previous verse), but he obviously follows the Greek text. He also retains the aorist of γιγνώσκω, but apparently finds it somewhat tautologous to then employ nouns of knowing (LXX's γνῶσις[33] and ἐπιστήμη), so substitutes a parallel phrase to "parables": πραγμάτων φύσεις, "the natures of things that are done". Σοφία and γνῶσις appeared together in LXX at the end of the previous verse and again at the beginning of this verse before cropping up yet again in the following verse; Gregory avoids repetitiveness

by employing them only in v. 18.
Ὠήθην δὲ τηνάλλως ἐπὶ τούτῳ φέρεσθαι may be a preface
which Gregory felt v. 18 needed, rather than a parallel to the end
of Koheleth's v. 17. But ᾠήθην (for LXX's ἔγνων?) and τούτῳ (for
LXX's τοῦτο?) suggest it is indeed intended as a paraphrase of
that clause, in which case it seems to be atypical of Gregory's
renderings of προαίρεσις πνεύματος in getting closer to the
meaning of "desire of wind" rather than "choice of spirit" (see
comments on 1:14, but cf. 2:17; 6:9). Τηνάλλως φέρεσθαι, "to gain
in vain, achieve nothing" captures the idea of "chasing of wind"
— i.e., a fruitless activity — whereas Gregory normally employs
a construction with πνεῦμα in a decidedly spiritual sense.

Οἴομαι appears again, carrying a quite different nuance than
that of LXX's γιγνώσκω. As in v. 16, the paraphrase gives the
impression that what is here expressed is a misguided opinion
once held by a Solomon who now knows better; the truth of the
matter (for Gregory) is that there is value in knowing parables
and the nature of things.

(18) ... καὶ σοφίᾳ μὲν γνῶσιν ἕπεσθαι, γνώσει δὲ πόνους
ἐπακολουθεῖν.

... and that just as knowledge comes with wisdom, so
distress comes with knowledge.

LXX followed the Hebrew text word-for-word, except that it
read דעת, "knowledge" instead of MT's כעס, "irritation" in the
first phrase. Gregory follows LXX (he overlooks the Greek
corrections of this first γνῶσις to "temper, anger" [Symmachus
ὀργή, Aquila and Theodotion θυμός]),[34] employing σοφία and
γνῶσις where LXX had them, while altering LXX's ἄλγημα, "pain,
suffering" to πόνοι, "pains, distress". Unconstrained by LXX's
formal correspondence method, he makes the verse more
precisely balanced, with a μὲν... δέ construction utilising two
infinitives meaning "to follow" (of ἕπομαι and ἐπακολουθέω).

Given its proverbial structure, this verse may have been a
quotation cited by Koheleth as an appropriate conclusion to his
quest for wisdom. In the paraphrase it is governed by οἴομαι (v.
17), and thus is branded as a mistaken aphorism.

Chapter Two

(1) Τοῦτο δὴ τοῦθ᾽ οὕτως ἔχειν νομίσας, ἔγνων ἐπὶ ἑτέραν ἰδέαν τραπέσθαι βίου, καὶ ἐκδοῦναι μὲν ἐμαυτὸν τρυφῇ, πεῖραν δὲ λαβεῖν ἡδονῶν ποικίλων. Νῦν τοίνυν συνῆκα ὡς τὰ τοιαῦτα μάταια σύμπαντα·

Since I believed that this was so, I decided to turn to a different lifestyle: to give myself over to self-indulgence and to gain experience of various pleasures. Then I realised that all such things are hollow.

In the guise of Solomon, Koheleth proceeded to his second experiment (concerning pleasure) because his first experiment (concerning wisdom) had proven to be futile, and stated already at the outset that this alternative approach to life is similarly futile. Gregory is happy to have Solomon place the ματαιότης stamp on the way of pleasure, but his opening phrase reminds the reader that the conclusion to the earlier experiment was only an opinion held (ἔχειν νομίσας) at a particular time: "Since I believed [wrongly] that this [*viz.*, the idea that wisdom is useless and distressing, 1:17,18] was so, I decided...." The implication is that no right-thinking individual would decide to indulge in the manner of living (ἰδέα βίου) which is to be described in the following verses.

Where Koheleth spoke of "testing out" (LXX πειράω), Gregory speaks of "surrendering oneself" (ἐκδίδωμι); while the former was an objective, clinical term depicting Koheleth as firmly in control of the situation, the latter is a subjective, moralistic term depicting Solomon as having lost control — for the moment. But LXX's πειράω is reflected in Gregory's πεῖρα: he paraphrases "seeing" (LXX ὁράω) very well in this context by "gaining experience" (πεῖραν λαμβάνω). For "merriment" (LXX εὐφροσύνη) and "good" (LXX ἀγαθός), Gregory employs the more loaded words "self-indulgence" (τρυφή) and "pleasures" (ἡδοναί), but he is content to simply retain the ματαιότης judgment, albeit in an adjectival form.

(2) καὶ γέλωτα μὲν εἰκῇ[1] φερόμενον ἐπέσχον, ἡδονὴν δὲ πρὸς τὸ σωφρονεῖν ἐκόλασα, πικρῶς ἐπιτιμήσας αὐτῇ.

I kept laughter from getting out of control, and I put limits on pleasure (which I regarded harshly), so as to learn moderation.

Instead of Koheleth's statement that laughter is foolish and his rhetorical question on what is achieved through merriment, Gregory's Solomon provides a moral example for his readers. To this end two verbs denoting a controlling activity — keeping something in check or holding something back — are employed: ἐπέχω and κολάζω. The two activities to be controlled are laughter (γέλως, taken straight from LXX) and pleasure (ἡδονή, here used by Gregory as a parallel to LXX's εὐφροσύνη, although he had just used τρυφή as that parallel and ἡδονή for LXX's ἀγαθός in the previous verse). Εἰκῇ φερόμενος, "being swept along heedlessly" is a kind of parallel to LXX's περιφορά, "a wandering"; πικρῶς ἐπιτιμάω, "to place a harsh value upon" is implied in Koheleth's rhetorical question; but σωφρονέω, "to practice self-control" is entirely of Gregory's making.

(3) Λογισάμενος δέ, ὅτι ψυχὴ δύναται στῆσαι μεθύουσαν καὶ ῥέουσαν ὥσπερ οἶνον σώματος φύσιν, ἐγκράτεια δὲ δουλοῦται ἐπιθυμίαν· προεθυμήθην κατιδεῖν, τί ποτε εἴη προκείμενον ἀνθρώποις σπουδαῖον, καὶ τῷ ὄντι καλὸν ὃ καταπράξονται παρὰ τουτονὶ τὸν βίον.

I reasoned that the soul is able to put a stop to the body's inclination to getting drunk and guzzling wine, and that desire can be mastered by self-control. I was eager to see what might be put before people as something excellent — something good to be achieved in life.

Gregory baulks at Solomon stimulating himself (LXX ἕλκω, literally "to draw, drag") with wine and embracing (LXX κρατέω, literally "to take hold of") foolishness; he prefers to have Solomon speak on self-control rather than self-indulgence. It is probably the appearance of "mind" (literally "heart": LXX καρδία) and "body" (LXX σάρξ) in the text which prompts Gregory's thesis on "soul" (ψυχή) and "body" (σῶμα), and it may even be that he read the former as "drawing" the latter — in the sense of attracting it away from wine. In the second case, LXX's κρατέω might readily be taken in its common sense of "rule, conquer, control", and hence give rise to Gregory's expression with "enslave" (δουλόω). "Desire" (ἐπιθυμία) would then appear to the Christian paraphrast as a suitable example of "foolishness" (LXX ἀφροσύνη) to be controlled through temperance.

Doubtlessly Gregory was encouraged in making this interpretation by the phrase "my heart guiding me in wisdom" (LXX καρδία μου ὡδήγησεν ἐν σοφίᾳ), a parenthetical clause indicating that all this indulgence was part of the experiment being thoughtfully conducted; the phrase allows Gregory to reason that a mind guided by true wisdom practices self-control rather than self-indulgence, and to paraphrase accordingly.

The last part of the verse is a much more straightforward treatment of Koheleth's words. Typically, the Semitism οἱ υἱοὶ τοῦ ἀνθρώπου (בני האדם) is replaced with the simple ἄνθρωποι, and other words are varied (καταπράσσω, "to accomplish" for LXX's commonplace ποιέω, βίος for LXX's ζωή, and σπουδαῖος and καλός for LXX's ἀγαθός), but here there is no forced interpretation. LXX standardised חחת השמים (normally חחת השמש)[2] into ὑπὸ τὸν ἥλιον — Gregory's οὗτος, which does service for Koheleth's refrain in this verse, seems to imply that there is another, later life above the sun, in heaven (if something good is achieved in this life).

(4) Διεξελήλυθα γὰρ τὰ λοιπὰ σύμπαντα ὅσ' ἀξιάγαστα νομίζεται, οἴκων τε ὑπερυψήλων ἀνορθώσεις καὶ φυτείας ἀμπέλων, ...

I passed through all the rest of those things which are regarded positively: restoring tall houses and planting vines, ...

The next verses simply itemise various "Solomonic" projects, and so there is little need for interpretive elements to intrude into Gregory's paraphrase.[3] Hence Gregory's subject-matter here is virtually identical with that of Koheleth: οἶκος, "house", as in LXX, and ἄμπελος, "vine" as the contents of LXX's ἀμπελών, "vineyard". Similarly with the activities concerned:

φυτεία, "a planting" from LXX's φυτεύω, "to plant", but for some reason not οἰκοδόμησις, "construction" from LXX's οἰκοδομέω, "to build" — Gregory speaks of an ἀνόρθωσις, "restoration" activity, perhaps because he had in mind Solomon's rebuilding of Gezer (1 Kings 9:17, where, however, οἰκοδομέω was still employed) rather than his building of the temple and royal palace in Jerusalem (1 Kings 9:10 referred to them as the two οἶκοι which Solomon built), or because in his experience in Neocaesarea and/or elsewhere the rebuilding of large houses had seemed a popular enterprise among the well-to-do, or was generally thought to be an ἀξιάγαστος, "admirable" thing.

(5) ... ἔτι δὲ παραδείσων κατασκευάς, καὶ παντοίων δένδρων καρποφόρων κτήσεις καὶ ἐπιμελείας·

... as well as establishing parks, and acquiring and cultivating all kinds of fruit-trees.

Again Gregory follows the text quite closely, making only those alterations which improve the style but do not change the meaning. LXX's prosaic ποιέω and φυτεύω are replaced by the more descriptive κατασκευή, "preparation" and the pair of κτῆσις, "possession" and ἐπιμέλεια, "attention". The Semitism ξύλον πᾶν καρποῦ (עץ כל-פרי) is Graecised into παντοίων δένδρων καρποφόρων. Κῆπος, "garden" is left out, perhaps because Gregory felt that παράδεισος, "park" meant essentially the same thing. It is interesting that he retains παράδεισος, rather than κῆπος or some alternative word, when that particular word in Patristic Greek carried the connotation of "Paradise"; it would seem that he wants to preserve this passage's affinity with the Genesis narrative, wherein the garden (LXX παράδεισος, Genesis 2:8) was described as containing all kinds of fruit-trees (Genesis 2:9; cf. 1:29).

(6) ὅπου δὲ καὶ δεξαμεναὶ μεγάλαι πρὸς ὑποδοχὰς ὑδάτων κατεσκευάσθησαν, εἰς δαψιλῆ ἀρδείαν τῶν φυτῶν ἀπονενεμημέναι.

Large reservoirs for the storage of water were also constructed, and assigned to the liberal irrigation of the plants.

The LXX translators often rendered ברכה, "pond, pool" as

κολυμβήθρα, "swimming-bath",⁴ a practice followed again here, even though the context indicated clearly that the purpose of the water-storages was for irrigation and not for swimming; Gregory's paraphrase does a better job in this context with δεξαμενή, "reservoir" (which was also the choice of Symmachus, while Aquila offered λίμνη, "pool").

His reference to ἀρδεία, "irrigation" takes its cue from LXX's ποτίζω, "to water", while ὑποδοχή, "reception" is his own addition for the sake of completeness — a reservoir must first receive water before it can disperse (ἀπονέμω) it. The expression "a thicket growing trees" (LXX δρυμὸν βλαστῶντα ξύλα) may have seemed somewhat awkward to Gregory, who makes do simply with "plants" (φυτά).

(7) Περιεβαλόμην δὲ καὶ οἰκετῶν πλῆθος, θεράποντας καὶ θεραπαίνας· ἄλλους μὲν ἔξωθεν κτησάμενος, ἄλλους δὲ καὶ παρ' ἐμαυτῷ γενομένους⁵ καρπωσάμενος. Ζώων δὲ τετραπόδων ἀγέλαι, πολλαὶ μὲν βουκολίων, πολλαὶ δὲ ποιμνίων ὑπὸ τὴν ἐμὴν ἦλθον ἐξουσίαν παρ' ὁντινοῦν τῶν πάλαι.

I surrounded myself with lots of servants, both male and female. I acquired some of them from outside my household, while others were produced within it. Herds of four-footed animals came under my control: many herds of cattle as well as many flocks of sheep, more than people had had in earlier times.

For "male servant" and "female servant" LXX employed two etymologically-unrelated words, δοῦλος and παιδίσκη (had the translator been concerned to provide perfectly balanced titles, he might have coupled δοῦλος with δούλη or παιδίσκη with παιδίσκος).⁶ Gregory, preferring a more perfectly-balanced style, opts for θεράπων and θεράπαινα. He could just as easily have opted for οἰκέτης and οἰκέτις, but he used the former by way of introduction as a general term for both sexes of domestic workers.

Περιβάλλομαι, "to throw round oneself" also functions by way of introduction as a general term for the "coming into possession of" two types of domestic workers, which are then itemised on the model of LXX: κτάομαι for those which are acquired from outside the household and γίγνομαι for those which arise from within it.[7] In making this distinction between bought and house-born servants, Gregory again strives for a balanced style, utilising an ἄλλους μὲν..., ἄλλους δέ construction.

Yet a third time in this verse Gregory prefaces his reproduction of a Kohelethine distinction with a general term to cover both distinct categories. The reproduced pair is βουκόλιον, "herd of cattle" and ποίμνιον, "flock of sheep", and Gregory uses ἀγέλη, "herd" by way of introduction. In this case, though, Gregory's introductory word seems to have a precursor: LXX κτῆσις, "possessions". The paraphrast probably reasoned that wealth was commonly measured by head of livestock, though he may have read κτῆνος, "flocks and herds" instead of κτῆσις — had he been able to read Hebrew, he might have taken MT's מקנה in its common sense of cows and sheep in herds and flocks.[8]

Koheleth was somewhat repetitious, speaking both here in v. 7 and almost immediately afterwards, in v. 9, of accomplishing "more than all who were before me in Jerusalem" (LXX ὑπέρ/παρὰ πάντας τοὺς γενομένους ἔμπροσθέν μου ἐν Ἰερουσαλήμ). Gregory reproduces the phrase somewhat more precisely in v. 9, but he avoids repetitiousness by departing considerably from it here: the specifics of antedating Solomon in David's city give way to the general term οἱ πάλαι, "the ancients" (cf. 1:10).

(8) Θησαυροί τε χρυσοῦ τε καὶ ἀργύρου προσέρρεον, δορυφόρους τέ μοι καὶ δασμοφόρους, τοὺς ἀπάντων βασιλεῖς πεποιημένῳ. Χοροί τε συνεκροτοῦντο παμπληθεῖς, ἀρρένων δέ[9] τε ὁμοῦ καὶ θηλειῶν εἰς τὴν ἐμὴν τέρψιν, παναρμόνιον ἐκπονούντων ᾠδήν. Συμπόσιά γε μὴν καὶ οἰνοχόους εἰς τοῦτο ἀπέταξα τῆς τρυφῆς μέρος ἐξ ἑκατέρου γένους ἀνθρώπων ἐξειλεγμένους, ...

Treasures of gold and silver flowed in, and the kings of all the nations were made my vassals and tributaries. Numerous choirs of male and female singers were carefully trained to perform harmonious songs for my enjoyment. There were drinking parties, too, with specially-appointed wine stewards of both sexes chosen for this part of the luxurious living.

Χρυσός and ἄργυρος are adapted from LXX's χρυσίον and

ἀργύριον, albeit in reverse order and once again prefaced by a general term: θησαυρός. Of greater interest is what Gregory makes of the second phrase, "the personal property of kings and provinces" (LXX περιουσιασμοὶ βασιλέων καὶ τῶν χωρῶν), which prompts him to describe the surrounding kings both as δασμοφόροι, "payers of tribute" to Solomon and as δορυφόροι, "vassals" (literally, "spear-bearers, attendants") of Solomon. Perhaps Gregory's cue for this was 1 Kings 3:13, where God promised Solomon that he would have no equal among kings in respect to both riches and honour; or 5:1,[10] where it was said that all the kingdoms over which Solomon ruled brought tribute to him and were his subjects all his life; or 10:24,25, where all the kings of the earth (in LXX) were reported to have sought an audience with Solomon to hear his wisdom and bring him gifts.[11] Any or all of these passages might have prompted Gregory to picture "the kings of all [the nations]" as Solomon's underlings in respect to being δορυφόρος as well as δασμοφόρος. Irrespective of any "historical" accuracy, the two words — both being formed from compounds of φέρω — provide a perfectly-balanced phrase; Gregory's penchant for such harmonious pairs has already been noted.

Solomon's penchant for harmonious songs is now noted by Gregory. The adjectives ἄρρην, "male" and θῆλυς, "female" (prefaced by χοροί, "choirs") do service for the masculine and feminine participles of LXX's ᾄδω, "sing",[12] though the cognate noun ᾠδή, "song" does appear in the paraphrase. LXX's ἐντρυφήματα, "pleasurable things" seems to be treated twice; perhaps Gregory took it as referring both to its preceding and following clauses, for he offers τέρψις, "enjoyment, delight" in the former and τρυφή, "luxury, delight" in the latter.

The hapax legomenon שׁדה, which appeared in the singular and then the plural form, has caused problems. Quite likely the word is a somewhat graphic one for "woman" (related to שׁד, "breast" or to שׁדד, "to overpower"?) and the juxtaposition of singular and plural should be rendered "women, and yet more women" (similar to רחם רחמתים, "a woman or two" in Judges 5:30, as Ibn Ezra was the first to note), the reference being thus to Solomon's famous harem, which fits well in this context of an enumeration of that king's accomplishments and particularly in the immediate context of "the delights (תענוגת) of the sons of men".[13] But LXX read Aramaic שדי, "to pour out" in שדה ושדות, and thus translated the expression as οἰνοχόοι[14] καὶ οἰνοχόαι, "male and female wine stewards", an οἰνοχόος being the person who pours out (χέω) the wine (οἶνος) for drinking. Accordingly Gregory refers to οἰνοχόοι... ἐξ ἑκατέρου γένους ἀνθρώπων, "wine stewards of both sexes", which makes a neat variation on his earlier χοροὶ... ἀρρένων... καὶ θηλειῶν.

(9) ... οὐδ' ἂν καταλέγειν ἔχοιμι, τοσοῦτον ὑπερέβαλον τούτοις τοὺς πρὸ ἐμοῦ βασιλεύσαντας Ἰερουσαλήμ. Εἶτα συνέβαινε, τὰ μὲν τῆς σοφίας μοι ἐλαττοῦσθαι, πληθύνειν δὲ τὰ τῆς οὐκ ἀγαθῆς ἐπιθυμίας.

I outdid the men who had ruled over Jerusalem before me to such an extent that I could not keep track of it all. So it was that my wisdom diminished and wicked desires grew.

In 1:16 LXX and Gregory had avoided the suggestion inherent in MT's wording that there had been a long line of kings ruling in David's city before Koheleth wrote. But here, where LXX again spoke of "all who were before me in Jerusalem" (this time in keeping with MT's wording), Gregory imports the idea of comparison specifically with former kings rather than generally with former wealthy and/or wise inhabitants of the city. "To rule Jerusalem" (βασιλεύω Ἰερουσαλήμ) — not "to reign in Jerusalem" (βασιλεύω ἐν Ἰερουσαλήμ) or "to rule Israel" — indicates that Gregory has in mind the Jebusite kings who ruled the city before Solomon's father made it his capital. Since Gregory believed that Solomon was the author of Ecclesiastes, he could hardly have him referring to a long line of Israelite kings in Jerusalem before that time, but it is a little puzzling that he should unnecessarily introduce the problem in this verse when he had avoided it in 1:16. And he now follows LXX's spelling of Ἰερουσαλήμ, when he had not done so in 1:12.

"My wisdom stayed (LXX ἵστημι) with me", Koheleth assured his readers; in other words, all of this experimentation described between v. 3 (where a similar rider appeared) and the present verse was conducted thoughtfully — Koheleth never lost his head in amongst all the indulgence, for wisdom stood firm in him. But such an understanding of the phrase does not make sense to Gregory, who can only reason that a person who gave himself over to self-indulgence was not acting in accordance with true wisdom. Thus he takes ἵστημι in the sense of "come to a halt, stagnate", and accordingly his paraphrase has wisdom decreasing (ἐλασσόω) while wicked desires are increasing (πληθύνω) — the latter phrase takes its cue from the following verse, albeit with an added moral censure (οὐκ ἀγαθός — i.e., κακός).[15]

1 Kings 5:9 (English 4:29) pictured Solomon's wisdom as being beyond reckoning, and 1 Kings 10:7 pictured his wisdom and his share of the good things of life as being beyond recounting. In this verse Gregory pictures Solomon's share of the good things of life as being beyond reckoning/recounting (καταλέγω),[16] but not his wisdom (at the point in time he is here describing). Koheleth's "Solomon" said that he "became great" (LXX μεγαλύνω); Gregory's Solomon says that his wisdom "became small" (ἐλασσόω).[17] The combination of wealth and foolishness would be familiar to readers of the New Testament, not least from 1 Timothy 6:9, which also warned of the harmful desires (ἐπιθυμίαι) to which the rich are subject — Gregory's version of the verse at hand contains the same (implied) warning, and is consistent with his combination of poverty and wisdom elsewhere in the paraphrase (6:8; 9:11,16).

(10) Παντὶ γὰρ ὀφθαλμῶν τε δελεάσματι, καὶ καρδίας ἀκράτοις ὁρμαῖς ἐφιεὶς πανταχόθεν προσπιπτούσαις, ἡδονῶν ἐλπίσιν ἐμαυτὸν ἐκδεδωκώς· καὶ πάσαις τρυφαῖς δειλαίαις,[18] τὴν ἐμαυτοῦ ἐγκατέδησα προαίρεσιν. Οὕτω γάρ μου αἱ ἐνθυμήσεις, εἰς δυσπραγίαν ἠνέχθησαν, ὡς ταῦτα μὲν εἶναι καλά, ταῦτα δέ μοι προσήκειν διαπράττεσθαι νομίζειν.

In the expectation of pleasures, I gave in to all the eyes' temptations and the heart's unrestrained passions, which launched their attacks from all directions. I bound my will to every wretched self-indulgence. My thinking was brought to

such a low state that I regarded these things as being good and
proper things to do.

Gregory is happy to take up the theme of the desires of
ὀφθαλμός and καρδία from Koheleth. The two negative
formulations, "I did not withold" (LXX οὐχ ὑφεῖλον and οὐκ
ἀπεκώλυσα), not necessarily carrying a negative moral judgment
(cf. 11:9), become one positive formulation, "I surrendered
myself" (ἐκδεδωκώς), evidently not carrying a positive moral
judgment (cf. 2:1). For what the eyes desire (LXX αἰτέω), Gregory
speaks of what is a temptation (δελέασμα) to them; and for what
provides merriment (LXX εὐφροσύνη) for the heart, Gregory
speaks of intemperate passion (ἀκράτη ὁρμή). As in 2:1, he
employs the loaded words ἡδοναί, "pleasures" and τρυφή, "self-
indulgence" — the latter this time on the basis of the LXX verb
εὐφραίνομαι rather than the noun εὐφροσύνη, and forming a
somewhat strange parallel to μόχθος, "toil, trouble". This word
(= MT עמל) was frequently employed by Koheleth, for whom the
struggle of life was a wearying experience, and Gregory normally
gives it an appropriate parallel by means of a cognate word (e.g.,
μοχθηρός, "laborious" in the next verse) or a synonymous term
(e.g., κάματος, "toil" in 2:19), but here he must have reasoned
that the heart does not make merry in μόχθος, but in τρυφή, and
paraphrased accordingly (quite the opposite of Symmachus'
positive viewing here of φιλοπονία, "industriousness"). As an
equivalent expression for καρδία in this context, Gregory speaks
of the will (προαίρεσις), describing it as being in bondage
(ἐγκαταδέω, "to bind fast in"). His use of προαίρεσις here may
well be prompted by LXX's employment of προαίρεσις πνεύματος
in the very next verse, on the basis of the thought that a self-
indulgent heart is under the influence of an evil spirit.

Another favourite word of Koheleth, who believed that
people should accept their lot in life and make the most of it,
was μερίς (חלק), "portion, share". Here he spoke of enjoyment as
being the μερίς received from μόχθος. For the latter Gregory had
spoken of τρυφή, so for the former he speaks of what was
thought to be "good" (καλός) and "to be fitting" (προσήκω).
While the text before Gregory merely remarked that "Solomon"
had enjoyed what came his way in life, Gregory remarks that

Solomon was misguided (εἰς δυσπραγίαν ἠνέχθησαν, literally "brought into misfortune") in enjoying the things he did.

(11) Εἶτα ποτὲ ἀνανήψας ἐγὼ καὶ ἀναβλέψας, κατεῖδον ἅπερ ἐν χερσὶν εἶχον, μοχθηρὰ ὁμοῦ καὶ παγχάλεπα, πνεύματος οὐκ ἀγαθοῦ ποιήματα. Οὐδὲν γὰρ ὁτιοῦν ὑπ' ἀνθρώπων ᾑρημένον, ἀποδεκτὸν εἶναί μοι νῦν καταφαίνεται καὶ περισπούδαστον ὀρθῷ λογισμῷ.

After a while I came to my senses and saw things clearly again. I saw that the very matters I had in hand were wicked and distressing, the work of an evil spirit. So now none of the things which are chosen by human beings seems to me to be acceptable or desirable to an upright mind.

Gregory now has Solomon recover his senses (ἀνανήφω) and recover his sight (ἀναβλέπω). The second verb is an alteration of LXX's ἐπιβλέπω, "to look upon, consider" all the things he had done, whereas the first verb looks like it might have arisen from MT's פנה, "to turn" to — i.e., to turn one's attention towards — all those things, which a pious interpreter might take as meaning a turning away from error (or even from the drunkenness of all the συμποσία of v. 8, for ἀνανήφω also means "to become sober again"). On the other hand, it may simply be that Gregory felt the progression of thought from v. 10 required a comment of this nature here; while Koheleth presented his standard conclusion of ματαιότης upon an overall survey of this experiment with physical pleasure, Gregory has presented the foregoing as a mistaken venture and so now must have Solomon's realisation of his mistake.

Gregory does not seem at all concerned about rendering Koheleth's terms consistently, for in the very next verse, which also opened in LXX with ἐπιβλέπω, he speaks of "thinking through" (συλλογίζομαι) various matters; such would have made a good paraphrase of Koheleth's expression here, too, but that does not suit Gregory's purposes, just as he would not wish to use ἀνανήφω and ἀναβλέπω again in the next verse, where the first of the matters referred to is σοφία, "wisdom". Gregory has Solomon turn **to** or **away from** matters, in accordance with the

value which the Church Father sees in those respective matters.
Five typically-Kohelethine expressions appeared in this
verse, none of them for the first time: μόχθος prompts the
adjective μοχθηρός, "toilsome, laborious", but probably in the
moral sense of "wicked"; ματαιότης becomes παγχάλεπος, "very
difficult, most grievous"; προαίρεσις πνεύματος is interpreted as
πνεύματος οὐκ ἀγαθοῦ ποιήματα, "actions of a spirit not good";
περισσεία is taken to be what is ἀποδεκτός, "acceptable" and
περισπούδαστος, "much desired, very admirable"; and ὑπὸ τὸν
ἥλιον means the area of activity of ἄνθρωποι. In all this
Koheleth's conclusion, that physical pleasure is no more
meaningful or useful than wisdom had proved to be, changes
into Gregory's conclusion, that physical pleasure is a wicked way
of life in contradistinction to the way of wisdom followed by the
righteous.

(12) Συλλογισάμενος οὖν τά τε σοφίας ἀγαθά, καὶ τὰ
ἀφροσύνης κακά, εἰκότως ἂν ἱκανῶς θαυμάζοιμι ἄνδρα
τοιοῦτον,[19] ὅς τις φερόμενος ἀλόγως· ἔπειτα ἑαυτοῦ λαβόμενος, εἰς
τὸ δέον ἐπιστρέψει.[20]

Since I have thought through the good qualities of wisdom
and the bad qualities of foolishness, I would naturally admire
the person who is swept along by foolishness — when that
person recovers his senses and returns to what is proper.

In the light of v. 13, which assigned value judgments to
wisdom and foolishness, Gregory feels justified in here referring
to the ἀγαθά, "good qualities" of the former and the κακά, "bad
qualities" of the latter, even though the text before him did not
assign value judgments at this point — and might even have
intended the very opposite of Gregory's meaning.[21] Σοφία and
ἀφροσύνη are taken directly from LXX; περιφορά, "senselessness" is not taken into the paraphrase, presumably because it
interferes with the neat wisdom-foolishness dichotomy, but it
probably lies behind the ἀλόγως, "irrationally" later in the verse.
The second half of this verse in MT reads strangely.
Literally, it is: "For what the person who will come after the
king? That which they have already done" (כי מה האדם שיבוא אחרי)

המלך את אשר־כבר עשוהו). This seems to mean that the successor of a
king pursues the same transitory and profitless activites as did
his predecessor and thus provides another example of the
eternal repetition of events; or perhaps it was intended to
indicate that no latter-day would-be Solomon should bother to
repeat Koheleth's experiment, since he would only be going
over the same ground and would not achieve anything; or it
may merely be another indication of Koheleth's concern about
what sort of person will succeed him and what that person will
do with what he inherits.[22] LXX did not latch on to any of these
possible meanings, but offered: "For who is the person who will
follow after counsel, insofar as he does it?" (ὅτι τίς[23] ἄνθρωπος, ὃς
ἐπελεύσεται ὀπίσω τῆς βουλῆς τὰ ὅσα ἐποίησεν αὐτήν;). Βουλή
presumably appeared in the translation on the basis of the
Aramaic verb מלך, "to counsel, advise", which must have made
in this verse more sense to the LXX translator than did the
Hebrew noun מלך, "king",[24] though the latter is readily accepted
by Targum and Peshitta (מלכא/ܡܠܟܐ),[25] and by Aquila and
Theodotion (βασιλεύς), if not by Symmachus (βουλή). The
resultant sentence in LXX seems to have been rhetorically asking
whether there is anyone who consistently follows good advice
— i.e., in the context, whether there is anyone who always acts
wisely rather than foolishly.

Gregory speaks of the person who comes to act wisely after
he had been acting foolishly. This treatment of the verse
probably arises from LXX, in that λαμβάνω, "to apprehend by the
senses" and ἐπιστρέφω, "to turn (from an error)" appear to paraphrase LXX's "following after counsel" rather than the notion of
"coming after the king." But the sequence of repentance after
acting ἀλόγως mirrors the picture Gregory has built up of a
sometime foolish Solomon coming to his right mind, and it
calls for any reader who is caught up in unwise activities or
opinions to do likewise — could the Hebrew בוא אחרי המלך have
suggested this idea of "follow the Solomonic example"?

(13) Φρονήσεως γὰρ καὶ ἀφροσύνης πολὺ τὸ μέσον, διαφορὰ
δὲ ἀμφοῖν τοσαύτη, ὅση περ ἡμέρας πρὸς νύκτα.

There is a great difference between thoughtfulness and

thoughtlessness; they are as different from each other as day is from night.

Gregory happily takes over this piece of conventional Wisdom. In φρόνησις, "thoughtfulness" he supplies a more precise antonym of ἀφροσύνη (which he has taken directly from LXX) than LXX's σοφία, which he had reproduced in the previous verse, and in ἡμέρα and νύξ he supplies the times associated with LXX's φῶς and σκότος respectively.[26] Koheleth's typical way of expressing the "advantage" (LXX περισσεία) of one thing over another gives way to Gregory's depiction of the "difference" (τὸ μέσον for the first occurrence, διαφορά for the second) between one thing and another.

(14) Ἔοικε τοίνυν, ὁ μὲν ἀρετὴν ἡρημένος, τρανῶς τε ἕκαστα καὶ ἄνω βλέποντι· τῆς τε ἑαυτοῦ πορείας, λαμπροτάτου φέγγους καιρῷ πεποιημένῳ· ὁ δ' αὖ κακίᾳ ἐμπεπλεγμένος, καὶ πλάνῃ παντοίᾳ ὡς ἐν σκοτομήνῃ πλανωμένῳ, τυφλός τε ὢν τὴν πρόσοψιν, καὶ[27] ὑπὸ τοῦ σκότους τῶν πραγμάτων ἀφῃρημένος.[28] Τέλος δὲ ἐπινοήσας ἑκατέρου τῶν βίων τούτων ἐγὼ τὸ διάφορον, εὗρον οὐδέν, ...

So the person who has chosen goodness is like someone who sees everything — including what is above — clearly; he has made his way in the time of brightest light. But the person who has become entangled in wickedness and all sorts of error is like someone who is wandering about on a moonless night; he is blind, since the darkness prevents him from seeing anything. When I thought about what difference there might be between the results of these two ways of living, I did not discover any.

Gregory provides definitions for the stock contrasts of the Wisdom school: the "wise person" (LXX σοφός) is the one who "chooses goodness" (ἀρετὴν αἱρέω), and the "fool" (LXX ἄφρων) is the one who gets himself "entangled in wickedness" (κακίᾳ ἐμπλέκω). To have "one's eyes in one's head" (LXX οἱ ὀφθαλμοὶ αὐτοῦ ἐν κεφαλῇ αὐτοῦ) is explained as meaning "to see everything clearly" (τρανῶς ἕκαστα βλέπω), and "to walk in darkness" (LXX ἐν σκότει πορεύομαι) is given in more concrete form as "to wander about on a moonless night" (ἐὰν σκοτομήνῃ πλανάομαι). Each of these gives rise to an antithesis: the wise person sees everything clearly, so in contrast the fool is unable to see anything at all; the fool makes his way in the time of deepest darkness, so in contrast the wise person makes his way in the time of brightest light.

The wise person also sees ἄνω, "on high, upwards", which recalls ἀνωτέρω τῶν ἄστρων in 1:3. The contrast of Proverbs 17:24 may be in view here: "a discerning person's face is set toward wisdom, but a fool's eyes are on the ends of the earth."[29] Or quite possibly it is Koheleth's frequent phrase "under the sun" which has prompted this adverb: the fool looks only at what is ὑπὸ τὸν ἥλιον, Gregory may be implying, while the wise person also looks ἄνω. Note, too, the contrast between the one who "takes for himself" (αἱρέομαι) goodness and the one who "has taken from him" (ἀφαιρέομαι) the ability to see goodness, and the comparison between "wandering" (πλανάομαι) about in darkness and becoming entangled in "error" (πλάνη).

Koheleth now contrasted the traditional Wisdom with his own empiricism. The contrast was forcefully put by the employment of a verb of knowledge and an emphatic pronominal expression (LXX ἔγνων καί γε ἐγώ), but it is considerably watered down by Gregory's employment of a verb of thinking and an unemphatic — due to its position — pronoun (ἐπινοήσας... ἐγώ). The knowledge that the same "happening" (LXX συνάντημα) happens to everybody, regardless of how they have conducted their lives, becomes the admission that no difference between the "end" (τέλος) of a good life and the "end" of a wicked life could be discovered merely by thinking about it. Gregory will move quickly in the next verses to assure his readers that this does not mean that there is no difference between the results of these two ways of living;[30] it just means that there was a time when Solomon was not as wise as he later became.

(15) ... καὶ ὡς κοινωνὸν ἀφρόνων ἐμαυτὸν καταστήσας, τὰ τῆς ἀφροσύνης ἐπίχειρα δέξομαι. Τί γὰρ ἢ τῶν σοφισμάτων ἐκείνων ἀγαθόν, ἢ ποία ὄνησις τῶν πολλῶν λόγων, ὅπου γε τὰ φλυαρίας ῥεύματα, ὥσπερ ἐκ πηγῆς ὁρμᾶται τῆς ἀφροσύνης;

If I make myself into an associate of fools, I will receive the

rewards of foolishness. What is the good of those clever arguments, or what is the use of lots of words, which are just like streams of nonsense pouring out of a fountain of foolishness?

Koheleth's realisation that the same "happening" (LXX συνάντημα) which happens to the fool would be his fate as well, the fact that he was a wise man making no difference in this matter, becomes in Gregory's paraphrase Solomon's recognition that the same "rewards" (ἐπίχειρα) which the fool receives were received by him as well, because of the fact that he had associated with fools. Accordingly, Koheleth's rhetorical question on what "advantage" (LXX περισσός)[31] there is to "being wise" (LXX σοφίζομαι), becomes in the paraphrase Solomon's rhetorical question on what "good" (ἀγαθός) there is in "clever arguments" (σοφίσματα). A second rhetorical question, on what "use" (ὄνησις) there is in "many words" (πολλοὶ λόγοι), arises from LXX's statement that the fool "prattles on superfluously" (ἐκ περισσεύματος λαλέω), which has no parallel in MT. "This is ματαιότης" leads Gregory to liken these clever arguments and multitudinous words to "nonsense" (φλυαρία) flowing in streams from a fountain of foolishness.

In placing περισσός in the phrase concerning Koheleth speaking (λαλέω) in his heart, and adding the phrase with περίσσευμα concerning the fool speaking (λαλέω), LXX seems to have been suggesting that the ματαιότης judgment is in this context a foolish judgment, and known to be so by Koheleth at the time of writing though not at the time that he had made the judgment. Gregory's tack is a different but related one: the φλυαρία judgment is a wise one, and known to be so by Solomon at the time of writing though not at the time when he had been an associate of fools. LXX's negative stance *vis-à-vis* the judgment was caused by its linkage here with the idea that there is no use in σοφία, while Gregory's positive stance is facilitated by his linkage of the judgment with the idea that there is no use in wordiness and σοφίσματα.

(16) Σοφῷ δὲ καὶ ἄφρονι κοινὸν οὐδέν, οὐ κατὰ ἀνθρώπων μνήμην, οὐ κατὰ Θεοῦ ἀμοιβήν. Τῶν δ' ἐν ἀνθρώποις πραγμάτων, ἔτι ἄρχεσθαι δοκούντων, ἤδη τὸ τέλος ἐπιλαμβάνει ἁπάντων.

Σοφὸς δὲ οὐδέποτε ἀσυνέτῳ τοῦ αὐτοῦ κοινωνεῖ τέλους.

A wise person and a foolish person have nothing in common, neither in terms of human remembrance nor in terms of divine recompense. As for human works, the end already overtakes them all while they still seem to be beginning. But a wise person never shares the same fate as a stupid person.

Koheleth stated that the wise person, "in common with" (LXX μετά) the foolish person, is quickly forgotten. But Gregory's Solomon states that these two types of people have "nothing in common" (κοινὸν οὐδέν) when it comes to being remembered.[32] Had not Solomon himself written in Proverbs 10:7 that the memory of the righteous is honoured while the name of the ungodly is extinguished?[33] Accordingly, Solomon is made to imply here, too, that the wise are remembered with honour — both by admiring human beings and by a rewarding God — while the fools are not — they are remembered as fools (if they are remembered at all) by their fellow human beings, and they receive the rewards of foolishness (cf. v. 15) from God. LXX's μνήμη is used for the human activity, and ἀμοιβή is introduced to cover the divine activity.

Concomitantly with the particular observation that both wise and foolish are forgotten, Koheleth offered the general observation that "everything" (LXX τὰ πάντα) is forgotten. Gregory refashions this into an observation that "human works" (ἐν ἀνθρώποις πράγματα) are cut short. As in 1:2, where he had made the same limitation of human πράγματα for τὰ πάντα, Gregory seems to be concerned that the works of God must remain unimpugned. The implied contrast is that what God does endures and is effective, and it is quite likely that Gregory is thinking here of God bringing about the frustration of human schemes (a kind of "man proposes, God disposes" dichotomy; cf. Proverbs 19:21). If "the end" (τὸ τέλος) is a parallel to "the coming days" (LXX αἱ ἡμέραι αἱ ἐρχόμεναι), then he could well be thinking eschatologically of "the day of the Lord" coming unexpectedly (cf. 1 Thessalonians 5:2).

Koheleth closed the verse with an exclamation of complaint that the wise person "dies" (LXX ἀποθνήσκω) just like the fool does — this is the "happening" he had in mind in the previous verses. If Gregory understood that this was a complaint, a nuance carried by LXX's καὶ πῶς, "how can it be?", he does not show it.[34] He handles this sentence as he did the opening sentence of the verse, putting forward the opposite contention that the two types of people do not "have in common" (this time he employs the verb κοινωνέω for LXX's μετά) the same τέλος. For variation, he uses ἀσύνετος instead of ἄφρων in this second instance, but he retains σοφός unvaried.

That Gregory's paraphrase gives the opposite meaning to the one given by the document he is paraphrasing does not necessarily indicate, at least in this instance, that he was knowingly contradicting that document. His mind-set would be such that he would seek an interpretation of this scriptural book which did not contradict the rest of Scripture, and in this verse his interpretation might genuinely arise from a literal reading of the text. If Solomon said that "there is no remembrance of the wise person in common with the fool", he must have meant that the remembrance of the wise person is not the same as the remembrance of the fool; and if he cried out, "how can it be that the wise person dies in common with the fool?", he must have meant that such a thing cannot happen, just as he had written in Proverbs 10:27ff. that the respective fates of these two types of people were very different indeed. Gregory's Solomon does not speak with a forked tongue.

(17) Ἐμίσησα τοίνυν καὶ τὸν σύμπαντά μου βίον, τὸν ἐν τοῖς ματαίοις ἀναλωθέντα, ὃν διήγαγον τοῖς περὶ γῆν πόνοις προστετηκώς.

So I hated all my life, which I had squandered on futile things, and which I had spent clinging to earthly concerns.

What exactly should be the object of μισέω, "hate"? Gregory lifts the verb in its exact form from LXX, but he limits the scope of its object from "life" (LXX ζωή) in general to "my life" (μου βίος).[35] While he might justify this on the basis of "I hated all my toil" (LXX μισέω with μόχθος μου) in the next verse, it has the effect in this verse of changing what appears to have been a

declaration of the hatefulness of life *per se* into a declaration of
the hatefulness of the kind of lifestyle that Solomon had been
pursuing until he came to his senses. Similarly, not "everything
is ματαιότης" for Gregory's Solomon, but only the things which
he thought were worthwhile in his prodigal lifestyle are in fact
μάταιος, and not all work ὑπὸ τὸν ἥλιον is to be condemned, but
only that work which is περὶ γῆν (and which by implication is
not concerned with things ἄνω, v. 14; cf. 1:3's περὶ γῆν and
ἀνωτέρω).

LXX's προαίρεσις πνεύματος may lie behind the ideas of
"squandering" (ἀναλόω) one's life and "clinging to" (προστήκομαι) earthly things, in that these could be considered as
examples of, or the result of, "choosing" (προαιρέω) to follow an
evil spirit (cf. 1:14) — or it might even be that προαίρεσις
πνεύματος has been thought by the paraphrast to be a parallel
expression to ματαιότης (cf. 6:9).

(18) Ὡς γὰρ συνελόντι φάναι, πάντα μοι λυπηρῶς
ἐκμεμόχθηται ὁρμῆς ἀλογίστου γενόμενα ποιήματα· καὶ
διαδέξεταί τις αὐτὰ ἕτερος, ...

**To put it simply: everything I had done was nothing but
painfully-achieved thoughtless passion; and someone else will
succeed to them ....**

Instead of repeating ἐμίσησα (as LXX did), Gregory introduces the verse with a rhetorical formula: ὡς συνελόντι φάναι,
"to tell in small compass" — or, as many a speaker untruthfully
says, "to cut a long story short". The idea that what Solomon
had done was now hateful to him is conveyed by the negative
nuances of λυπηρῶς, "painfully" and ἀλόγιστος, "thoughtless".
LXX's μοχθέω gives rise to ἐκμοχθέω, "to work out with toil,
achieve by great exertion," but Koheleth's characteristic phrase
ὑπὸ τὸν ἥλιον is ignored in this and in the following verses,
probably because it was becoming too repetitive for Gregory.

To "leave" (LXX ἀφίημι) what one has toiled for to someone
who comes after one,[36] means that someone else is going to
"succeed to" (διαδέχομαι) those things — αὐτά is left hanging,
but is defined in v.19.

(19) ... εἴτε σοφός, εἴτε ἠλίθιος, τὰς ψυχρὰς τῶν ἐμῶν καμάτων ἐπικαρπίας.

... — that is, to the trivial profits of my efforts — whether he is wise or foolish.

Σοφός is once again adopted from LXX, but once again LXX's ἄφρων receives a variation: ἠλίθιος — Gregory seems to have a lot more synonyms of "foolish" at his disposal than synonyms of "wise". A simple juxtaposition in an εἴτε... εἴτε formula replaces the rhetorical question of his predecessor.

Now the αὐτά of the previous verse, the things to which someone is going to succeed, is defined: αἱ τῶν ἐμῶν καμάτων ἐπικαρπίαι, "the profits of my labours", an excellent rendering of LXX's μόχθος μου, "my labour" in this context. LXX's ματαιότης is paralleled by ψυχρός, literally "cold", but metaphorically "vain, feeble, ineffectual"; however, the judgment is not identically placed. Koheleth placed his ματαιότης judgment on the state of affairs whereby someone who may be a fool would succeed to what the wise Koheleth had spent a great deal of effort in acquiring, but Gregory places his ψυχρός judgment on the things themselves which the formerly unwise Solomon has spent his time in acquiring.

(20) Ἀπολαβομένῳ δέ μοι ταῦτα καὶ ἀπορρίψαντι, ...

But when I cut myself off from these things and renounced them, ...

Koheleth now "turned (MT סבב) to let [his heart] despair (יאש piel)" over these things, so disconcerted was he by the worthlessness and pointlessness of all his toil under the sun. LXX had a little trouble with this idiom, and rendered it as "turning about (ἐπιστρέφω) to bid farewell to (ἀποτάσσομαι)" his heart over these things. But any reader of the New Testament would be familiar with these two verbs in the senses of "repenting" and "renouncing" respectively, such that LXX, either wittingly or unwittingly, has opened up the possibility of taking this verse as an account of the giving up of former labours. That is precisely the way in which Gregory takes it, as is evident from his employment of ἀπολαμβάνω, "to take back, cut off" and ἀπορρίπτω, "to throw away, renounce" for the two verbs. It fits well with the picture he has developed of a repentant Solomon (cf. v.11).

(21) ... κατεφάνη τὰ τῷ ὄντι ἀγαθὰ προκείμενα ἀνθρώπῳ, σοφίας τε γνῶσις, καὶ κτῆσις ἀνδρείας. Εἰ δέ τις τούτων μὲν οὐκ ἐφρόντισεν, ἑτέρων δὲ ἐπτόηται, ὁ τοιοῦτος εἵλετο μὲν πονηρὰ ἀντὶ ἀγαθῶν, ...

... the true good, which is set before a person, became clear: knowledge of wisdom and possession of virtue. If someone takes no thought for these things, but becomes passionately excited about other things, that person is choosing evil instead of good.

To work with σοφία and γνῶσις means, for Gregory, to have σοφίας γνῶσις, "knowledge of wisdom". Koheleth also listed כשרון, "skill, success", which LXX rendered as ἀνδρεία, "manliness, virtue".[37] Gregory happily adopts this in the form κτῆσις ἀνδρείας, "possession of virtue" to balance his σοφίας γνῶσις formulation. He proclaims these things as constituting that true "good" (ἀγαθός) which is "set before" (πρόκειμαι) a person, and thus provides a result for the quest he had announced in v. 3: the desire to discover what might be "set before" (πρόκειμαι) people as being "good" (σπουδαῖος and καλός); that is what he had wanted to "see" (καθοράω), and now it can "be clearly seen" (καταφαίνομαι).

"Not working with [literally: 'in'] it" (LXX οὐ μοχθέω ἐν αὐτῷ) means, for Gregory, "paying no heed to these things" (οὐ φροντίζω τούτων), to which he adds the further wickedness of "being passionately excited about other things" (πτοέομαι ἑτέρων). There is no mention in the paraphrase of LXX's μερίς, but such unwise and unvirtuous excitements might be considered to be the "lot" of a foolish person.

Πονηρός is closely modelled on LXX's πονηρία, but it is set in a quite different context: for Koheleth it was a great evil, and another example of ματαιότης, that someone who had not worked for it would receive the fruits of another's labour; for Gregory, the evil is what is chosen by someone who does not follow the way of wisdom and virtue — an observation about injustice has become one about unrighteousness.

(22) ... μετῆλθε δὲ κακίαν ἀντὶ χρηστότητος, καὶ μόχθον ἀνθ᾽ ἡσυχίας, ...

He seeks wickedness instead of goodness, and distress instead of quietness.

Koheleth asked the question, "What does a person get for his efforts?", to be answered in the following verse. Gregory answers the imaginary question, "What does an evil person get for his efforts?", and in doing so anticipates something of the following verse.

Μόχθος is taken straight from LXX, and κακία is what Gregory regards as the natural inclination of the human heart (LXX προαίρεσις καρδίας, "choice/purpose of the heart"). He juxtaposes each with its respective opposite number: ἡσυχία and χρηστότης.

(23) ... ταράχοις ποικίλοις περιελκόμενος, νύκτωρ τε καὶ μεθ᾽ ἡμέραν συνεχόμενος ἀεί, σώματός τε ἐπείγουσι καμάτοις, καὶ ψυχῆς φροντίσιν ἀδιαλείπτοις, σφαδαζούσης αὐτῷ τῆς καρδίας, ἀλλοκότων ἕνεκα πραγμάτων.

He is pulled about by various troubles, continually being afflicted both night and day with pressing work for his body and constant anxieties for his mind, while he struggles in his heart over strange matters.

Gregory continues to apply Koheleth's bleak picture of life exclusively to the life of the wicked, who thus are pictured as getting their just deserts for having chosen wickedness. "All his days" (LXX πᾶσαι αἱ ἡμέραι αὐτοῦ) at the beginning of the verse and "in the night" (LXX ἐν νυκτί) towards the end are brought together by Gregory as "both by night and by day" (νύκτωρ τε καὶ μεθ᾽ ἡμέραν). LXX's ἄλγημα, "pain, suffering" is rendered by "toil" (κάματος) which "weighs down" (ἐπείγω) the sinner.

In reading the next phrase, "the irritation of his task" (MT כעס עינינו), LXX made the first word the genitive, and rendered "the distraction of his soul" (θυμοῦ περισπασμὸς αὐτοῦ).

Περισπασμός finds its equivalent in Gregory's φροντίς, "anxiety", which is "never ceasing" (ἀδιάλειπτος), and Gregory develops the idea of θυμός by employing ψυχή as the aspect of the human being which carries the burden of φροντίς. Ever seeking a balanced formulation, he then introduces σῶμα as the aspect of the human being which carries the burden of κάματος. LXX's καρδία is retained, and the reason why it cannot "rest" (LXX κοιμάομαι) is because it "struggles" or "convulses" (σφαδάζω) over various matters. The whole is prefaced by Gregory with the general comment that the person he is describing — the person who neglects wisdom and virtue (v. 21) — must suffer no end of "trouble" (τάραχος).

Koheleth's ματαιότης judgment was made of the suffering inherent in human life. Gregory's ἀλλόκοτος ("strange, monstrous, unwelcome") judgment is made of the matters over which the fool's heart is struggling. Once again he has greatly reduced the scope of the critique.

(24) Οὐ γὰρ τὸ τέλειον ἀγαθὸν περὶ βρῶσίν τε καὶ πόσιν ἰζάνει· εἰ καὶ μάλιστα ἐκ Θεοῦ ἀνθρώποις γίνονται αἱ τροφαί·

The perfect good does not lie in eating and drinking, although people's nourishment certainly comes from God.

Four times in his book (2:24; 3:12,22; 8:15) Koheleth employed an οὐκ ἔστιν ἀγαθόν (אין טוב) formulation, each time — except in this verse — following it up with a clause beginning with εἰ μή (כי אם or מאשר). "There is no good, except..." evidently meant "the only good is...", or "there is nothing better than...." Because the subject-matter was the same in all four contexts, it would seem that Koheleth meant to say the same thing here, and the most likely explanation for the absence of "except" is a haplographic error in the transmission of MT: a *mem* stood originally before the *shin* (cf. מאשר, 3:22), but it was inadvertently dropped by a scribe because the word immediately before it ended in *mem*.[38] LXX, eager to stick closely to the Hebrew text, did not feel at liberty to insert εἰ μή into the formulation at this point and thus bring this verse into line with the other instances.[39]

But for whatever reason, "except" was absent from the text of 2:24 in front of Gregory, and that suited his purposes well. He does not agree with any "eat, drink, and be merry" philosophy, so at 3:22 and 8:15 he prefaces such sentiments with the past tense of δοκέω to indicate that this was a view once mistakenly held by a now much wiser Solomon. At 3:12 he concedes that enjoyment is good, but adds the rider, "if righteousness guides one's actions".

But here at 2:24 he does not have to add any reservations or qualifications to what the text literally says: βρῶσις, "eating" (for LXX's ἐσθίω) and πόσις, "drinking" (for LXX's πίνω) are not really ἀγαθός. Taking this first sentence as though there was not meant to be an "except" in it, necessitates taking the second sentence as though it were an adversative expression — "'x' is not the Good, **but** it does come from God" — rather than a justificatory expression — "'x' is good; **after all**, it does come from God" — but this presents no problem to Gregory, who begins it with εἰ καὶ μάλιστα, "although certainly". LXX's τοῦτο is identified as τροφή, "nourishment", presumably covering both βρῶσις and πόσις of the first sentence.

(25) οὐδὲν γὰρ τῶν πρὸς σωτηρίαν ἡμῖν δεδομένων ἔξω τῆς αὐτοῦ ὑπάρχει προνοίας.

None of the things which are provided for our preservation come into being without his providence.

Koheleth asked, "Who יאכל and who יחוש apart from me?" The first verb presented no problem, and LXX dutifully repeated ἐσθίω, as in the previous verse. The second verb might be interpreted as "to refrain" (if the Masoretic *shin* is repointed as *sin* and the word is thus read as יחוס, as it is in the case of LXX's φείδομαι) or "to gorge oneself" (thus some LXX manuscripts and Theodotion repeat πίνω, as in the previous verse for שתה).[40] If Gregory read φείδομαι, he does not make any use of the idea in his paraphrase. A reading of πίνω seems more likely, since what is provided for human "preservation" (σωτηρία) is equivalent to what is provided as human "nourishment" (τροφή in the previous verse, a blanket term for "eating" and "drinking"). The pronoun "me" in MT seems strange — perhaps

Koheleth was saying that he alone has earned the right to do as he will with what he has toiled for.[41] But LXX's (and Peshitta's) emendation to "him", supported by several Hebrew manuscripts, makes better sense in the context: no-one can do anything unless God wills it.[42] Gregory agrees: nothing exists without the πρόνοια, "foreknowledge, providence" of God. But if Koheleth's point was that God can be unfair in what he wills, Gregory's is different: God will always provide what is necessary.

(26) Ἀλλ' ὁ μὲν ἀγαθὸς ἀνήρ, σοφίας ἐκ Θεοῦ τυχών, εὐφροσύνης ἔτυχεν οὐρανίου· ὁ δ' αὖ πονηρός, θεηλάτοις ἐλαυνόμενος κακοῖς, πλεονεξίαν νοσῶν, πολλά τε ἀθροῖσαι σπουδάζει, καὶ τὸν ὑπὸ Θεοῦ τετιμημένον ἐναντίον τοῦ πάντων Δεσπότου ὀνειδίσαι σπεύδει, δῶρα προτείνων ἄχρηστα, δολερά τε ὁμοῦ καὶ μάταια τῆς ἑαυτοῦ ἀθλίας ψυχῆς σπουδάσματα πεποιημένος.

The good person, who gets wisdom from God, also gets heavenly joy. But the evil person is harassed by troubles sent from God. Suffering from greed, he eagerly gathers a great deal for himself, and he eagerly reproaches the person who is honoured by God in the presence of the Lord of all. He also offers useless gifts, making the eager pursuits of his wretched soul both deceitful and futile.

Koheleth complained again of what was ματαιότης: a person can toil away only to have someone else receive the benefits of that toil. He had already complained about this in vv. 18-21, but now he directed the complaint towards the responsible party — the God who blesses the person who is "ἀγαθός (טוב) before him" and who curses the ἁμαρτάνων (חוטא), "sinner". Since Koheleth had pictured himself as one of those who had toiled for someone else's benefit, and since he described the situation as a great πονηρία (v. 21) and as ματαιότης (several times, culminating in the end of this verse), he would appear to have been speaking in somewhat ironic terms of the person to whom God has taken a liking and the person to whom he has taken a disliking; the former is ἀγαθός in God's eyes, for unfathomable reasons, while the latter misses out (ἁμαρτάνω [אטח]), for equally unfathomable reasons.⁴³ Gregory naturally takes the words in their conventional senses. The person who is ἀγαθός before God is ὁ ἀγαθὸς ἀνήρ, and the sinner is ὁ πονηρός. The good person receives σοφία and εὐφροσύνη, as in LXX, but LXX's γνῶσις is missing from Gregory's enumeration of blessings — although the addition of the adjective οὐράνιος, "heavenly" might indicate where this will be complete. The evil person "suffers from greed" (πλεονεξίαν νοσέω — LXX unambiguously had περισπασμός here; cf. v. 23), and so he spends his time "gathering" (ἀθροίζω does service for both προστίθημι and συνάγω of LXX).

The evil person also upbraids the good person, in Gregory's version. Ὀνειδίζω, "to reproach, impute" may have occurred to the paraphrast on the basis of προστίθημι, "to add", which can also mean "to impute". This time the person who is ἀγαθός before God is the one whom God honours (τιμάω, the opposite of ὀνειδίζω — yet another example of Gregory's love for a balanced composition), but "before God" also gives rise to "in the presence of the Lord of all" (Θεός and Δεσπότης πάντων are presumably the same person, since they both arise from the single θεός of the biblical text and since Gregory uses the two synonymously in 12:13 — so Solomon is not speaking prophetically of Christ, but is speaking ironically of the evil person reproaching before God the very person who is honoured by God himself). The three occurrences of LXX's δίδωμι, "to give" are treated by τυγχάνω, "to get" (i.e., "to be given"); θεήλατος, "sent by God" and πλεονεξία, "gain"; and δῶρον, "gift" respectively, so Gregory is well able to provide variation in the paraphrase.

But at the same time he is varying the meaning. It is no longer Koheleth's complaint that some people get a good deal from God and some get a bad deal, which is not as it should be; it is now Solomon's observation that good people get good things and bad people get bad things, which is as it should be. It is no longer Koheleth's frustration at one person receiving the benefits of someone else's hard work; it is now Solomon's indignation at bad people saying bad things about good people. Koheleth said that such a situation is an example of ματαιότης, but Gregory lays the judgment ἄχρηστος, "useless" on the gifts which sinners offer — presumably to God to gain his favour, and thus the blessings of the righteous or his support in their dispute with the righteous — and δολερός, "deceitful" and μάταιος on their eager pursuits (note the use of σπουδάζω and σπεύδω, "to do eagerly" and σπούδασμα, "a thing eagerly done", all in reference to the activities of the evil person, who is θεήλατος, "driven by God").

LXX's προαίρεσις πνεύματος this time finds its equivalent in ἀθλία ψυχή, "wretched soul" or "a soul subject to the toils of conflict". Normally Gregory takes πνεῦμα in this expression as referring to an evil spirit at work in people's hearts, but here he takes it as referring to the hearts of the people themselves: the person who has chosen (προαιρέω) evil is in a wretched spiritual condition.

Chapter Three

(1) Χρόνος δὲ οὗτος πάντων γέμει τῶν ἐναντιωτήτων,[1] ....

This age is full of all the most contrasting things:

Koheleth here introduced his famous Catalogue of Times (vv. 2-8) with the thesis that everything has its appointed time. Such a thesis was nothing new, since much instruction in the ancient Near Eastern wisdom tradition was devoted to the discernment of the right time, place, and extent for human activity.[2] The world in which human beings find themselves has its seasonal variations, and each individual life has its own particular seasons, and so in the natural process of events certain activities are suitable only for certain times. If a person acts at the appropriate time, his activity will be successful, but if he acts at an inappropriate time, even his most strenuous efforts will not suffice to avert failure.

But Koheleth did not present this thesis of everything having its appointed time in order to advise his students or readers that it is possible for them to seize upon the proper time for their sundry activities. The feeling conveyed by his Catalogue of Times was one of despair at the constant changing of the times, leading to the conclusion in v. 9 that human activity is therefore meaningless. This feeling was evoked by the juxtaposition of forceful contrasts: birth/death, planting/uprooting, killing/healing, wrecking/building, weeping/laughing, mourning/dancing, and so on. For each event or activity there is an antithesis, such that event and counter-event, far from complementing each other, cut across each other in meaningless ambiguity. The world thus described is enigmatic, discordant, and contradictory.[3]

Gregory, unlike other early interpreters,[4] grasped Koheleth's point and makes it explicit in his paraphrase, lest anyone should miss it. Here in v. 1, introducing the Catalogue of Times, Gregory notes that the human affairs to be catalogued are characterised by a superlative degree of ἐναντίος, "opposite, contrary, reverse". Later in v. 8, concluding the Catalogue, he reiterates the point by noting that these affairs swing rapidly between "supposed goods" and "acknowledged evils". In the intervening verses he keeps the contrasting affairs short and sharp, thus building up the same feeling as that engendered by Koheleth's short and sharp antitheses.

But Koheleth's expression ὑπὸ τὸν οὐρανόν (חתת השמים) again provides Gregory with an escape clause from an all-pervasive critique of life. Talk of "a time" (LXX χρόνος) which is "under heaven" allows the frame of reference to be limited to "this age" (χρόνος οὗτος — cf. Gregory's use of οὗτος for LXX's ὑπὸ τὸν ἥλιον in 2:3). Doubtless the paraphrast means to imply that there is "an age to come" wherein the present ambiguities and discords of "this age" will no longer be operative and wherein what now seems to be meaningless will be seen to have a meaning. This betrays a confidence which was certainly not evident in the work he is paraphrasing.

(2) ... τοκετῶν, εἶτα θανάτων, βλαστήσεως φυτῶν, εἶτα ἀνατροπῆς·

Births, and then deaths; the growth of plants, and then their uprooting; ....

Koheleth was extremely terse in his Catalogue of Times, simply repeating the formula "a time of [such-and-such] and a time of [its opposite]." A paraphrast might well be tempted to considerably expand and vary the formula. Gregory does vary the formula: in this verse he employs εἶτα, and in subsequent verses simply καί (vv. 3,4) or τε... καί (v. 3), νῦν μὲν... νῦν δέ (vv. 5,6), ποτὲ μὲν... ποτὲ δέ (v. 5), ἄλλοτε... ἄλλοτε (v. 7), ποτὲ μὲν... ἄλλοτε δέ (v. 8), and again εἶτα (vv. 7,8). But he does not expand on the activities enumerated, since his concern is to depict the rapid changing of the times, and his formula here — "[such-and-such], εἶτα (and then, thereupon, soon) [its opposite]", equally as terse as Koheleth's — achieves this admirably.[5]

Throughout the first half of his version of the Catalogue, Gregory opts for the employment of nouns, often cognate to the verbs of LXX. Thus he opens with τοκετός, "birth" (from LXX's τίκτω, "to give birth to") and θάνατος, "death" (from LXX's ἀποθνήσκω, "to die"). LXX's φυτεύω, "to plant" gives rise to

Gregory's φυτόν, "plant", which he depicts as first undergoing βλάστησις, "growth" and then ἀνατροπή, "overthrowing" (evidently taking LXX's ἐκτίλλω, "to pluck up" as connoting a more wanton destruction [cf. Symmachus ἐκριζόω, "to root out"] than gentler souls might prefer him to indicate).[6]

(3) ἰάσεων καὶ ἀναιρέσεων, οἴκων τε εὐορθώσεως καὶ καταλύσεως, ...

... healings and killings, the construction and destruction of houses, ...

Gregory continues with his simple juxtaposition of contrasting nouns, all four of which in this verse — ἴασις, ἀναίρεσις, κατάλυσις, and εὐόρθωσις — are of the same type. Only the first is drawn from a cognate verb in LXX (ἰάομαι), though the paraphrast's reference to houses (οἶκοι) is obviously related to LXX's housebuilding (οἰκοδομέω).

It is noteworthy that Gregory has reversed the order of these particular times. Koheleth depicted a time of killing before a time of healing, and a time of tearing down before a time of building. Gregory's reversal brings the pattern of the events depicted in this verse into line with the pattern established in the preceding verse: in each pair the constructive activity is itemised first (birth, planting, healing, and building) and the concomitant destructive activity follows it (death, uprooting, killing, and tearing down). To use the terms which Gregory himself employs in v. 8 to summarise the Catalogue of Times, the pattern is one of change from ἀγαθός to κακός — by changing the order of the times catalogued here, Gregory has made this verse conform to his later summary.

Koheleth's sequence of destruction and reconstruction was all too common in the ancient world, and made a good parallel to the killing/healing sequence of this verse and to the war/ peace sequence of v. 8. Gregory had spoken of the reconstruction (ἀνόρθωσις) of houses in 2:4, when — as is also the case here — Koheleth had simply mentioned building (LXX οἰκοδομέω). If Koheleth's order in this verse had been retained, Gregory could have used the concept of reconstruction again. Instead, he is forced to speak of the construction (εὐόρθωσις) of houses prior to their destruction (κατάλυσις).

(4) ... κλαυθμῶν καὶ γελώτων, κοπετῶν καὶ ὀρχημάτων.

... weeping and laughing, mourning and dancing.

Gregory's treatment of this verse is very straightforward, conforming perfectly to the patterns already noted. All four nouns — which appear in the plural, difficult to bring across in an English translation — are drawn directly from the cognate LXX verbs: κλαυθμός from κλαίω, "to weep"; γέλως from γελάω, "to laugh"; κοπετός from κόπτω, "to mourn"; and ὄρχημα from ὀρχέομαι, "to dance". The antithetical activities are simply divided by καί, the short and simple juxtapositioning of opposites conveying the feeling of rapid changes of mood and fortune.

In one respect, Gregory's careful structuring of his material breaks down in this verse. Throughout the Catalogue of Times he has imposed a pattern of citing first the positive or joyful activity and then its negative or sorrowful counterpart, even where this pattern has necessitated a reversal of Koheleth's order of events, as it does in vv. 3, 5a, and 7b. Here, too, Gregory's pattern calls for a reversal of Koheleth's antitheses, but on this occasion alone in the body of the Catalogue — the final programmatic citation of the states of human affairs in v. 8 is a special case — the paraphrast allows his otherwise consistent structure of Ἀγαθός Times preceding Κακός Times to be varied.

(5) Νῦν μὲν συνάγει τις τὰ ἀπὸ γῆς, νῦν δὲ ἐξέβαλε· καὶ ποτὲ μὲν ἐπιμέμηνε γυναικί, ποτὲ δὲ αὐτὴν ἀποστυχεῖ.

At this moment a person gathers together the things of the earth, but at another moment he throws them away; at one time he dotes upon a woman, but at another time he loathes her.

Koheleth's reference to a time for scattering stones and a time for gathering them together is something of a puzzle, since such activities do not seem as commonplace as the others he catalogued. He may have had in mind the practice of destroying the fertile fields of an enemy by scattering stones over them (2

Kings 3:19,25) and the opposite practice of clearing the ground of one's own fields for the purpose of planting (Isaiah 5:2),[7] in which case it would be a variation on the thoughts of vv. 2 — "a time to plant and a time to pluck up what is planted" — and 8 — "a time for war and a time for peace". Alternatively, he possibly had in mind the scattering of stones from a structure (cf. the depiction of walls and houses being destroyed in Ezekiel 26:12) and the collecting of stones for a new structure (cf. the gathering of wood to rebuild the temple in Haggai 1:8), in which case it would be a return to the thought of v. 3 — "a time to tear down and a time to build".[8]

Gregory offers no explanation of the scattering and gathering of "stones" (LXX λίθοι) specifically, but rephrases the expression as one concerning "the things of the earth" (τὰ ἀπὸ γῆς) in general. This neat paraphrase removes the possibility that readers might be puzzled about what Koheleth meant, without adding anything unwieldy to the text by way of explanation and thus upsetting its compact structure. The structure does change somewhat at this point of the paraphrase, in that Gregory now employs verbs to denote the sundry activities listed in the second half of the Catalogue of Times, whereas in the first half he employed nouns for this purpose, but the pattern of activities is still — after the momentary lapse in the previous verse — a positive action followed by its negative counterpart, a pattern which again requires (in the case of the first pair in this verse) a reversal of Koheleth's order of affairs.[9]

For the first pair of verbs, Gregory is content to more or less straightforwardly adopt his predecessor's vocabulary: the "gathering" is denoted by LXX's συνάγω and the "throwing away" by ἐκβάλλω, a slight fine-tuning of LXX's βάλλω. But for the "embracing" (LXX περιλαμβάνω) and the "being far off" (LXX μακρύνομαι) from embracing, he prefers to portray more graphically the alarming fickleness of human infatuation by employing the verbs ἐπιμαίνομαι, "to be mad after, dote upon" and ἀποστυγέω, "to hate violently, loathe". Gregory might well have had the story of Amnon and Tamar (2 Samuel 13) in mind as the biblical example *par excellence* of what he here depicts, but

60 GREGORY'S ECCLESIASTES

he would also have seen Solomon — to his mind the originator of the thoughts he is paraphrasing — as the embodiment of this change of passion. In 7:26 Gregory's Solomon confesses that he had been seized by a fatal passion for women, and goes on to display a current passionate feeling of antagonism towards their kind. Who better than the legendary lover, now reformed, to make mention of the ebb and flow of the passions?

(6) Καὶ νῦν μὲν ἐζήτησέ τις ὁτιοῦν, νῦν δὲ ἀπώλεσε· καὶ νῦν μὲν ἐφύλαξε, νῦν δὲ προήκατο·

Now he searches for something, but then he loses it completely; now he keeps it, but then he lets it go.

Koheleth here placed two closely allied couplets, the first half of the verse contrasting the acquisition of possessions with their loss, and the second half contrasting the careful guarding of what one has with a lack of care or even wilful abandonment of it.[10] Gregory assists this linking by offering parallel νῦν μὲν... νῦν δέ constructions, the same construction as he employed for the similar thought of gathering together and then throwing away the things of the earth in the first half of the previous verse. He again mostly reproduces LXX's verbs — ζητέω, "to seek, search for"; ἀπόλλυμι, "to lose utterly"; φυλάσσω, "to keep, guard" — but since in the previous verse he made use of ἐκβάλλω, "to throw away", he now characteristically introduces some variety in the vocabulary by inserting προΐεμαι, "to let go, abandon". His formulation conveys a feeling of the fickleness of human emotions, at one time investing considerable attention and care in a thing but later not caring at all.

(7) ἄλλοτε ἀπέκτεινεν, ἄλλοτε ἐφονεύθη· ἐλάλησεν, εἶτα ἡσύχασεν·

At one time he kills, and at another time he is killed; he speaks, and then he keeps quiet; ....

Perhaps Koheleth intended with this verse to continue the thought of carefulness/carelessness towards possessions expressed in the previous verse, now in regard to one's clothing (at one time thoughtlessly damaging and at another time painstakingly repairing an item of clothing) and conversation (at one time having the presence of mind to keep tight-lipped about some matter and at another time being unable to prevent oneself from blurting everything out). Or he might well have had in view the ancient mourning customs of rending one's garments (and then sewing up the rent after the mourning period has passed) and observing the period when speech is forbidden (and then speaking again after the mourning period). Gregory does not link the two couplets in either of these ways; on the contrary, he takes considerable liberties with the first one.

How does Gregory derive "kill and be killed" from "rend and sew"? LXX's ῥήγνυμι, "to tear up" may have suggested to him a rather gruesome form of death. In Matthew 7:6 this verb was used to describe animals tearing into a human being, a situation which was later actually facilitated by certain persecutors against Christian martyrs; such atrocities may have been fresh in Gregory's mind as a result of the Decian persecution and so prompted him to render ῥήγνυμι as ἀποκτείνω, "to kill, slay". Or perhaps Gregory had once witnessed or heard a graphic report of a brutal slaying in which someone had literally been torn up by a sword-wielding killer, and this naturally came to mind when he considered what Koheleth had written. We might then expect the antithesis of "tearing up" — LXX ῥάπτω, "to sew together" — to be rendered by an equivalent of ἰάομαι, "to heal", which is the antithesis of LXX's ἀποκτείνω in v. 3, but Gregory offers φονεύομαι, "to be killed". Perhaps the metaphorical meaning of ῥάπτω ("to devise, plot")[11] suggested to Gregory the process of retributive killing, and/or he is being mindful of the biblical principle, "Whoever sheds human blood, shall have his blood shed by human hands" (Genesis 9:6).

No liberties are taken with the second couplet, apart from once again reversing the order of the antithetical components in order to have what might be regarded as the more ἀγαθός activity precede what might be regarded as the more κακός activity (it would seem that Gregory regards the time of silence as being occasioned by misfortune, judging by the pattern he imposes again here; he may even be linking the time of speaking with the time of killing — the killer boasting about what he has done — and the time of silence with the time of being killed — the boaster is permanently silenced). Λαλέω, "to speak" is again LXX's word, while ἡσυχάζω, "to keep quiet" closely paraphrases LXX's σιγάω. The formulation, consisting of the two verbs separated by εἶτα, could not be more compact.

(8) ἠγάπησεν, εἶτα ἐμίσησε. Τὰ γὰρ ἐν ἀνθρώποις πράγματα ποτὲ μὲν πολεμεῖται, ἄλλοτε δὲ εἰρηνεύεται, ὀξυρρόπως τῶν πραγμάτων ἐξ ἀγαθῶν εἶναι δοκούντων εἰς ὁμολογούμενα κακὰ μεταπιπτόντων.

... he loves, and then he hates. Human affairs are at one time in a state of war, but at another time in a state of peace — these affairs rapidly change from supposed goods to acknowledged evils.

Koheleth's Catalogue of Times here came to a close with two final couplets. In the first of these Gregory is satisfied with LXX's μισέω, "to hate", but he prefers — as does Aquila — ἀγαπάω to LXX's φιλέω, "to love", perhaps (in Gregory's case) because ἀγάπη was such a meaningful word for the Greek-speaking Christians, ἀγαπάω thus being the standard antonym of μισέω in the Christian literature. In the second couplet Gregory employs verbs which are cognate to LXX's nouns: πολεμέω from πόλεμος, "war" and εἰρηνεύω from εἰρήνη, "peace". This is the reverse of what he did in the first half of the Catalogue; viz., the employment of nouns which were for the most part cognate to LXX's verbs. Koheleth used verbs throughout the Catalogue, with the exception of the final couplet concerning a time for war and a time for peace, where the change from verbs to nouns emphasised the completion of the list of times.[12]   Gregory changed from nouns to verbs in the middle of the Catalogue, and now sticks with the employment of verbs to the end, but he marks the completion of the list of times by offering a summary of what has been at work in each of the antithetical affairs: events which a person might regard positively (birth, the growth of a plant, healing, the construction of a house, laughing, dancing, gathering together the things of the earth, doting upon a woman, searching for something, keeping it, being rid of an enemy, speaking, and loving — in general, being at peace with oneself and the world) quickly give way to those which people commonly regard negatively (death, the uprooting of a plant, killing, the destruction of a house, weeping, mourning, throwing away the things of the earth, loathing a woman, losing something completely, letting it go, being killed, keeping quiet, and hating — in general, being at war with oneself and the world).[13] As Gregory phrased it in v. 1, "this age is full of all the most contrasting things".

(9) Παυσώμεθα τοίνυν ἐξ ἀνονήτων μόχθων.

So let us refrain from useless labours.

Koheleth here repeated the "programmatic question"[14] he had asked at the very beginning (1:3), putting it to the reader again in the light of the Catalogue of Times as a kind of introduction to the characteristic conclusions he draws from the Catalogue. The rhetorical question was, in effect: "What advantage accrues to the person who has to undergo this incessant routine of planting / plucking / killing / healing / wrecking / building / weeping / laughing / mourning / dancing / scattering / gathering / embracing / refraining / gaining / losing / keeping / discarding / tearing / sewing / hushing / speaking / loving / hating / fighting / pacifying?" The implied answer is: "No permanent advantage or satisfaction can be gained from toiling in a world marked by such maddening ambivalence."

As in 1:3, Gregory changes Koheleth's rhetorical question into an assertion that human beings are toiling away at the wrong things; in this case, he fashions it into a call to his readers to have done with such things. The question concerning the profitability (LXX περισσεία) of toiling (LXX μοχθέω) is answered by the judgment that the toil (μόχθος) in which people are engaged is unprofitable (ἀνόνητος). Gregory does not make this judgment on all human activity, but only on those activities directed towards earthly rather than heavenly concerns. In 1:3 he complained about people having given themselves over to the pursuit of the transitory (πρόσκαιρος, "lasting but for a time"; cf. 3:13); now he admonishes them to forgo these pursuits entirely.

(10) Ταῦτα γὰρ ἅπαντα, ὥς γέ μοι δοκεῖ, κέντροις ἰοβόλοις ἀνθρώπους ἐξοιστρεῖν ἐτέθη.

For all these things — as it seems to me, at any rate — are arranged to madden people with poisonous stings.

In 1:13 Koheleth had stated his view that God has burdened human beings with an evil task (LXX περισπασμός, "distraction, disturbance"), an assertion repeated here, though the word "evil" (LXX πονηρός) is omitted.[15] In 1:13 Gregory had removed the word "God" (LXX θεός) in favour of an impersonal construction which allowed the blame for the human plight to be shifted from the divine shoulders, a tactic which he now repeats. Ἐτέθη, "it is set, laid down, arranged" (aorist passive of τίθημι) has no stated agent; although Gregory may have God in mind as the one who afflicts people who indulge in the multifarious earthly activities enumerated in the preceding verses (after all, he noted in 2:26 that God harasses the evil person),[16] it would seem from the immediate mention of "an evil observer of the times" — καιροσκόπος δή τις πονηρός of v. 11 is the very next expression after ἐτέθη — that Gregory wants to shift the blame for human suffering from God to God's antagonist (see the comments on this "evil observer" under the following verse).

Although Koheleth did not actually assign the adjective πονηρός to περισπασμός in this instance, it is evident that the same negative value-judgment he applied in 1:13 is also to be applied here. So Gregory is quite justified in saying that the effect of these various human tasks is "to madden" (ἐξοιστράω) people, to make them wild, as if they had been stung with "poisonous stings" (κέντρα ἰοβόλα). In 12:11 it is the sayings of the wise which are depicted as having the effect of a (βού)κεντρον, in the positive sense of rousing the mind, but here it is the doings of the foolish which Gregory likens to a κέντρον, in the negative sense of infuriating the mind; while a κέντρον can be an instrument for guiding, it can also be an instrument of torture.

(11) Καιροσκόπος δή τις πονηρὸς τὸν αἰῶνα τοῦτον περικέχηνεν, ἀφανίσαι ὑπερδιατεινόμενος τὸ τοῦ Θεοῦ πλάσμα, ἐξ ἀρχῆς αὐτῷ μέχρι τέλους πολεμεῖν ᾑρημένος.

Indeed, an evil observer of the times has this age in his jaws, and strives with a great effort to wipe out the image of God, having chosen to fight against him from the beginning until the end.

"He has put the αἰών (עלם) in their heart" is the most disputed phrase in Ecclesiastes,[17] but its juxtaposition with the phrase "yet so that a person might not find out the work which God has done from beginning to end" suggests that the former has much to do with the human desire to achieve the latter. In 7:27,28 Koheleth recorded that he had wanted to discover "the sum" of things, but could not; and in 8:17 he noted that people seek to find out "all the work of God... that is done under the sun", but cannot. 3:11 makes excellent sense as a kind of parallel to these two verses. The human being has αἰών, "eternity" in his heart — his Creator has made him a thinking being, and he wants to pass beyond his fragmentary knowledge and discern the fuller meaning of the whole pattern[18] — but the Creator will not let the creature be his equal. As surely as God has put αἰών in the human heart (a consciousness that there is more than the immediate καιρός of this or that [vv. 2-8] in which the creature finds itself), he has also put a veil upon the human heart, so that the finite human mind is unable to reach beyond the καιρός into the αἰών to see as God does.

To Gregory αἰών suggests the present time, ὁ αἰὼν οὗτος. This expression was a familiar one from the New Testament, where it denoted the present age which is under the rulership of the devil but which will soon come to an end when Christ ushers in the age to come, ὁ αἰὼν μέλλων. In particular it is worth noting 2 Corinthians 4:4, where it was said that "the god of this age (ὁ θεὸς τοῦ αἰῶνος τούτου) has blinded the minds of the unbelievers, to keep them from seeing... Christ, who is the image (εἰκών) of God". Gregory seems to be making a similar assertion, that an evil Being has the present age in his power and seeks to wipe out the image (πλάσμα) of God.

The Being in question is depicted as "an evil observer of the times" (καιροσκόπος τις πονηρός), presumably because he keeps a close watch on the καιροί (vv. 2-8) so that he may take advantage of any opportunity to do his evil work; the blame for the καιροί constantly changing from ἀγαθός to κακός (v. 8) is doubtlessly to be seen as the result of the timely activities of this καιροσκόπος, and fighting (πολεμέω) in the human sphere in v. 8 is to be seen as a result of this Being's being at war (πολεμέω) against what is of God. Gregory's belief that the world is currently in the grips of an evil Being is graphically portrayed by the verb περιχάσκω, "to close the jaws over, take into the mouth", which seems to characterise this "observer" as a predator (cf. 1 Peter 5:8, where the devil is depicted as "prowling around like a roaring lion, seeking someone to devour") who has his prey precisely where he wants it. What he wants is to defeat God, by destroying God's image in the world (this probably means subverting everything and everybody in God's creation to his own evil ends, so that nothing good is left, or — à la 2 Corinthians 4:4 — preventing people from seeing Christ; i.e. — à la Koheleth — preventing them from finding out the work which God has done). This struggle has been going on since "the beginning" and will continue until "the end" (ἀρχή and τέλος respectively, as in LXX).

Gregory's interpretation of this verse is rather apocalyptic. On three counts it is reminiscent of the famous passage in Revelation 12:7-12 concerning war in heaven. Firstly and most obviously, both Gregory and the visionary of Revelation speak of fighting (πολεμέω) on the part of the evil one against the forces of God. Secondly, the imagery employed by the apocalypticist to depict the evil one is "the great dragon" and "that ancient serpent", both of which accord with the paraphrast's image of the evil one "closing his jaws over" this age. And thirdly, the same passage in Revelation mentions how the evil one has come to earth greatly agitated "because he knows that his time (καιρός) is short", providing further reason for Gregory to style him as a καιροσκόπος who is "greatly exerting himself" (ὑπερδιατείνομαι) during the present age.

Koheleth's opening remark that "he has made everything

beautiful (LXX καλός) in its time" — i.e., God has created the whole set-up in such a way that nothing happens in the world sooner or later than he wants it to happen (cf. Genesis 1:31, "God saw everything that he had made, and it was very good [LXX καλός]", because it corresponded exactly to what he intended) — does not quite fit into Gregory's scheme of things in this passage. Since he has treated the Catalogue of Times pessimistically, he is unable to incorporate the thought of everything being καλός in his paraphrase. He introduced the Catalogue by saying that "this age (χρόνος οὗτος) is full of all the most contrasting things" (v. 1), and now he gives the reason for this unhappy state of affairs: "an evil observer of the times has this age (αἰὼν οὗτος) in his jaws." For the Church Father, πονηρός rather than καλός characterises the present time.

(12) Πέπεισμαι τοίνυν τὰ μέγιστα ἀγαθὰ ἀνθρώπῳ εὐθυμίαν καὶ εὐποιΐαν ὑπάρχειν, ...

Accordingly, I am persuaded that the greatest good for a person is cheerfulness and kindness, ...

Here was the second instance of Koheleth's οὐκ ἔστιν ἀγαθόν (אין טוב) expression, and the first instance of that expression being followed by a clause beginning with εἰ μή (כי אם). It is the only instance in which Gregory unambiguously assents to Koheleth's opinion as expressed by the "there is no good except..." formula, although even here he qualifies his approval. In 2:24 the absence of εἰ μή allowed Gregory legitimately to avoid any suggestion of an "eat, drink, and be merry" sentiment, and in 3:22 and 8:15 he presents the sentiment as a view once mistakenly held by a Solomon who has since come to his senses. But here in 3:12 there is no hint that Solomon may be mistaken in "being persuaded" (πείθομαι, for LXX's γιγνώσκω, "to know") that enjoyment is good; the qualification soon appears, however — in the next verse, which is still part of the same sentence in the paraphrase — that this applies only "if righteousness guides one's actions".

The reason for Gregory's approval of Koheleth's enjoinment to enjoyment in this case is that the concomitant activities of "being joyful" (LXX εὐφραίνομαι) were not "eating" (LXX ἐσθίω) and "drinking" (LXX πίνω), which sound suspiciously like the pagan philosophy, but just "doing good" (LXX ποιέω ἀγαθόν), which sounds decidedly more Christian. By ποιέω ἀγαθόν (עשה טוב), Koheleth may actually have meant something like "do oneself good, enjoy oneself, make the most of something" (so Ibn Ezra; cf. ὁράω ἀγαθόν [ראה טוב], "see good" in the following verse, and ποιέω κακά [עשה רע], "do oneself harm" in 2 Samuel 12:18),[19] but since Koheleth used the expression in the ethical sense in 7:20, Gregory is quite justified in interpreting it in the same way here. In point of fact, Koheleth mentioned "eating and drinking" in the very next verse, so that it is evident that his sentiments here were identical with those he expressed on the other occasions on which he employed the οὐκ ἔστιν ἀγαθόν formula, but Gregory ignores those references. His paraphrase covers only the two activities mentioned in the verse at hand, with two finely-balanced nouns: εὐθυμία, "cheerfulness" (for LXX's εὐφραίνομαι) and εὐποιΐα, "kindness" (literally, "the doing of good", for LXX's ποιέω ἀγαθόν). The formula itself, "there is no good except..." (LXX οὐκ ἔστιν ἀγαθὸν εἰ μή) is well handled by the paraphrase "the greatest good is..." (τὰ μέγιστα ἀγαθὰ ὑπάρχειν).

(13) ... καὶ μέν τοι καὶ τὴν πρόσκαιρον ταύτην ἀπόλαυσιν ἐκ Θεοῦ παραγενέσθαι μόνον, εἰ δικαιοσύνη τῶν πράξεων[20] ἡγοῖτο.

... and that this temporary enjoyment comes solely from God, if righteousness guides one's actions.

Each time Koheleth employed the οὐκ ἔστιν ἀγαθόν formula, he followed it with a clause referring to the God-givenness of the situation (2:24ff.; 3:13,22; 8:15) and thus sought to validate the advice given in the formula.[21] Gregory agrees that everything good comes from God, but does not agree with Koheleth on what is good. "To see good" (LXX ὁράω ἀγαθόν) he correctly understands as "see as enjoyable" (hence his use of ἀπόλαυσις, "enjoyment" or an advantage attained from something), but he ignores Koheleth's characteristic reference to "eating and drinking" because, as he has already said in 2:24, "the perfect good (τὸ τέλειον ἀγαθόν — cf. τὰ μέγιστα ἀγαθά in 3:12) does not lie in eating and drinking".

Gregory, as if to compensate for deleting a significant part of the verse (the matter of eating and drinking), makes two additions, both of which can be well defended. The first of these is the note that one's enjoyment is only πρόσκαιρος, "temporary", a comment quite in keeping with Koheleth's sentiments, and a particularly timely word in view of the just-completed catalogue of the rapidly-changing καιροί in vv. 2-8. The second addition is the note that God only grants this enjoyment εἰ δικαιοσύνη τῶν πράξεων ἡγοῖτο, "if righteousness guides one's actions", a comment not so clearly in keeping with Koheleth's sentiments — but doubtless Gregory would defend it on the basis of the thought expressed in 2:26 that God only gives joy to the person who "pleases" (literally, "is ἀγαθός before") him, in contrast to the "sinner" (ἁμαρτάνων); to a pious interpreter, this can only mean that God gives joy solely to the person who is δίκαιος, even though that joy can only be πρόσκαιρος in a world which is in the grip of an evil καιροσκόπος.

(14) Τῶν δὲ αἰωνίων καὶ ἀφθάρτων πραγμάτων, ὅσα ὁ Θεὸς παγίως ὥρισεν, οὔτε τι ἀφελεῖν, οὔτε τι προσθεῖναι δυνατόν. ῷ τινι οὖν, ἀλλ᾽ ἔστιν, ἐκεῖνα φοβερά τε ὁμοῦ καὶ θαυμαστά·

But it is not possible either to take anything away from, or to add anything to, those eternal and incorruptible things which God has firmly laid down. To anybody, those things are both fearful and wonderful.

Gregory evidently approves of this verse, as he takes nothing away from it, nor adds anything to it, unlike his treatment of the previous verse. He even faithfully reproduces LXX's very words for "taking away from" (ἀφαιρέω) and "adding to" (προστίθημι), although in reverse order. Whatever God does, lasts "forever" (LXX εἰς τὸν αἰῶνα), said Koheleth; whatever God has established, is "eternal and incorruptible" (αἰώνιος καὶ ἄφθαρτος), says Gregory. In Koheleth's version there seems to have been a contrast with the human situation depicted in v. 11 (human beings only have the thought of αἰών implanted in their

hearts),[22] while in Gregory's version the same contrast is with
the human situation depicted in v. 13 (human beings are in a
πρόσκαιρος situation), although Gregory may also intend a
contrast with the satanic situation he has depicted in his
reworking of v. 11 (the evil observer of the times will only be
able to do his evil work during ὁ αἰὼν οὗτος, whereas the good
work of God is αἰώνιος).

Koheleth rounded off this verse with the explanation that
God has created a situation in which his creatures are powerless
against what he does, because he wants them to "fear" (LXX
φοβέομαι) him. It seems quite likely that φοβέομαι (ירא) here
expressed an actual "fear" (if not indeed terror) which compels
acceptance of the human situation and resignation towards it
(since God and humans are in their respective places, as
Koheleth noted in 5:1), rather than the reverent "fear of the
Lord" (φόβος κυρίου), a relationship of faith and piety, which is
to be found elsewhere in Scripture (e.g., Psalm 111 [LXX 110]:10).[23]
Gregory captures the ambivalence of the verb φοβέομαι by
paraphrasing with two adjectives: φοβερός, "fearful, dreadful"
and θαυμαστός, "wonderful, admirable"; in this way he conveys
both the actual fear of the ungodly and the reverent fear of the
faithful, while suggesting that every human being (ὅστις οὖν,
"whosoever") ought to stand in awe and admiration of the
omnipotent God.

(15) καὶ τὰ μὲν γενόμενα, ἕστηκε· τὰ δὲ ἐσόμενα, ἤδη κατὰ τὸ
προεγνῶσθαι γεγένηται. Θεῷ δὲ κέχρηται ὁ ἀδικούμενος βοηθῷ.

**Those things which have taken place, have endured; and
those things which will take place, have already occurred — as
far as foreknowing is concerned. And the person who is
wronged has a helper in God.**

Koheleth rounded off the section on the Times with a
repetition of the idea expressed in 1:9 that things repeat
themselves. It was worth repeating that observation in the light
of the Catalogue of Times, which had not explicitly stated
(although the implication was obvious) that these various
antithetical events and activities repeat themselves. But in the

light of this verse's immediate context of v. 14, Gregory feels it best to link this verse with the idea of the omnipotence and omniscience of God, and places the first part of v. 15 in the same sentence as his categorising of God's work in v. 14 as "both fearful and wonderful". Thus Koheleth's phrase, "that which has been, is already [or: now]" (LXX τὸ γενόμενον ἤδη ἐστίν), linked with his statement in v. 14 that everything which God does, lasts "forever" (LXX εἰς τὸν αἰῶνα), yields Gregory's contention here that "these things which have taken place [at the behest of God], have endured" (τὰ γενόμενα, ἔστηκε). And if in this context Koheleth remarked that "that which is to be, has been already [or: now]" (LXX ὅσα τοῦ γίνεσθαι, ἤδη γέγονεν, which Gregory closely paraphrases with τὰ ἐσόμενα, ἤδη... γεγένηται), he must have been referring — in Gregory's view — to the omniscience of God, who "foreknows" (προγιγνώσκω) already at this time what is going to take place in future times.

"God seeks what is pursued" is at first sight a puzzling phrase, but there are two ways which commend themselves as offering a solution to the puzzle in this context. One is to take "seek" (LXX ζητέω) and "pursue" (LXX διώκω) as synonyms, as they were in Psalm 34:15 (English v. 14, Greek 33:15), "seek peace and pursue it" (LXX ζήτησον εἰρήνην καὶ δίωξον αὐτήν), and thus arrive at the meaning, "God keeps on seeking what he has sought before"24 — "there is nothing new under the sun" (1:9) because God repeats himself, and brings about precisely the same events as he had brought about previously; he brings back a time for war after a time for peace which followed a previous time for war, and similarly with all the other antithetical καιροί. The second way of solving this puzzle by means of the context is to understand "what [or: who] is pursued" (LXX ὁ διωκόμενος) as having a nuance derived from the Catalogue of Times (vv. 2-8): each καιρός is followed by its opposite number in the Catalogue at such a pace (usually there were only two words in each Hebrew stich, and one of those in the construct state) that one can well imagine the latter καιρός chasing the former out of the way, only to be pushed off the scene again by its opposite — acts and events occur continually, each pursuing the other in a revolving circle;25 the time to build, for example, is nudged out

of the way by the time to break down, until it itself is brought
back by God for a time.

Whichever of these two possible solutions captures the
precise sense of ὁ διωκόμενος (whether it is God or the opposing
καιρός which does the pursuing, or even whether — since God
is in control of the καιροί — both are meant), they both point to
an understanding of this fascinating phrase which is shared by
the Vulgate's *et Deus instaurat quod abiit*, "and God restores
what has elapsed".[26] But other ancient interpreters did not take
such heed of the context in their attempts to unravel Koheleth's
phrase. By itself, ὁ διωκόμενος (נרדף) sounded to them like "what
[*or*: who] is pursued" in the negative sense of "hunted" or
"persecuted". Thus the Targum renders the phrase as "the LORD
will seek the poor and needy from the hands of the wicked who
pursued (רדף) him", and the Peshitta speaks of God seeking the
"one who is persecuted" (ܡܬܪܕܦܐ). Even Gregory, who — as
noted earlier — had an eye on the context of this verse
(although, it is true, he did not take the first part of the verse as
referring to the καιροί and so cannot be expected to understand
this final phrase as making the same reference), interprets the
phrase in the same way: "the pursued", in his view, is "the
person who is wronged or injured" in some way (ὁ ἀδικούμενος), and the statement that God "seeks" such a person is the
assurance that God is the "helper" or "rescuer" (βοηθός) of the
wrongfully or injuriously pursued.[27]

(16) Εἶδον ἐν τοῖς κάτω μέρεσι, κολάσεως μὲν βάραθρον τοὺς
δυσσεβεῖς δεχόμενον, εὐσεβέσι δὲ χῶρον ἕτερον ἀνειμένον.

**I saw in the lower regions a pit of punishment awaiting the
ungodly, but a different place set apart for the godly.**

Koheleth now bemoaned the fact that he had seen "wickedness" or "injustice" (רשע) in "the place of judgment" (מקום המשפט,
presumably the law-courts) and in "the place of righteousness"
(מקום הצדק, which may be a synonym of מקום המשפט for the sake of
emphasis, or may denote the sphere of religion).[28] The
repetition of the phrase שמה הרשע ("wickedness was there" — in
the very places where one would look for justice and integrity)

demonstrated Koheleth's abhorrence of corruption (cf. the repetition of his lament in 4:1 that "there was no comforter for them", *viz.* the oppressed).[29] The text read a little differently in LXX. "The place of judgment" (τόπος τῆς κρίσεως) and "the place of righteousness" (τόπος τοῦ δικαίου) were still there, but the former had become the place of "the ungodly person" (ὁ ἀσεβής, evidently vocalising רשע with double *qametz* rather than the Masoretes' *seghol* and *patach*), while the latter had become the place of "the godly person" (ὁ εὐσεβής, which was either an early mistake on the part of a copyist,[30] or a deliberate adjustment on the part of the translator or a later scribe in the interest of orthodoxy).

Not surprisingly, Gregory's paraphrase is in keeping with LXX.[31] He exults over "a pit of punishment" (κολάσεως βάραθρον) which awaits the ungodly and "a different place" (χῶρος ἕτερος) which awaits the godly; he employs LXX's εὐσεβής to denote the latter fortunate individuals, but prefers δυσσεβής over ἀσεβής to denote the former unfortunate individuals. Evidently Koheleth's talk of places of judgment and of righteousness, particularly in the LXX form of juxtaposing the godly and the ungodly, has brought to the Christian paraphrast's mind the separation of the sheep from the goats (Matthew 25:31-46); in view of his treatment of v. 11 as having to do with the present age being in the control of an evil Being, it is not surprising that Gregory would view v. 16 as having to do with the age to come rectifying this unhappy situation (cf., for example, Revelation 14:9-11; 20:1-3,10,15 on the idea of "a pit of punishment" for the evil Being and those who follow him, and Revelation 21:1-4 on the idea of "a different place" for those who follow God; Matthew 25:34,41,46 reflected the same ideas).

In 1:14 Gregory paraphrased LXX's ὑπὸ τὸν ἥλιον by κάτω, to indicate that "a strange, foul spirit" was operative below the heavenly realm. As his paraphrase of Koheleth's frequent expression on this occasion he offers ἐν τοῖς κάτω μέρεσι, "in the lower regions", to indicate the proper destination of all who succumb to that spirit. It is unlikely that Gregory intends ἐν τοῖς κάτω μέρεσι to apply also in regard to the different place set apart for the godly, since he would most likely view that place as being in the heavenly realm; even if he were thinking of the "new earth" (γῆ καινή, Revelation 21:1) in contrast to the "new heaven" (οὐρανὸς καινός, *ibid.*), which in itself would be a surprising distinction to make, he would hardly link this place with the pit of punishment of the ungodly as being both ἐν τοῖς κάτω μέρεσι. There is no doubt, though, that for Koheleth "the place of judgment" and "the place of righteousness" were both ὑπὸ τὸν ἥλιον — i.e., in the sphere of human activity and experience. And for Koheleth, "I saw" (LXX εἶδον) referred to the quite straightforward, down-to-earth observation of just what was going on around him; but for Gregory in this instance, εἶδον denotes a visionary "seeing" on the part of "a prophet wiser than anyone else" (1:1).

(17) Ἐλογισάμην δὲ πάντα ὅμοια ὑπάρχειν παρὰ Θεῷ νομίζεσθαι καὶ κρίνεσθαι, ταυτὸν εἶναι δικαίους καὶ ἀδίκους, λογικὰ καὶ ἄλογα. Χρόνον τε γὰρ ἅπασιν ὁμοίως ἐπιμεμετρῆσθαι, καὶ θάνατον ἐπηρτῆσθαι,...

I concluded that with God everything is considered and judged to be equal — it is the same for the righteous as for the unrighteous, for those with reason as for those without reason. Time is measured out equally to all, and death hangs over them.

Since Gregory interpreted the previous verse as having to do with eschatological judgment, it might be expected that he would take the same line with v. 17. This verse, which speculated that "God will judge the righteous and the wicked", would appear to have been an excellent candidate upon which to base a paraphrase concerning future retribution.[32] But to Gregory's mind the operative phrase is "I said in my heart" (LXX εἶπα ἐγὼ ἐν καρδίᾳ μου), which appeared at the beginning of both this and the following verse. This indicates to Gregory, as it did in 1:16 (where ἐλάλησα appeared instead of εἶπα) and 2:1, that the human thoughts of the man Solomon were being presented here in contrast to the divine wisdom which the prophet Solomon presented elsewhere. So Gregory again employs λογίζομαι to denote this fallible human reasoning, all too prone to arrive at conclusions which are wide of the truth. He

interprets v. 17, together with the following verses to the end of
this chapter, as being Solomon's thoughts at a particular time
that the fates of human and animal, and of the righteous and
unrighteous, are the same. Gregory does not, at this point in his
version of Ecclesiastes, say outright that these thoughts were
misguided; he merely presents them as conclusions which have
been drawn. It is left to Chapter Nine to clear up any possibility
of misunderstanding in this matter. There, in vv. 1-3, the idea
that the same fate awaits both the righteous and the unrighteous
is repeated, and at that stage of his sermon Gregory's Solomon
states clearly that that was what he had thought at one time but
now knows to be a false and foolish opinion.

So for the moment this false and foolish opinion is
expressed without comment, save for the ἐλογισάμην, "I
concluded by (human) reasoning" which stands at its head. It
seems as if God "regards" (νομίζω expands on what Gregory
understands LXX to have meant by κρίνω, "to judge", which he
also includes in his paraphrase) all his creatures to be the same,
whether they be "righteous" (δίκαιος, as in LXX), or
"unrighteous" (ἄδικος, a more precise antithesis than LXX's
ἀσεβής), or whether they be "with reason" (λογικός) or "without
reason" (ἄλογος). The latter two antitheses are transposed here
from Koheleth's talk in the following verses of "human beings"
(LXX υἱοὶ τοῦ ἀνθρώπου) and "animals" (LXX κτήνη), it suiting
the paraphrast's purpose to have the subject-matter of this
passage as a whole introduced in the opening sentence governed
by λογίζομαι. Similarly, Koheleth's reassertion that there is a
time for everything is interpreted by Gregory in the light of the
thought in the following verses that the fates of human beings
and animals are the same: the same amount of time is
"measured out" (ἐπιμετρέομαι) to both types of creature, and the
same death "hangs over" (ἐπαρτάομαι) both. It is perhaps
possible that the little word ἐκεῖ, "there", which MT (שׁם) placed at
the end of this verse and LXX at the beginning of the next,[33] and
which the Targum sees as an allusion to the judgment after
death, has prompted Gregory to make reference to death here,
but more likely the paraphrase stems from the context of this
verse rather than from any particular element in the verse itself.

(18) ... ταυτόν τε εἶναι παρὰ Θεῷ κτηνῶν τε καὶ ἀνθρώπων φῦλα, διαφέρειν δὲ ἀλλήλων, μόνῳ τῷ ἐνάρθρῳ τῆς φωνῆς·

With God the races of animals and humans are equal, differing from each other only in the articulation of the voice.

Koheleth's construction of this verse was a little contorted, but his basic meaning is clear enough: human beings are really the same as animals. Gregory paraphrases this quite straightforwardly, not even repeating λογίζομαι or an equivalent to cast doubt over the truth of the assertion, even though Koheleth repeated the phrase εἶπα ἐγὼ ἐν καρδίᾳ μου (אמרתי אני בלבי) — Gregory evidently believed that placing that qualifier once at the beginning of the passage (v. 17) with a reminder at the end (μοι ἐδόκει, "it seemed to me", v. 22), was sufficient to set the right tone for these conclusions. Λογικά and ἄλογα had been Gregory's own way of denoting the two types of creatures (v. 17); here he is content to make use of LXX's κτήνη and ἄνθρωποι (LXX actually had the Semitism υἱοὶ τοῦ ἀνθρώπου, which Gregory has characteristically Graecised).

In just one respect, Gregory's Solomon says, human beings and animals do "differ" (διαφέρω) from each other, and that is in "the articulation of the voice" (ὁ ἔναρθρος τῆς φωνῆς). This observation arises from Koheleth's expression "in regard to the matter of (על־דברת) human beings", which LXX had rather mechanically translated as "in regard to the speech (περὶ λαλιᾶς — cf. Peshitta ܕܒ̈ܢܝ) of human beings" and thus provided the catalyst for Gregory's interpretation. Even so, Gregory arrives at quite a different meaning for the verse than that of LXX: the earlier Greek translation seems to have been saying that in their talking, too, human beings are shown to be nothing more than animals (this presumably means that, despite their assumed intelligence and superiority, humans demonstrate by what they say that they are still on the level of an instinctual beast), but Gregory has Solomon say that in their talking, alone, human beings can be seen to be different from animals (this means that humans are able to make articulate sounds, in contrast to the dumb beasts).

(19) συμβαίνειν δὲ αὐτοῖς ἅπαντα παραπλήσια, καὶ τὸν θάνατον χωρεῖν, οὐδὲν μᾶλλον ἐπὶ τὰ λοιπὰ τῶν ζώων, ἤπερ καὶ ἐπ᾽ ἀνθρώπους. Πνεῦμα γὰρ πᾶσιν ὅμοιον εἶναι, καὶ πλέον ὑπάρχειν ἐν ἀνθρώποις μηδέν, ἀλλὰ πάντα ἑνὶ λόγῳ εἶναι μάταια, ...

Everything happens similarly with them, and death comes to other living things no more than it does to human beings. For all have the same breath, and there is nothing more in a human being; but all are, in a word, hollow.

Gregory continues to present Koheleth's thoughts in an unadulterated fashion at this stage of the paraphrase,[34] speaking of the common destiny of ἄνθρωποι and the other "living things" (ζῷα makes a change from κτήνη, which was becoming a little monotonous in LXX). These two types of creatures have one and the same "fate" (LXX συνάντημα) in store for them, said Koheleth; i.e., says Gregory, they each have the same kinds of things "happen" (συμβαίνω)[35] to them — in particular, as he had already foreshadowed in v. 17, they each have "death" (θάνατος, as in LXX) awaiting them; this is because both types of creatures have the same "breath of life" (πνεῦμα, as in LXX) in them.

So to say that the human being "has no advantage" (LXX τί ἐπερίσσευσεν...; οὐδέν)[36] is to say that the human has "nothing more" (πλέον... μηδέν) than this common πνεῦμα, and to say that "all is ματαιότης" means that one is of the opinion that all creatures are equally μάταιος.

(20) ... ἀπὸ τῆς αὐτῆς γῆς λαβόντα τὴν σύστασιν, καὶ εἰς τὴν αὐτὴν γῆν ἔξοντα τὴν ἀνάλυσιν.

They were constructed from the same earth, and they will depart to the same earth.

Literally, Gregory's paraphrase reads: "... receiving the[ir] composition from the same earth, and having the[ir] departure (ἀνάλυσις, a euphemism for death) to the same earth." This is still governed by the πάντα of v. 19, so it is a relatively simple rephrasing of Koheleth's "all (LXX τὰ πάντα) come from the dust, and all return to the dust". The substitution of γῆ, "earth" (as in Symmachus' translation) for LXX's χοῦς, "dust" makes the allusion to Genesis 3:19 (God's words to Adam, "you are γῆ and to γῆ you shall return") all the stronger for the Greek reader — as it already was for the Hebrew reader, since עפר, "dust" was used both in the Genesis verse and in this verse of Ecclesiastes (Gregory will perform this effective substitution again in 12:7). It is typical of Gregory to strive for a finely-balanced composition, which he achieves with the matching antitheses of λαβόντα τὴν σύστασιν and ἔξοντα τὴν ἀνάλυσιν. Koheleth's own construction here, with his equally balanced if more prosaic clauses, facilitates Gregory's penchant in this instance, and so the latter's ἀπὸ τῆς αὐτῆς γῆς and εἰς τὴν αὐτὴν γῆν closely models LXX's ἀπὸ τοῦ χοός and εἰς τὸν χοῦν.

(21) Ἄδηλον γὰρ εἶναι περί τε τῶν ἀνθρωπίνων ψυχῶν, εἰ ἀναπτήσονται ἄνω, καὶ περὶ τῶν λοιπῶν ἃς τὰ ἄλογα κέκτηνται, εἰ κάτω διαρρυήσονται.

It is uncertain, in regard to the souls of human beings, whether they will fly upwards, and in regard to the others which the animals possess, whether they will fall downwards.

The view was evidently held by at least some in Koheleth's day that the "breath of life" (LXX πνεῦμα) of human beings returned to God upon death, while the "breath of life" of animals went to the earth. Koheleth was sceptical about making such a distinction, although in 12:7 he made use of the idea of the breath of life returning to the God who gave it, in an obvious allusion to the Creation story. Gregory registers this scepticism — which Koheleth conveyed by means of a rhetorical question, "who knows?" (LXX τίς οἶδεν) — with the expression ἄδηλον εἶναι, "to be unknown, unseen, uncertain".

Ψυχή, which would suggest to his readers the human "soul", is employed by the Christian paraphrast for the πνεῦμα which is in human beings, but he does not wish to use this same word for the πνεῦμα which is in animals, lest he be thought to be suggesting that animals, too, have a "soul"; to avoid this theological problem he speaks vaguely of τὰ λοιπά, "the other ones" — i.e., whatever other kind of life-essence it may be that animates the animals. In v. 19 Gregory had allowed Koheleth's assertion, that both types of creatures have the same "breath of life" (πνεῦμα) in them, to stand, but now, when Koheleth asserted that in this matter as well he knew of no difference between the πνεῦμα of the one and the πνεῦμα of the other, Gregory quietly makes a distinction between the ψυχή of the human creature and the "other kind" of the non-human creatures. These latter creatures are styled τὰ ἄλογα, "the ones without speech or reason", recalling Gregory's antithesis in v. 17: λογικός and ἄλογος for the two types of creatures.

For the concept of the human life-essence "going up" (LXX ἀναβαίνω), Gregory employs the same verb as he uses in 12:7: ἀναπέτομαι, "to fly up". Thus he answers the scepticism of this verse, "it is uncertain whether the human ψυχή will fly up", with the statement of faith in the later verse, "the human ψυχή can have salvation by acknowledging and flying up to its Creator". (Some manuscripts of Gregory's paraphrase have ἀνίσταμαι, "to rise up" rather than ἀναπέτομαι in 3:21;[37] this loses something of the close affinity with 12:7, but alludes to the New Testament teaching of a resurrection from the dead.) The opposite process of "going down" (LXX καταβαίνω) is described as "falling away" or "slipping through" (διαρρέω), which seems to depict the earth swallowing up or absorbing these less fortunate creatures — the idea of the earth reclaiming its own may be a favourite image of Gregory, for he appears to present a similar picture with regard to human beings in 5:14 and 12:4.

(22) Καὶ ὅ μοι ἐδόκει μηδὲν ἕτερον ὑπάρχειν ἀγαθόν, εἰ μὴ τρυφὴ καὶ τῶν παρόντων χρῆσις. Οὐ γὰρ εἶναι πάλιν ᾠήθην, ἐπὶ τὴν ἀπόλαυσιν τούτων ἐλθεῖν δυνατόν, ἅπαξ ἀνθρώπῳ θανάτου γευσαμένῳ.

There seemed to me to be no other good than self-indulgence and making use of what is at hand, because I did not think it possible to return again to the enjoyment of these things once a person had tasted death.

Gregory is uncomfortable with the recurrent conclusion that one ought to be joyful in one's life-situation. As he did in the description of the Solomonic lifestyle in Chapter Two,

Gregory takes "being joyful" (LXX εὐφραίνομαι) in an Epicurean sense of "eating, drinking, and being merry", and so again offers τρυφή, "self-indulgence" as his censorious equivalent. This he couples with τῶν παρόντων χρῆσις, "the use of what is at hand", which he apparently takes Koheleth to have meant in speaking of what is a person's "lot" (LXX μερίς). His rewording of Koheleth's characteristic phrase, "there is no good except..." (LXX οὐκ ἔστιν ἀγαθὸν εἰ μή...), is on this occasion the least paraphrastic of Gregory's four parallels: μηδὲν ἕτερον ὑπάρχειν ἀγαθόν, εἰ μή..., "there is no other good than..." (cf. 2:24; 3:12; 8:15).

Δοκέω, "to think, seem" and οἴομαι, "to think, imagine" put these musings into the perspective in which Gregory would have his readers see them. Ostensibly "it seemed to me" (μοι ἐδόκει) is a parallel of "I saw" (LXX εἶδον), but the implications of the two expressions are quite different: Koheleth entertained no doubts as to the validity of his conclusion, whereas Gregory is drawing attention to the fallibility of Solomon's human reasoning. This erroneous thinking, which an older and wiser Solomon now recognises as such, is more clearly unmasked at other points of the paraphrase, such as 2:10,11 and 8:15-17; for the moment, Gregory is content with a somewhat more subtle approach, and throughout this passage (3:17-22) he has allowed Koheleth to speak his mind relatively freely, relying on the weight of other passages to apply the corrective only hinted at here with λογίζομαι at the beginning of the section (in v. 17) and now δοκέω and οἴομαι at its close.

The final thought of this chapter, expressed once again by means of a rhetorical question, was that it is not possible for anyone "to see what will happen after him". "After him" (LXX μετ᾽ αὐτόν) means, of course, "after his death", and Gregory paraphrases accordingly (ἅπαξ ἀνθρώπῳ θανάτου γευσαμένῳ, "once a person has tasted death"). But then he interprets "seeing" (LXX ὁράω) in the light of "seeing good" (LXX ὁράω ἀγαθόν) in v. 13, and so speaks here — as he did there — of "enjoyment" (ἀπόλαυσις) which does not last. Thus Gregory's understanding of this clause is that it referred, not to the impossibility of knowing what will happen after one's death, but to the impossibility of engaging in earthly pleasures after one's death.

Chapter Four

(1) Ἀπὸ δὲ τούτων ἀπασῶν ἐμαυτὸν ἐπιστρέψας τῶν ἐννοιῶν κατεσκεψάμην καὶ ἀπεστράφην πάντα εἴδη συκοφαντιῶν τὰ ἐν ἀνθρώποις πλαζόμενα, ἐξ ὧν τινὲς μὲν ἀδικούμενοι δακρύουσι καὶ θρηνοῦσι, βίᾳ καταβεβλημένοι τῶν ἐπαμυνόντων, ἢ ὅλως παρα-μυθησομένων αὐτοὺς πάσης πανταχόθεν κατεχούσης ἀπορίας· οἱ δὲ χειροδίκαι εἰς ὕψος αἴρονται, ἐξ οὗ καὶ πεσοῦνται.

Turning myself from all these thoughts, I looked closely at, and turned away from, all the forms of oppression that are devised by human beings, as a result of which some people, being treated unjustly, weep and wail. They are struck down by the power of those who ought to help them, or on the whole ought to comfort them in all the troubles that press down upon them from every side. But those who "make might their right" are raised to a height from which they will also fall.

It suits Gregory's purposes to take Koheleth's expression "and I turned" (LXX καὶ ἐπέστρεψα ἐγώ) in this instance as denoting a departure from previous thoughts; that is to say, the ideas put forward in the preceding verses, to the effect that human beings and animals are equally hollow and could well come to the same end, are not to be persevered with — ἐπιστρέφω, "to turn around", can also mean "to repent". When καὶ ἐπέστρεψα ἐγώ occurs again only six verses later, however (in v. 7), Gregory's purposes are not served by the same nuance, for in that instance the preceding verses have put forward the idea that there is a decided difference between the way in which a wise person fares and the way in which a foolish person fares, a view with which Gregory is much more in sympathy. So in the latter case the paraphrast does not interpret the expression "and I turned" as denoting any radical change, but rather as delineating a smooth transition to a new thought, which is not at all to be seen as calling into question what had just been spoken of. With such subtle differences of turning the same phrase, the interpreter can imply much.

LXX's ἐπιστρέφω in this verse, within the context of observing the suffering of the oppressed, suggests to Gregory also a second meaning, namely the idea of "turning away from" (ἀποστρέφω) the unbearable sight of such suffering. For the Christian writer, there can be no calm and detached "seeing" (LXX ὁράω) of the ways in which human beings treat each other and a cool recording of the facts as observed; a "close viewing" (κατασκέπτομαι) of just what goes on among the powerful and the powerless leads to aversion. Koheleth certainly appeared to be sympathetic towards those who suffer oppression, and it may well be that he felt himself to be disadvantaged by an alien or unfriendly power, but by and large he gave the impression of being quite well off in comparison to the οἱ πολλοί. Gregory, on the other hand, is known to have suffered persecution, along with his flock, at the hands of anti-Christian powers,[1] so it is not surprising to find a somewhat stronger note of personal feeling about oppression in the Christian version of Koheleth's thoughts.

"Oppression" (MT עשקים, and assuming — with the Targumist but against Symmachus — this first occurrence to be an abstract noun rather than the plural passive participle of the verb עשק, "to oppress")[2] was rendered in LXX by συκοφαντία, which means particularly "slander" or some kind of false accusation or prosecution, and Gregory reproduces the word. LXX Ecclesiastes employed συκοφαντία also for both occurrences of the noun עשק, in 5:7 and 7:7, and at those places Gregory again takes his cue from that, a somewhat surprisingly slavish following of the choice of word of the Greek text before him.[3] Perhaps his own experience of the persecution of the Christians, which often enough took the form of malicious untruths being spread about in the market-places and upheld in the law-courts, explains Gregory's retention of LXX's rather particular expression when he might have replaced it with a more general expression in this context. His personal experience of oppression may also explain why Gregory is moved to emphasise the "tear" (LXX δάκρυον) of the oppressed by adding "wailing" (θρηνέω) to the "weeping" (δακρύω).

Koheleth noted that the oppressors have "power" (LXX ἰσχύς, Gregory βία), which by implication the oppressed obvious-ly do not have — and not only that, but they do not even have anyone to comfort them in their affliction. This latter harsh truth was hammered home by Koheleth through a repetition of the phrase καὶ οὐκ ἔστιν αὐτοῖς παρακαλῶν (ואין להם מנחם), "and they have no comforter".

Gregory, as noted earlier, is not fond of repetitiveness in his paraphrase, and so he offers two parallels to παρακαλέω: ἐπαμύνω, "to come to aid, assist" and παρα- μυθέομαι,[4] "to encourage, console", and against these two he places the opposite notion of καταβάλλω, "to strike down".

Gregory's phrasing here is not as clear as it might be,[5] but he seems to be presenting the ironic contrast of those who ought to be offering help and comfort being the very ones who are doing the oppressing. The notion that God places certain people in a position of power in order that they might use their power for the good of those over whom they have been placed, but so rarely do they do so, is a very biblical idea: in particular, one might think of Ezekiel's lament that the "shepherds" who are to feed God's flock have been feeding themselves, even to the extent of feeding upon that very flock (Ezekiel 34). Thus Gregory's ironic twist to this verse is quite in keeping with the biblical tradition — and so too is his additional assertion that the powerful who misuse their power will be brought low. "Those who 'make might their right'" (οἱ χειροδίκαι, literally "those who assert their right by hand") is based on Koheleth's "those powerful oppressors" (LXX ἀπὸ χειρὸς συκοφαντούντων αὐτοὺς ἰσχύς, literally "power from the hand of those who oppress them"), but Koheleth gave no sign of confidence concerning any future "falling down" (πίπτω) for those who have been "raised up" (αἴρομαι).

(2) Τῶν δὲ ἀδίκων καὶ θρασέων, οἱ μὲν ἀποθανόντες, ἄμεινον παρὰ τοὺς μέχρι νῦν ζῶντας ἔπραξαν.

As for the unrighteous and arrogant, those who are dead are in a better state than those who are still alive.

Koheleth's "commending" (LXX ἐπαινέω) of the dead is not warmly endorsed in the paraphrase, even though it notes that certain people "are in a better state" (ἄμεινον πράσσω) when they are dead. The Hebrew sage was quite general in his scope: the

dead person, irrespective of his righteousness or unrighteousness, is better off than the living person, because the living
person is constantly aware of the oppression that is going on
among the living, while the dead person is completely oblivious
to it all (this implicit point is made explicit in the following
verse); if anything, it is the righteous dead who are particularly
better off, since they when alive would be more disturbed by
their awareness of the unrighteousness that reigns in this world,
even when it did not affect them personally. The Christian
interpreter is more particular in his scope: he will not allow the
implication that death is a release for the righteous as well as the
unrighteous from a life which is futile; only the life of the
unrighteous (ἄδικος, to which θρασύς, "bold, arrogant" is added
for good measure in this context of oppression) is futile, and so it
is only that life which can be said to be better ended.

    At first sight it might be thought somewhat puzzling that
the Christian writer should say that an unrighteous person is "in
a better state" when dead, for one would expect him to rather
warn that judgment awaits the unrighteous after their time of
unhindered activity in this life has passed. He has, after all,
already stated in 3:16 his view that there is "in the lower regions
a pit of punishment awaiting the ungodly". But the answer to
this puzzle probably lies in the apocalyptic interest of Gregory,
which we have already noted in the previous chapter (and
which will become even more noticeable in the final chapter).
The Last Days of the earth, according to the words of Jesus, will
be "the days of punishment" (Luke 21:22), "days of distress
unequalled from the beginning... until now, and never to be
equalled again" (Mark 13:19); the unrighteous in those days,
according to the words of the Apocalypse, will have poured
upon them "the seven bowls of the wrath of God" (details in
Revelation 16), not to mention being in the midst of the sundry
cataclysmic struggles going on at that time. So it is that Gregory
can say that the unrighteous who are dead (before these terrible
Last Days) are more fortunate than the unrighteous who are still
alive (when the imminent eschaton of this world arrives).[6]

(3) Αἱρετώτερος δὲ τούτων ἀμφοτέρων, ὁ ὅμοιος αὐτοῖς ἐσόμενος, μηδέπω δὲ[7] γεγονώς, ὅτι οὔπω τῆς κατὰ ἀνθρώπους ἥψατο πονηρίας.

And better than both of these is the one who, if he is going to be like them, has not yet been born, because he has not yet taken part in human wickedness.

What was said of the preceding verse applies also to the verse now at hand: Koheleth was quite general in his scope, while Gregory restricts the observation to the unrighteous. Here Koheleth sadly asserted that it is better never to have been born, for then one would never have seen the evil of this world. This is a sentiment that has often enough been expressed by thinkers in all ages,[8] and it is not unique even in the biblical collection (cf. Job 3:13-16; Jeremiah 20:18) nor in the tradition which followed — the schools of Hillel and Shammai, which could not agree on whether the words of Koheleth should be included in the biblical collection, did agree that it is better not to be born than to be born![9] But this is not a sentiment that Gregory is prepared to echo. For him, this observation can be made only of "the one who is going to be like them" (ὁ ὅμοιος αὐτοῖς ἐσόμενος), the "them" being "the unrighteous and arrogant" mentioned in the previous verse, who are in for a decidedly unpleasant future; anybody who, like them, lays hold of wickedness in this world, will share in that very same future, and so would be better off with no future at all.

"Taking part in" (ἅπτω) the wickedness in the world seems to be the very opposite, in fact, of what Koheleth meant by "seeing" (LXX ὁράω) that wickedness. He may well have been using "see" in the straightforward sense of a person observing the evil that is being done in the world around him, or he might even have been using it in the experiential sense of evil actually being done to the person in question, but it is unlikely that he was using it in an active sense of the evil being perpetrated by that person himself. It was because Koheleth "saw all the oppression that takes place under the sun" (v. 1) that he now proclaimed it better not to be alive, so as not to "see the evil that is done under the sun" (this verse); the meaning of the verb "to see" in these two phrases is surely identical, and it is only Gregory's agenda, not permitting him to ascribe futility to the righteous life, which causes him to vary the meaning as he does. Koheleth stamped both the beginning (v. 1) and the end (this verse) of this short comment on oppression with his characteristic phrase ὑπὸ τὸν ἥλιον, and Gregory almost as equally characteristically paraphrases it on both occasions by expressions which focus the observations on the sphere of (sinful) human activity, though being careful — as a lover of variation — never to employ precisely the same expression: ἐν ἀνθρώποις in the first instance, and κατὰ ἀνθρώπους in the second (cf. πρὸς ἀνθρώπων in 1:9 and ὑπ᾽ ἀνθρώπων in 2:11). Gregory is always happy to pontificate about human sinfulness being to blame for anything that is wrong with this world, even when the biblical writer's view ranged more broadly than that, but in this passage Koheleth was presumably speaking only of human activities, so it is quite appropriate for his paraphrast to depict "the evil deed" (LXX τὸ ποίημα τὸ πονηρόν) that is done under the sun as "the wickedness" (ἡ πονηρία) that is done by human beings.

(4) Φανερὸν δέ μοι ἐγένετο καὶ ὁπόσος ἀνδρὶ φθόνος παρὰ τῶν πέλας ἔπεται, οἶστρος ὑπάρχων πονηροῦ πνεύματος·

It also became evident to me, how great a jealousy from one's associates pursues a person — it is the sting of an evil spirit — ....

"Jealousy" (קִנְאָה) is the root cause of all human toil, according to Koheleth; people fret so much and thus work so hard because they are envious of their fellows or because they want to outstrip their neighbours, but this, too, is a profitless, pointless pursuit. A more positive soul might interject at this point that this "jealousy" can sometimes be a good thing or at least have a good result, if people are prompted to emulate their fellows in doing something worthwhile. Hence the Targum, latching on to the double sense of the Hebrew root קנא, which has to do with "passion" — on the negative side, "jealousy", but on the positive side, "zeal" — adds a lengthy note to this verse to the effect that if a person's קנאה prompts him to do good, that is good in Heaven's judgment, but if his קנאה prompts him to do evil, that is bad in Heaven's judgment.

Perhaps LXX wished to perform a similar softening of Koheleth's pronouncement by its choice of a Greek equivalent for קנאה. Ζῆλος, "zealous imitation, emulation" was employed by certain classical ethicists to denote a noble passion, the opposite of φθόνος, "envy, jealousy" (although other writers used these two words as interchangeable denotations of the baser impulse), Philo using it exclusively in connection with praiseworthy qualities.[10] But if it was LXX's intention to suggest the possibility of interpretation which we find openly expressed in the Targum, then it has not successfully suggested this to Gregory, who changes the word from the possibly positive ζῆλος into the unambiguously negative φθόνος. The latter is doubtlessly the more appropriate choice in translating Koheleth's sentiments, for his now very familiar "futility and a striving after wind" judgment clearly showed that he saw no good in this human passion and the useless "toil" it leads to (LXX's μόχθος here may be reflected in Gregory's depiction of the passion in question as "being busy with" or "pursuing" [ἕπομαι] a person).

The ματαιότης part of this judgment is by now far too familiar for Gregory to bother with any sort of equivalent to it in his paraphrase, but the προαίρεσις πνεύματος part enables him again to locate the reason why some people are in so lamentable a situation: it is because of the "evil spirit" (πνεῦμα πονηρόν, by simple definition equivalent to the πνεῦμα οὐκ ἀγαθόν of 2:11) at work in the world. The observable fact that some people are smitten by jealousy is a sign of where the "sting" (οἶστρος) of this evil spirit has struck — but it is by their own choice (LXX προαίρεσις) that they have left themselves open to being stung, as Gregory will make clear in his interpretation of the following verse. Gregory seems to be rather fond of this image of human beings being stung by a wicked Being, for back in 3:10,11 he had introduced the notion of poisonous "stings" (κέντρα) inflicted upon hapless victims by an "evil observer of the times" (καιροσκόπος πονηρός), who is doubtlessly to be identified with the πνεῦμα πονηρόν mentioned here.

(5) καὶ ὅτι ὁ ὑποδεξάμενός τε αὐτόν, καὶ οἱονεὶ προστερνισάμενος, οὐδὲν ἕτερον ἔχει, ἢ τὸ διεσθίειν τὴν ἑαυτοῦ ψυχήν, καὶ διαπρίειν τε καὶ δαπανᾶν μετὰ τοῦ σώματος ἑαυτοῦ λύπην ἀπαραμύθητον, τὴν τῶν ἄλλων εὐπραγίαν τιθέμενον.[11]

... and that the person who takes it in and, as it were, clutches it to his breast, takes part in nothing other than the eating of his own soul and the cutting and consuming of it, along with his own body. He regards the success of others as an inconsolable pain.

What appears to have been a short proverbial saying on the ruinous effects of doing no work, is treated at some length in the paraphrase as an elucidation on the crippling effects of jealousy. Koheleth's proverb was in juxtaposition with the preceding verse, where he had commented that all human work, motivated as it is by jealousy, is meaningless; he here noted that doing no work at all leads to starvation, and he juxtaposed this also with the note of the following verse that tranquility is better than striving. Gregory's elucidation flows on harmoniously from the previous verse, where he commented that jealousy is "the sting of an evil spirit"; he now notes that this passion can consume the person who allows it to take control of him, and he will move on to conclude in the following verse that it is better to opt for tranquility than to leave oneself open to the craftiness of this evil spirit.

To say that "the fool folds his hands" (LXX ὁ ἄφρων περιέλαβεν τὰς χεῖρας αὐτοῦ) is to say that his hands are idle and not engaged in work (cf. Proverbs 6:10).[12] But to call the person foolish who does not work, when working had just been pronounced foolish, is a somewhat abrupt change (though typical of Koheleth, and indeed of Wisdom generally, to have placed contrasting thoughts side by side in order to obtain a more rounded picture), whereas Gregory is able to present a smoother style (likewise typical of his work, and indeed of early biblical interpreters generally) by taking this foolish person as being identical with the foolish person, driven by jealousy, just mentioned in v. 4. "Folding one's hands" in this context suggests to Gregory the picture of "clasping to one's breast" (προσστερνίζομαι) or wholeheartedly embracing the dangerous passion of jealousy, and indeed the idea of "embracing" is eminently readable from LXX's περιλαμβάνω (cf. 3:5). The concomitant notion of the fool "taking in" or "submitting to" (ὑποδέχομαι) this emotion, with which Gregory begins his version of this verse, may well arise from LXX's talk of "choosing" (προαίρεσις) a spirit at the end of the previous verse. To say further, "and he eats his flesh" (LXX καὶ ἔφαγεν τὰς σάρκας αὐτοῦ), is to say that the fool destroys himself (cf. Isaiah 49:26), for if he does no work at all he will have nothing to eat and so will waste away.[13] For Gregory, interpreting in the context of v. 4's pronouncement on jealousy, "eating one's flesh" suggests a somewhat different metaphor: the destructive emotion of jealousy, churning around inside a person, eats away at his mind/heart/soul (ψυχή) as well as at his flesh (σῶμα). So powerful and dangerous is this destructive force, that it elicits no less than three paraphrases for Koheleth's simple "eating" (LXX ἐσθίω): "eating up" (διεσθίω), "sawing up" (διαπρίω), and "using up" (δαπανάω). As well, Gregory feels it valuable to add some reason why the foolish person is so cut up by jealousy: anything which in someone else's perspective is a good thing (εὐπραγία, "success", a condition of well-being), is in his perspective a bad thing (λύπη, "pain" of body or mind, a condition of distress).

(6) ῞Ελοιτο δ' ἄν τις εὖ φρονῶν θατέραν ἐμπλῆσαι τῶν χειρῶν, σὺν ῥᾳστώνῃ καὶ πραότητι, ἤπερ ἀμφοτέρας σὺν μόχθῳ, καὶ δολεροῦ πνεύματος πανουργίᾳ.

The person who thinks rightly would prefer to fill one of his hands with rest and gentleness, than both of them with distress and the trickery of a treacherous spirit.

᾽Αγαθὸς "Α" ὑπὲρ "Β" (ב" "מן "א" טוב), literally "good (is) 'A', more than 'B'" — i.e., "'A' is better than 'B'" — is a formulation which was employed frequently by Koheleth, particularly in the collection of proverbs in Chapter Seven. Generally Gregory assents to his predecessor's value-judgment, although not infrequently in such a way as to yield a somewhat more orthodox flavour to the comparison; his preferred equivalent to ἀγαθὸς... ὑπέρ is mostly a verb or adjective expressing the preferability or desirability of "A" over "B". This pattern is already set here at 4:6, where Gregory affirms that one ought to "prefer" (αἱρέομαι) "A" to "B", with the latter carrying a different nuance than the one which Koheleth seems to have intended.

The preferred option is paraphrased straighforwardly enough, allowing for Gregory's penchant for balance: because the second clause contains two words denoting the worse state of affairs, he feels it necessary to offer in the first clause two near synonyms for the better state of affairs — ῥᾳστώνη, "rest, ease" and πραότης, "mildness, gentleness" for Koheleth's single ἀνάπαυσις (נחת), "rest". In fact Koheleth may have purposefully placed one descriptive element in the first clause and two in the second, since he was contrasting one handful of something good with two handfuls of something bad, but if so the deft touch is lost on Gregory.

In rephrasing matters here, Gregory inserts a preposition (σύν) into the two clauses (as does Symmachus [μετά]);[14] and he speaks of "one of the hands" and "both [of them]" (θατέρα... τῶν χειρῶν and ἀμφότεραι — cf. Symmachus ἀμφότεραι χειρῶν) in preference to LXX's "a handful" and "two handfuls" (δράξ and δύο δρακές).

The proscribed option gives a further example of the way in which Gregory takes Koheleth's familiar expression προαίρεσις πνεύματος (רעות רוח): as denoting the activities of an evil spirit, causing trouble in the world. On this occasion he describes the πνεῦμα as "treacherous" (δολερός) and he depicts its activities as "trickery" (πανουργία), but he will not have us believe that human beings are the innocent victims of this treacherous trickery; as with the previous case (v. 4) of προαίρεσις πνεύματος, he will mention the matter of human προαίρεσις when he moves on to the next verse in the paraphrase.

The paraphrast is less inventive here with μόχθος, this being — out of 22 occurrences of the noun in LXX — one of only two occasions (cf. 2:22) on which he simply reproduces it. But he does incorporate a special note of approval on the thought expressed in this verse: it is "right thinking" (εὖ φρονέω) to prefer the one handful of rest to the two handfuls of distress.

(7) Ἔστι δέ τι καὶ ἕτερον, ὅπερ οἶδα συμβαῖνον παρὰ τὸ προσῆκον, ἀνδρὸς ἕνεκα προαιρέσεως οὐκ ἀγαθῆς.

There is also another thing, which I know happens contrary to what is proper, as a result of the wicked choice of human beings.

Koheleth's expression "and I turned" (LXX καὶ ἐπέστρεψα ἐγώ) indicated, as it did in v. 1, that the author was about to cite a new case of futility under the sun. Gregory correctly captures this sense here by introducing the new case with the note that "there is also another thing" (ἔστι δέ τι καὶ ἕτερον) to be mentioned at this point. The different treatment which Koheleth's expression received at its previous appearance, and the reasons for that difference, have already been commented on at v. 1.

The case that is to be described is an example of "futility" (LXX ματαιότης) in that, in Gregory's view, it happens "contrary to what is proper" (παρὰ τὸ προσῆκον), and this solely because of the foolishness of human beings — that it takes place "under the sun" (LXX ὑπὸ τὸν ἥλιον) means for Gregory that it takes place in the sphere of human activity (normally Gregory employs ἄνθρωπος to designate this, but here alone he uses ἀνήρ, probably because he sees the case to follow as having to do with the male of the species). Gregory's expression "wicked choice" (προαίρεσις οὐκ ἀγαθή) takes up two thoughts from what has gone before: the noun arises directly from LXX's use of it in the preceding verse and *passim*, and the negated adjective has already been so employed to describe the chosen spirit itself in 2:11 (cf. 4:4); thus it is decreed that the explanation for the world's problems lies in the way in which human beings have exercised their free will.

(8) Ὃς μεμονωμένος πάντοθεν, καὶ οὔτε ἀδελφὸν ἔχων, οὔτε υἱόν, κτήμασι δὲ πολλοῖς εὐθηνούμενος, ἀπληστίᾳ συζῶν, χρηστότητι ἑαυτὸν οὐθ' ὅλως ὁτιοῦν ἐπιδοῦναι θέλει. Ἡδέως οὖν ἂν αὐτὸν ἐροίμην, ὅτου χάριν ὁ τοιοῦτος μοχθεῖ, τὸ μὲν ἀγαθόν τι δρᾶσαι προτροπάδην φεύγων, ποικίλαις δὲ τοῦ χρηματίσασθαί ποθεν ἐπιθυμίαις διασπώμενος.

The person who is entirely alone, having neither brother

nor son, but abounding in great possessions, passes his life in
insatiability. In no way whatsoever does he want to give himself
to goodness. So I would gladly ask that person why he toils in
such a way, fleeing with headlong speed from doing anything
good, and distracted by various desires to make money from any
source.

A further example of ματαιότης under the sun is now
placed on record: a case of there being "one" (LXX εἷς) but not "a
second" (LXX δεύτερος) — i.e., as Gregory puts it, a case of a
person "being left alone" (μονόομαι); the reversal in the
paraphrase of the order of mention of LXX's υἱός and ἀδελφός
places the two absent generations in their chronological order,
but may well be quite arbitrary. Despite being completely alone,
this "one" continues to labour on in order to gain more wealth,
since "his eye is not satisfied with wealth" (LXX ὀφθαλμὸς[15]
αὐτοῦ οὐκ ἐμπίπλαται πλούτου), which indicates to Gregory both
that this person has already amassed great possessions (κτήματα)
and that he is driven on by nothing other than sheer greediness
(ἀπληστία). Against this vice of ἀπληστία, Gregory holds the
virtue of χρηστότης, "goodness (of heart), kindness", a notion he
borrows — probably mistakenly, as we shall see presently —
from LXX's ἀγαθωσύνη later in the verse, where he paraphrases
it again in an analogous way.

Koheleth now rather abruptly put the question, "for whom
am I toiling, and depriving myself of good?" The putting of this
question in the first person, when the one who is toiling had
been spoken of in the third person, means that the interpreter
has to make a decision: either the sudden question about what
"I" am doing reveals that Koheleth was really talking about his
own personal experience in this verse, recalling what he asked of
himself when he began to realise that he was leading a foolish
way of life; or it is a matter of literary identification with the one
who toils, imagining that person asking a question which he
ought to put to himself but in fact never does.[16] The second
possibility may be the more likely — hence many translators
supply some such introduction to the question as the Revised
Standard Version's "so that he never asks" (cf. Vulgate *nec*
recogitat dicens, and Targum ולא יימר בלביה) — but in any case the

first possibility is not open to an interpreter who believes Ecclesiastes to have been spoken or written by Solomon, since it is well known that he was succeeded on the throne by his son Rehoboam.

So Gregory, being unable to opt for the first alternative, takes an inventive tack. He skirts around the problem of the question being put in the first person, by transposing it into indirect speech (third person), purporting to be what Solomon (speaking in the first person) would ask the one who toils (who would be spoken to in the second person!) if he came face to face with him. There is no textual support for the third person at this point in the biblical text, but it is interesting to note that despite this at least two modern translations/paraphrases — Today's English Version and the Living Bible — have also rephrased the question in the third person; of these three, however, only Gregory retains a concession to Koheleth's "I", by saying that "I would ask him" (αὐτὸν ἐροίμην).

What Solomon would ask, then, is why this person "toils" away (μοχθέω, as in LXX) like he does, and why he "flees with headlong speed" (προτροπάδην φεύγω) from doing "the good" (τὸ ἀγαθόν). This latter phrase is Gregory's equivalent to his predecessor's talk of "depriving" (LXX στερίσκω) oneself of "good" (LXX ἀγαθωσύνη), an expression which was most likely intended by Koheleth as the antithesis of his oft-mentioned counsel to "see good" in one's work. By "seeing good" in one's work, Koheleth meant finding enjoyment or something worthwhile in it (see Gregory's paraphrase of ὁράω ἀγαθωσύνην in 5:17), so by "depriving oneself of good" in all this toiling, he presumably meant that the lonely person finds nothing enjoyable or worthwhile in his incessant working to gain more wealth. But Gregory's paraphrase here speaks rather of the lonely toiler missing out on the opportunity of "doing" (δράω) rather than "seeing" good, and hence gives an ethical rather than existential meaning to the word "good".[17] So incensed is Gregory with the refusal of the wealthy loner to use that wealth for good in the world — the Church Father may well have seen many examples of this in his own time — that he paraphrases this matter twice in the one verse, first in the context of the description of the person's situation (as commented on earlier) and then this second time within its original context of the question that ought to be asked about that situation. The situation itself was described by LXX as a bad "distraction" (περισπασμός, cf. 1:13 and parallels), and so Gregory comments on the lonely toiler being "distracted" (διασπάω) by various passions for "making money" or "transacting business for oneself" (χρηματίζομαι). That this is also ματαιότης goes without saying.

(9) Πολλῷ δὲ τούτου βελτίους οἳ κοινωνίαν ἅμα βίου ἐστείλαντο, ἐξ ἧς καρποῖντο ἂν τὰ βέλτιστα;

How much better than this are those who have taken on a communal way of life, from which they may reap the best fruits!

The question mark at the end of Gregory's version of this verse is puzzling. Koheleth was certainly not asking a question here, and indeed Gregory's own sentence makes good sense read as a statement ("Much better than this are those...."), following which the γάρ of the next statement (v. 10) provides a lead-in to certain corroborative evidence. Further, if Gregory did intend this verse to form an introductory question to the evidence which is to be tabled in the following verses, it would seem to call for the use of πόσῳ ("How much better than this are those...?") rather than πολλῷ.[18] It is tempting to dismiss the interrogative marker altogether as having been inadvertently transposed from the previous verse, where there definitely was a question, but at that place an interrogative marker would also have appeared somewhat strange in the paraphrase, since the question there — although carrying a question mark in LXX — was placed by Gregory in indirect speech.

If the question mark is to be accepted here, and not simply ignored,[19] then the question it marks must be a rhetorical one ("Are those who have taken on a communal way of life... much better than this [one of the previous verse who has not]?"), with an implied answer ("Yes, for the reasons which will be given in the following verses" — the "yes" is obviously not stated, but this implied answer might be thought to be taken up by the γάρ of v. 10). The English translation above ("How much better than this are those...!") attempts to capture something of this rhetorical device — if indeed that is what it is — by wording the verse rhetorically as an exclamation.

In any case the point made by the verse is clear enough, despite a possible confusion with στέλλομαι — the New Testament used this verb exclusively in the sense of "to shrink from, avoid", but such a meaning here would be quite inconsistent with all that follows in vv. 10-12, so Gregory must intend some such meaning as "to put on", or the active voice's (στέλλω's) sense of "to set in order, equip oneself". Koheleth's two uses of "good" (LXX ἀγαθός) are reformed into the comparative and superlative degrees: "better" (βελτίων, better Greek than ἀγαθὸς... ὑπέρ [מ ...טוב]) and "best" (βέλτιστος, a defensible interpretation of Koheleth's point). To say that people who live together rather than alone have a good "reward" (LXX μισθός) for their labour, means for Gregory that they are able "to reap the fruits" (καρπόομαι) bestowed by a life lived in common with others.

(10) Δύο γὰρ ἀνδρῶν τοῖς αὐτοῖς πράγμασιν ὀρθῶς προσκειμένων, εἰ καὶ θατέρῳ τινὶ προσπέσῃ τι· ἀλλὰ μὴν οὐ μικρὰν ἐπικουρίαν ἔχει, τὸν αὐτῷ συνόντα. Μεγίστη δὲ καὶ συμφορὰ ἀνθρώπῳ δυσπραγοῦντι, καὶ ἡ ἐρημία τοῦ ἀνακτησομένου.

For when two people rightly devote themselves to the same things, if something happens to one of them he certainly has no small help in his companion. The most hazardous state for a person is to suffer misfortune and have no-one to help him recover.

Aside from the qualification that the benefits are greater if the participants approach the lifestyle "rightly/justly" (ὀρθῶς), contained in an introductory phrase commending the joint pursuit of common objectives, Gregory's paraphrase is quite direct.[20] If a person "falls" (LXX πίπτω), as Koheleth expressed it, Gregory reasons that it is because something else — and this τι must obviously be a misfortune of some kind, as is confirmed by δυσπραγέω, "to be unlucky" later in the verse — "falls upon" him (προσπίπτω); and if his fellow "raises" him (LXX ἐγείρω), it is by means of "reviving" or "restoring" him (ἀνακτάομαι) after the unlucky blow has struck.

Actually Koheleth used the plural of the verb πίπτω (יפלו) and thus might have wished to suggest — unless it is to be taken as an indefinite singular ("if either of them falls")[21] — the solidarity of two companions in a common misfortune, but Gregory may feel that a companion (συνών, for LXX's μέτοχος) is better able to help if he is not himself affected by the mishap.

Koheleth now proclaimed, "אילו the one who falls with no-one to lift him up." To some interpreters אילו looks like Aramaic אילו ending in shureq, "if, whereas", which is evidently what Koheleth meant with אלו at 6:6,[22] but the Masoretes read אילו here as two words — as indicated by the double accentuation — and ending in cholem: אי לו, "woe to him!", which is evidently what Koheleth meant with אי לך ("woe to you!") in 10:16. The Masoretic reading is shared by LXX, which translated אילו as οὐαὶ αὐτῷ, and Gregory paraphrases this by speaking of the case at hand as "the greatest misfortune" (μεγίστη συμφορά) that can happen to a person.

Ἐρημία, "solitude, wilderness, absence of" is obviously employed by the Church Father in a very negative way. If Gregory was at all a supporter of the eremite lifestyle, then it certainly does not show in the manner in which he transmits this passage (vv. 9-12) on the differences between a solitary and a corporate way of life; he readily reasserts, with no qualifications — other than the ὀρθῶς — Koheleth's view that two together are better off than one alone.

(11) Οἱ δ' αὖ ὁμοδίαιτοι, καὶ τὴν εὐπραγίαν αὐτοῖς ἐδιπλασίασαν, καὶ πραγμάτων ἀβουλήτων χειμῶνα παρεμυθήσαντο· ὥστε καὶ μεθημέραν τῇ ἐπ' ἀλλήλοις λαμπρύνεσθαι παρρησίᾳ, καὶ νύκτωρ φαιδρότητι σεμνύνεσθαι.[23] Ὁ δὲ βίον ἀκοινώνητον ἕλκων, φρικώδη τινὰ ἑαυτῷ διεξάγει ζωήν, ...

Those who live with others double their well-being and soften the storm of unfortunate circumstances, so as to distinguish themselves by their frankness to each other by day

and to be highly regarded for their cheerfulness by night. But the person who leads a solitary life is leading a life which can bring him horror.

"If two people lie down together", said Koheleth, "they have warmth." While it is not impossible that he had in mind the marriage bed (as the Targumist assumes by carefully noting that he is speaking here of a man and his wife), it is more likely in the context of the surrounding verses that his illustration was of travelling companions who huddle together on a cold night under the same blanket (a view which is supported by the *Aboth* of Rabbi Nathan [ch. 8], where it is said that sleeping together is a sign of friendship).[24] Gregory takes "lying down" together (LXX κοιμάομαι) as a metaphor for "living with others" generally (ὁμοδίαιτος), and by running his paraphrase of this verse and the following one together as one unit he naturally interprets the picture as having to do with comradeship rather than marriage.

"They have warmth" (LXX θέρμη αὐτοῖς, literally, "[there is] warmth to them"), a phrase which could hardly have been expressed any more compactly than it was, gives rise to a considerably longer paraphrase, as Gregory waxes lyrical on the benefits of the corporate life.   In doing so, he clearly demonstrates his love for counterbalanced expressions: firstly the "doubling" (διπλασιάζω) of good fortune is juxtaposed with the "lessening" (παραμυθέομαι) of bad fortune, and then what is particularly noticeable about the comrades "by day" (μεθημέραν) is balanced by what is particularly noticeable about them "by night" (νύκτωρ). In giving such a lengthy treatment to so short a Kohelethine statement, and especially in speaking so positively of a life lived with others, it would also appear that Gregory is demonstrating where his own sentiments lie: "frankness" (παρρησία) and "cheerfulness" (φαιδρότης) are, in Gregory's view, the distinguishing features of good companionship; by implication the uncompanionable person has no-one with whom to share his sorrows and his joys, but must keep it all to himself. Precisely why Gregory should have felt moved at this point to picture what is noticeable about companions "by day" and "by night" is not immediately clear, but it would seem that the idea of κοιμάομαι (שכב) here has put the thought of νύξ before him, to which he has then supplied the complementary notion of ἡμέρα. Koheleth himself did speak of both day and night together in two different verses (2:23 and 8:16), and there too Gregory employs μεθημέραν and νύκτωρ, so by introducing the pair here in 4:11 he is showing a certain fondness for this device.

The contrary situation to two companions keeping each other warm was put by Koheleth as a rhetorical question, "how shall one be warm?" (LXX ὁ εἷς πῶς θερμανθῇ;). This "one" is obviously on his own, and Gregory depicts him as living an unsocial (ἀκοινώνητος) lifestyle, in contrast to those who live a social lifestyle (κοινωνία, v. 9). His lack of warmth, which conjures up — alongside the earlier probable picture of travelling companions huddling together to keep warm on a cold night outdoors — the picture of a solitary traveller shivering by himself under the stars, suggests to Gregory a trembling arising from a different cause: φρικώδης refers to something "horrible", something "that causes shuddering or horror", and an example of such a thing will be given in the very next verse. An example of Gregory's care not to be repetitive with words or phrases is seen right here, for his sentence structure here requires him to express the idea of "leading a [particular kind of] life" twice, so he employs firstly ἕλκω and βίος, then διεξάγω and ζωή.

(12) ... οὐκ ᾐσθημένος, ὡς εἰ καὶ ἐπίθοιτό τις ἀνθρώποις συμπεφραγμένοις, θρασέως καὶ οὐκ ἀσφαλῶς βουλεύεται,²⁵ καὶ ὅτι οὐδὲ σχοῖνος τριπλῇ ῥᾳδίως ἀπορρήγνυσθαι πέφυκεν.

He does not understand that if someone were to attack a closely-formed group of people, he makes a rash and unsafe decision, and that a triple cord is not easily broken.

This is Gregory's implied example of the kind of terrifying thing (φρικώδης, in the previous verse) that can happen to a person who leads a solitary life — a lifestyle chosen out of ignorance (οὐκ αἰσθάνομαι, in this verse) concerning the dangers inherent therein: the person who decides to live by himself does not seem to realise that there is safety in numbers, and therefore by implication that there is danger in solitariness. After the build-up of φρικώδης, something more than mere implying might be expected from Gregory. Indeed, Koheleth could be read as expressing the danger clearly, if "the one" (LXX ὁ εἷς) is taken as referring to the one being attacked, for then the point was being explicitly made that it is easier to overpower a person who is by himself. In MT this reading is hampered by the lack of an את before האחד, but since the objective marker is not consistently applied its absence here need not rule out such an interpretation, and in LXX the passive voice of the verb (ἐπικραταιωθῇ) indicates that at least the LXX interpreter believed ὁ εἷς to be the one subject to attack and not the perpetrator of the attack. Gregory, however, depicts one (τις) attacking more than one (ἄνθρωποι, a plural noun), which might even be the opposite of Koheleth's picture — if יתקפו is read as a plural verb (as opposed to MT's vocalisation of it as a singular verb with suffix) along with אחד as the object, for such a reading yields the sense of more than one attacking one. Gregory's interpretation of some individual τις doing the attacking might owe something to Symmachus' rendering of יתקפו as ὑπερισχύσῃ τις, "(some)one will overpower", but if he is following that particular translator on that score he is asserting his own idea on the matter of who is attacked, for Symmachus agrees with LXX (against Targum and Peshitta) that אחד refers to the εἷς who is vulnerable to a successful attack.

The paraphrase expands Koheleth's "the two" (LXX οἱ δύο) into an indeterminate number of people "packed closely together, formed in close order or rank" (συμφράσσω); Koheleth said that they can more readily "withstand" an attacker (LXX ἵστημι κατέναντι αὐτοῦ, literally, "stand against him"), so Gregory comments that the attacker would be acting "rashly" (θρασέως) and "unsafely" (οὐκ ἀσφαλῶς) in "attacking" them (ἐπιτίθεμαι) — i.e., attempting, in Koheleth's word, to "overpower" (LXX ἐπικραταιόω) them.[26]

Koheleth's proverbial saying, "the triple cord is not quickly broken", using the image of the strength of a rope made from three strands, was evidently meant to express the strength of unity: if two together are stronger than one apart, then three together are even stronger still.[27] But since Gregory has not made use of the number "two" since the beginning of v. 10 in his treatment of this passage, saying now that "three are even better than two" would not make much sense in his paraphrase. So he contents himself with merely restating the proverb, but even so he is not content with LXX's choice of vocabulary. For "triple" he prefers the more common τριπλόος to LXX's ἔντριτος, and for "cord" he employs σχοῖνος rather than the diminutive σπαρτίον. LXX's adverb ταχέως, "quickly" is replaced by ῥᾳδίως, "easily", and only the verb ἀπορρήγνυμι, "to break" is thought worthy of retention.

Despite his variation from LXX in the matter of vocabulary, Gregory here is really only translating rather than paraphrasing the proverb, "the triple cord is not quickly broken"; that is to say, he does not offer a rephrasing of the proverbial saying — for example, "it is an even more rash and unsafe decision to rush upon three people who are together than it is to attack two companions" — which would involve him in a more particular decision regarding its interpretation. Could this be a deliberate backing off on Gregory's part from foreclosing other possible interpretations? The proverbial form of Koheleth's phrase here has created a fertile field for imaginative Christian interpreters to apply this saying to the doctrine of the Trinity, and to the union of faith, hope, and love (1 Corinthians 13:13) in the Christian life, and so on.[28] Quite obviously such ideas were not in Koheleth's mind when he wrote his original work, but the use of this saying in such a way may have been in the mind of Koheleth's Christian paraphrast when he decided not to tamper with the phrasing of Ecclesiastes at this point.

(13) Ἐγὼ δὲ προκρίνω νέον πένητα σώφρονα, γέροντος βασιλέως ἄφρονος, ᾧ ἐνθύμιον οὐ γεγένηται, ὡς ....

I prefer a young poor person who is wise to an old king who is foolish, to whom the thought has not occurred that ....

"To prefer [here προκρίνω] 'A' to 'B'" is Gregory's preferred way of treating LXX's ἀγαθὸς "A" ὑπὲρ "B" (cf. αἱρέομαι in v. 6). He also prefers, as he has frequently demonstrated, a perfectly balanced formulation, and so here he slightly rearranges the order of words on the "B" side to parallel the order of words on the "A" side, so that both phrases match up exactly: firstly the age-marker ("young" [νέος for LXX's παῖς] versus "old" [γέρων for LXX's πρεσβύτερος]), secondly the status-marker ("poor" [πένης, as in LXX] versus "royal" [βασιλεύς, as in LXX]), and thirdly the intelligence-marker ("wise" [σώφρων for LXX's σοφός] versus "foolish" [ἄφρων, as in LXX]). This last pair is in itself a further example of Gregory's craft, for he has supplied LXX's ἄφρων (literally, "without sense") with σώφρων (literally, "of sound sense"), a direct opposite which is etymologically — and visibly — related to it.

The foolish old king which Koheleth pictured here "does not know how to take heed (LXX προσέχω) any longer", which to Gregory means that he has not given much thought (ἐνθύμιος) to the matters raised in the following verses; hence Gregory styles this last phrase as an introduction to what is about to be said. What Koheleth was about to say (in vv. 14-16) seems to have been a kind of case study of the interplay between a foolish old king and a wise young poor person, the latter supplanting the former (v. 14) to popular acclaim (v. 15) which does not last (v. 16). Commentators have frequently felt that this case study must have been of a particular historical incident, and many theories as to the respective identities of the old ruler and the young usurper have been postulated;[29] indeed, there is no end of possibilities for the imaginative interpreter, but Gregory sensibly refrains from choosing a particular case from history or legend. If Koheleth was citing an actual case, then it is not known to Gregory, but the pattern of which Koheleth spoke is an all too familiar one in human affairs, and indeed this is very likely what the writer of Ecclesiastes intended: not a particular event, but a typical pattern. Gregory's paraphrase keeps it that way, avoiding the trap which so many other commentators found too inviting.

Gregory is rewarded for his efforts by being cited by name at this point in the *Commentary on Ecclesiastes* of Jerome. The great biblical scholar of the late fourth century names only five exegetes who have contributed to his understanding of

Ecclesiastes,[30] and Gregory becomes one of this select band when
Jerome notes that

> *vir sanctus, Gregorius Ponti episcopus, Origenis auditor in* Metaphrasi
> Ecclesiastae *ita hunc locum intellexit: Ego vero praefero adolescentulum
> pauperem et sapientem regi seni et stulto; cui nunquam venit in mentem
> quod...*"[31]
> ("the holy man Gregory, bishop in Pontus and student of Origen, in the
> *Paraphrase of Ecclesiastes* understands the passage here in this way: 'I
> prefer a young person who is poor and wise to a king who is old and
> foolish, to whose mind it has never occurred that...'").

It is evident that Jerome is here quoting Gregory's paraphrase
directly, since the Latin runs almost word-for-word with
Gregory's Greek (although Jerome, in placing *rex* before *senex*,[32]
has followed Koheleth's order of words and in so doing has
undone Gregory's fine-tuning). The quotation proceeds — with
some variation at the end of v. 15 — to the end of v. 16, and thus
demonstrates Jerome's approval of, or at least interest in, the
earlier Father's understanding of this passage.

(14) ... δυνατόν ἐστι, τῶν μὲν ἐκ τοῦ δεσμωτηρίου τινὰ εἰς τὸ
βασιλεῦσαι καταστῆναι, αὐτὸν δὲ τῆς ἀδίκου δυναστείας, δικαίως
ὕστερον ἐκπεσεῖν.

**... it is possible to bring someone from the prison to the
throne, the one who has unjust power to be later justly thrown
out.**

An anonymous person is elevated from the "prison" (not
surprisingly Gregory replaces LXX's Semitic οἶκος τῶν δεσμίων[33]
with the Hellenic δεσμωτήριον — Symmachus does the same
thing with φυλακή) to "become king" (βασιλεύω, as in LXX). In
MT אצי is vocalised as the perfect tense, "he came out", but LXX
read it as an imperfect, "he will come out", and thus translated it
by the future of ἐξέρχομαι. The first reading makes the opening
phrase sound like the recording of an event that has taken place
in the past, while the second reading makes it sound like a
prophecy of an event that is yet to take place. It might be
expected that someone with an interest in eschatology would
exclusively latch on to the direction in which LXX pointed, but
Gregory paraphrases well by using the infinitive of καθίστημι,
"to bring into a certain state" (along with δυνατόν ἐστι, "it is

possible") to label this a typical event, one that has happened in the past and will happen again in the future, whenever kings are old and foolish enough not to take heed of the situation.

The kind of king who is in danger of losing his throne to an erstwhile prisoner, in the opinion of the Church Father, is not just an "old" and "foolish" king (γέρων and ἄφρων, v. 13), but more particularly an "unjust" ruler (ἄδικος, this verse), for that kind of sovereign is likely to be "justly" (δικαίως) thrown out of office. Thoughts of justice may have been put in Gregory's head by the mention here of "the prisoners" (LXX οἱ δέσμιοι, literally, "the bound"), for tyrants are quick to imprison any who would oppose or inhibit their tyranny. Koheleth made no mention of the justice or otherwise of what he recorded here — in fact, judging by his refrain in the opening verse of this chapter, "they [i.e., the oppressed] have no comforter", he was unlikely to have been thinking of the overthrow of an oppressive tyrant, but rather of what happens when kings of whatever ilk grow old and less astute at protecting their royal power — but Koheleth's failure to ascribe a moral judgment is frequently "rectified" by his paraphrast.

In the second phrase, for MT's ילד niphal, "to be born", LXX used γίγνομαι, which can also mean "to become".[34] Thus the Hebrew phrase, "he was born poor in his kingdom", was consistent with the picture of a poor person ascending to the throne (and its riches), while the Greek phrase, "he was born [or: he became] poor in his kingdom", introduced the possibility of taking the expression as denoting the opposite process, namely the royal (and accordingly rich) person descending to poverty. This provides the basis for Gregory's contention that the king can "be thrown out" (ἐκπίπτω) of his position of "power" (δυναστεία), a contention which calls for unrighteous kings to repent of their ways if they wish to avoid such a fate; the warning is so phrased that the one who has been raised from the prison to the throne to replace a tyrant should similarly take heed, and exercise his power more justly than his predecessor did.

(15) Συμβαίνει γὰρ τοὺς ὑπὸ τῷ νέῳ μέν, ἔμφρονι δὲ τασσομένους, ἀλύπους εἶναι τοὺς ὅσοι προγενέστεροι.

For it is the case that those who are under the young person, and who are classed as sensible, are free from distress, though they are older than him.

Koheleth noted how everyone who is living and moving under (LXX ὑπό) the sun is with (LXX μετά) the young usurper, which would seem to have been a description of how popular a revolution against tyranny is at the time, at least until it becomes a manifest tyranny itself.

Gregory places the people under (ὑπό) the youth rather than with him or under the sun, and depicts them as being "free from distress" (ἄλυπος) if they are among the ranks of the "sensible" or "prudent" (ἔμφρων). In introducing the notion of ἔμφρων to this verse, Gregory is harking back to the mention in v. 13 of σώφρων on the part of the young person and ἄφρων on the part of the old king; his point is probably that those who did not share in the foolishness and unrighteousness of the king have nothing to fear in the accession to the throne of the wise and righteous successor, but only those who, along with the king himself, cannot be regarded as ἔμφρων, will suffer λύπη under the new regime (either pain of body, in being punished for their unrighteousness, or pain of mind, in no longer having the opportunity for unrighteousness which they enjoyed under the old regime, may be intended here).

Gregory takes no special notice of Koheleth's mention of the young person in question being "second" (LXX δεύτερος), a reference which has caused some confusion among other commentators: was Koheleth now speaking of another youth than the one of whom he had just been speaking, or does "second" mean "successor"?[35] To Gregory's mind, the same hypothetical young person as before is still in view, and so he sees no need to offer any parallel to δεύτερος in his paraphrase.

Koheleth ended the verse with the note that this young person "will stand in his place" (LXX στήσεται ἀντ' αὐτοῦ) — presumably in the place of the old king, having taken over his throne. At this point Jerome's quotation of Gregory's paraphrase (mentioned in the comments on v. 13) is most interesting, for Jerome has Gregory ending his version of the verse with a reference to that king: *sub rege sene ante versati sint*,[36] "they previously lived under the old king", which

presupposes something like ὑπὸ τῷ βασιλεῖ γέροντι πρὶν
ἀνεστραμμένοι ὦσι in the Greek text — or *versati sint* may be
rendering ἐστραμμένοι ὦσι and thus might be rendered "they
were troubled/disturbed". But the text of Gregory's paraphrase
which has come down to us has τοὺς ὅσοι προγενέστεροι, literally
"the [accusative article] as many as are older [nominative
noun]", which appears somewhat disjointed. Jerome may have
had before him a better manuscript than any that has survived
to this day, or he may have taken it upon himself to improve
what had been passed down to him (and since then to us). His
rendering is not un-Gregorian, for it seems to provide the
notion of distress (*versor* [στρέφομαι?]) under the old ruler
(*senex* [γέρων?]) as a counterbalance to the notion of an absence
of distress (*absque moerore* [ἄλυπος]) under the young ruler
(*adolescens* [νέος]), and for that reason looks authentic.   If
Jerome's reading is accepted, Gregory is making a point of saying
that those who suffered under the old unrighteous king are
released from their suffering by the young righteous king; if it is
not, he is asserting that people who are older than a young king
have nothing to worry about if he is a righteous king.

(16) Οἱ γὰρ μετέπειτα γενόμενοι, διὰ τὸ ἑτέρου ἀπειράτως
ἔχειν, οὐδὲ τοῦτον ἐπαινεῖν δύνανται, ἀγόμενοί τε γνώμῃ ἀλογίστῳ,
καὶ ὁρμῇ πνεύματος ἐναντίου.

**Those who are born later, who have not had experience of
another person, are not able to praise this one. They are led by
an unreasoning judgment, and by the impulse of a hostile spirit.**

Koheleth spoke of the endless number of people who were
"before them" (LXX ἔμπροσθεν αὐτῶν), and then of "the later [*or:*
last] ones" (LXX οἱ ἔσχατοι);   by this he no doubt meant the
countless generations who lived before the time of the two kings
pictured in vv. 13-15, and the generations who come after that
time.   Gregory takes the second group as being οἱ μετέπειτα
γενόμενοι, "those who are born later" (than the time of the
unrighteous king, and so have experienced only the rule of the
righteous king);   the first group he styled at the end of the
previous verse as being προγενέστεροι, those who are "earlier in

birth" (than the righteous king, and so have experienced the rule of the unrighteous king as well as that of his successor) — it is possible that the προγενέστεροι, which appears a little strange in its present position in the text (see comments on v. 15), was originally part of a treatment of the opening phrase of this verse, which goes unparaphrased in Gregory's text as we have it.

The later generations do not "rejoice" (LXX εὐφραίνομαι) in the successor of the old king, according to Koheleth; that is, according to Gregory, they cannot "praise" (ἐπαινέω) him, because these later people have never lived under the "other" ruler (ἕτερος), and so they are not able to fully appreciate "this" ruler (οὗτος) under whom they do live. Their failure to acknowledge the righteousness of their king, who had replaced the unrighteous king before their time, is in Gregory's view what Koheleth was here labelling ματαιότης and προαίρεσις πνεύματος. The προαίρεσις is twofold: both a "judgment" (γνώμη) made by the human beings, and behind it the "impulse" (ὁρμή) provided by a spiritual being. The spiritual being at work is unambiguously a "hostile" or "contrary" one (ἐναντίος), opposing righteousness in the world and thus prompting human beings to form an opinion about the righteous king which is "unreasoning" (ἀλόγιστος, doing service for LXX's ματαιότης here?). There may be an intended contrast between this irrationality (ἀλόγιστος) of the later people and the rationality (ἔμφρων, v. 15) of the earlier people, who would have well appreciated the life free from distress under the new king after the life full of distress under the old king.

With this, the case study on the foolish old king and the wise young king is drawn to a close (so, too, is Jerome's quotation of Gregory's paraphrase), and Koheleth moved on to new matters, though Gregory's Solomon will do his best to make the transition somewhat less abrupt, by beginning the new verse with a δέ, by styling it as advice analogous to what the foolish old king should have borne in mind (vv. 13,14) — viz., advice to be careful to lead one's life righteously, addressed to the leader of the ἐκκλησία (or perhaps to any member of the ἐκκλησία, which would be less of a parallel to the talk here of secular rulers, but see the comments on ἐκκλησιάζω in v. 17) —

and by referring there, as he has in this section (at v. 13), to the "foolish" (ἄφρων).

(17)³⁷ Ἐκκλησιάζων δὲ πρὸ ὀφθαλμῶν ἔχε τόν τ᾽ ἑαυτοῦ βίον ὀρθῶς διαπορεύεσθαι, καὶ ὑπὲρ τῶν ἀφρόνων εὔχεσθαι, ὅπως ἐπίσταιντο σύνεσιν λαβόντες, ἐκκλίνειν τὴν πρᾶξιν τῶν πονηρῶν.

In speaking to the assembly, keep this before your eyes: to lead your own life correctly and to pray for the foolish, that they may be able to gain understanding and turn from the actions of the wicked.

At 1:12 and 12:9 the title ἐκκλησιαστής prompts Gregory to style the writer of Ecclesiastes as the one "speaking to the assembly" (ἐκκλησιάζω — cf. λέγω τῇ τοῦ Θεοῦ Ἐκκλησίᾳ at 1:1). Here at 4:17, where Koheleth mentioned "going to the house of God" (LXX πορεύομαι εἰς οἶκον τοῦ θεοῦ), Gregory employs ἐκκλησιάζω again. If he means this verb in the same sense in which he employs it elsewhere, then what we have here is Solomon, as the Preacher *par excellence*, offering advice to other preachers. It may be, though, that at this point Gregory intends the more general sense of "attending the ἐκκλησία (τοῦ θεοῦ)" rather than specifically addressing it, in which case Solomon is offering advice to all church-goers, and perhaps particularly to the laity rather than to the clergy. This latter meaning would be more in keeping with what Koheleth said, for he gave no evidence of having had priestly service in view.³⁸

The advice was, "watch your foot!" (LXX φύλαξον πόδα³⁹ σου); i.e., "take care" — in Gregory's version, "keep [certain things] before [your] eyes!" (πρὸ ὀφθαλμῶν ἔχε). The first thing that the preacher — or church-goer generally — ought to be careful about, according to the paraphrase, is that he is living his life "correctly" (ὀρθῶς, in which there may be echoes of LXX's ἀκούω, "listen", taken in the sense of "obeying" what one hears in the ἐκκλησία). Secondly, he should pray for the foolish. This is Gregory's equivalent to LXX's ὑπὲρ δόμα τῶν ἀφρόνων θυσία.⁴⁰ He may have interpreted this in the light of Proverbs 15:8, "the sacrifice of the wicked is an abomination to the LORD, but the prayer of the upright is his delight", and felt that if Solomon —

who to Gregory's mind also wrote the book of Proverbs — was here in Ecclesiastes admonishing his readers not to offer the sacrifice of the foolish (i.e., the wicked), this was equivalent to him calling on them to offer the prayer of the upright.[41]

Koheleth's truncated expression at the end of the verse, "they do not know to do wrong" (LXX οὔκ εἰσιν εἰδότες τοῦ ποιῆσαι κακόν), which probably was meant to convey the idea that the fools do not realise that their sacrifices are foolish ("they do not know that they are doing wrong"),[42] is naturally taken in a moral sense by Gregory. Having placed it in the context of prayer for the foolish, he is able to style it in a positive fashion, expressing the hope that, in effect, "they may know how not to do wrong" — if they had "understanding" (σύνεσις), implies Gregory, perhaps thinking of Job 28:28 (which employed ἐπιστήμη for "understanding" [cf. Gregory's ἐπίσταμαι, "to understand, be able"]), they would depart from evil (αἱ πράξεις τῶν πονηρῶν, "the doings of the wicked"). Koheleth's scorn for those who offer sacrifices has become Solomon's concern for those who do not yet have their lives on the right path.

Chapter Five

(1)[1] Γλώσσης δὲ φείδεσθαι καλόν, καὶ εὐσταθούσῃ χρῆσθαι καρδίᾳ ἐν τῇ περὶ λόγους σπουδῇ. Οὐ γὰρ χρὴ ἀλογίστως αὐτῶν ἔχοντα, κἂν ἄτοπα, ἢ τὰ ἐπὶ νοῦν ἐλθόντα, ταῦτα προΐεσθαι διὰ τῆς φωνῆς· ἀλλ᾽ ἐνθυμουμένους, ὅτι εἰ καὶ πολὺ ἀφεστήκαμεν οὐρανοῦ, γινώσκειν χρή, ὅτι ἐπ᾽ ἐπηκόῳ φθεγγόμεθα Θεοῦ, καὶ ἔστι λυσιτελὲς λαλεῖν ἀπεριπτώτως.

It is good to use the tongue sparingly, and to be subject to a calm heart when expressing oneself in words. For it is not proper for thoughtless and unnatural things, or whatever comes to mind, to be said out loud; but — even bearing in mind that we are far separated from heaven — it is proper to be aware that we speak in the hearing of God, and it is advantageous to speak unerringly.

A paraphrast is at liberty to reshuffle somewhat the thoughts of his predecessor: so it is that Gregory's opening phrase, "use the tongue sparingly" (γλώσσης φείδεσθαι), seems to be more a reflection of Koheleth's closing phrase, "let your words be few" (LXX ἔστωσαν οἱ λόγοι σου ὀλίγοι), while his closing phrase, "speak unerringly" (λαλεῖν ἀπεριπτώτως),[2] seems to be more a reflection of the original writer's opening phrase, "do not be hasty with your mouth" (LXX μὴ σπεῦδε ἐπὶ στόματί σου); such a reshuffling does not misrepresent the original work, for it is still passing on the same advice to the reader.

Koheleth's parallel phrase, "do not let your heart be hasty to utter a word" (LXX καρδία σου μὴ ταχυνάτω τοῦ ἐξενέγκαι λόγον), gives rise to Gregory's injunction to "be subject to a calm heart" (εὐσταθούσῃ χρῆσθαι καρδίᾳ) when one wishes to put one's thoughts into words. The use of σπουδή, "haste, exertion" for the exercise of speech in this phrase obviously reflects LXX's σπεύδω, "hasten, exert oneself" in the opening phrase, and suggests a rather impulsive exercise of speech which a calm heart is able to temper. Gregory feels that it is helpful to spell out briefly here an antithesis to the exercise of a sparing tongue and a calm heart; viz., the uttering (προΐημι, "let slip" seems to also carry the nuance of an impulsive action later to be regretted) of whatever thoughts happen to spring to mind (τὰ ἐπὶ νοῦν ἐλθόντα), which will mean that many thoughts only fit to be labelled as ἄτοπος, "unnatural, disgusting" will be expressed out loud. This speaking "thoughtlessly" (ἀλογίστως) is labelled as improper (οὐ χρή) and set in juxtaposition to what is proper (χρή): speaking "unerringly" (ἀπεριπτώτως), as in the hearing of God.

It is not entirely clear what Koheleth meant to imply by offering, as a reason for keeping one's words to a minimum, the observation that God is in heaven while the human speaker is on earth. The implication may have been that God is far removed from the affairs of human beings and takes no interest in what happens to them, so there is no point in addressing lengthy prayers to him or in calling upon Heaven to bear witness to some grievance or undertaking; on the other hand, the implication may have been that God is great and powerful in contrast to human smallness and limitation, so it is not wise to "big-note oneself" before him by means of extravagant oaths or gratuitous advice to other people.[3] It would seem, however, in the immediate context of speaking "before God" (LXX πρὸ προσώπου τοῦ θεοῦ, which is well paraphrased by Gregory's ἐπ' ἐπηκόῳ Θεοῦ, "in the hearing of God") and in the broader context of making vows before a God who is to be feared (vv. 4-7), that it is quite in order to draw the latter implication from Koheleth's observation. Gregory seeks to convey the idea that God's being in heaven means that he is above the earthly realm in two senses — sitting in a far different place, but at the same time overseeing what goes on in this place — so he notes that while it is true to say that we are a long way from heaven (πολὺ ἀφεστήκαμεν οὐρανοῦ), we should also be aware that God hears every word we say.[4]

Koheleth was fond of weighing things on the scale and attributing profitability or (more often) non-profitability to them (cf. the frequent use of περισσεία [יתרון], 1:3 and passim). While he did not explicitly give a value-judgment here in 5:1, there is certainly no doubt as to what his attitude was. Thus Gregory's talk of carefulness in speech being λυσιτελής, "profitable, advantageous" is admirably Kohelethine.

(2) "Ωσπερ δὲ φροντίσι ψυχῆς ποικίλαις παρέπεται ὀνειράτων παντοδαπῇ φαντασίᾳ·⁵ οὕτω καὶ ἀφροσύνη φλυαρία συνέζευκται.

Just as every kind of imagination of dreams comes with complex concerns of the mind, so also silly talk is connected with foolishness.

Koheleth's proverbial saying is rendered without expansion by Gregory. Dreams (LXX ἐνύπνιον) arise when there is much by which to be distracted or disturbed (LXX περισπασμός, cf. 1:13), said the proverb; that is, says the paraphrase, fantasies appear in the mind (ὀνειράτων⁶ φαντασία, "the imagination of dreams", an expression which seems to emphasise the non-reality of these phenomena) when it is overwhelmed with deep concerns (φροντίδες). The many words uttered by the fool can be neatly summed up in the word φλυαρία, "silly talk, nonsense". As always when Koheleth employed an identical expression in sequential clauses (LXX ἐν πλήθει..., καὶ... ἐν πλήθει, "in many..., and... in many"), Gregory prefers to avoid such repetitiveness: ποικίλος, "diversified, complex" for the first occurrence, and no parallel at all in the second instance.

(3) Ἐπαγγελία δὲ δι᾽ εὐχῆς γινομένη, τέλος λαμβανέτω δι᾽ ἔργου. Ἀφρόνων δὲ ἴδιον, τὸ ἀποβλήτους εἶναι· σὺ δὲ ἀληθὴς ἔσο,....

A promise made with a vow ought to be fulfilled in deed. It is a characteristic of fools to be worthless; so you ought to be truthful, ...

God has been left out of the Christian paraphrase, for while Koheleth referred explicitly to vows made "to God" (LXX τῷ θεῷ), Gregory makes no mention of the deity. Either he feels that to add τῷ θεῷ is to employ a somewhat tautologous phrase — because people invariably call upon God or Heaven in their vow-formulae — or he feels that it is too restrictive — because people frequently make empty vows to their fellows without any reference to God, and these kinds of vows should also be considered. In either case, there is no intention on Gregory's part to leave God out of the picture; on the contrary, he has just told us in v. 1 that whatever we say is spoken in the hearing of

God, and he will remind us of this again in v. 5. There is ample indication in the context that it is God who stands as the Witness of all "vows" (Gregory copies εὐχή from LXX and adds ἐπαγγελία, "promise" for good measure), and that it is he who expects such vows to be made good (λαμβάνω τέλος, "receive fulfilment", placing as subject the object of LXX's ἀποδίδωμι, "fulfill").

In the second part of the verse Koheleth had no explicit reference to God, and again neither does Gregory. The statement that "there is no pleasure in fools" (LXX οὐκ ἔστιν θέλημα ἐν ἄφροσιν) did not say precisely who is displeased by them. Koheleth's phrase may have been deliberately vague in this respect; that is, he may well have had in mind both the One by whom the vow is made — God is allegedly on record as being displeased with people who do not fulfill what they have vowed (Deuteronomy 23:21-23) — and also the one to whom the vow is made — the person who is given an undertaking by someone who does not fulfill it is unlikely to be pleased by such behaviour. If this is the case, then Gregory's paraphrase has rightly preserved the wider scope at this point:[7] in describing the fool as ἀπόβλητος, "to be thrown away as worthless", it is not said that only God takes this attitude to the casual vow-maker, and thus we may infer that both God and all right-minded people are unimpressed by an activity which is typical of fools.

If the reader wishes to be counted among the right-minded, and not to be characterised as a fool, he is then advised to be ἀληθής, "truthful". As a paraphrase of "fulfill what you vow" (LXX σὺν ὅσα ἐὰν εὔξῃ ἀπόδος), this obviously means: Be true to your word! — don't say anything which you have little or no intention of carrying out in deed.

(4) ... γινώσκων ὡς πολλῷ ἄμεινον μὴ εὔξασθαί σε, μηδὲ ὑποσχέσθαι τὶ δρᾶσαι, ἢ εὐξάμενον, εἶτα παραλιπεῖν.

... knowing that it is much better for you not to vow or promise to do something, than to vow and then not do it.

This is a particularly straightforward rendition of Koheleth's advice. As he did in the previous verse, Gregory adds the idea of "promising" (this time employing ὑπισχνέομαι) to that of "vowing" (retaining LXX's εὔχομαι); the intention behind this addition may be to ensure that the reader does not think only of formal vows made with ceremony, but is mindful also of less formal undertakings that equally ought not to be made lightly. A negative phrase, LXX's μὴ ἀποδοῦναι ("not fulfill"), is covered by a negative verb, παραλείπω ("leave remaining, fail to do"). The positive degree, LXX's ἀγαθόν (standing for טוב), is sensibly replaced in an improved Greek rendering by the comparative degree, ἄμεινον (cf. Symmachus βέλτιον).

(5) Δεῖ δὲ παντοίως φεύγειν τὴν τῶ[ν οὐ]⁸ καλῶν ῥημάτων ἐπιρροήν, ὡς ἀκουσομένου Θεοῦ. Τῷ γὰρ ταῦτα ἐνθυμουμένῳ πλέον οὐδέν ἐστιν, ἢ τὸ αἰσθάνεσθαι τῶν ἑαυτοῦ ἔργων ὑπὸ Θεοῦ διαφθειρομένων.

You ought to avoid by all means the stream of bad words, since God will hear them. The person who sets his heart on such things gets no more from them than to see his works destroyed by God.

Koheleth warned that one's mouth can "lead (one's self) into sin" (LXX ἐξαμαρτάνω), by which was presumably meant — following on directly from the previous verse — that if a vow is made and not subsequently fulfilled, then the act of allowing the words to pass one's lips is the act of setting oneself up to commit a sin (namely, the sin of failing to do what one has vowed to do). But the warning might be read as having a wider reference, to the danger of hasty or thoughtless talk generally, and this is the way in which Gregory reads it. What one must guard against (φεύγω, "avoid, flee from", a strenghtening of LXX's μὴ διδώμι, "not allow"), counsels the Church Father, is "the stream of bad words" (ἡ τῶν οὐ καλῶν ῥημάτων ἐπιρροή). This phrase is reminiscent of Gregory's talk in 2:15 of "the streams of nonsense" (τὰ φλυαρίας ῥεύματα) which the fool spouts forth; οὐ καλός here in 5:5 might be a judgment passed on casual promises, but more likely Gregory is referring again to foolish talk in general.

The activity of speaking to "the messenger" (המלאך) was now mentioned by Koheleth. In the Midrash *Koheleth Rabbah* this is taken as a reference to an earthly מלאך, such as an official who comes to collect the dues on a vow which had been earlier recorded, in which case the lame excuse "It was a mistake!" (MT שגגה היא — LXX ᾿Αγνοιά ἐστιν) is an attempt to escape from the requirement of paying what had been pledged; in the Targum it is taken as a reference to a heavenly מלאך, an avenging angel who will exact punishment on Judgment Day from all those who have uttered shameful words, in which case the lame excuse is an attempt to avoid punishment for one's verbal sins. But to the LXX translator this מלאך was no less than God (ὁ θεός — cf. Peshitta ܐܠܗܐ) himself, who was elsewhere reported as having presented himself to human beings in angelic form (e.g., in Jacob's dream [Genesis 31:11-13] and in Moses' burning bush [Exodus 3:2-6]); to refer here in v. 5 to one's speaking "in the presence of God" (πρὸ προσώπου τοῦ θεοῦ) might be seen as tidying up Koheleth's work by bringing this reference into line with v. 1, where he had used precisely that phrase.[9] Gregory — as we would expect — offers a paraphrase of the phrase which appears in LXX (he is not distracted by Symmachus, Aquila, and Theodotion "correcting" LXX to ὁ ἄγγελος), but — as we would also expect — not precisely the same paraphrase as he had offered in v. 1. There he had warned us "that we speak in the hearing of God" (ὅτι ἐπ' ἐπηκόῳ φθεγγόμεθα Θεοῦ); here he warns us "that God will hear" (ὡς ἀκουσομένου Θεοῦ) the words that we speak.

Gregory ignores Koheleth's citation of the wrongdoer's excuse, "It was a mistake!", and speaks instead of the wrongdoer "setting his heart on" (ἐνθυμέομαι) such things as bad words; it would appear that he regards this imbuing of oneself with what is οὐ καλός as providing a more significant reason for God to completely destroy (διαφθείρω, as in LXX) one's work (simply ἔργον, a de-semitisation of LXX's τὰ ποιήματα χειρῶν σου [מעשה ידיך], "the works of your hands"). Nor does he mention God's becoming angry (LXX ὀργίζομαι);[10] perhaps he feels that it is not proper to speak of such emotions on the part of the Deity, for after all Gregory's God is a long-suffering judge who does not punish swiftly (8:11) but who will bring down a just judgment at the right time (8:5).

(6) "Ὥσπερ γὰρ τὰ πολλὰ ἐνύπνια μάταια, οὕτω καὶ τὰ πολλὰ ῥήματα. Φόβος δὲ Θεοῦ, ἀνθρώπων σωτήριος, σπάνιος δέ.

Just as many dreams are empty, so also are many words. But the fear of God is the salvation of human beings, although it is rare.

The original version of this verse ran as follows: "In many dreams and futilities and many words, fear God."[11] This appears to have been a continuation of Koheleth's advice to his readers not to become involved in the practices of fools: as he had advised us in 4:17 to be careful when entering the house of God to go there to listen rather than to offer the sacrifice of fools, so he advised us here to be careful to remain mindful of God rather than to act like the fools who are exercised by dreams and endless foolish talk (cf. v. 2) — in the midst of all the many "futilities" being indulged in around us by those less wise than us, we ought to simply "fear God".[12]

Gregory reads the verse differently. He ignores or discounts the καί on the front of ματαιότητες, and thus is able to read the first several words of the sentence (LXX ἐν πλήθει ἐνυπνίων [καὶ] ματαιότητες) as a clause in its own right with subject and predicate ("in many dreams are futilities"), and then to take the following words (LXX καὶ λόγοι πολλοί) as an answering clause ("also many words"). This reading yields the sense: "As in many dreams there are futilities, so also (in the case of) many words." Koheleth had just used a ὅτι... καί (וְ ...כִּי) construction in this way in v. 2, so overlooking the inconvenient καί on the front of ματαιότητες here in v. 6 turns this verse into a parallel of the earlier verse — both are now drawing an analogy between dreams on the one hand and foolish talking on the other. So Gregory styles the first half of his version of this verse as a "just as..., so also" (ὥσπερ..., οὕτω καί) sentence, just as he did with his version of v. 2. This time he is content to employ LXX's word for "dream" (ἐνύπνιον), but he again rejects LXX's word for "word" (λόγος is replaced by ῥῆμα).

As mentioned above, the original version of this verse ended with the admonition, "fear God!" (LXX σὺν[13] τὸν θεὸν φοβοῦ). Gregory opts for a considerably less direct style, trans-

forming an imperative (φοβοῦ!) into an observation (concerning
the φόβος Θεοῦ).
His observation is twofold. Firstly, he wants to make it
clear to the reader why it is in the reader's interests to have this
"fear of God", and so he notes that here is the key to "salvation"
(σωτήριος). If he means by this that here is a key to gaining some
— though not guaranteed — success in the business of life by
wisely avoiding the sorts of pitfalls that the fools fall into, then
the paraphrast is arguably warranted in adding this observation
to Koheleth's words; but if, as appears more likely, he is
suggesting that the God-fearing person can confidently expect to
receive the reward of eternal life for his piety in this life, then he
is transmitting a decidedly more optimistic view than the one
which appears to have been transmitted by Koheleth's words.
Secondly, the Church Father adds a pessimistic observation: this
salvatory fear of God is σπάνιος, "rare", a scarce commodity,
seldom found. This statement does not accord well with the
tradition that bishop Gregory Thaumaturgos converted to the
fear of God all but seventeen of the people in his city of
Neocaesarea,[14] and might lead us to doubt the veracity of that
legend. It does, however, accord with Koheleth's views on the
rarity of upright people — barely one person in a thousand
(7:28)! But more to the point here at 5:6, Gregory's observation
that the fear of God is rare accords perfectly with Koheleth's
observation in the very next verse that the poor are invariably
oppressed in this world; this addition in the paraphrase — along
with the immediately following ὅθεν, "for which reason", with
which Gregory begins his paraphrase of v. 7 — serves the
function of providing a smooth transition from the topic that
has been in focus in the preceding passage (4:17–5:6 had to do
with verbal activities) to the topic which will be in focus in the
subsequent passage (with v. 7 there is a return to the matter of
economic activities). If one is aware that the fear of God is rare,
says the Church Father, then one is not surprised to see that
there is so much oppression going on under the sun.

(7) ῝Οθεν [οὐ]¹⁵ χρὴ θαυμάζειν ἀφορῶντα πρός τε πένητας
συκοφαντουμένους, καὶ πρὸς δικαστὰς παραλογιζομένους. Χρὴ δὲ

ἐκτρέπεσθαι τὸ τῶν δυνατωτέρων μείζονας εἶναι δοκεῖν.

For that reason you should not be surprised to see the poor being oppressed and the judges defrauding them. But you should avoid imagining yourself to be greater than those who are more powerful than you.

Gregory agrees with Koheleth's remark that the oppression of the poor should not surprise us, but the reason which the Hebrew sage gave as the grounds for this lack of surprise — namely the existence of a corrupt system of officialdom — becomes in the paraphrase a warning against acting above one's station in life. Koheleth's ὅτι (כי), which introduced his reason for expecting to find the poor suffering oppression, is ignored by Gregory, whose ὅθεν points back to what he has put forward as the real reason for the wise observer to be unsurprised by these matters — namely the rarity of the fear of God (v. 6).

As it did in 4:1, LXX chose again here to speak of "oppression" as συκοφαντία (for MT's עשק in this instance), and Gregory again follows suit. Συκοφαντία carries a rather particular meaning — "slander", a false accusation/prosecution — but such a narrowing of Koheleth's scope of reference may not be completely out of place in this present context of the denial of justice. The "seizure of judgment and justice" (LXX ἁρπαγὴ κρίματος καὶ δικαιοσύνης) is explained by the Church Father as the defrauding (παραλογίζομαι) of the poor out of what is rightfully theirs by the judges (δικασταί) who are supposed to protect people's rights. At 4:1 Gregory had presented the ironic contrast of those who ought to be offering help to the oppressed being the very ones who are doing the oppressing, and he now treats 5:7 in a similar vein: these judges, whose job it is to uphold the law and to impose punishments on the wicked oppressors, are in fact acting as wicked oppressors themselves by defrauding the innocent oppressed.

Koheleth's description of successive "high ones" (LXX ὑψηλοί) "watching" (LXX φυλάσσω) over other "high ones" conjured up a vivid picture of a satrapial system, each official looking for ways in which to feather his own nest at the expense of the lesser officials under him, with those citizens at the very bottom of the hierarchy — the poor — ending up by far the worst off.

(The impression that the reference was to such a system was enhanced by the use of the term מדינה, "province, satrapy" [in LXX a χώρα, "land, region"] in the first part of the verse.) For Gregory, Koheleth's observation that there is a ὑψηλός above a ὑψηλός and there are ὑψηλοί above them, is a word of warning to anyone who thinks that he is a great and powerful person: he should be mindful that, no matter how mighty he considers himself to be, there are always "mightier ones" (δυνατώτεροι) above him. The implication in this advice to avoid thoughts of grandeur is that the person who raises himself above his rightful place will be brought low by the people who are in reality more powerful than he. Gregory's paraphrase of the following verse hints at what is in store for such a person, and it may be that he has in mind, as the most powerful one who sees to it that the right thing eventually happens, God himself.[16]

(8) Κἂν γὰρ ἐκγένηται τοῦτο, ἀλλ᾽ οὖν τῶν ἐσομένων σοι φοβερῶν, οὐ ῥύσεταί σε ἡ καθ᾽ αὐτὴν πονηρία.

Even if this were to come about, wickedness by itself will not save you from the terrible things which will happen to you.

This verse was possibly the most intractable in the entire book of Ecclesiastes. Literally, it read: "The advantage of earth [or: a land] is in all, a king to [or: of] a cultivated field (LXX περισσεία γῆς ἐν παντί ἐστι, βασιλεὺς τοῦ ἀγροῦ εἰργασμένου)." In the Targum the verse is taken as meaning that tilling the earth has a great advantage over anything else, because even the king is dependent on the produce of the earth and on the agriculturalists who work to produce it, particularly in a time of crisis; while *Koheleth Rabbah* records the interpretation of "the advantage of the earth is in all [things]" as indicating that absolutely everything the earth produces — even such seemingly disadvantageous products as flies and gnats — are essential parts of the world's composition, and the interpretation of the second phrase (MT מלך לשדה נעבד), read as "a king makes himself servant to the field", as indicating that no matter how powerful a king may be, he remains a slave to the soil in that he can achieve nothing if his land is unproductive.

Two other possibilities of interpretation suggest themselves as ways of making sense out of Koheleth's cryptic expression: "an advantage to a country for all [the people who live in it] is to have a king over cultivated land" (i.e., to have stable and strong government protecting the agricultural areas from oppression at the hands of petty officials or destruction at the hands of invading armies); or "the profits from a land are taken by all [the corrupt officials mentioned in the previous verse], with the king himself being served by the fields" (i.e., the highest of the corrupt officials reaping the benefits of the labours of the oppressed is no less than the king himself).[17] If there is any relation at all between what Koheleth was saying and what Gregory represents him as saying at this point, it could only be seen if we assumed that the paraphrast has taken this last line of interpretation, for underlying Gregory's version of this verse is the contention that power is invariably exercised wickedly.

But it is perhaps not surprising if Gregory has despaired of making sense out of his predecessor's puzzling words in this verse, and has issued instead to the reader a warning which he believes ought to follow up what has just been said in v. 7, even if it bears little if any relation to what Koheleth was talking about here in v. 8. In v. 7 the Christian paraphrase had counseled the reader not to imagine himself to be greater than those who are more powerful than he, and so now that advice is underpinned by the foreshadowing of certain undefined "terrible things" (φοβερά) that will befall the person who does not take heed of it. The opening phrase, "even if this were to come about..." (κἂν γὰρ ἐκγένηται τοῦτο...), postulates the unlikely scenario of the imaginings in v. 7 actually taking place — in other words, "even if you really did become greater than those who had been more powerful than you..." — while the closing phrase, "... wickedness by itself will not save you" (... οὐ ῥύσεταί σε ἡ καθ' αὐτὴν πονηρία), indicates that Gregory has in mind in all this the wicked use of power over others, and not the holding of positions of power *per se* — the person who oppresses and defrauds those who are less powerful than he (v. 7), the paraphrase is saying, will find that his wicked ways will be of no avail when his evil deeds catch up with him (v. 8; cf. Gregory's paraphrase of 8:8). These undefined φοβερά which will befall the wicked can be taken as having a double reference: on the one hand, in the context of the closing phrase of v. 7, to the nasty way in which the power-wielders are likely to eventually treat anyone who thinks (and acts as if) he is greater than they; and on the other hand, in the context of the opening phrase of v. 8, to the retribution which God will eventually pour upon those who are in reality the power-wielders in this world.

(9) ῞Ωσπερ δὲ κτῆμα τὸ ἐξ ἁρπαγῆς βλαβερώτατον καὶ ἀνοσιώτατον, οὕτω καὶ ἀνδρὶ ἐπιθυμητῇ χρημάτων οὐκ ἐκγίνεται[18] κόρος, οὔθ' ἡ παρὰ τῶν πέλας εὔνοια· κἂν ὁτιοῦν μάλιστα πάμπολυ ἀργύριον ἐπικτήσωνται. Τοῦτο μὲν γὰρ μάταιον.

Just as a possession gained through robbery is most hurtful and unholy, so also a person who covets possessions never has his fill, nor the good-will of his neighbours — even if he were to acquire the greatest possible amount of money. For this is futile.

Koheleth began a series of reflections on the futility of wealth with the observation that the person who loves (LXX ἀγαπάω) money (LXX ἀργύριον) is never satisfied (LXX πίμπλαμαι), which Gregory paraphrases by saying that the person who covets (ἐπιθυμέω) possessions (χρῆμα — he uses ἀργύριον later in the verse) never has his fill (ἐκγίνεται κόρος), but before he does so he prefaces the observation with what he evidently regards as being a pertinent analogy to this situation: the person who acquires property by forceful means (ἁρπαγή, "seizure, robbery") is doing something which is both hurtful (βλαβερός) and unholy (ἀνόσιος). LXX had employed ἁρπαγή in v. 7 to depict the wresting of justice from the oppressed, and it may be that which has suggested to Gregory that reference should be made here to such criminal activity (where the word had appeared in v. 7 he himself had spoken of the poor being defrauded by the judges), while the notions of βλαβερός and ἀνόσιος might be thought by a pious interpreter to be obviously implied by talk of the love of money, "the root of all evils" (1

Timothy 6:10). It is also not impossible that an interpretation of the previous verse lies behind the reference at this point to acts of seizure: if "the increase of a land is in all" is construed as "the products of the land are taken by all [the corrupt and wicked people]", this could suggest the forceful acquisition by powerful and/or criminal elements of what is not rightfully theirs.

Koheleth then proceeded with his own analogy to the situation of a person who loves money never being satisfied: the situation of a person who loves wealth never having any produce! This rather strange juxtaposition of "in wealth, no produce" (בהמון לא תבואה) understandably caused some difficulties for interpreters,[19] and LXX preferred to read the לא in this second stich as לו and accordingly translated the phrase as ἐν πλήθει αὐτῶν γένημα, "produce in its abundance".[20] Gregory speaks of there being no "good-will" (εὔνοια) among his neighbours for the person who heaps up great wealth. Such a paraphrase appears to understand that there was a negative in Koheleth's second stich, just as there was in his first (Gregory used οὐκ in his treatment of the first stich, and he begins his treatment of the second with οὔθ'). But it may be that Gregory's expression ότιοῦν μάλιστα πάμπολυ ἀργύριον, "the greatest possible amount of money" is his paraphrase of LXX's phrase ἐν πλήθει αὐτῶν γένημα, with the clause on neighbourly ill-feeling reflecting his own additional thought on what is the lot of a person who covets such things (perhaps alluding to the jealous feelings of the neighbours already raised by the paraphrast in 4:4, where he also employed the expression παρὰ τῶν πέλας) rather than what he specifically read in the text before him.

The verse concluded with the standard Kohelethine view, καί γε τοῦτο ματαιότης (גם־זה הבל), "this, too, is futility". This precise phrase occurred 13 times in LXX Ecclesiastes,[21] and Gregory is very inventive with the number of variations he can devise with which to render it; only here does he offer a formulation which closely mirrors the original phrasing: τοῦτο μὲν γὰρ μάταιον, "for this [viz., the acquisition of the greatest possible amount of money] is futile". (At 7:6 Gregory's phrasing approximates this, but there the adjective is placed first and is not a cognate of ματαιότης.)

(10) Ἀγαθότης δὲ τοὺς συνόντας αὐτῇ ὑπερευφραίνουσα, ἀνδρείους ἀπεργάζεται τοῦ καθορᾶν ἕκαστα τῶν πραγμάτων παρέχουσα τὴν δύναμιν.

But goodness is a great joy for those who partake in it; it makes them strong, furnishing them with the ability to perceive all things.

Whenever Koheleth used the word "good" (טוב or טובה), which he did quite frequently, his pious interpreters are inclined to invest in that word a moral force; on six occasions (4:8; 5:17; 6:3,6; and 7:14; in addition to the verse now at hand) LXX appears to particularly invite such an interpretation by translating טובה as ἀγαθωσύνη, "goodness, kindness".[22]   What Koheleth actually said in the present verse was ברבות הטובה רבו אוכליה, "when the good becomes numerous, those who eat it become numerous", which at face value seems to have been saying that the more there is to eat, the more people there are to eat it; in the context of the discussion on wealth, and in particular in the immediate context of the following reference to the questionable benefit which is derived by its owners (i.e., those who own this increased "good"), there was every indication that he had in mind increased success in the accumulation of worldly goods, and a concomitant increase in the numbers of people who believe they ought to have a share in one's blessings! But the LXX version of this thought, ἐν πλήθει τῆς ἀγαθωσύνης ἐπληθύνθησαν ἔσθοντες αὐτήν, could be read as "in the abundance of goodness/kindness, those who eat it prevail [or: are made full]", which might suggest — if "eating" is taken in a metaphorical sense — that goodness has a satisfying effect on those who partake in it; and in place of the "benefit to its owners" (כשרון לבעליה) in the following sentence LXX spoke of the ἀνδρεία τῷ παρ' αὐτῆς, the "virtue of the one[23] who is near to it", which in turn suggests the morally good qualities of the person who performs acts of kindness (or perhaps those qualities rubbing off onto the person who observes such behaviour).

Accordingly, Gregory's paraphrase speaks of a moral good rather than material goods.[24] What is at issue here for the Church Father is unambiguously ἀγαθότης, "goodness, loving-kindness"; and to say, as LXX seemed to, that those who "eat" (ἐσθίω) goodness "are made full" (πληθύνομαι), really means that goodness "is a great joy" (ὑπερευφραίνομαι — literally, "rejoices exceedingly") to "those who partake in it" (οἱ συνόντες αὐτῇ, an expression which also does service for LXX's ὁ παρ' αὐτῆς, "the one who is near to it" of the following sentence). The ἀνδρεία, "virtue" ("manliness") at which LXX had hinted (where Koheleth had spoken of a כשרון, "benefit" or "use") is seen in that the person who has to do with goodness is made thereby ἀν-δρεῖος, "strong" ("manly"). It is evident that Gregory's version of this verse presents a striking contrast to what had been in view in his version of the previous verse: there the pursuit of wealth had been depicted as being a hurtful activity and as resulting in ill-feeling; here the pursuit of goodness is depicted as being a strengthening activity and as resulting in joyous feelings. It is not at all evident that Koheleth was similarly meaning to present a contrast in these two verses — in fact, he appears to have been offering in the second of these verses corroborative evidence for the contention he had made in the first of them, that the pursuit of wealth is ματαιότης, rather than putting forward some other pursuit which does not fall under this judgment.

Koheleth's ironic comment that the only benefit for the owner of the increased goods is that he is able to "see" (LXX ὁράω) his goods increased, becomes Gregory's decidedly more cryptic statement that the person who has to do with goodness receives thereby the ability to "perceive" (καθοράω) "all things" (ἕκαστα τῶν πραγμάτων). Precisely what Gregory means by this phrase is not clear, but it is certainly not a seeing with "one's eyes" (LXX ὀφθαλμοὶ αὐτοῦ), but rather with one's mind. If πράγματα is to be taken in the sense of "deeds" or "actions", then the meaning may be that the person who partakes in goodness is able to see each and every human activity for what it is; he is not seduced into thinking, for example, that the forceful acquisition of a possession which is not rightfully his is a beneficial and justifiable activity, for he can see that it is on the contrary a most hurtful and unholy activity (v. 9). If, on the other hand, πράγματα is to be taken in the sense of "matters" or

"affairs", then the meaning may be that the participant in
goodness is able to keep everything in perspective; he is not
under the misapprehension, for example, that being wealthy is
as desirable as it is often made out to be, for he can see its
considerable disadvantages (vv. 11,12) and in particular its
transitory nature (vv. 13,14) — perhaps the person mentioned
here, who "perceives all things", is to be contrasted with the
person mentioned in v. 15, who "is not conscious of" (οὐκ
ἐνθυμέομαι) certain important matters.

(11) Μέγα δὲ καὶ τὸ μὴ προστετηκέναι τοιαύταις φροντίσιν· ὁ
μέν γε πένης, κἂν δοῦλος ᾖ, καὶ μὴ ὑπερεμπλήσας τὴν ἑαυτοῦ
γαστέρα, προσηνοῦς μεταλαμβάνει τῆς διὰ τοῦ ὕπνου ἀνέσεως·
πλούτου δὲ ἐπιθυμία σύνεστι ἀγρυπνίαις καὶ καμάτοις ψυχῆς.

It is important not to adhere to concerns such as these: the
poor person, even if he is a slave and does not fill his stomach to
capacity, at least gets his share of the gentle relaxation of sleep;
but the desire for wealth is linked to sleeplessness and troubles
of mind.

Gregory prefaces this verse with a short introduction which
alerts the reader to the importance of not succumbing to
concerns "such as these" (τοιαῦται) — i.e., to concerns such as
those that will be elaborated upon in the following verses, all
having to do with the "desire for wealth" (πλούτου ἐπιθυμία).
Having made that addition, he proceeds to give, for the first time
in many verses, a comparatively straightforward paraphrase of
Koheleth's words.[25]
    Koheleth spoke of the עבד having a "sweet sleep" (LXX
γλυκὺς ὕπνος), which latter expression Gregory nicely paraphrases as "the gentle relaxation of sleep" (προσηνὴς ἡ διὰ τοῦ
ὕπνου ἄνεσις), but what he makes of the individual in question
is more interesting. In MT the word is vocalised as a participle,
"the worker, the one who tills (the soil)"; it would appear that to
the eyes of the LXX translator, however, the word was a
segholate noun, "the slave, servant", and thus is to be rendered
δοῦλος (cf. Peshitta ܪܚܠܐ, which could mean either "[agri-
cultural] worker" or "servant"). Gregory speaks of the πένης,

"the day-labourer, poor person", who may even be a δοῦλος.
This gives the impression of being a paraphrase both of the
Masoretic and of the Septuagintal understanding of the word, by
giving first of all a more general equivalent to MT's "worker"
than the choice of LXX, but following this with LXX's "slave" as
a particular sub-category (the poorest of the poor). Koheleth
assured the reader that this person's sleep is sweet "whether he
eats little or much" (LXX εἰ ὀλίγον καὶ εἰ πολὺ φάγεται), which
Gregory apparently understands to have been saying that the
poor person eats neither too little nor too much, in contrast to
the rich person who eats far too much, for he notes that this
person "does not over-fill" his stomach (μὴ ὑπερεμπίπλημι,
which would indicate that he consumes a reasonable rather than
an unreasonable amount of food and drink).

As for the opposite kind of person, Koheleth presented his
interpreters with the expression השבע לעשיר. This is vocalised in
MT as a nominal construction, and on the same understanding
Symmachus translated it as ἡ πλησμονὴ τοῦ πλουσίου, "the
satiety of the rich", but it might be vocalised as a verbal
construction and hence translated à la LXX as ὁ ἐμπλησθεὶς τοῦ
πλουτῆσαι, "the one who is satiated with becoming wealthy".
Gregory does not speak of the person per se but of the
phenomenon: πλούτου ἐπιθυμία, "the desire for wealth". This it
is that "does not permit him to sleep" (LXX οὐκ ἔστιν ἀφίων
αὐτὸν τοῦ ὑπνῶσαι), and the paraphrase spells out more clearly
that such "sleeplessness" (ἀγρυπνία) is a result of the "troubles of
mind" (κάματοι ψυχῆς) which inevitably accompany the desire
for wealth. No doubt the vast majority of Gregory's flock were
poor, and perhaps a good number of them were slaves; it must
have been very reassuring for them to be told that in reality they
were better off than the rich people they envied.

(12) Τί δ' ἂν γένοιτο τούτου ἀτοπώτερον, ἢ τὸ μετὰ πολλῆς
σπουδῆς καὶ ἐπιμελείας ἀποθησαυρίζοντα τὸν πλοῦτον συντηρεῖν,
μυρίων ἑαυτῷ φυλάσσοντα κακῶν ἀφορμήν;

**What could be more absurd than hoarding and preserving
wealth with much trouble and care, when this is fostering the
means for countless evils to oneself?**

Twice within this passage on the futility of wealth (at the outset of this verse and again at the outset of v. 15) Koheleth used the expression רעה חולה, literally "a sick evil", by which he presumably meant a situation of considerable repulsiveness, "a sickening evil". At v. 15 LXX translated word-for-word (though appearing to have regarded חולה rather than רעה as the noun in this construction), without giving particular attention to what Koheleth might have meant by the expression, with πονηρὰ ἀρρωστία, "an evil sickness"; here at v. 12 the πονηρά was dispensed with and only the ἀρρωστία remained,[26] making it look as though Koheleth was speaking of an illness which he had observed under the sun. This rendering does, however, make some sense in the context, for what was in view at the close of this verse was the harm (LXX κακία, literally "evil") that is caused to the hoarder of riches by his activities; it might be said that a person who is subject to an all-consuming passion for wealth is suffering from an illness.

But if LXX's ἀρρωστία seems to have pointed in this interpretive direction, it is not taken up by Gregory, who remains close to what seems to have been the intended meaning of the original work: what Koheleth had pronounced "sickening", the Church Father labels "absurd" (ἄτοπος, "out of place, strange"). But Gregory makes an interesting variation on Koheleth's thoughts, in the way in which he applies the verb φυλάσσω (שמר), "to guard". In the text before him it was clear that "wealth" (LXX πλοῦτος) is guarded, and that this results in "evil" (LXX κακία) to the owner of that wealth; but Gregory applies φυλάσσω not only to the πλοῦτος, in which context he spells out the two-fold action of first hoarding it up (ἀποθησαυρίζω) and then being in a position to guard it (συντηρέω), but also to the κακία (κακόν in his version), in which context he places the verb φυλάσσω itself. In treating the matter at hand in this way, Gregory is bringing out more clearly an irony that might be thought to have been understated by Koheleth : the lover of wealth, in being concerned that his inordinate share of the good things of this world be preserved, is in fact only ensuring that his inordinate share of the bad things in life is preserved.

It is rather noticeable that Gregory is more comfortable with Koheleth's contention concerning the futility of the pursuit of wealth than he is with some of Koheleth's contentions concerning the futility of other pursuits. When Koheleth said (in 1:18), "the more wisdom, the more sorrow", Gregory strongly hints that this is a mistaken belief which Solomon grew out of. When Koheleth said in effect (in 2:23), "the more work, the more pain", Gregory wants it to be understood that this applies only to the person who has chosen wicked pursuits. But when Koheleth said in effect (in the verse now at hand), "the more wealth, the more harm to oneself", Gregory paraphrases without the slightest murmur of reservation.

(13) Καὶ τὸν πλοῦτον ἐκεῖνον ἀνάγκη ἀπολέσθαι ποτὲ καὶ διαφθαρῆναι, εἴτε γένοιτο τῷ κτησαμένῳ τέκνα, εἴτε καὶ μή·

This wealth necessarily slips away at some stage and is completely destroyed, whether the person who acquired it has children or not.

As he often does, the paraphrast renders a Kohelethine verb (on this occasion ἀπόλλυμαι [אבד], "to be lost/destroyed") by a pair of closely-related verbs (here ἀπόλλυμαι itself and διαφθείρομαι, both essentially meaning "to be utterly destroyed", with the former perhaps connoting a coming undone before the ultimately final blow delivered in the latter). Gregory does not speculate on what distracting or disturbing thing (LXX περισπασμός) might occasion the loss of riches; he merely says that such an occurrence will inevitably (ἀνάγκη, "of necessity") eventuate sooner or later.

Koheleth now spoke of fathering a child, and then said "and there is nothing in his hand" (LXX καὶ οὐκ ἔστιν ἐν χειρὶ αὐτοῦ οὐδέν). In the context of the loss of wealth that had just been mentioned, the meaning of this phrase must have been that the father has been rendered unable to pass any of that wealth on to his child, a meaning which is essentially unaffected by whether "his hand" is taken to be a reference to that of the father, who has nothing to hand on to the next generation, or to that of the child, who is thus left empty-handed.[27]

But Gregory has a novel approach to the phrase, not relating it at all to the idea of lost wealth. He appears instead to take it as a contrast to the preceding phrase, "and he fathers a child" (LXX καὶ ἐγέννησεν υἱόν), such that the empty-handed person is the antithetical case of the person who does not father a child. Accordingly, he treats these two phrases as having put forward alternative possibilities: either a person acquires children (εἴτε γένοιτο τῷ κτησαμένῳ τέκνα) or he does not (εἴτε καὶ μή), but either way it makes no difference to what was said in the first half of the verse concerning the inevitability of the utter destruction of worldly wealth. Perhaps Gregory thinks that Koheleth was warning those people who have children not to be under the mistaken impression that God will allow them to retain their riches for the sake of the children; they are just as subject to this immutable law as are those who have no such "altruistic" excuse for hoarding wealth.

(14) αὐτόν τε εἰ καὶ μὴ βούλοιτο προσήκει τοιοῦτον εἰς τὴν γῆν[28] πεσεῖν καὶ ἀπελθεῖν, οἷος καὶ ὁπότε εἰς τὸ εἶναι παρὼν ἐτύγχανε. Κεναῖς δὲ χερσὶν ἀπιέναι μέλλων, ...

Even if he does not want to, such a person is destined to fall into the earth, and to depart from life in the same condition in which he had formerly been destined to come into being. Having to depart with empty hands ....

To keep repeating oneself does not make for a good address, although some points do need to be repeated, would seem to be the paraphrast's view. Koheleth told his readers twice in this verse that a person "goes" from this life (first LXX used ἐπιστρέφω, and then the notion was repeated with πορεύομαι) in the same condition as he "came" to it (first ἐξέρχομαι, then ἥκω), before saying it for a third time in the very next verse. Gregory puts this antithesis of coming and going as such only once before the reader — a person "goes away" (ἀπέρχομαι) just as he "arrived" (πάρειμι) — although he will paraphrase the notion again in a different way at its next occurrence. But the idea of departing this life is worth repeating, since people — particularly rich people — ought to give more thought to this matter than they generally do, as Gregory will note in his paraphrase of the following verse (already here μὴ βούλομαι, "to not be willing" hints that such people do not have a proper attitude towards death).

Hence we find coupled with ἀπέρχομαι the rather more graphic εἰς τὴν γῆν πίπτω, "to fall into the earth" (a phrase which recalls Genesis 3:19's talk of the human body returning to the earth whence it came and which Gregory will call into service again with some relish in his paraphrase of 12:4), and the idea is brought up explicitly once more by Gregory in the last part of this verse by means of ἄπειμι, "to go away, depart".

For Koheleth (as for the writer of Job [1:21]), the best word for portraying the fact that a human being comes into the world with nothing and goes out of the world with nothing was "naked" (LXX γυμνός). Gregory prefers not to offer a paraphrase of this nakedness;[29] he evidently feels that the matter is sufficiently handled by the concept with which this verse concludes — viz., empty-handedness (LXX οὐδέν... ἐν χειρὶ αὐτοῦ), the consciousness of which Gregory particularly links to the perception of evil mentioned in the following sentence (the beginning of v. 15).

(15) ... αὔξει τὴν ἑαυτοῦ κακίαν, ὥσπερ οὐκ ἐνθυμούμενος, ὅ τι ἐπίκειται αὐτῷ τέλος τοῦ βίου τῇ γενέσει ὅμοιον, καὶ ὅτι ἀνόνητα μοχθεῖ, εἰς δέ τινα μᾶλλον ἀνέμου ὁρμήν, ἥπερ τῇ ἑαυτοῦ σπουδῇ χαριζόμενος, ...

... magnifies the evil for him, as he does not consider that an end to life similar to its beginning hangs over him, and that he labours unprofitably — more a desire for the wind than an exertion on something of advantage to him.

Koheleth's bitter comment that "this, too, is a sickening evil" (MT גם־זה רעה חולה) — LXX called it a πονηρὰ ἀρρωστία, an "evil sickness", cf. v. 12) would appear to have been his own attitude to the situation, just as the frequent comment "this, too, is futility" placed his personal stamp of dissatisfaction on so many other things which he had observed in the world (note that when the רעה חולה comment first appeared but three verses previously it was explicitly introduced as a pronouncement

made upon something which Koheleth "saw under the sun");
moreover, this matter of what happens after one's death to the
things for which one has toiled so strenuously during one's life
was a matter of considerable personal feeling on Koheleth's part,
as was evidenced by the latter part of Chapter Two as well as by
the passage now at hand. But to Gregory the fact that one has to
leave this life with empty hands is not a matter which should
trouble a righteous mind, for it is only an evil from the
perspective "of him" (ἑαυτοῦ); i.e., from the perspective of the
wicked hoarder of riches, who does not seem to be aware
(ἐνθυμέομαι) of the simple truth which Koheleth now repeated
once more: as a person "comes" (LXX παραγίγνομαι), so he
"goes" (LXX ἀπέρχομαι), or in Gregory's words, as is a person's
"beginning" (γένεσις), so is his "end" (τέλος).

Koheleth's rhetorical question "what surplus/profit is there
for him?" (LXX τίς περισσεία αὐτῷ) receives the correct answer
that there is none (his labours are ἀνόνητος, "unprofitable,
useless").   "Toiling for the wind" (LXX μοχθέω εἰς ἄνεμον) is
rendered as "desire for the wind" (ἀνέμου ὁρμή), and Gregory
feels that this image may be better understood if it is juxtaposed
with an antithetical activity, "an exertion on something advantageous" (τῇ σπουδῇ χαριζόμενος, literally "doing something
agreeable with exertion"), which is to say that "to toil for [or: to
desire] the wind" is to exert oneself on something which is not
advantageous.

Μοχθέω εἰς ἄνεμον (עמל לרח) looks like an equivalent
expression to the frequent προαίρεσις πνεύματος (רעות/רעיון רח),
and Gregory's ἀνέμου ὁρμή would work well as a possible
paraphrase of that expression, but LXX always used πνεῦμα
rather than ἄνεμος in that context and Gregory almost always
spiritualises it, even at 4:16 where he approximates ἀνέμου ὁρμή
with ὁρμή πνεύματος. In fact, here at 5:15 was one of only two
occasions in Ecclesiastes when LXX's choice for רח was ἄνεμος
rather than πνεῦμα (the other was 11:4), and it seems to be a
principle of Gregory's never to use ἄνεμος when the text before
him had πνεῦμα. Although he is not always able to spiritualise
πνεῦμα (cf., e.g., 1:6, where he still uses the word even though we
might have expected him to employ ἄνεμος, as he does in v. 7),

the Church Father's interpretation of it is much more often than
not in that direction; certainly his almost monolithic understanding of προαίρεσις πνεύματος as referring to "spirit" rather
than "wind" prevents him from offering ἀνέμου ὁρμή as a paraphrase of that expression, even though his κενὴ ἐπιθυμία,
"empty desire" in 6:9 seems to indicate an awareness of the
possibility of this interpretation.

(16) ... καταναλώσας τὸν ἑαυτοῦ βίον σύμπαντα, ἕν τε
ἐπιθυμίαις ἀνοσιωτάταις, καὶ ἐν ὁρμαῖς ἀλόγοις, ἔτι δὲ λύπαις καὶ
ἀρρωστίαις. Καὶ συνελόντι φάναι, σκότος μέν εἰσι τῷ τοιούτῳ αἱ
ἡμέραι· πένθος δὲ ἡ ζωή.

He spends his whole life in most unholy passions and
irrational desires, with pains and illnesses as well. To put it
briefly: to such a person the days are darkness and life is sadness.

Gregory inverts the two halves of this verse, styling the
now first half as a continuation of what has already been said
concerning the suffering which the hoarder of wealth brings
upon himself, and the now second half as a résumé (συνελόντι
φημί, "to declare in brief") of all that. The "all his days" (LXX
πᾶσαι αἱ ἡμέραι) of Koheleth's first half is treated in a number of
ways by the paraphrase: it finds its way into Gregory's first half
as "his whole life" (ὁ ἑαυτοῦ βίος σύμπας) and it also appears in
its rightful place in Gregory's second half, both in the sense of
"life" (ζωή) and in the sense of actual "days" (ἡμέραι).

According to MT, the pursuer of wealth "eats in darkness"
(בחשך יאכל)[30] throughout his days, but LXX read ואבל instead of
יאכל, and so presented the individual in question as spending his
days "in darkness and mourning" (ἐν σκότει καὶ πένθει).
Accordingly, Gregory says that the person who is consumed by a
desire for wealth sees only σκότος and πένθος.

LXX closed the verse with three nouns depicting the
suffering of the pursuer of wealth: θυμός, "emotion";[31]
ἀρρωστία, "illness";[32] and χόλος, "anger". In the case of the last
two nouns the paraphrast is content to present them unadorned,
reproducing ἀρρωστία while preferring λύπη, "pain, distress" to
χόλος, but θυμός captures his paraphrastic interest, giving rise to

Gregory's ἐπιθυμία, "passion, desire", which is styled as "unholy" (ἀνόσιος) and supplied with a companion emotion in ὁρμή, "impulse, desire" (repeated from v. 15), which in turn is styled as "irrational" (ἄλογος) and thus helps to form the kind of balanced construction of which Gregory is so fond.

(17) Ἀγαθόν γε μὴν ἐκεῖνο καὶ οὐκ ἀπόβλητον· Θεοῦ γάρ ἐστι δῶρον, τὸ δυνηθῆναι ἀπολαῦσαι ἄνθρωπον τῶν ἑαυτοῦ καμάτων[33] ἐν εὐφροσύνῃ, ...

But certainly this is good and not to be rejected: it is a gift of God for a person to be able to enjoy in cheerfulness the things for which he has worked, ...

The conclusion to Koheleth's investigations, that the best thing for a human being to do is to find moderate enjoyment in the simple things of life, was introduced this time not only by his usual word of approval, ἀγαθός (טוב), but also by καλός (יפה, "beautiful, proper"); Gregory includes ἀγαθός unmodified, and paraphrases καλός by means of a negative equivalent, οὐκ ἀπόβλητος ("not to be rejected"). Ἐκεῖνος, where we might have expected Gregory to employ οὗτος, is perhaps a little confusing, as it might be taken as directing the approval back to the matters which have just been in view, but there can be no doubt that Gregory does not approve of the wicked pursuit of wealth but rather wishes to uphold the goodness of the matters he now raises in the remainder of this new sentence (vv. 17 and 18). When "good" appeared again, in the expression ὁράω ἀγαθωσύνην (ראה טובה), "to see good", Gregory understands this to mean "to enjoy", which he covers by ἀπολαύω. We might have anticipated a moral twist being given to ἀγαθωσύνη (cf. comments on v. 10), but Gregory is happy enough to speak of plain and simple εὐφροσύνη, "merriment, cheerfulness" at this point. A moral rider will not be delayed long, however, for an important qualification on this matter of enjoying the fruits of one's labours will be made by the paraphrast in the following verse, which is still part of the same sentence in the paraphrase. This is exactly the same approach as he had followed at 3:12, the only other instance — out of no less than six occasions on which

Koheleth reported his conclusion regarding enjoyment of the small pleasures offered by life — of Gregory actually voicing some approval of this conclusion. But he cannot bring himself to include Koheleth's "eating" (LXX ἐσθίω) and "drinking" (LXX πίνω), since in tandem with "being merry" (i.e., participating in εὐφροσύνη) this might give the impression of condoning a certain well-known but un-Christian philosophy of life.

To see good "in all his labour" (LXX ἐν παντὶ μόχθῳ αὐτοῦ), then, is to be able to enjoy "the things for which he has laboured" (οἱ ἑαυτοῦ κάματοι). This ability "is a gift of God" (Θεοῦ ἐστι δῶρον), Gregory says, paraphrasing the thought of the following verse, where Koheleth did indeed say that this ability "is a gift of God" (LXX δόμα Θεοῦ ἐστιν). But in this particular verse, when Koheleth talked of God "giving" (LXX δίδωμι) something to a human being, it was not exactly the ability to enjoy the fruits of one's labours that was in focus; rather, Koheleth was saying that God gives to a human being a certain "number of days of his life" (LXX ἀριθμὸς ἡμερῶν ζωῆς αὐτοῦ). Gregory does not say a word about this matter; perhaps he feels that it is untidy to include the notion at this point when he is going to speak of "measuring out one's life" (συμμετρέομαι τὸν ἑαυτοῦ βίον) in the very next sentence (v. 19).

(18) ... θεόσδοτα, καὶ οὐχ ἁρπακτικὰ³⁴ δεξάμενον κτήματα.

... if they are possessions given by God and not gained through robbery.

It is rare for the paraphrase to express things more briefly than they were expressed in the original version of Ecclesiastes, but Gregory evidently feels that the thoughts of this verse have been adequately covered in the preceding verse, the only matter needing to be taken up being the question of how one acquires the things for which one has worked. Gregory wants to make it clear that the only kinds of "possessions" (κτήματα, for LXX's ὑπάρχοντα) which one can rightfully enjoy with God's blessing are those which have been "given by God" (θεόσδοτος, for LXX's ἔδωκεν ὁ θεός); to this end he adds the contrasting phenomenon of possessions which have been "gained through robbery" (ἁρπακτός).[35] At the beginning of this passage on the futility of wealth Gregory had added a cautionary note concerning the harmful and unholy nature of gaining a κτῆμα "through robbery" (ἐξ ἁρπαγῆς, v. 9), and so the note here serves to reinforce what he has already said. Like his addition to 3:13, "if righteousness guides one's actions" (εἰ δικαιοσύνη τῶν πράξεων ἡγοῖτο), it ensures that Solomon cannot be taken as giving blanket approval to the enjoyment of one's possessions without reference to any moral imperative.

(19) Οὔτε γὰρ λύπαις οὗτός γε νοσεῖ, οὔτε ὡς ἐπὶ πολὺ ἐνθυμήσεσι πονηραῖς δουλεύει· συμμετρεῖται δὲ τὸν ἑαυτοῦ βίον εὐποιΐαις, τοῖς πᾶσιν εὐθυμούμενος, καὶ ἀγαλλιώμενος τῇ τοῦ Θεοῦ δωρεᾷ.

Such a person is neither afflicted with pains nor generally subject to evil thoughts, but measures out his life with good deeds, being cheerful in all things and rejoicing in the gift of God.

If Koheleth claimed that the person who enjoys the gift of God does not "remember the days of his life" (LXX μιμνήσκομαι τὰς ἡμέρας τῆς ζωῆς αὐτοῦ) because God keeps him "occupied" or "distracted" (LXX περισπάω) with that enjoyment, the meaning would appear to have been that this lucky individual does not spend his time brooding over the brevity and inscrutability of life, but simply enjoys the time that has been allotted to him. Gregory pictures the God-gifted individual "measuring out his life" (συμμετρέομαι τὸν ἑαυτοῦ βίον) with good deeds, which seems to imply that the person so measuring does indeed "remember the days of his life". But the earlier text's "not remember" lies behind Gregory's depiction of this person as not "being subject to evil thoughts" (ἐνθυμήσεσι πονηραῖς δουλεύω), as is indicated by the ὡς ἐπὶ πολύ, "for the most part" on the front of that phrase, clearly prompted by LXX's πολλά, "much"; and he couples this non-subjection to evil thoughts with a depiction of the God-gifted individual not "being afflicted with pains" (λύπαις νοσέω), to show that this person is quite the opposite of the person described in v. 16 and the preceding verses. Gregory takes μιμνήσκομαι to mean something like "have in one's mind or experience", and so pictures the righteous person as not sharing the afflictions and attitudes which occupy the thoughts of the unrighteous person. As for God keeping the righteous person busy, to Gregory this is really just another way of saying what was already referred to in the last two verses; *viz.*, the notion of "the gift of God", which is expressed as ἡ τοῦ Θεοῦ δωρεά at this point in the paraphrase. The "enjoyment" (LXX εὐφροσύνη) consists of "rejoicing" (ἀγαλλιάομαι) in this gift and "being cheerful" (εὐθυμέω) in all things, not forgetting that a righteous person is also to fill his days with "good deeds" (εὐποιΐα).

Chapter Six

(1) Παρέξομαι δὲ τῷ λόγῳ, τὴν μάλιστα ἐπιπολάζουσαν ἀνθρώποις κακοπραγίαν.
I will now make mention of the most prevalent human misfortune.

A new example of evil under the sun was introduced by Koheleth with his characteristically terse εἶδον (ראיתי), "I saw". Gregory has Solomon display greater rhetorical flair by announcing παρέξομαι δὲ τῷ λόγῳ, "I will now make mention" (*or:* "I will now bring up [the following matter] in [my] address [to the assembly]"). "Evil" (LXX πονηρία) is on this occasion alone rendered as κακοπραγία, "misfortune" (cf. βλάβη, 8:9), although a moral implication seems again to be drawn from LXX's πονηρία in the following verse, where Koheleth spelt out this latest example of "evil". To say that the evil in question is "great" (LXX πολύς) is presumably to make a comment on its quantitative greatness (that it is a common evil, one that occurs frequently among people), though it might be understood as a comment on its qualitative greatness (that it is an overwhelming evil, one that weighs heavily upon a person).[1] Gregory opts for the first of the two alternatives and thus speaks of the misfortune as "being prevalent" (ἐπιπολάζω) — in fact, he goes so far as to say that it is the most (μάλιστα) prevalent human misfortune of all. Gregory often paraphrases "under the sun" (LXX ὑπὸ τὸν ἥλιον) by a phrase denoting "among human beings" (πρὸς ἀνθρώπων, 1:9; ὑπ᾽ ἀνθρώπων, 2:11; ἐν ἀνθρώποις, 4:1; κατὰ ἀνθρώπους, 4:3) or one along similar lines, but in this verse LXX mentioned ὁ ἄνθρωπος anyway, so Gregory would no doubt regard it as engaging in tautology to offer in addition a parallel to "under the sun".

(2) Ὅταν Θεὸς μὲν τὰ καταθύμια αὐτῶν ἅπαντα ἐπιχορηγήσας, μηδενὸς οὑτινοσοῦν τῶν εἰς ἐπιθυμίαν ἐλθόντων αὐτὸν ἀφέληται, μὴ περιουσίας, μὴ πολυδοξίας, μὴ τῶν λοιπῶν περὶ ὅσα ἄνθρωποι ἐπτόηνται· ὁ δὲ τοῖς πᾶσιν εὐθηνούμενος, ὥσπερ τούτῳ μόνῳ θεηλάτῳ κακῷ συνεχόμενος, τῷ μὴ ἀπολαύειν,

ἑταίρῳ τῷ αὐτοῦ ταμιεύσεται,[2] πεσὼν ἄκαρπος καὶ ἑαυτῷ, καὶ τοῖς πλησίον. Τοῦτο μέγα τεκμήριον καὶ ἔλεγχον περιφανῆ ὑπερβαλλούσης ἐγὼ τίθεμαι πονηρίας·

Whenever God grants to someone everything that is in his mind and takes from him nothing at all that entered his fancy — neither wealth, nor honour, nor any of the other things over which people become passionate — the one who thus has everything in abundance, as if the only ill inflicted on him from heaven were the non-enjoying of it, stores it up for an associate of his and it falls without profit either to himself or to his neighbour. This I regard as a sure sign and clear proof of extraordinary evil.

The alternative situation to that depicted in 5:18 was presented here: the person to whom God grants the good things of life in abundance (as before), but to whom he does not grant the ability to enjoy them. In 5:18 Gregory was unusually brief, but here he is willing to paint the picture in full. "Wealth" (περιουσία, for LXX's πλοῦτος) and "honour" (πολυδοξία, for LXX's δόξα) are both itemised, and "possessions" (LXX ὑπάρχοντα) is broadened to take into account "any of the other things over which people become passionate" (τὰ λοιπὰ περὶ ὅσα ἄνθρωποι ἐπτόηνται).

In order to create the kind of balanced formulation so close to his heart, Gregory brings forward Koheleth's idea of "lacking nothing that one's soul desires" (LXX οὐκ ἔστιν ὑστερῶν τῇ ψυχῇ αὐτοῦ ἀπὸ πάντων, ὧν ἐπιθυμήσει), inserting it in the opening part of the sentence, so that — in the form "[God] takes from him nothing at all that entered his fancy" (μηδενὸς οὐτινοσοῦν τῶν εἰς ἐπιθυμίαν ἐλθόντων αὐτὸν ἀφέληται) — it stands in direct juxtaposition to its positively-formulated counterpart, "God grants to him everything that is in his mind" (Θεὸς μὲν τὰ καταθύμια αὐτῶν ἅπαντα ἐπιχορηγήσας). The latter expression is Gregory's paraphrase of Koheleth's simple "God gives to him..." (LXX δώσει αὐτῷ ὁ θεός..., the gifts in question being subsequently itemised as above).

Ἀπολαύω, "to enjoy" is an excellent paraphrase of LXX's ἐσθίω, "to eat" in this context, but has the Church Father removed a little of the punch from his predecessor's assertion? Koheleth was quite adamant that (for some inscrutable reason) God has not "empowered" (LXX ἐξουσιάζω) this particular person to enjoy the good things of life that have fallen to him, just as (for some equally inscrutable reason) God has empowered another particular person (5:18) to enjoy those very same blessings that have come his way. Gregory removes the punch by employing, in place of a direct reference to θεός as the One ultimately responsible for this situation, the adjective θεήλατος, "caused by a god", which has a slight distancing effect, similar to speaking in English of something being "providential" or "destined" rather than speaking directly of God. Nor does Gregory actually say that the person under consideration has not been "empowered" or "enabled" to enjoy what has been granted to him; he simply states that this person does not enjoy these blessings. Moreover, he places the whole clause under the adverb ὥσπερ, "as it were", which has the effect of suggesting that it only appears (to the foolish human involved) as though the heavens have had a hand in this sorry state of affairs. In fact, Gregory's opening ὅταν, "whenever" suggests that there is a kind of natural inevitability in the situation here described: it always seems to happen that a person who has everything in abundance becomes an unhappy miser, spending his days in the pointless activity of simply "storing up" or "managing" (ταμιεύω) endless possessions, rather than getting satisfaction out of a reasonable amount of worldly goods. Thus Gregory sees a reiteration here of the major point Koheleth had just made in the second half of the previous chapter.

Koheleth was evidently much troubled by the thought that a person can engage in a great deal of toil, only to have some other person enjoy its fruits, since he inserted a variation on that thought here. On this occasion the possibility was canvassed that what rightfully belongs to one person may fall to a "stranger" or "foreigner" (LXX ξένος). Gregory's ἑταῖρος seems to convey the idea of a "comrade" or "friend" rather than someone unknown to the person originally granted such abundant blessings, which suggests that the word may be a scribal error from an original ἕτερος[3] (employed by Gregory in a similar context in 2:18), but the parallel use of the word πλησίον, "neighbour" strengthens the implication of a closer, more familiar relationship between the two people concerned than that which Koheleth appears to have intended in this case. In defence of the paraphrase, it might be argued that in Koheleth's view every person is intrinsically a stranger to every other person, even to those who are near to him,[4] so that when he spoke of a ξένος (נכרי) he may actually have had in mind even a ἑταῖρος or πλησίον. Whether that was the case or not, there is no question that Koheleth envisioned this other person eating (i.e., enjoying) the very blessings that the first person had been unable to eat, for he stated this explicitly; but Gregory says that it is completely "fruitless" or "unprofitable" (ἄκαρπος) for both people — bringing forward the ματαιότης judgment from its position in the following clause, where it did not refer to the second person as also being unable to enjoy the blessings that the first person was unable to enjoy, but to the futility of a system in which the first person's blessings are enjoyed by another. Koheleth's lament that a stranger can gain the benefits of what might at first have fallen to oneself, has become Solomon's observation that no good for anyone will come of the situation in which a person receives in abundance everything he might desire.

Koheleth described this whole matter as "a sickening evil" (LXX ἀρρωστία πονηρά, literally "an evil sickness"; cf. πονηρὰ ἀρρωστία, 5:15). For the Hebrew sage, it was a repulsive thing that, for some inscrutable reason, God should not allow a person to enjoy those good things of life which, after all, God himself has showered upon him. Gregory describes the situation a little differently, seeing in it an obvious indication (μέγα τεκμήριον and ἔλεγχος περιφανής both mean essentially the same thing and in tandem strengthen the assertion) that a particularly bad πονηρία is operative here, though on the part not of the divine but of the human agent. For the Church Father, the sight of wealth, honour, or any other humanly-desired thing being hoarded for its own sake to no-one's benefit is a clear sign of wickedness on the part of those engaged in such an activity.

The punctuation of the present edition of Gregory's text,

with a full-stop preceding and a colon following this clause, directs the reader to the case in point to be presented in the next verse: the case of a man who is blessed with many children and a long life, but who has no goodness in his soul.

(3) ἄνδρα τε ἐκεῖνον, ὃς πλείστων πατὴρ ὀνομασθεὶς τέκνων ἀσινῶς, βιοὺς δὲ χρόνον μακρόν, οὐκ ἐπλήσθη χρηστότητος τὴν ψυχὴν ἐπὶ τοσοῦτον, θάνατον[5] πεῖραν οὐ λαβών· τοῦτον ἔγωγε, οὔτε τῆς πολυπαιδίας, οὔτε τῆς πολυημερίας ζηλώσαιμ' ἄν· καὶ προκρίνω δὲ αὐτοῦ ἄωρον γαστρὸς μητρῴας ἐκπεσὸν ἔμβρυον.

A man who, securely bearing the name of father of many children, has a long life (having no experience of death), but whose soul is not filled with goodness over so much — I would be envious neither of this fellow's many children nor of his many days; I regard as preferable to him the foetus which falls prematurely from its mother's womb.

Gregory neatly encapsulates the two most highly-desired blessings of Koheleth's day in the pair πολύπαις, "many children" and πολυήμερος, "many days". He removes any possible problem of over-exaggeration in his predecessor's hyperbolic "to father a hundred" (LXX γεννάω ἑκατόν) by speaking in less arbitrarily-precise numerical terms: a man may be the father of πλεῖστα τέκνα, "very many children" (or perhaps "the most children [that any one man has ever fathered or could ever father]"). Koheleth seemed a little repetitious on the matter of a long life, saying first that "he lives many years" (LXX ἔτη πολλὰ ζήσεται) and then immediately thereafter that "many are the days of his years" (LXX πλῆθος ὅ τι ἔσονται ἡμέραι ἐτῶν αὐτοῦ), so Gregory conflates Koheleth's twin expressions into one paraphrase concerning the man who has "life for a long time" (βίοι χρόνον μακρόν).

The use of the plural (rather than βίος) in this latter expression might suggest to the reader that not only the father of this large family, but also each of his children, has this blessing of longevity — an impression which is perhaps strengthened by Gregory's treatment of the phrase "he has no burial" (LXX ταφὴ οὐκ ἐγένετο αὐτῷ), as we shall see presently. This phrase evoked the picture of a person not receiving a proper, dignified burial, a dishonourable fate which was widely regarded with horror in ancient times.[6] In the context, Koheleth seems to have been asking the reader: What is the use of a large family and a long life if you do not enjoy what you have and nobody cares about you when you die? But Gregory's interpretation is: "he has no experience of death" (θανάτου πεῖραν οὐ λαβών). At face value this might be taken to mean "he does not die", in which case the Church Father's understanding of the passage would seem to be along the lines of "even if this fellow were to live forever,[7] I would still not envy him"; however, such an understanding is contradicted by Gregory's clear statement in v. 6 that this fellow does die. More likely Gregory's rendering here in v. 3, with λαμβάνω in the aorist tense, is intended to mean that the man depicted here is to be considered as having not yet died and thus as continuing his seemingly blessed existence as Solomon speaks,[8] in which case the Church Father is saying something like "even if this fellow has not died after so many years of life, he is in a worse situation than the foetus which died before it had any years of life" — or, in other words, "the one who has had no experience of life is to be preferred to this one who has had no experience of death". A third possibility, hinted at above in connection with the phrase βίοι χρόνον μακρόν and not mutually exclusive of the meaning just mentioned for the phrase θανάτου πεῖραν οὐ λαβών, is that the latter phrase indicates that this long-lived patriarch of a large family has a further good fortune: during his long life not a single death occurs in his family to bring him sorrow.[9]

Despite these supreme blessings, Koheleth presented this man as not "being satisfied" (LXX ἐμπίμπλαμαι) with "the good" (LXX ἡ ἀγαθωσύνη) that he has. But a different understanding of these words is open to the pious interpreter: this man is not "filled" with "goodness". Gregory ensures that his readers will receive this more pious message by employing πίμπλαμαι (which may in fact have stood in the Greek text before him)[10] and, more significantly, χρηστότης, which can only mean "goodness (of heart)", "kindness", or the like, and not worldly goods, material blessings, or the like. LXX's ψυχή is helpful in spiritualising this matter.

The physical matter of a miscarriage (LXX ἔκτρωμα), to which the seemingly-blessed man is unfavourably compared, is explained by the paraphrast as a foetus (ἔμβρυον) which falls (ἐκπίπτω)[11] prematurely from its mother's womb.

(4) Ἐκεῖνο γὰρ ὥσπερ ἦλθε ματαίως, οὕτως ἄπεισι καὶ λαθραίως ἐν ἀμνηστίᾳ, ...

Just as that foetus came in vain, so it also leaves secretly in oblivion, ...

Just as the unexpressed subject of the pre-Gregorian version of this verse was evidently the ἔκτρωμα which had just been mentioned (as becomes clearer in the following verse), so too Gregory's ἐκεῖνο, "that one" evidently refers to the ἔμβρυον he has just mentioned. The use of the adverb ματαίως makes for better Greek than LXX's ἐν ματαιότητι (a simple transferral into Greek of Koheleth's Semitic formulation בהבל). Gregory also seems to feel that ἄπειμι, "leave" is an improvement on LXX's straightforward πορεύομαι, "go" (though he is satisfied with the equally prosaic ἔρχομαι, "come"); and he excises Koheleth's persistent talk of "darkness" (LXX σκότος), probably because the idea is covered by the talk of "not seeing the sun" in the very next verse (part of the same sentence as this verse in both LXX and Gregory's paraphrase).

"His name is covered" (LXX ὄνομα αὐτοῦ καλυφθήσεται) is explained as meaning that there is "a forgetting" (ἀμνηστία) of the stillborn child;[12] i.e. it moves "secretly" or "furtively" (λαθραίως) into a state of oblivion.

(5) ... οὐχ ἀψάμενον κακῶν, οὐδὲ προσβλέψαν ἡλίῳ. Τοῦτο κουφότερον, ἤπερ τῷ πονηρῷ, ...

... without having taken part in evils or seen the sun. This is a lighter matter than for the wicked man, ...

The miscarried foetus' failure to experience life was expressed in two ways by Koheleth: it does not "see" (LXX ὁράω, which Gregory paraphrases by προσβλέπω) the sun, and it does not "know" (LXX γιγνώσκω). The latter expression, taken straightforwardly, neatly encapsulates the notion of the foetus failing to have reached consciousness. Gregory makes the point that the foetus does not "take part in evils" (ἅπτω κακῶν), which by implication all liveborn humans inevitably do.[13] Alternatively, he might simply mean by this expression that the foetus does not have experience of the various ills which beset human life,[14] but his very similar expression "take part in human wickedness" (ἅπτω τῆς κατὰ ἀνθρώπους πονηρίας) in the parallel case of 4:3, where the unborn was similarly being compared to the born, supports the former interpretation.

"There is rest for this one more than for this one", said Koheleth (LXX ἀνάπαυσις τούτῳ ὑπὲρ τοῦτον), presumably meaning that the first one — the miscarried foetus — is free of the experiences which cause the second one — the long-lived man — so much disquiet.[15] Gregory notes that the situation of the former — whose identity is not explicitly defined, just as it was not in the original Ecclesiastes, but who is evidently the miscarried foetus — is "lighter" or "easier" (κουφότερος) than the situation of the latter — who is identified as ὁ πονηρός, "the wicked one" and is evidently the long-lived man. He can be described as "wicked" because, as is stated twice, he has nothing to do with "goodness" (χρηστότης, v. 3; ἀγαθότης, v. 6).

Gregory has skilfully balanced the contrast between the two individuals: failure to "look upon" (προσβλέπω, in this verse) the sun is a less deplorable fate than failure to "look upon" (ἐπιγιγνώσκω, in the following verse) goodness; it is better not to have had the opportunity of engaging in "evil" (κακός, in the opening phrase of this verse) than to have so completely immersed oneself in it as to be described as "evil" (πονηρός, in the closing phrase) oneself.

(6) ... κἂν χιλίοις ἔτεσι τὴν ἑαυτοῦ ζωὴν ἀναμετρησαμένῳ ἀγαθότητα μὴ ἐπιγνῷ.[16] Τέλος δὲ ἀμφοῖν θάνατος.

... **even if he measures his life at a thousand years, to not see goodness. The end of both is death.**

In v. 3 Koheleth had spoken exaggeratedly of a hundred

children, and now in v. 6 he spoke in equally exaggerated terms
of a lifetime measuring "a thousand years twice over" (or χιλίων
ἐτῶν κάθοδος, "the return of a thousand years", as LXX phrased
it). Gregory again uses less precise numerical figures, but on this
occasion he does retain the hyperbolic χίλιοι rather than replace
it with something like πλεῖστος, "very many" (or in this context
perhaps "the greatest number [of years anyone could possibly
dream of living for]"), with which he replaced the hyperbolic
ἑκατόν in v. 3.

Koheleth's characteristic ὁράω ἀγαθωσύνην (ראה טובה), "to
see good", which Gregory had accurately paraphrased as
ἀπολαύω, "to enjoy" on its last occurrence (5:17), here again
receives the Church Father's characteristically moral interpretation: "to look upon [or: acknowledge, approve] goodness"
(ἐπιγιγνώσκω ἀγαθότητα — cf. πίμπλεμαι χρηστότητος for LXX's
ἐμπίπλεμαι ἀγαθωσύνης in v. 3). But Koheleth's closing
rhetorical question has its meaning accurately conveyed by
Gregory's rendering: the "one place" (LXX τόπος εἷς) to which all
are destined to go is the destination (τέλος, "end") called "death"
(θάνατος).

(7) Ἐλεγχομένου ἄφρονος, μάλιστα τῷ πλησμονὴν μηδεμιᾶς
λαμβάνειν ἐπιθυμίας.

A foolish person is most clearly shown for what he is in his
finding no satisfaction in any passion.

All of a person's "toil" (LXX μόχθος) is "for his[17] mouth"
(or: goes "into his mouth", LXX εἰς στόμα αὐτοῦ), according to
Koheleth. It seems that either this made little sense to Gregory
(the Targumist understands it to mean that a person toils for
food), or it did not suit his purposes to make use of the idea, and
so he leaves it unparaphrased. But the second half of the verse,
which stated that a person is never "satisfied" (literally "filled",
LXX πληρόομαι), is treated by Gregory, who says that no
"satisfaction" (literally "filling", πλησμονή) is found. LXX's
ψυχή, the seat of the appetite (in its widest sense), is well
paraphrased by ἐπιθυμία, "desire" or "passion".

But Gregory's remarks are not applied to Everyman; it can

only be said of the "fool" (ἄφρων) that his desires are never
satisfied. True, Koheleth did make a short reference to the
ἄφρων (כסיל) in the very next verse, but there was no linking of
only that kind of person to the human situation depicted in the
verse now at hand; on the contrary, Koheleth appears to have
concluded there that both the foolish person and the "wise
person" (LXX σοφός) are in the same disadvantageous position.
As far as the Church Father is concerned, however, anyone who
indulges in human passions, which are of course ultimately
unsatisfying, "proves" (ἐλέγχω) himself to be a fool, in the same
way as the hoarding of various humanly-desired things is
"proof" (ἔλεγχος, v. 2) of wickedness on the part of the people
who indulge in that activity.

(8) Ὁ δὲ σώφρων, τούτοις οὐκ ἐνίσχεται τοῖς πάθεσιν. Ὡς δ᾽
ἐπὶ τὸ πλεῖστον εὐθύτης ζωῆς ἄνθρωπον τῇ πενίᾳ ὁδηγεῖ.

**But the wise person is not caught up in these emotions.
Righteousness of life mostly leads a person to poverty.**

In 2:16, where Koheleth had appeared to state clearly that
the respective fates of the wise and the foolish are identical,
Gregory had just as clearly stated that these two kinds of person
never share the same fate. Not surprisingly, then, when here in
6:8 Koheleth's rhetorical question appears to have invited an
analogous conclusion — that the wise have no advantage over
the foolish (presumably for the reason presented in the previous
verse, that nobody can find ultimate satisfaction in life) —
Gregory again contradicts his predecessor. He wants it to be
understood that the wise do have an important advantage in
life: unlike the person in view in the previous verse (whom
Gregory has taken to be specifically the foolish person), the wise
person is not "caught up" in or "held fast" by (ἐνίσχω) those
human passions which totally control a fool's life.

Koheleth followed up with a parallel rhetorical question:
מה־לעני יודע להלך נגד החיים, "what [advantage] has the poor person in
knowing how to walk over against life?"   "Advantage" (יותר)
was not actually repeated between the מה and ל in this second
question, but is to be understood; and "knowing how to walk

over against life" evidently meant knowing how to conduct oneself in life (unless one takes החיים to mean "the living", in which case the meaning concerned conducting oneself properly in front of other people). Possibly because of the absence of יותר, LXX did not style this second half of the verse as a question, but as a corroborative assertion strengthening the opening question: ... διότι ὁ πένης οἶδεν πορευθῆναι κατέναντι τῆς ζωῆς, "... since the poor person knows how to walk over against life." While the Hebrew question suggested that there is no value to a poor person in knowing how to live (because he lacks the means for enjoying life), just as there is no value to a wise person in being wise (because he can no more achieve satisfaction in life than can the fool), LXX's rendering suggested that a further reason why there is no particular value in being wise (in addition to the fact that the wise person is just as dissatisfied as the fool) is that even a poor person knows how to live (and therefore has as much vital practical knowledge as does a supposedly superior wise person).

But that is not the way Gregory Thaumaturgos is disposed to read this text. Mention of a person who "knows how to walk over against life" sounds to him like a definition of a righteous person, one who walks in the way of εὐθύτης, "righteousness". To say that this right-living individual is "a poor person" (LXX πένης) makes sense in such an interpretation, because "poverty" (πενία) is in fact generally the lot of the righteous, who are not driven by the selfish and greedy passions that so afflict the unrighteous; these unholy desires lead wicked people to hoard possessions (cf. 5:12-16), but righteousness leads good people to act unselfishly and justly, which in most cases (ὡς ἐπὶ τὸ πλεῖστον, "for the most part", perhaps an escape clause to protect the reputations of the righteous rich; cf. ἔθω in 9:11) means that they remain poor in worldly possessions.

(9) Ἐξίστησι δὲ πολλοὺς ὀφθαλμῶν λίχνων θεάματα, τὴν ψυχὴν ἐρεθίζοντα, ἐπ' ἀνόητον σπουδὴν ἕλκοντα, διὰ τῆς τοῦ ὀφθῆναι κενῆς ἐπιθυμίας.

The things that are seen by greedy eyes drive many people out of their senses, exciting their mind and drawing them into a

useless pursuit through the empty desire to be seen.

Gregory completely ignores Koheleth's "'Α' is better than 'Β'" formulation (LXX ἀγαθὸς "Α" ὑπὲρ "Β", cf. 4:6) in this instance, presumably because he can see nothing ἀγαθός in what was described here. As in 11:9, the Church Father is not prepared to give free rein to the "sight of the eyes" (LXX ὅραμα ὀφθαλμῶν, which Gregory here translates by θεάματα ὀφθαλμῶν, adding later in the verse the concomitant notion that people desire not only to see but also "to be seen" [ὀφθῆναι]). No matter that Koheleth was plainly saying here that the "sight of the eyes" is **better** than the "wandering of the soul" (i.e., it is better to enjoy the simple pleasures at hand than to long for unattainable things); Gregory is convinced that, people's eyes being invariably λίχνος ("greedy", a comment actually in keeping with the observation Koheleth made in 1:8), the "sight of the eyes" leads to the "wandering of the soul" (i.e., a person can so easily be led astray by what he looks upon with covetous or lustful eyes), and so he treats the two expressions as part and parcel of the same foolish behaviour. As for the "wandering of the soul" itself (LXX πορευόμενος ψυχῇ), this is a most serious matter for Gregory: "exciting" (ἐρεθίζω) the ψυχή, "deranging" (ἐξίστημι) it, "drawing" (ἕλκω) it away from the proper path.

Koheleth, too, although he would hardly have conceived of it in quite the same way as his Christian interpreter, was not impressed with the insatiable appetites of human beings, as he emphasised here by means of his thematic ματαιότης and προαίρεσις πνεύματος. This was the last occurrence in Ecclesiastes of the latter expression, which on most of its previous appearances had prompted Gregory to speak of an evil spirit at work in the world or within wicked human beings. In the present context of people being driven out of their senses and having their minds excited by what their eyes see we would expect Gregory to use the same interpretation. But here he actually does treat ματαιότης and προαίρεσις πνεύματος as parallel expressions denoting futile activities, and paraphrases with two parallel expressions of his own: ἀνόνητον σπουδή, a "useless pursuit" and κενὴ ἐπιθυμία, an "empty desire". Unless we are to make the unlikely supposition that Gregory has ignored προαίρεσις πνεύματος here (because he saw no value in speaking of the evil spirit at this point) and is only paraphrasing ματαιότης (for which in fact he does employ both ἀνόνητος and κενός in 1:2), it would appear that Gregory is well aware of the possibility of interpreting Koheleth's expression as "desire/choice of wind", denoting an aimless and futile striving after something transitory and unattainable, but that he has chosen not to apply that interpretation on most of the occasions the expression appeared in Ecclesiastes (cf., e.g., comments to 1:14, but note also the two other non-spiritual Gregorian interpretations of προαίρεσις πνεύματος in the instances of τηνάλλως φέρεσθαι, "to gain in vain, achieve nothing" in 1:17 and τοῖς περὶ γῆν πόνοις προστήκομαι, "to cling to earthly concerns" in 2:17).

(10) Τὰ μέν τοι νῦν γεγεννημένα ἤδη ἔγνωσται· καὶ σαφὲς τυγχάνει, ὡς τοῖς ὑπὲρ αὐτὸν ἄνθρωπος ἀντιτάσσεσθαι οὐχ οἷός τε.

Surely the things which have now come into being were already known, and it is clear that a person cannot fight against those that are above him.

If something "is called by its name" (LXX καλεῖται ὄνομα αὐτοῦ), reasons Gregory, it "is known" (γιγνώσκομαι, bringing LXX's verb forward from the second phrase); and if something is known, it "is clear" (σαφὲς τυγχάνει, perhaps more literally: "has [the quality of being] clear"). It was not entirely clear, however, exactly what Koheleth thought was "known" concerning human beings: whether the phrase ἐγνώσθη ὅ ἐστιν ἄνθρωπος (נודע אשר־הוא אדם) ought to be taken in its own right as saying that it is known that human beings are just that — human, and not divine — (à la the Midrash Koheleth Rabbah), or ought to be taken as the beginning of what follows — "it is known in regard to human beings that they cannot contend" etc. — (à la Gregory),[18] but either way it is clear that Koheleth had in mind the limitations that have been placed upon humankind.

There is something, claimed Koheleth, against which a human being cannot contend (LXX's κρίνω means "judge", but here probably should be taken in the sense of "accuse, bring to trial", or the like, which gives rise to Gregory's ἀντιτάσσομαι, "to set oneself against, meet in battle"). But just who or what is this thing, which is "stronger than" (LXX ἰσχυρὸς[19] ὑπέρ) a human being? Since the subject matter was expressed in the singular, it might be readily thought that the reference is to God, as it explicitly was in the very similar thought of 3:14,15,[20] but Gregory, latching on to LXX's ὑπέρ, speaks in the plural of "those that are above him" — with a built-in ambiguity: because the Greek construction with ἀντιτάσσομαι requires the dative case, the reader cannot be sure whether τοῖς ὑπὲρ αὐτόν is masculine, and thus meant to denote "those people [or: superhuman powers] who are above him", or neuter, and thus meant to denote "those things which are above [or: beyond] him".

If Gregory has the former in mind, he is possibly returning to the thought he expressed in 4:1 of those humans who are above (on a ὕψος, "height") oppressing the ones below them, who are powerless to do anything but weep and wail; or he may be introducing the thought he will express in 12:3 of those agents of God who are "above" (ὑπέρτερος), before whom even supposedly powerful humans are powerless. If, on the other hand, Gregory has "things" in mind, he is returning to the thought he had expressed in 3:14 of "those eternal and incorruptible things" (τὰ αἰώνια καὶ ἄφθαρτα πράγματα) which God has firmly laid down, and which cannot possibly be altered by humans. In view of the similarity of thought between Koheleth's versions of 3:14 and the verse now at hand, this last alternative is the most likely, but it may be that Gregory is happy to have created an ambiguity at this point, thus allowing for a wider reference than any one of these alone.

(11) Φλυαρίαι γε μὴν κατὰ ἀνθρώπους στρέφονται, τὴν τῶν χρωμένων ἄνοιαν ἐπαυξάνουσαι.[21] Μηδαμῶς γὰρ πλέον τι ὠφελουμένου ....

Silly talk is prevalent among human beings, increasing the foolishness of those who indulge in it. A person gains no great advantage whatsoever ....

Another ambiguity follows immediately, both in the text before Gregory (LXX's λόγοι, as also MT's דברים before it,

primarily means "words", but may denote "things" more generally) and in the text which he produced (Gregory's φλυαρίαι may
mean either "silly talk" or "silly activities"): there are many
words/things which "increase" (LXX πληθύνω, Gregory ἐπαυ-
ξάνω) "futility" (LXX ματαιότης, Gregory ἄνοια, the latter meaning specifically "foolishness"). Either meaning of the subject —
"words" or "things/activities" — makes sense in this context,[22]
but it is possibly best to opt for the more primary meaning in
both versions.

It being the case that so many words/things increase futility,
Koheleth repeated his programmatic question: What profit (LXX
περισσόν) is there for a human being? When this question was
first asked at the beginning of Ecclesiastes (in 1:3, with περισσεία),
Gregory's equivalent was ὄφελος ("profit, advantage"). Only
when περισσόν appears for the last time at the end of the book
(in 12:12), does Gregory again employ ὄφελος. Throughout the
rest of Ecclesiastes he adopts several other means of
paraphrasing this notion, but here in the middle of the book he
makes use of the verbal cognate of ὄφελος: ὠφελέομαι, "to derive
profit/advantage". The thought itself Gregory applies to what
follows, most probably because the LXX text he was using placed
this phrase at the head of a new chapter.[23]

(12) ... τοῦ γινώσκοντος τὰ αὐτῷ συμβησόμενα παρὰ τὸν βίον
καταθύμια· θῶμεν γὰρ[24] τοῦτο· ὅμως δὲ καὶ τῶν ἀνθρώπων
περιεργίᾳ ἐπιτεχνᾶται, ὡς καὶ τὰ μετὰ θάνατόν τινος ἑκάστου
ἐσόμενα, πολυπραγμονεῖν τε καὶ δοκεῖν εἰδέναι.

**... from knowing in his mind the things that will happen to
him in life (let us imagine this); nevertheless, with human
forwardness he contrives to pry into and supposedly know the
things that will happen after everyone's death.**

Koheleth's first rhetorical question in this verse expressed
scepticism concerning human ability to know what is "good"
(LXX ἀγαθός) in life. Since Gregory believes that God has
revealed what is good for people to do,[25] he prefers to think that
the scepticism was directed only to the matter which Koheleth
addressed in his second rhetorical question, concerning human

inability to know what is going to "be" (Gregory retains LXX's εἰμί in the second sentence, but imports the notion to the first sentence in the form of συμβαίνω, "happen").

The Church Father is happy to express a sceptical view of human knowledge of the future, and so he adds the short clause θῶμεν τοῦτο, "let us imagine this"; i.e., "let us imagine for the moment that it is possible (though of course we know it is not) for someone to know what will happen to him in the future" — and even if it were possible, Gregory has already stated at the outset of the sentence (the last clause of v. 11) that a person would in any case gain no great advantage from such knowledge. This is not necessarily a Kohelethine view, for Koheleth gave the impression that it would be advantageous to know the future (7:14; 8:6-8; 9:12; 10:8,9; 11:1-6), but Gregory wants to dissuade people from becoming too curious about matters which God has kept from their knowledge.

No mention is made in the paraphrase of the "futility" (LXX ματαιότης) of a life which passes so quickly that it can be likened to a "shadow" (LXX σκιά). Perhaps Gregory was too tired of Koheleth's continual harping on ματαιότης, and he may even have been a little confused by LXX's ἐν (presumably reading *beth* rather than MT's *kaph*), which turned the phrase into the somewhat puzzling observation that life is lived in a shadow — certainly ὡς (had *kaph* been read) would have made better sense here, drawing a familiar Wisdom analogy of life flitting like a shadow (cf. Job 8:9), but ἐν can also be made to yield sense in this context, similar to the idea expressed in Ecclesiastes 5:16 of human life being spent "in darkness" (LXX ἐν σκότει). Gregory, however, may not have been able to see a way for this matter to readily fit into his restyling of the context as having to do with human ignorance of what is to happen in the future.

This ignorance was indeed the point at issue in Koheleth's second rhetorical question, but even here Gregory does not seem to have got it quite right. The first question dealt with a person's "life" (LXX ζωή, Gregory βίος), and the second with what happens "after him" (LXX ὀπίσω αὐτοῦ) — i.e., after his death, but Gregory says μετὰ θάνατόν τινος ἑκάστου, "after everyone's death". Unless he is thinking of what might happen in the world — if indeed the world were still to exist — after all human life has ended in an Eschaton (cf. his interpretation of 12:1-7), Gregory is referring to what happens to people after they die, even though such an interpretation is inconsistent with Koheleth's clear ὑπὸ τὸν ἥλιον, which must have been referring to what happens in this world. Koheleth's lament that no-one can "tell" (LXX ἀπαγγέλλω) us what the future holds has become Solomon's comment that no-one can "know" (ὁράω) what happens in the after-life, so no-one should "pry into" (πολυπραγμονέω) the matter.

Chapter Seven

(1) Μνήμη δὲ ἀγαθὴ ψυχῇ προσηνεστέρα, ἥπερ σώματι ἔλαιον· καὶ βίου ἔξοδος, ἀμείνων γενέσεως

A good remembrance is more pleasant for the soul than oil is for the body, and the end of life is better than the beginning.

In tentative answer to the question "what is good?" (LXX τί ἀγαθόν) of the previous verse, Koheleth now strung together, in this and the following verses, a number of ἀγαθὸς "A" ὑπὲρ "B" ("ב" מן "א" טוב) statements, a formulation which he had first employed in 4:6. On this occasion, Gregory uses the comparative of ἀγαθός — ἀμείνων, "better" — for the second comparison (Koheleth did not actually repeat ἀγαθός in that clause, but it is clearly understood), and the comparative of προσηνής — προσηνέστερος, "gentler, more pleasant" — for the first comparison. 'Αγαθός itself Gregory assigns to μνήμη ("remembrance"), his equivalent to LXX's ὄνομα ("name"), while LXX's ἔλαιον, which was styled as ἀγαθός, is presented without adjectival qualification in the paraphrase. Although Koheleth's initial ἀγαθός (טוב) was governing the whole clause rather than qualifying ὄνομα (שם), speaking of "a name" without adjectival qualification in this context nevertheless evidently did mean "a good name" (cf. שם in Proverbs 22:1, where LXX translated ὄνομα καλόν),[1] so Gregory's transposition of ἀγαθός is a defensible paraphrase.

Since Koheleth moved on immediately after "oil" to speak of the "day of death" (LXX ἡμέρα τοῦ θανάτου), a commentator seeking a connection between the two halves of this verse might readily interpret the mention of oil as being a reference to the practice of anointing a body for burial, from which point it is a short step for the pious commentator to interpret the mention of a good name (or reputation) as being a reference to the merits attaching to a person as he moves from this life to a life after death. This would seem to be the interpretation that Gregory is suggesting with his talk of "a good remembrance" for the ψυχή being better than oil for the σῶμα. In the case of a person whose life has warranted a good μνήμη, the Church Father can agree with Koheleth that the end of his life is better than its beginning, since a Christian looks forward to a better life for the faithful on the other side of the grave.

The original Ecclesiastes contained a pleasant play on words here with the juxtaposition of שם and שמן. The later Semitic versions have been unable to reproduce this exactly, offering instead the pair שׁמא and משׁחא (Targum), ܫܡܐ and ܡܫܚܐ (Peshitta) — שׁמא/ܡܫܚܐ means "fat", and so will not work here in Aramaic and Syriac. A Greek version, of course, cannot even attempt to mimic Koheleth's particular play on words, as is evident with LXX's ὄνομα and ἔλαιον, but Gregory — probably unintentionally — does present his readers with a play on words of a different kind: taking up LXX's γένεσις for the beginning of life, he juxtaposes ἔξοδος for its end, thus employing the Greek titles of the first two books of the Bible.

(2) καὶ αἱρετώτερον πενθεῖν, ἢ κωμάζειν, καὶ τὸ παρεῖναι τοῖς λυπουμένοις, ἢ τοῖς μεθυσκομένοις. Ἔστι γὰρ οὕτω, λαβόντα τινὰ τοῦ βίου τέλος μὴ εὐλαβηθῆναι περὶ τῶν ἀμφ᾽ αὐτόν.

It is more desirable to mourn than to make merry, and to be with those who are grieving rather than with those who are drunk. In this way a person coming to the end of life is not concerned about what is around him.

"Better" is now paraphrased by αἱρετώτερος, "more desirable". The repeated Semitic expression "to go to the house of..." (LXX πορευθῆναι εἰς οἶκον... [...לכת אל-בית]) is replaced by the single Greek verb "to be with..." (παρεῖναι), while the single Kohelethine references to mourning (LXX πένθος) and drinking (LXX πότος) are each covered twice by the paraphrast: λυπέομαι, "to grieve" in addition to πενθέω for the more desirable activity, and κωμάζω, "to make merry" and μεθύσκομαι, "to be(come) drunk" for the less desirable activity. In paraphrasing the same notions twice, Gregory's intention may be to suggest in the first instance the private activities of mourning a loved one or alternatively pursuing a hedonistic lifestyle, and in the second instance the public activities of calling on the bereaved in order to offer solidarity to them or alternatively associating with revellers in order to get drunk with them.

Koheleth then stated somewhat abruptly that "this" (LXX οὗτος) is the "end" (LXX τέλος) of every human being. The "this" was not actually defined, but in view of the following advice to "the living" (LXX ὁ ζῶν) to take this matter to heart it would seem that the reference was to the "house of mourning" earlier in the verse (and to the "day of death" in the previous verse): everyone will sooner or later end up as the object of mourning, a matter which can be reflected upon when participating in mourning over those who have already died. Thus Gregory speaks of the "end of life" (τοῦ βίου τέλος) as being in view here.

The advice to "take [this] to heart" (LXX δίδωμι εἰς καρδίαν) was doubtlessly counselling the reader to be aware of his own mortality. For Gregory, such a course results in the person who has associated with mourners rather than drunkards being unconcerned about "anything around him" (τὰ ἀμφ' αὐτόν), presumably because he has focussed his thoughts on the eternal joys of the life to come rather than on the transitory pleasures of this life. If indeed the paraphrast is directing the reader's thoughts beyond the things of this mortal life, it need hardly be noted that he has moved beyond the realm of Koheleth's thoughts.

(3) Γέλωτος δὲ θυμὸς ἔμφρων προτιμότερος· αὐστηρᾷ γὰρ διαθέσει προσώπου, κατορθοῦται ψυχή.

Prudent anger is preferable to laughter, for the soul is kept upright by a stern facial expression.

"Better" is now paraphrased by προτιμότερος, "preferable". However, LXX's choices for the two alternative activities, "laughter" (γέλως) and "irritation" (θυμός), are retained unparaphrased, even though the latter word is generally used of "anger", whereas the present context would appear to call for the meaning "sorrow" and accordingly also might be thought to call for a paraphrase to clear away possible ambiguity. The θυμός is strictly speaking the "soul" or seat of various emotions, including sorrow, so it may be that both the LXX translator and the Christian paraphrast intend the meaning "sorrow" to be read here, but the most natural interpretation remains "anger". And since it is somewhat dangerous to allow a free rein to human emotions, Gregory adds to his version the rider ἔμφρων, "sensible, prudent" — only a controlled, proper use of anger is to be preferred.

Koheleth continued with the observation that through the possession of a countenance bearing the label "badness" (LXX κακία) the heart "is made good" (LXX ἀγαθύνομαι) — in other words: through the contemplation of serious matters such as death, which causes a person to wear a severe or sad facial expression, the mind is improved. In Gregory's words: through the possession of a countenance that can be described as "stern" or "harsh" (αὐστηρός) the soul "is kept upright" (κατορθόομαι). Although ψυχή could possibly be understood as "mind" rather than "soul", and hence as a concept as equally this-worldly as LXX's καρδία, Gregory's paraphrase seems again — as in the previous verse — to direct the reader's thoughts on towards the possibility of an afterlife: the point of keeping one's soul upright, or of purifying one's soul through sobriety, is so that one will receive the reward that awaits the righteous.

(4) Αἱ μὲν τοίνυν τῶν σοφῶν ψυχαί, σκυθρωπάζουσι καὶ συστέλλονται, αἱ δὲ τῶν ἀφρόνων ἐπαιρόμεναι διαχέονται.

Accordingly, the souls of the wise are sad and subdued, while those of the fools are excited and intemperate.

The thought of the previous verses is continued, and Gregory again employs ψυχή to carry the notion of LXX's καρδία. In a similar way to his treatment of v. 2, Gregory covers each of the alternative activities twice, but as we have come to expect he does not repeat himself in the typical Kohelethine fashion seen on this occasion in the use of the expression οἶκος πένθους (בית אבל) in both that verse and the verse now at hand; in view of the intervening verse, the paraphrast broadens the focus from "mourning" in particular to "being of a sad countenance" (σκυθρωπάζω) and "being subdued" (συστέλλομαι) in general, and over against this he places — as his equivalent to Koheleth's talk of "merriment" (LXX εὐφροσύνη) — the opposite pair of "being excited" (ἐπαίρομαι) and "being dissipated/dissolute" (διαχέομαι).

(5) Πολὺ δέ ἐστιν εὐκταιότερον ἐπίπληξιν σοφοῦ ἑνὸς δέξασθαι, ἢ ὅλου χοροῦ ἀνθρώπων φαύλων καὶ δυστήνων ᾀδόντων γενέσθαι ἀκροατήν.
It is far more desirable to receive a rebuke from one wise person than to become a listener to a whole chorus of common and wretched people singing.

"Better" is now paraphrased by πολὺ εὐκταιότερος, "far more desirable". In the previous verse Gregory had been content to leave unparaphrased LXX's consistent vocabulary for the "wise" (σοφός) and the "foolish" (ἄφρων); on this occasion he is again content with a simple σοφός to depict wise people, but foolish people are characterised as both φαῦλος, "common, low, petty" and δύστηνος, "wretched". The double-barrelled shot at the latter may be occasioned by the fact that Koheleth spoke of them in the plural, while he spoke of the former in the singular. Certainly this difference in number is emphasised by Gregory through specific mention of "one" (εἷς) wise person contrasted with "a whole chorus" (ὅλος χορός) of foolish people.

It is not self-evident what Koheleth meant by the "song" (LXX ᾆσμα) of the fools. He may have been speaking literally of the boisterous songs much enjoyed in the houses of merriment frequented by fools (places just mentioned in the previous verse), or he may have been speaking metaphorically of the praise and flattery so readily dispensed in large doses by fools (as a direct contrast to the "rebuke" [LXX ἐπιτίμησις, Gregory ἐπίπληξις] offered by the wise);[2] it may even be that both of these characteristic actions of fools were in Koheleth's mind at this point. By making reference to the "singing" (ᾄδων) of the fools, Gregory appears to retain — intentionally or unintentionally — the open-endedness of the original. This impression is strengthened by his talk of a person becoming an ἀκροατής of fools and their songs, since ἀκροατής can carry the nuance not just simply of a "listener" but also of a "disciple", someone who hearkens to or obeys the words of another (in the bad sense, this means someone who is taken in by the words of another, which in this context may suggest a person who foolishly accepts the words of praise and flattery bestowed on him by fools), and ᾄδων can mean "praising" as well as the more straightforward "singing".

(6) Τῶν γὰρ ἀφρόνων ἀνθρώπων ὁ γέλως, ἀκανθῶν πολλῶν λάβρῳ πυρὶ καιομένων ἤχῳ προσέοικεν. Ἄθλιον δὲ καὶ τοῦτο, ...

For the laughter of foolish people is like the boisterous sound of many thorns burning in a fire. This is also a miserable thing, ...

In making a most apt analogy between the sound of thorns crackling under a heated pot and the laughter or senseless talk of fools, Koheleth also demonstrated his literary skills by playing with the sounds of words: the words for "thorns" (סירים) and "pot" (סיר) sound identical (and almost like the word for "song" [שיר] in the immediately preceding phrase [v. 5]). The word-play is naturally lost in translation,[3] with LXX employing ἄκανθαι for סירים (Gregory is happy with this Greek word in this context) and λέβης for סיר (Gregory feels it is more relevant to focus on the "fire" [πῦρ] and the "burning" [καιόμενος] which produces the sound, than to mention a utensil which may derive utility from the burning process).

The paraphrase presents the analogy in the opposite way to the original work: the sound of the fools is placed in the opening position, followed by the sound of the thorns. Since the noise made by fools is the matter already familiar to the reader through its mention in the previous verse, and the sound of the thorns is now introduced to the reader as an analogous noise, Gregory's rearrangement of Koheleth's order makes for a more logical sequence of thought. As for the respective sounds themselves, Gregory speaks in the first instance of "laughter" (γέλως, as in LXX) and in the second instance of a "sound, roar, wail" (ἦχος is a more colourful word for this noise than is his predecessor's φωνή, and Gregory employs it because he wants to depict the roaring blaze of a large fire composed of many thorns, but in doing so he makes the implied analogy with the "voice" of the fool less obvious). He also presents the analogy by means of a verb (προσέοικα, "to be like, resemble") rather than particles (LXX ὡς..., οὕτως..., "as..., so...").

At this point Koheleth reiterated a judgment he had made on so much of what he had observed under the sun: "This, too, is futility" (LXX καί γε τοῦτο ματαιότης). Since Koheleth generally made this judgment as a conclusion to whatever matter he had been discussing, it seems reasonable to take it here too as referring back to what had just been spoken of — the laughter or senseless talk of the fool. However, the immediately following ὅτι (כי) with which the next verse begins might suggest that the οὗτος (זה) in question is the matter about to be raised: "This [following matter] is also [an example of] futility, [namely] that [such and such takes place]".[4] MT places the soph pasuq at the end of the הבל phrase, thus making the most straightforward interpretation a linking of this judgment with what has just been pictured. The LXX editor follows the same tradition and, by placing a colon before the ματαιότης phrase and a full-stop after it, directs the reader's thoughts back to what has come before rather than forward to what follows. Gregory's editor, however, in placing a full-stop before the ἄθλιος ("miserable, wretched") phrase and a comma after it, directs the reader's thoughts on to the next verse.

(7) ... κακόν γε μὴν μέγιστον ἡ συκοφαντία· αὕτη γὰρ σοφῶν ἐπιβουλεύει ψυχαῖς, καὶ ἐπιχειρεῖ διαφθείρειν τὴν γενναίαν ἔνστασιν τῶν ἀγαθῶν.

... and the greatest evil: oppression — because it conspires against the souls of the wise, and attempts to corrupt the noble way of life of good people.

Before proceding to the matter at hand, Gregory goes even further than the ἄθλιος judgment he has just pronounced: the thing of which he is about to speak is nothing less than κακόν γε μὴν μέγιστον, which might almost be translated as "really and truly the greatest evil!" This particularly nasty thing is then introduced as συκοφαντία.

LXX Ecclesiastes consistently employed συκοφαντία when Koheleth spoke of עשק (or עשקים), and Gregory always accepts this LXX word as appropriate (cf. 4:1 and 5:7). עשק generally means "oppression", and this would still yield good sense here in 7:7, where Koheleth can be read as saying that an oppressive system is able to subvert the wisdom of a wise person and make him into a fool — that is to say, a corrupt system encourages the people of skill and intelligence to use their abilities in corrupt ways, such as for self-enrichment, and hence brings those people down to the level of fools.[5] Συκοφαντία particularly means "slander", and this meaning can also be made to yield some sense in the present context, where Koheleth could be taken as saying that a slanderous accusation is able to damage the reputation of a wise person and make him appear to be no better than a fool (this is, after all, the one place where the Peshitta version of Ecclesiastes retains the Syriac root ܥܠܒ — which means "slander" more often than it means "oppress" — for the Hebrew עשק); in view of the consistent use of συκοφαντία for עשק throughout LXX Ecclesiastes, however, it is plausible that "oppression" in general was still the meaning in the mind of the LXX translator at this point.

There is a similar dual possibility of interpretation in Gregory's paraphrase, because he again copies the LXX word, as he has in the other two instances. "Oppression" makes excellent sense in his paraphrase of the verse at hand (as indeed it does in those previous instances), since the Church Father warns here of a danger to the souls of the wise in the attempted corruption of the noble way of life which good people pursue; this sounds very much like a warning that those people who allow themselves to be seduced out of a noble lifestyle by the earthly rewards that a corrupt system offers are endangering the heavenly rewards that would await them if they were to remain wise. Alternatively, Gregory may particularly be warning the wise about the dangerous evil of "slander", which can ruin their lives; this could be meant either in the sense of good people being brought down by false accusations which are made against them, or in the sense of noble people bringing themselves down to the level of fools by falling prey to the sinfulness of spreading malicious rumours about other people.

The bringing down of the wise was expressed by LXX through περιφέρω, "to carry to and fro, be unsteady or wavering"; further, the forces of foolishness are able to "destroy" (LXX ἀπόλλυμι) the heart of the wise. As MT now reads, they are able to do this by means of a מתנה — a "gift" or "present", in this context presumably some kind of bribe or other reward for participation in corrupt behaviour. But LXX appears to have associated this word with מתנים, "loins", the seat of strength, and accordingly translated with εὐτονία, "strength, vigour" (in Codex Vaticanus this appears as εὐγένεια, "nobility", a reading which would more naturally give rise to Gregory's equivalent of γενναῖος, "noble").

In paraphrasing this notion of wise people being brought down, Gregory basically follows LXX, although he places the imperilled part of a human being (ψυχή, for LXX's καρδία) in the first part of the warning. As in LXX, both clauses are governed by συκοφαντία, and there is no mention of anything like a מתנה. Gregory appears to be demonstrating a greater confidence than Koheleth in saying that oppression or slander "attempts" (ἐπιχειρέω) to bring good people down; he may be suggesting to his readers that they do not have to succumb to the temptation to take part in this great evil. At the same time, in styling it as "the greatest evil...", because it [does such and such]", the Church Father is perhaps betraying less than complete confidence in the ability of his congregants to keep themselves safe from corruption. Συκοφαντία, says Gregory, "conspires against" (ἐπιβουλεύω) good people, and puts its hand to "destroying" or "corrupting" (διαφθείρω) their nobility.

(8) Λόγων[6] δὲ οὐκ ἀρχόμενον, ἀλλὰ παυόμενον ἐπαινεῖν προσήκει, καὶ τὸ μέτριον ἦθος ἀποδέχεσθαι, καὶ μὴ τὸ μετεωριζόμενον καὶ τετυφωμένον.

It is proper to applaud a person who finishes a speech, not someone who begins one, and to approve a moderate disposition, not one that is excited and crazed.

The notion of one matter being "better" than another (LXX

ἀγαθὸς... ὑπέρ, cf. vv. 1-3,5) is now paraphrased by an injunction
to "approve" (ἐπαινέω for the first set of alternatives, ἀποδέχομαι
for the second) the one matter and not the other.

The first two antithetical matters had to do with a דבר.
Now Koheleth may have had in mind here any "thing" in
general — earlier in the chapter he had commented that the end
of one's life is better than the beginning of it (v. 1), and that the
wise person's thoughts are on such matters (v. 4) — or he may
have been thinking of the spoken "word" in particular — he
went on in the following verses to mention some unwise things
which people are prone to say (particularly in v. 10, but v. 9 and
even the latter half of the verse now at hand could be
interpreted as having to do with rash speech). LXX Ecclesiastes
almost always translated דבר by λόγος (in this case by the plural
form, which Gregory copies),[7] a translation which might suggest
to the interpreter that "word" rather than "thing" is in view.[8] In
also using the word λόγος here, Gregory most likely intends his
readers to think of human speech rather than of things in
general.

To express the two alternatives in the first half of the verse,
Gregory opts for participles, from παύομαι, "to cease" (for LXX's
ἐσχάτη, the "end") and from ἄρχομαι, "to begin" (for LXX's
ἀρχή, the "beginning"). Similarly, to express the proscribed
alternative in the second half of the verse, he again uses
participles, from μετεωρίζομαι, "to float in mid air, be excited"
and from τυφόομαι, "to be in the clouds, be crazed" (these two
colourful verbs are both inspired by LXX's ὑψηλὸς πνεύματι,
"haughty of spirit"). The prescribed alternative, however, more
closely follows the formulation of the original: Gregory speaks
of μέτριος ἦθος, a moderate disposition or temperate character,
where LXX spoke of μακρόθυμος [πνεύματι],[9] a long-suffering
spirit or patient mind.

(9) Πάνυ δὲ χρὴ θυμοῦ φείδεσθαι, καὶ μὴ[10] εἰς ὀργὴν
προχείρως καταφέρεσθαι, ᾗτινι ἄφρονες δουλεύουσιν.

**One should certainly use anger sparingly, and not be easily
led into wrath, the slaves of which are fools.**

In v. 3 Gregory had felt constrained by LXX's use of the word θυμός to counsel his readers that "anger" is a good thing, although he had immediately qualified this by adding that it was only "prudent" (ἔμφρων) anger which Solomon had in mind. No doubt the Christian paraphrast is glad of the opportunity now presented by v. 9 to make it clear that any imprudent exercising of anger is by no means to be countenanced.

Koheleth made use of a cognate verb and noun in the two halves of this verse, the verb θυμόω (כעס), "to be(come) angry" in the first phrase and the noun θυμός (כעס), "anger" in the second phrase. Such a device, common in Semitic languages, is not one that appeals to Gregory in his task of re-expressing Ecclesiastes in good Greek. He employs θυμός in his own introductory phrase concerning the need to keep anger in check, but the notion of becoming angry is expressed by means of the etymologically quite unrelated words εἰς ὀργὴν καταφέρομαι, "to be brought to anger" (cf. Symmachus' ὀργή here).

That anger comes "to rest" (LXX ἀναπαύω) in the "bosom" (LXX κόλπος) of fools means for Gregory that foolish people allow themselves "to be slaves" (δουλεύω) to anger; the wise person, on the other hand, has mastery over his emotions, and does not allow himself to be easily carried away by natural impulses.

(10) Ἁμαρτάνουσι δὲ οἱ λέγοντες τοῖς προτέροις ἀμείνονα δεδόσθαι βίον, ...

People who say that a better life was given to those who lived in earlier times are wrong.

Koheleth put forward a common human complaint concerning what moderns term "the good old days" (LXX αἱ ἡμέραι αἱ πρότεραι... ἀγαθαί), and castigated the complaint as being an unwise one. The complaint itself was styled as a question in *oratio recta* by Koheleth, but Gregory prefers an abbreviated reporting of the substance of the complaint in *oratio obliqua*, and while Koheleth put the matter in terms of previous times being thought to have been better than present times (which left open the possibility that the complaint may be about "the good old days" earlier in one's own lifetime), Gregory expresses it purely in terms of earlier generations being thought to have had a better life than the present generation. Koheleth's customary way of expressing this concept of something being "better" than something else (literally, "good more than" — LXX ἀγαθὸς ὑπέρ) is here simply expressed by the comparative adjective ἀμείνων, "better". And the closing comment that the complaint is not made "wisely" (LXX ἐν σοφίᾳ, literally "in wisdom")[11] has been abbreviated to a single-worded indication right at the outset that the people who make the complaint are "erring" (ἁμαρτάνω — possibly Gregory is even wanting to suggest that they are "sinning" in making such a complaint, but more likely he sees this as a matter of misjudgment rather than misconduct).

(11) ... καὶ οὐ συνιᾶσιν, ὅτι πάμπολυ διαφέρει σοφία τῆς τῶν χρημάτων περιουσίας· καὶ τοσοῦτόν ἐστι φανερωτέρα,[12] ....

They do not perceive that wisdom is very different than abundance of possessions; it is so much brighter ....

Gregory appears to have read this verse as another of Koheleth's frequent ἀγαθὸς "A" ὑπὲρ "B" ("ב" מן "א" טוב) sayings. No versions of the Greek (or of the Hebrew) text that have come down to us have anything other than the preposition "with" (μετά [= עם]) where Gregory seems to have read "than" (ὑπέρ [= מן]), though Gregory might have found support for his reading from the Syriac version, which does have ܡܢ here — although the Peshitta's rendering of this verse owes more to what is said in 9:18 than to what is in view here, and Gregory does not follow the Peshitta in referring to "weapons" (ܡܐܢܝ ܩܪܒܐ; cf. 9:18's ܡܐܢܐ ܩܪܒܐ, where LXX has σκεύη πολέμου) rather than an "inheritance" (LXX κληροδοσία, which he retains in the form of χρῆμα, "goods, property"). Ecclesiastes as we have it says at this point that wisdom is a good thing "with" (either in the sense of "in common with" or "accompanied by") possessions — i.e., wisdom is a good and useful thing to have, just as possessions are good and useful things to have; or: wisdom is good and useful, when one also has possessions. But the paraphrase says that wisdom "differs greatly" (πάμπολυ διαφέρω) from the mere abundance of possessions.

However, it is more likely that this change which Gregory has introduced was not made on the basis of reading or expecting a ὑπέρ (or a ‑ܡ or a מ) here, but simply on the basis of interpreting what Koheleth actually said at this point as being a false view which he was characterising. On a number of occasions in the following two chapters Gregory employs the device of having Solomon indicate that what he is currently putting forward is a view which he had once mistakenly held (e.g., 8:15; 9:1) or which is still mistakenly held by foolish people (e.g., 9:3,10). Here at 7:11 Gregory styles the verse as a continuation of the errors of the people in view in the previous verse, where indeed Koheleth himself had stated plainly that he was referring to a mistaken view. Thus it seems plausible that the text in front of the Church Father indeed read "good is wisdom **with** an inheritance", and that Gregory has interpreted this as being a further Solomonic depiction of what comes from the mouths of fools: the same people who were quoted in v. 10 as asking "Why were the old days better than these?" are now being quoted as saying "Wisdom is no better than an inheritance". This may be the understanding which lies behind the paraphrase's contention that, just as certain people err in thinking that a better life was given to those who lived in earlier times (v. 10), so they err in failing to see the difference between wisdom and possessions.

Koheleth rounded off this verse by further noting that wisdom, along with an inheritance, is of some advantage to "those who see the sun" (LXX θεωροῦντες τὸν ἥλιον). By this latter phrase he doubtlessly meant "those who live ὑπὸ τὸν ἥλιον", but the phrase "seeing the sun" strikes Gregory as a metaphor for something being "visible" or "bright" (φανερός or φανός),[13] and he puts forward the opinion that wisdom is "more conspicuous" or "brighter" than possessions, a notion which he sees as being linked to what is said at the beginning of the next verse. Meanwhile the notion of an "advantage" (LXX περισσεία) is redirected back into the context of the fool being attracted to possessions — an "abundance" (περιουσία) thereof.

(12) ... ὅσον ἄργυρος λαμπρότερος φαίνεται τῆς ἑαυτοῦ σκιᾶς. Ζωὴ γὰρ ἀνθρώπου, οὐκ ἐξ ἐπικήρου πλούτου κτήσεως, ἀλλ᾿ ἐκ σοφίας περιγίνεται.

... — as much as silver shines more brightly than its own shadow. For a person's life gains an advantage, not from the possession of perishable riches, but from wisdom.

בצל החכמה בצל הכסף, Koheleth now proclaimed rather cryptically; "[to be] in the shade of wisdom [is to be] in the shade of silver". LXX translated this as ἐν σκιᾷ αὐτῆς ἡ σοφία ὡς σκιὰ τοῦ ἀργυρίου, "wisdom in its shadow [is] as the shadow of silver", which suggests an extra he where MT has only one (a reading of בצלה החכמה and hence a possible case of dittography in the manuscript before the Greek translator or of haplography in the manuscript tradition leading to MT), and further suggests a possible reading of the second *beth* as a *kaph* (although the ὡς may have been deliberately introduced without any Hebrew textual warrant simply to make for a more intelligible translation).[14]

Given the climate in the land of the Bible, "shade" (צל) is eminently understandable as a metaphor for a place of shelter from danger (e.g., Isaiah 32:2), so it would seem that Koheleth, following on from his observation that wisdom and possessions are both good and advantageous things, was here making an analogy between the protective power afforded by wisdom and the protective power afforded by money.[15]   But Gregory interprets Koheleth's analogy in a quite different way. His paraphrase has just noted that wisdom is particularly "visible" or "bright" (φανερός or φανός), and so now an analogy is drawn with the phenomenon of silver "being visible" or "shining brightly" (φαίνω), in contrast to its shadow. From Koheleth's somewhat cryptic paralleling of wisdom's shadow with silver's shadow, Gregory extracts a parallel between the brightness of wisdom and the brightness of silver: just as silver is more clearly visible or shines more brightly than its shadow, so is wisdom a much more conspicuous or brighter thing than the abundance of possessions (of the previous verse).

Gregory then rounds off his treatment of these two verses by stating plainly that one "gains an advantage" or "achieves

superiority" (περιγίγνομαι) in life through wisdom and not
through wealth. Koheleth indeed agrees that there is an
advantage (LXX περισσεία, literally "surplus, abundance") in
wisdom,[16] in that it is a life-preserving thing, but this context, in
which he has been noting the parallel usefulness of wisdom and
wealth, does not suggest that he was wanting to deny the
advantages of wealth in life. Nevertheless, it must be said that
Gregory's interpretation of these two verses (11 and 12) makes
for a smooth paraphrase of what is a somewhat difficult original.

(13) Τίς δὲ καὶ δυνήσεται, εἰπέ μοι, τὴν τοσαύτην καὶ οὕτω
χρηστὴν τοῦ Θεοῦ πρόνοιαν ἐξειπεῖν;

**Tell me: Who will be able to declare the providence of God,
which is so great and so kind?**

Koheleth here returned to one of his central themes: the
powerlessness of human beings over against God. He invited
his readers to "consider" (LXX εἶδον) what God has done, and
then asked them a rhetorical question concerning human ability
to do anything about it; Gregory simply invites his readers to
"tell" him (εἶπον) the answer to the rhetorical question, but his
version of the question concerns human ability to adequately
capture in words the greatness of what God has done.

Mention of God's "works" (LXX ποιήματα)[17] brings to
Gregory's mind divine "providence" (πρόνοια). Naturally, the
Church Father will not countenance the possibility that anything
which God has done might have been "done crookedly" (LXX
διαστρέφω) and would be better if it were "straightened" (LXX
κοσμέω); from Gregory's viewpoint everything that God does is
"so great" (τοσοῦτος) and "so good/kind/worthy" (οὕτω χρηστός)
that it defies description.

(14) ἢ τίς ἀνακαλέσασθαι τὰ δοκοῦντα παρημελῆσθαι ὑπὸ
Θεοῦ δικαίως;

**Or who will be able to truly recall things which supposedly
have been abandoned by God?**

This verse would have made a good summary of and
conclusion to the famous poem at the beginning of Chapter

Three: there are "good times" (LXX ἡμέρα ἀγαθωσύνης) and
there are "bad times" (LXX ἡμέρα κακίας), God having made
"the one corresponding to the other" (LXX τοῦτο σύμφωνον
τούτῳ), so that the unfortunate human being has no idea what
will happen "afterwards" (LXX ὀπίσω αὐτοῦ, "after him" [i.e.,
after he has died] or "after it" [i.e., after the particular τοῦτο in
which he currently finds himself]) and accordingly should just
accept the situation as it is.

Gregory makes no connection with Koheleth's earlier
Catalogue of Times, even though he had recognised that the
catalogue couples times that can be labelled as ἀγαθός with times
that can be labelled as κακός (see his paraphrase of 3:8). The
reason why he does not make a connection must be that he does
not want the blame for the human plight to be directed at God.
The text before Gregory here at 7:14 said plainly that it is God
who has made both τοῦτο (i.e., the time of ἀγαθωσύνη) and
τοῦτο (i.e., the time of κακία), but since Gregory had earlier
studiously avoided naming God as the instigator of the
unpredictable changes from one to the other (see his paraphrase
of 3:10) it is hardly surprising that also now he holds back from
such an assertion. All he will say is that there are things which
might "seem" (δοκέω) to "be abandoned" or "be disregarded"
(παραμελέομαι) by God.

Yet even this assertion is qualified at both ends. At the
beginning of Gregory's version of this verse ἢ τίς
ἀνακαλέσασθαι, "or who will [be able] to recall?" carries on the
rhetorical question of the previous verse and implies that no-
one is actually able to come up with a case of God having
abandoned something (or someone) he had created. And at the
end of the verse δικαίως can be read in two ways, both of which
further qualify the assertion. If δικαίως is to be linked with the
"recalling" activity of human beings, it emphasises human
inability to come up with a genuine case of divine
abandonment: "who will be able to **truly** recall [such a case]?" If,
on the other hand, it is to be linked with the alleged
"abandoning" activity of God, the δικαίως makes it clear that,
even if God were to actually abandon something (or someone)
he had created, it would be with good reason: "supposed things

which have been **justly** abandoned by God."

It is perhaps worth noting that Gregory, as well as being uninterested in Koheleth's references in this verse to respective times of good and evil, is also undistracted on this occasion by LXX's clumsily literalistic περὶ λαλιᾶς, "concerning speech" (for MT's על־דברת, "concerning the matter of"; Symmachus, too, thinks these words are best left out, a precedent Gregory might have done well to follow also in 3:18) — unless it was this talk of "speech" that suggested to the Church Father the idea of human beings trying to put forward an accusation against God.

(15) Πράττων δὲ οὐκ ὀρθῶς πρότερον ἔγωγε κατενόησα τὰ σύμπαντα, καὶ δίκαιον ἐμμένοντα τῇ δικαιοσύνῃ, καὶ μέχρι θανάτου μὴ ἐξιστάμενον, ἀλλὰ καὶ δι' αὐτὴν ἐπιβουλευόμενον, καὶ ἀσεβῆ συναποθνήσκοντα τῇ ἑαυτοῦ κακίᾳ.

In my former condition of unrighteousness I observed everything, including a righteous person holding fast to righteousness and not letting go of it until death, but also being treated treacherously because of it, and an ungodly person dying with his wickedness.

Koheleth's expression ימי הבלי, "the days of my futility" is an excellent Hebraic way of denoting a futile or — going back to the basic meaning of הבל as a transitory "breath" — a fleeting life. LXX Ecclesiastes' agenda of closely mimicking the Hebrew construction resulted in the less than excellent Greek expression ἡμέραι ματαιότητός μου. Gregory's use of οὐκ ὀρθῶς, "not righteously" as his equivalent of LXX's ματαιότης in this instance, along with his insertion of the word πρότερος, "earlier, former" into his paraphrase of this expression, results in the less than Kohelethine assertion that the only time that a person's life can be said "to be in a condition of" (πράττω) futility is when that person is living unrighteously. In Gregory's understanding, Solomon, at the time of delivering his Ecclesiastes oration, was looking back on a life that included times when he was not as wise as he had become by the time he came to put these thoughts together (cf., e.g., the paraphrase of 1:16; 9:1-3); if, therefore, Solomon refers to his "days of futility", he must be referring to those former days of foolishness from which he had risen to wiser heights.

What Koheleth presented here was a classic problem for the pious *Weltanschauung*. The traditional school of thought had taught that "the fear of the LORD prolongs life, but the years of the wicked will be short" (Proverbs 10:27). The problem, as Koheleth observed, is that the way of the world does not conform to that simple pattern, but that in fact often a righteous person will "perish" (LXX ἀπόλλυμαι) while an unrighteous person will "last [for a long time]" (LXX μένω).[18] The solution to this conundrum, in the view of many a pious interpreter (such as the Targumist in his paraphrase at this point), is to be found beyond the grave, where all will be set right, the righteous person being rewarded for his merit and the unrighteous person being requited for his evil doings. But Gregory simply refuses to see the problem here; in his version of affairs, "perishing" is to be ascribed to the unrighteous person, who "dies together with" (συναποθνήσκω) his wickedness, and "lasting" is to be ascribed to the righteous person, who "abides in" or "holds fast to" (ἐμμένω) his righteousness.

Gregory would no doubt defend his paraphrase by claiming that "the righteous one perishing in his righteousness" (LXX δίκαιος ἀπολλύμενος ἐν δικαίῳ αὐτοῦ) is a reference not so much to the possibility of an untimely death coming upon such a person as to the fact that the one who is truly righteous retains his righteous character throughout his life, no matter what might militate against such steadfastness[19] — such as "being treated treacherously" or "being the object of plots" (ἐπι- βουλεύομαι), which might be a concession to the generally-understood meaning of Koheleth's phrase as having to do with the righteous person's life being cut short. Further, Gregory's defense would continue, "the wicked one lasting in his wickedness" (LXX ἀσεβὴς μένων ἐν κακίᾳ αὐτοῦ) is a reference not so much to the possibility of a long life being enjoyed by such a person as to the fact that the one who is truly wicked persists in his wickedness throughout his life, no matter what opportunities for repentance are set before him.

The impression with which the reader is left from these

two documents, *The Words of Koheleth* on the one hand and *A Paraphrase of Solomon's "Ecclesiastes"* on the other, is quite different. Koheleth's observation of a good person perishing while an evil person lives on served to underline his contention that his — and by implication also the reader's — life can be characterised as ματαιότης: what is the point of a life that can be cut short at any time for no apparently just reason? Solomon's (i.e., Gregory's) observation of a good person remaining faithful throughout his life while an evil person dies in his evil serves as an example to anyone who is, like Solomon had been, living οὐκ ὀρθῶς — Solomon himself had evidently taken heed of the moral lesson in what he had observed, and by the time of delivering this address to the assembly had reformed his former ways; so, too, should the reader of Gregory's paraphrase model himself on the example of a righteous person holding fast to his righteousness rather than the example of an ungodly person perishing along with his wickedness.

(16) Χρὴ δὲ δίκαιον ὄντα μὴ πάνυ τοιοῦτον εἶναι δοκεῖν, μηδὲ ἄγαν σοφὸν καὶ ὑπερμέτρως· ὅπως μή τι πταίσας, πολλαπλασίονα ἁμαρτήσῃ.

A righteous person should not pretend to be exceedingly righteous nor excessively and immeasurably wise, lest he make a false step and sin all the more excessively.

Since no guarantee of success and happiness in life comes with the possession either of righteousness (as the observation recorded in the previous verse has made plain) or of wisdom (as the Solomonic masquerade in the opening two chapters had made plain), Koheleth now advised his readers against seeking to be very righteous or very wise; one may very well receive nothing but ruination for all one's efforts. But Gregory did not concede in his paraphrase of the previous verse that the righteous life can serve as an example of futility, and neither did he concede in his paraphrase of the earlier Solomonic experiences that wisdom is ultimately futile, so it is not surprising that he does not exactly advise his readers at this point that striving to be very righteous and very wise may not be worth the effort.

Koheleth's expression "to be very righteous" (LXX γίγνομαι δίκαιος πολύ) seems straightforward enough, conjuring up a picture of the person who studiously follows all the religious rules to the letter. But the parallel expression "to be very wise" (LXX σοφίζομαι περισσά) provided the pious interpreter with the handle he needed, since σοφίζομαι, and/or the חכם hithpael which it translated, might be thought to carry the nuance here of "playing the wise man" in the reprehensive sense of pretending to be what one is not.[20] Such a possibility is not supported by the only other biblical use of חכם hithpael, in Exodus 1:10, where it evidently meant "to behave wisely/cleverly", and LXX's κατασοφίζομαι meant "to be wiser/cleverer than, to outwit" one's opponents. But if this possible nuance is taken up, Koheleth's comments in this verse could be construed as having to do, not with the ultimate futility of being a very wise (or very righteous) person, but with the inadvisability of playing the part of a very wise (or very righteous) person when one is not in reality such a person at all.

This interpretation requires that the interpreter overlook the obviously-intended parallelism of these two expressions with the pair "to be very wicked" (LXX ἀσεβέω πολύ) and "to be stubborn" (LXX γίγνομαι σκληρός — MT had said היה סכל, "to be foolish") in the following verse, where the meaning can hardly be that one should not **play the part** of a very wicked or foolish/stubborn person when one is not in reality such a person at all, but simply that one should not **be** too wicked or foolish for one's own good. But Gregory is keen to detect a difference between giving people the advice, "Do not be very righteous and very wise" — advice which the supremely righteous and wise Solomon would surely never give — and giving them the advice, "Do not be very wicked and very foolish/stubborn". So he is happy to take up the possible nuance offered by the formulation of the verse now at hand: a person should not "appear" or "pretend" (δοκέω) to be excessively righteous or excessively wise. And just in case there is any possibility of misunderstanding left in the verse, Gregory makes it clear, by beginning with δίκαιος ὄντα, that one should certainly be righteous (and presumably also wise, although he leaves that unmentioned).

What happens to the person who is — or, in Gregory's paraphrase, pretends to be — exceedingly righteous and wise? Koheleth presented the probable fate of such a person by means of the verb שׁמם hithpolel, which can mean either "to be desolate" or "to be astonished". If the first meaning is adopted for this occurrence, Koheleth can be seen as having pointed to the material harm that can unexpectedly fall upon such a person, whereas if the second meaning is adopted, he appears to have been pointing to the mental distress that would accompany the blow. Either way, in view of the already-mentioned parallelism with the following verse, a meaning analogous to v. 17's "to die before one's time" (LXX ἀποθάνῃς ἐν οὐ καιρῷ σου) seems most appropriate; hence למה תשׁומם should probably be translated as "Why ruin yourself?" LXX's choice of the Greek verb ἐκπλήσ-σομαι (as also Symmachus' ἀδημονέω), came down on the side of the meaning "to be astonished" rather than "to be desolate" (although it might be argued that another possible meaning of ἐκπλήσσομαι, "to be driven away", is relevant here as a depiction of the social ostracism likely to be inflicted upon an excessively pious and clever person).

For Gregory, what is likely to happen to the person who pretends to be more righteous or wise than he really is, is that he will "make a false step" (πταίω), and this will be more reprehensible than for an ordinary person to make some slip; when one "makes an error" or "sins" (ἁμαρτάνω), the sin is "many times greater" (πολλαπλάσιος) if one has set oneself up as being a greater person. There may be something of an echo here of Jesus' saying (in Luke 12:47-49), "That servant who knew his master's will, but did not make ready or act according to his will, shall receive a severe beating, but he who did not know, and did what deserved a beating, shall receive a light beating; for every one to whom much is given, of him will much be required" — hence the more righteous a person is or purports to be, the more he is expected to live a righteous life, and the greater his guilt if he does not act according to the will of God.

(17) Καὶ μὴ ἔσο τολμηρὸς καὶ προπετής, μή σε θάνατος ἁρπάσῃ ἄκαιρος.

And do not be daring and reckless, lest an untimely death snatch you away.

In the previous verse Gregory had seen the likely consequences of pretending to be what one is not, but here in the same formulations he sees the likely consequences of being what one should not be. Evidently he is happy to have his readers warned against being wicked, while he is not at all happy to have them warned against being righteous.

"To be wicked" (MT רשע, LXX ἀσεβέω) and to be "foolish" (MT סכל) or "stubborn" (LXX σκληρός) in the context of "dying before one's time" (LXX ἀποθάνῃς ἐν οὐ²¹ καιρῷ σου) means, according to Gregory, that one acts in a "daring" (τολμηρός) and "reckless" (προπετής) manner, such that one is likely to be overtaken by "an untimely death" (θάνατος ἄκαιρος). By means of πολύς (הרבה) Koheleth indicated that, as in the previous verse, he was thinking of the attributes in question as being present to a greater than normal degree (he certainly did not hold that wickedness per se is likely to result in an early death, as is clear from his comment at v. 15); in offering no equivalent to this word Gregory demonstrates that he is of the opinion that any amount of recklessness is sufficient to carry its perpetrator into an early grave.

(18) Μέγιστον δὲ ἀγαθὸν ἀντιλαμβάνεσθαι Θεοῦ, καὶ ἐν τούτῳ ὄντα μηδὲν ἁμαρτάνειν. Τῶν γὰρ ἀμιάντων χειρὶ ἀνάγνῳ ψαύειν, μυσαρόν. Ὁ δὲ μετὰ φόβου Θεοῦ ὑπείκων ἅπαντα διαφεύγει τἀναντία.

The greatest good is to take hold of God and, abiding in this, not to sin at all. To touch undefiled things with a defiled hand is an abomination; but the one who acts in accordance with the fear of God escapes everything that is contrary.

As a concluding remark to the two admonitions of verses 16 and 17, Koheleth advised his readers to grasp both of them: for best results in life — although of course Koheleth offered no guarantees — a person should hold fast to "this" rule of behaviour (LXX οὗτος — that is to say, the avoidance of extreme righteousness and cleverness) and also not abandon "this" other rule of behaviour (LXX οὗτος — that is to say, the avoidance of extreme wickedness and foolishness); · in this way the right-thinking person is more likely to "get through" (LXX ἐξέρχομαι) the various situations of life.

But Gregory did not see Koheleth's dichotomy — "this" on the one hand and "this" on the other hand — as being connected to the previous admonitions. Instead, he interprets the first οὗτος as being a reference to "undefiled" things (ἀμίαντος) and the second οὗτος as being a reference to "defiled" things (ἄναγνος), but with these kinds of opposing concepts there can be no question of grasping both; rather, the person who takes hold of what is undefiled — ultimately: God — "escapes" (διαφεύγω) the contrary things of life.

It is evidently the LXX text in front of Gregory that has given rise to his defiled/undefiled contrast here. MT presented a clear case of synthetical parallelism in the twin lines תאחז בזה, "take hold of this" and מזה אל-תנח את-ידך, "do not let go of this with your hand". For the first of these lines LXX offered as its equivalent ἀντέχεσθαί σε ἐν τούτῳ, "hold on to this", but in the second line we read ἀπὸ τούτου μὴ μιάνῃς τὴν χεῖρά σου, "do not defile your hand by this". Very likely the original LXX equivalent to נוח hiphil was ἀνίημι, "to let go, slacken",[22] but at some point, probably due to a dittographical error arising from the preceding μή, ἀνῇς became μιάνῃς. This idea of μιαίνω, "to defile, stain" had obviously entered the LXX text by the time Gregory Thaumaturgos came to interpret Ecclesiastes, for he is led to paraphrase the expression here as a warning against "touching undefiled things with a defiled hand" (τῶν ἀμιάντων χειρὶ ἀνάγνῳ ψαύειν).

The first line, "take hold of this", is accordingly paraphrased by Gregory as an injunction to "take hold of" (ἀντιλαμβάνω) God and, moreover, to continue to have one's being (εἰμί) "in this" (reproducing LXX's ἐν τούτῳ).[23] Since God is depicted as the one who is to be taken hold of, it would make sense if he were to be pictured also as the one in whom people should continue to have their being, and accordingly by ἐν τούτῳ Gregory may mean "in him"; but the use of οὗτος to refer to God sounds awkward, and so it may be preferable to understand "this" as a reference to the activity recommended in the previous clause, such that Gregory is here telling his readers to stick with a policy of taking hold of God rather than to allow themselves to take hold of sin instead.

Indeed, Gregory says that the person who follows this policy "does not sin at all" (μηδὲν ἁμαρτάνω). This expression could be taken to mean that it is not at all sinful to take hold of God and to remain steadfast in such a course of action, but that would be a singularly unnecessary observation for Gregory to make, for surely no-one would suggest that taking up and persisting in a godly lifestyle might be a sinful thing. Perhaps some sense can be given to this meaning by reading the clause now at hand in connection with v. 16's warning about the great sin of a righteous person who, after pretending to be exceeedingly righteous, makes a false step; Gregory might be wanting to put forward here the contrast of a person who persists in true righteousness and does not make a false step — i.e., he may be warning his readers that it is sinful to take hold of God if one does not remain steadfast in this course of action. Nevertheless, μηδὲν ἁμαρτάνω makes it look as though Gregory is saying that the person who has his being in God no longer commits any sins at all, and it is not impossible that the Church Father intends to make such a statement, given the Pauline teaching of the believer being "dead to sin and alive to God" (Romans 6:11), even though the contention does not fit well in the context of the forthcoming v. 20.

The one who is most likely to come through in the game of life is "the one who fears God" (LXX φοβούμενος τὸν θεόν). In Kohelethine usage, this expression should probably be taken as indicating the person who is mindful of human powerlessness over against God (cf. 3:14), and hence in this context the person who will not try to tempt fate by acting in either of the two extremes Koheleth had just mentioned. But in Gregorian usage, "the one who complies [or: acts in accordance] with the fear of God" (ὁ μετὰ φόβου Θεοῦ ὑπείκων) is the same person as the one who was supposedly in view in the first οὗτος clause, namely the Christian who has taken hold of God and now abides in him, no longer acting in accordance with his original sinful nature.

This person, continues Gregory, escapes "everything that is contrary" (ἄπαντα τἀναντία). Τὰ ἐναντία in this context may simply mean anything that is opposed to God, or anything that is contrary to the fear of God. But there may also be an intentional allusion here to the Catalogue of Times in Chapter Three, for there Gregory had noted that this present age is filled with "all the most contrasting things" (πάντα ἐναντιότητα, 3:1), so many rapidly-changing (v. 8) but consistently-useless (v. 9) human activities and emotions, due to the work of an Evil Being who is opposed to God (v. 11). If by this expression here in 7:18 Gregory wishes to recall the earlier Catalogue of Times, he is reminding his readers that the only way to escape from the endless round of contrary labours under the sway of the Being opposed to God is to submit oneself in reverence to God.

(19) Σοφία δὲ βοηθείας, στίφους ἀνδρῶν τῶν δυνατωτάτων ἐν πόλει μείζονα δύναται, ἢ καὶ συγγινώσκει δικαίως πολλάκις τῶν δεόντων ἀποτυγχάνουσιν.

Wisdom is of more help in a city than a band of the strongest men, and it often justly pardons those who fail in their duty.

Wisdom "is strong" (עז) for a wise person, said Koheleth, giving him a strength greater than ten rulers in a city. LXX apparently read or postulated עזר here, for the Greek version spoke of wisdom "helping" (βοηθέω) the wise person. The Targumist made the same reading or postulation, as evidenced by his use of סיע ithpaal, "to be helped", but the Peshitta attests to the MT reading in its employment of ܚܝܠ pael, "to make strong". Gregory seems to be aware of more than the Septuagintal understanding of this verse, for he says that wisdom is a "help" (βοήθεια) which "is more able, stronger" (μείζων δύναμαι) than the strongest men.

"The strongest men" (ἄνδρες δυνατώτατοι) is probably not exactly what Koheleth had in mind. He styled these people as שׁלּיטים, "rulers", which LXX translated as ἐξουσιάζοντες, "those who exercise authority". Gregory's expression might also be taken as denoting the most powerful men in the city, in the sense of the political leaders or authority-wielders, except that he styles these men as being grouped in a στῖφος, a compact fighting unit of combatants in close array, thus indicating that he has in mind physical strength rather than civic power. To speak of an indeterminate group of men rather than specifically "ten" (LXX δέκα) may not be inappropriate, since Koheleth may well have been using this number in the indefinite sense of "many", although in the context of the πόλις (עיר) it is possible that he is making a reference to the δέκα πρῶτοι who governed Hellenistic cities.[24]

Gregory adds his own homiletical thought to this verse: a further valuable aspect of wisdom is that it can "pardon" (συγγιγνώσκω) "those who fail in their duty" (τῶν δεόντων ἀποτυγχάνοντες). This thought has evidently been prompted by the following verse's note that there is no truly "righteous" (LXX δίκαιος) person on earth who never sins; Gregory's paraphrase of v. 20 clearly shows that he is in agreement with Koheleth on that matter, but before proceeding to it he notes that wisdom is able to act "righteously" (δικαίως) on behalf of the person who falls short of the standard of total righteousness. This can be interpreted in two ways: either Gregory is meaning to suggest to his readers that they should not despair if they occasionally make some small slip — providing, that is, they are generally living a wise/righteous lifestyle, for then their overall adherence to wisdom/righteousness will mean that the small slip can be forgiven by God — or he is wanting to suggest that the wise/righteous person, because he knows that no-one on earth is able to live perfectly all the time (despite the suggestion in the paraphrase of v. 18 that the person who abides in God is no longer subject to sin), ought to be ready to forgive those who stumble. Gregory appears here to be offering counsel in the vein of 1 Peter 4:8, "love one another earnestly, because love covers over many sins".

(20) Ἄπταιστος γάρ ἐστιν οὐδὲ εἷς.

For there is not one who does not stumble.

Koheleth's observation that no-one on earth always does

good and never sins, a view that is shared by many biblical writers (e.g., 1 Kings 8:46; 1 John 1:8), is so straightforwardly true that Gregory handles it with uncustomary brevity. His use here of ἄπταιστος, "not stumbling" for Koheleth's dual concepts of "doing good" (LXX ποιέω ἀγαθόν) and "not sinning" (LXX οὐχ ἁμαρτάνω) recalls his use of πταίω, "to stumble" in v. 16; such a connection with the earlier verse is entirely appropriate, for the realisation that no-one can be perfectly righteous ought to dissuade a person from seeking to become — or, in Gregory's version, pretending to be — excessively righteous.

(21) Ἀσεβῶν δὲ λόγοις, οὐδ᾽ ὁπωσοῦν τι χρὴ προσιέναι, ὅπως μὴ τῶν κατὰ σοῦ λόγων αὐτήκοος γενόμενος, ὥσπερ δούλου πονηροῦ φλυαρίας·

You should in no way whatever pay attention to the words of ungodly people, lest you become an earwitness of words spoken against yourself, such as the silly talk of a wicked servant.

Koheleth now proceeded with the advice not to take much notice of the things which "they say" (ידברו) behind your back. Since he had just clearly stated that everyone is a sinner, the "they" he had in mind at this point is potentially every human being. Nevertheless, LXX (as also Peshitta and Targum) was of the view that the people in question here are particularly wicked or ungodly people, and so styled this verse as having to do with the things which "ungodly people say" (λαλήσουσιν ἀσεβεῖς);[25] accordingly, Gregory, too, focuses specifically on the words of the ἀσεβεῖς in his paraphrase.

The danger in "paying attention" to these words (LXX θῆς καρδίαν σου, literally "giving your heart" to the words, which Gregory expresses by means of προσίημι, "letting [the words] come near" to you) is that you are likely to hear someone speaking ill of you. The case which Koheleth put forward was that of your own "servant" (LXX δοῦλος) "cursing" (LXX καταράομαι) you. Gregory cites this case as the "silly talk" (φλυαρία) of a wicked δοῦλος, but he cites it clearly as just one possible example of the broader notion of "the words spoken against yourself" (οἱ κατὰ σοῦ λόγοι) which you can overhear if you listen to what ungodly people are saying. At 6:11 Gregory had noted that φλυαρία is prevalent among human beings, so his readers should not be surprised to hear here that their own servants, if they have any, might very well be indulging in such foolishness.

(22) ἔπειτα δηχθεὶς τὴν καρδίαν, ὕστερον ἐν πολλαῖς πράξεσιν εἰς τὸ ἀντικαταράσασθαι καὶ σὺ ἐκτραπῇς.

Then, stung at heart, you also might afterwards turn to cursing in return in many actions.

As a good reason for following the advice of the preceding verse and not taking too much notice of the bad things people say about you behind your back, Koheleth pointed out that you yourself no doubt frequently say bad things about other people behind their backs. "Your heart knows" (ידע לבך) that this is the case, said Koheleth; that is to say, "you know in your heart" that it is true. But the people who produced the LXX text read a *resh* instead of a *daleth* here — a reading of ירע לבך , "he will injure your heart" — and were unable to decide between two alternative renderings of this expression, πονηρεύσεταί σε, "he will do you harm" and κακώσει καρδίαν σου, "he will mistreat your heart", both of which have been included in the Greek version that has come down to us. If the text in front of Gregory included both of these alternative translations, he has sensibly decided to paraphrase them in just one expression: "stung at heart" (δηχθεὶς τὴν καρδίαν).

LXX's double rendering of ידע לבך involves also a double rendering of פעמים רבות, "many times": firstly πλειστάκις, "very often" and secondly καθόδους πολλάς, "repeatedly". Presumably Koheleth was referring to the many occasions on which the reader has spoken ill of other people rather than the frequency with which he has occasion to recall in his heart that he has done so, but by retaining the Hebrew word order in both of its renderings LXX made it appear that the reference was to the frequency with which the servant or other ungodly person is going to do harm to the reader and mistreat his heart. Gregory does not retain this positioning; in the paraphrase it is clear that the reference is to the number of curses which the reader directs towards other people, and not to the number of occasions on which he has been stung at heart by the words of others.

In Gregory's version, however, the reader is not depicted as cursing "many times", nor even of cursing "in many words", but rather of cursing "in many actions" (ἐν πολλαῖς πράξεσιν). Perhaps the Church Father was of the opinion that people curse their fellows more by the bad things they do to them than by the bad things they say of them, or he reasoned that the way in which a master responds to the disloyal talk of a servant is not with mere words but with firm punishments. Koheleth was talking about having cursed people in the past, and so being understanding of someone whom you now overhear cursing you, but Gregory is talking about how you, if you overhear someone cursing you today, might curse other people (or specifically this particular person) in the future. For Gregory, then, the real danger of paying attention to the words of ungodly people is that you can be led to "turn aside" (ἐκτρέπω) from a godly life "into" (εἰς) the trap of doing the same things that you have witnessed the ungodly doing: in this case, you will turn to "cursing in return" (ἀντικαταράομαι, arising from LXX's two-fold καταράομαι, which appears once in the preceding verse with the reader as the object and once again in the verse now at hand with the reader as the subject).

(23) Ἔγνων δὲ ταῦτα ἐγὼ ἄπαντα, σοφίαν ἐκ Θεοῦ λαβών, ἣν ὕστερον ἀποβαλών, οὐκέτι οἷός τε ἤμην ὅμοιος εἶναι.

I knew all these things, having received wisdom from God — which I later rejected, and was no longer able to be the same.

Everything he had been saying had been "tested" (LXX πειράω) by means of wisdom, Koheleth assured his readers, but nevertheless he had to admit that his quest for ultimate wisdom had been unsuccessful — it remained "far" (MT רחוק, which LXX appears to have read as a verb, translating with μακρύνομαι, "to be far off") from him, as indeed it does from all human beings (v. 24). Gregory's Solomon does not speak of having conducted a wise experiment (nor did he speak in such terms at 2:1) and of having found himself unable to achieve what he had aspired to; rather, he speaks of having "known" (γιγνώσκω) the truth of what he says, but later having found himself unable to be "the same" (ὅμοιος) as he was at the time when he had known that wisdom.

In Gregory's hands, then, Koheleth's recognition that wisdom is "far" from him becomes Solomon's confession that he "rejected" (ἀποβάλλω) wisdom after earlier "receiving" (λαμβάνω) it from God. Gregory has already provided evidence that he is working with just such a model of Solomon's life: for example in 2:9, where he has Solomon tell us that his wisdom diminished as he allowed himself to become more and more involved in a hedonistic lifestyle. In 12:10 Gregory's Solomon will reveal to us that he returned to a God-pleasing lifestyle when he was an old man (in time to deliver this wise address to the assembly of God's people before his long lifetime came to an end). This accords with the view of Rabbi Judan, recorded in *Koheleth Rabbah* 1:12, that Solomon experienced three phases in his life, being "wise, foolish, and again wise" (חכם טפש וחכם) — as opposed to Rabbi Oniah's view that the process was "foolish, then wise, then foolish again" (טפש חכם וטפש).[26] The idea that Solomon lost but later regained wisdom does not exactly accord with the biblical account of his life, which speaks of his heart being turned after other gods when he was old (1 Kings 11:4) and makes no suggestion of any change of heart before the end, but Gregory finds it a convenient theory for interpreting the book of Ecclesiastes. Here in 7:23, then, the older and wiser Solomon looks back with regret on his earlier foolishness, which caused him so many problems that could have been avoided had he remained on the straight and narrow path of wisdom/ righteousness.

(24) Ἔφυγε γὰρ ἀπ' ἐμοῦ σοφία εἰς μῆκος ἄπειρον, καὶ εἰς βάθος ἀμέτρητον, ὡς μὴ εἶναι αὐτῆς λαβέσθαι μηκέτι.

For wisdom fled from me to an infinite distance and an immeasurable depth, so that I could no longer take hold of it.

רחוק מה־שהיה, "far off is that which is", remarked Koheleth at the outset of this verse, commenting on human inability to understand all that exists or happens in this world; LXX appears to have read an additional *mem* here — i.e., ממה (= מן מה) — and so translated the expression as μακρὰν ὑπὲρ ὃ ἦν, "[that which is] far beyond what was" (cf. Peshitta ܡܢ ܡܐ ܕܗܘܐ). Further, lamented Koheleth, it is עמק עמק, "deep, deep", the repetition emphasising the impenetrableness of ultimate wisdom concerning the way of the world; LXX styled it as βαθὺ βάθος, "[at] a deep depth".[27] Gregory brings the two expressions nicely into balance by paraphrasing both of them by means of a noun indicating distance and an adjective indicating immeasurability: μῆκος ἄπειρον, "an infinite distance" for the first phrase and βάθος ἀμέτρητον, "an immeasurable depth" for the second.

Gregory also neatly balances his paraphrase of this verse with that of the preceding verse. There he noted that Solomon had "received" (λαμβάνω) wisdom from God, and now he notes that Solomon was later unable to "take hold of" (λαμβάνω) that wisdom. The reason for this lamentable situation is expressed in two ways in these two verses: v. 23 has Solomon say that he "rejected" (ἀποβάλλω) wisdom after God had granted it to him, and v. 24 has him paraphrase that by saying that wisdom "fled" (φεύγω) from him. And while the previous verse paints the sad picture of a once blessed man who was "no longer" (οὐκέτι) the same, the verse now at hand paints the same picture in terms of a man who once had wisdom in his grasp but then was "no longer" (μηκέτι) able to take hold of this most precious possession.

Koheleth's plaintive cry, "who can discover it?" (LXX τίς εὑρήσει αὐτό;) indicated clearly enough that he was character-ising here the plight of Everyman: ultimate wisdom is far from all who live under the sun. But Gregory interprets the verse as having to do specifically with Solomon's lack of wisdom during the dark days of his life; by implication, this is not necessarily a universal human affliction, for the reader can take heed of the great man's experience and accordingly need not be subject to that same dearth of wisdom with which Solomon had allowed himself to be afflicted at that time.

(25) "Ωστε ὕστερον καὶ τοῦ ἐπιζητεῖν αὐτήν, τέλειον[28] ἀπεσχόμην· καὶ οὔτε ἐνεθυμούμην ἔτι τοῦ κατανοεῖν τὰς τῶν ἀσεβῶν ἀφροσύνας καὶ βουλὰς ματαίας, καὶ ἀλύοντα βίον.

So after that I abstained altogether from seeking it; nor did I give any further thought to understanding the follies and empty counsels of ungodly people, and their meandering life.

In informing his readers of his investigation into practical wisdom, Koheleth said that "I and my heart" (LXX ἐγὼ καὶ ἡ καρδία μου) turned to the matter. This is an unusual expression without any precise parallel in the Hebrew Bible, but it is not an entirely unintelligible one, for a person may speak of his heart or soul as something distinguishable from himself (cf. Luke 12:19: "I will say to my soul, 'Soul, you have...'").[29] Many MT manuscripts, however, have the more straightforward expression "I in my heart" (אני בלבי instead of אני ולבי), as in 2:1, a reading shared by the Targum (אנא...בלבי). Gregory makes no direct reference to the καρδία in his paraphrase, but it may lie behind his choice of the verb ἐνθυμέομαι, "to lay to heart, think out", since one's θυμός is equivalent to one's καρδία in this context of the seat of thought.

Koheleth spoke plainly of his quest for σοφία (חכמה) and his attempt at an "accounting" (ψῆφος [חשבון]) of things; in fact, he could hardly have spoken more emphatically of such a quest than he did by employing here no less than three verbs in immediate succession to describe his intention: "to know" (LXX γιγνώσκω), "to investigate" (LXX κατασκέπτομαι), and "to seek" (LXX ζητέω) wisdom. Gregory, however, has Solomon speak of completely "abstaining" (ἀπέχομαι) from "seeking after" (ἐπιζητέω) wisdom. Perhaps the Christian interpreter might point to LXX's κυκλόω, "to turn (around)" as indicating a turning away from the quest for wisdom — Gregory has already demonstrated a tendency to interpret Koheleth's use of expressions for "turning" as indicating a change from past attitudes (cf. 2:11,20) — but in the present context of his paraphrase of the passage now at hand this would more readily indicate a turning back to the way of wisdom after the earlier abandonment of it. The main reason for Gregory saying that

wisdom was not being sought, when Koheleth said that it was
being sought, is that Gregory can make better sense of the passage
by so saying: the preceding verses have been paraphrased as a
confession of the Solomonic abandonment of wisdom, and the
following verse will be paraphrased as an example of what the
fallen Solomon experienced, so the present verse is best treated
as a further depiction of the depths to which the great man sank
at that unfortunate time of his life.

The Masoretes read רשע כסל as "the wickedness of folly", but
LXX read it as ἀσεβοῦς ἀφροσύνη, "the folly of the wicked
person", and Gregory follows suit, though he expresses it in the
plural and adds definite articles (αἱ τῶν ἀσεβῶν ἀφροσύναι).
Koheleth's final two abstract nouns for "folly", סכלות and הוללות,
set in immediate juxtaposition in a way that was probably meant
to suggest equivalence — "foolishness equals senselessness" —
were then treated by LXX as further marks of the ἀσεβής, who, in
addition to ἀφροσύνη, is characterised by ὀχληρία[30] καὶ περιφορά,
"troublesomeness and circumlocution"; hence Gregory paraphrases these twin matters as pertaining to the ἀσεβεῖς, who, in
addition to ἀφροσύναι, are characterised by βουλαὶ μάταιαι καὶ
ἀλύων βίος, "empty counsels and a meandering life". When
Gregory's Solomon says that he gave no further thought to
"understanding" (κατανοέω, for LXX's γιγνώσκω) these characteristics of the ungodly, he presumably means that he pursued such
empty counsels and lived such a meandering life, not being
cognisant of the fact that these things were ungodly and unwise.

(26) Οὕτω δὲ διακείμενος, εἰς αὐτὰ διηνέχθην,[31] καὶ ἐπιθυμίᾳ
συσχεθεὶς θανατηφόρῳ, ἔγνων τὴν γυναῖκα, γῆν[32] τινα, ἢ εἴ τι ἕτερον
τοιοῦτον ὑπάρχουσαν. Καρδία μὲν γὰρ αὐτῆς σαγηνεύει τοὺς
παριόντας, χειρὶ δὲ χεῖρα[33] συνάψασα μόνον, κατέχει ἢ εἰ δεσμοῖς
περιβάλλουσα εἷλκε. Μόνος δ' ἂν ἀπ' αὐτῆς ῥυσθείης, τὸν Θεὸν
ἵλεω καὶ ἐπόπτην ἐσχηκώς· ὡς ὅ γε ἁμαρτίᾳ δεδουλωμένος οὐκ ἂν
ἐκφύγοι.

**Being in such a state, I was carried on to those things, and
trapped by a fatal desire, I learned that Woman is a snare or
something similar. Her heart ensnares those who pass by, and
just by joining hand to hand she holds you as securely as if she**

were dragging you along bound with chains. You can only get
away from her by having a gracious and watchful God, since the
man who is enslaved by sin cannot escape.

The "things" (αὐτά) to which Gregory alludes in his
introduction to this verse are evidently those things he has just
mentioned in the previous verse: the foolish and empty things
in which ungodly people involve themselves as they live their
meandering life. Because Solomon had abandoned the way of
wisdom, he gave himself over to the wicked counsels of such
people and accordingly left himself open "to being carried this
way and that" (διαφέρομαι) in precisely such a meandering life.

Gregory seems to relish the opportunity provided here to
present Woman (ἡ γυνή, as in LXX) as a particularly dangerous
creature. Many interpreters have wanted to limit Koheleth's
reference as being only to a particular kind of sinful and
licentious woman rather than being a wholesale condemnation
of women in general,[34] but Gregory does not style the verse as
having to do only with the loose woman. An interpreter
wishing to limit the reference to adulterous women who seek to
erotically trap a man into sexual immorality might point to the
sentiments expressed by Koheleth in 9:9 as indicating that he did
not paint all women in the same scarlet colours, but Gregory
paraphrases that verse, too, as having to do with the immorality
into which women lead men. However, it should not surprise
us that a celibate Church Father — and particularly one who had
learned his Christianity from Origen, a man so concerned to
avoid the snares and traps of women that he had castrated
himself — wants his (male) readers to be well aware of the
dangerous nature of Woman.

A woman is more bitter[35] than "death" (LXX θάνατος),
Koheleth said bitterly; that is, says Gregory, it is "fatal"
(θανατηφόρος, "death-bringing") to become involved with her.
Koheleth vividly pictured the powerful attraction Woman
exercises over Man by means of three closely parallel nouns:
מצודים, "snares", חרמים, "traps", and אסורים, "chains". MT links the
first two nouns together by means of a *darga* accent sign, such
that they are twin depictions of a woman's heart,[36] but LXX took
the first as a depiction of the woman and only the second as a

depiction of her heart, so that is the way in which Gregory paraphrases; the third noun unambiguously refers to the woman's hands in all three versions.

No problems are presented by the Greek treatments of Koheleth's second and third images: LXX translated חרמים as σαγῆναι, "nets" (specifically the large dragnets used in fishing), so Gregory speaks of a woman's heart "ensnaring" (σαγηνεύω) the passerby; and אסורים was translated as δεσμοί, "fetters, chains", which Gregory also uses in his longer paraphrase concerning the way in which a woman's hands hold a man captive. But the first image has not been so smoothly treated: LXX's equivalent of a מצוד was a θήρευμα, and Gregory's paraphrase has γῆ. Θήρευμα sounds more like the object that is caught in a trap, the "prey" or "game", than the instrument that is used to trap that object, but since Koheleth was picturing the woman as the huntress rather than the hunted, we would expect to read θήρατρον, "net, trap" — as the instrument of the chase, this would be a more straightforward equivalent of מצוד — or perhaps θηρέτρια, "huntress" — if the translator wished to make the imagery apply more directly to the woman. Γῆ, however, makes no sense at all in this context, unless we are to assume that Gregory wishes to say that a woman is nothing but a piece of dirt! It would appear that the text has suffered in transmission at this point, the γῆ which appears there being the remnant of a longer, more appropriate paraphrase of θήρευμα. Since σαγήνη appears a little later in LXX's version of the verse, and since Gregory there employs σαγηνεύω in his paraphrase, it may be that the paraphrase originally made use of σαγήνη here in introducing the notion of a woman's effectiveness at entrapment; but perhaps it is more likely that πάγη, "snare, trap" originally stood in the text at this point, since it is easier to imagine a scribe having found illegible or inadvertently dropped merely the beginning of [πα]γην than having done similarly with both the beginning and the end of [σα]γην[ην], and also since we have come to expect Gregory to strive for variety of vocabulary in his paraphrase.[37]

It is perhaps worthy of note that twice within this depiction of womanly wiles Gregory uses the expression ἢ εἰ, literally "or if", an unusual combination of these two particles. In the second instance, where Gregory's meaning would appear to be that the woman's hand in a man's hand holds him as securely "as if" she had bound him in chains, we might expect that this would be expressed by the standard ὡς εἰ (or ὡσεί). In the first instance, as an afterthought to the depiction of the woman as a snare, Gregory adds "or some other such thing" (ἢ εἴ τι ἕτερον τοιοῦτον); here it is the use of εἰ which is surprising, though presumably it is to convey some such sense as "perhaps" or "even". Interestingly, just such a use of ἢ εἰ appears in Gregory's *Panegyric to Origen*, where he speaks of God granting gifts to Origen more than to most people, and then adds "or perhaps more than to anybody of the present time" (ἢ εἰ καὶ παρὰ πάντας ἴσως τοὺς νῦν ἀνθρώπους);[38] here the sense of "perhaps" is already present in ἴσως, but perhaps εἰ is added in order to emphasise the postulatory nature of the assertion. The point to be drawn from the use of this unusual ἢ εἰ combination in the *Panegyric*, which is indisputably the work of Gregory Thaumaturgos, and in the *Paraphrase of Ecclesiastes*, which is of less indisputable authorship,[39] is that it lends support to the view that the same man wrote both works.[40]

There is one man who can escape a woman's clutches, according to Koheleth: the one who is "ἀγαθός (טוב) before God", as opposed to the doomed ἁμαρτάνων (חוטא).   In Kohelethine terms, the former category is the person whom God chooses to bless, for reasons known only to the Deity himself, while the latter category is the person whom God chooses not to bless, for the same inscrutable reasons (see the comments on 2:26). In Gregorian terms, the man who is able to escape (ῥύομαι in the first clause) from the fatal female is the one who "has a gracious and watchful God" (τὸν Θεὸν ἵλεω καὶ ἐπόπτην ἔχω), while the man who is unable to escape (ἐκφεύγω in the second clause) is "the one who is enslaved by sin" (ὁ ἁμαρτίᾳ δεδουλωμένος). It seems that, in the view of the Church Father, "being ensnared" (LXX συλλαμβάνομαι) by a woman is equivalent to "being enslaved" (δουλόομαι) to sin; the (male) reader is thus exhorted to cling to a gracious God rather than to a guileful goddess.

(27) Ζητήσας δ᾽ ἐγὼ διὰ πασῶν γυναικῶν σωφροσύνην αὐτῶν, ...

I searched among all women for self-control on their part,....

In describing his systematic and thorough method of
investigation, Koheleth, the appearance of whose *nom de
plume*[41] here is ignored by Gregory, told his readers that his
modus operandi was μία τῇ μιᾷ (אחת לאחת) — i.e., "[examining]
one [thing in relation] to another", or "[adding] one [thing] to
another" — in order to make an "accounting" of things (MT
חשבון, which LXX rendered as λογισμός, presumably vocalising
the Hebrew word analogously to v. 29 rather than to v. 25, where
ψῆφος was seen as the appropriate Greek word). Gregory
interprets the clause in relation to its context: since Solomon
has just spoken of the nature of Woman, and in the next verses
will present the results of the accounting he has made of her
(and of her male counterpart), this systematic study of "one after
another" here mentioned is to be understood as his search
through the entire race of women (διὰ πασῶν γυναικῶν) — and
who better than Solomon, husband of so large a number of
women, to conduct such a search? — for a particular quality
which a woman ought to possess.

Koheleth did not actually specify what quality he had been
looking for in human beings, but just informed his readers (in v.
28) that only "one man in a thousand" measured up to his
exacting standards, while not even "one woman in that
number" made the grade. Presumably it was wisdom (or, in
more traditional religious terms, righteousness — cf. LXX's
εὐθής, "straight, upright" in v. 29) which Koheleth had in mind,
and so he was pessimistically concluding that a mere 0.1% of the
men in this world are truly wise and hence worthy of respect
and admiration, while an even smaller percentage of women —
if any at all — qualify. Gregory specifies here in v. 27 the
particular quality which he feels Solomon was seeking in people,
a quality which all truly wise/righteous people possess:
σωφροσύνη, "self-control". In the context of the previous verse's
talk of the female ensnaring the male, it is easy to see why
Gregory regards this particular virtue as one to be earnestly

sought. Rather than a woman taking the role of a sexual
huntress, the Church Father doubtlessly is of the view that she
ought to be chaste and modest, restrained and obedient — in a
word, she should exercise σωφροσύνη.

(28) ... εὗρον ἐν οὐδεμιᾷ. Καὶ ἄνδρα μέν τις ἐν χιλίοις γνοίη
ἂν σώφρονα, γυναῖκα δὲ οὔ.

... but I found it in none. You might find one self-
controlled man among a thousand, but not one woman.

Gregory reports Koheleth's finding (concerning the dearth
of worthy men and women) in terms of the virtue he has
already introduced in his paraphrase of the previous verse:
Solomon was looking for people who are σώφρων, "self-
controlled", and he found that, while chaste and temperate men
are extremely rare, chaste and temperate women are practically
non-existent.

Koheleth's opening admission of failure — LXX οὐχ εὗρον,
"I did not find [it]" — may well have been referring to his quest
"to find an accounting" of things (LXX εὑρίσκω λογισμόν at the
end of the preceding verse), but the way in which Gregory has
paraphrased v. 27 means that he must apply this phrase to the
same matter as that to which LXX's closing οὐχ εὗρον of v. 28
refers; thus Gregory's version says εὗρον ἐν οὐδεμιᾷ, "I found
[self-control] in none [of all those women among whom I
searched for it]". What he found, Koheleth told his readers, was
that just one ἄνθρωπος (אדם) in a thousand measured up to his
exacting standards, while not even one γυνή (אשה) in that
number made the grade. Since ἄνθρωπος obviously refers to
that half of the human population which is not to be denoted as
γυνή, Gregory correctly uses the generally more gender-specific
ἀνήρ for that group.

(29) Κατενόησα δὲ ἐκεῖνο μάλιστα, ὅτι ἄνθρωποι ὑπὸ Θεοῦ
ἁπλοῖ ταῖς ψυχαῖς γενόμενοι, ἑαυτοῖς ἐπισπῶνται λογισμοὺς
ποικίλους καὶ ζητήσεις ἀπεράντους, ...

This is what I learned most: that human beings were made
with a simple mind by God, but they busy themselves with

complex reasonings and endless questionings.

Koheleth introduced the results of his investigations by saying that he found "only this" (MT לבד... הז) or "[nothing] but this" (LXX πλὴν... τοῦτο); since he had just presented other results of his investigations, he must have meant by this phrase that this was his most fundamental conclusion in regard to his findings, a notion which Gregory captures by saying that he learned "this most of all" (ἐκεῖνο μάλιστα).

This principal finding relates to ὁ ἄνθρωπος (האדם), whom God made "straight" (LXX εὐθής), but who has sought out "many devices" (LXX λογισμοὶ πολλοί). Gregory understands that ὁ ἄνθρωπος here refers to the entire human race[42] — unlike v. 28, where ἄνθρωπος was juxtaposed with γυνή and accordingly was paraphrased as referring specifically to the ἀνήρ side of the human coin. God made the human mind "simple" (ἁπλόος), says Gregory, but unfortunately human beings have decided to pursue "complex reasonings and endless questionings" (λογισμοὶ ποικίλοι καὶ ζητήσεις ἀπέραντοι).

Chapter Eight

(1) ... καὶ σοφίαν ζητεῖν προσποιούμενοι, περὶ ῥημάτια κατατρίβονται.¹ Σοφία δὲ ἐν ἀνθρώπῳ ἐξεταζομένη, καὶ διὰ προσώπου φαίνεται φωτίζουσα τὸν κεκτημένον· ὥσπερ οὖν ἀναίδεια, μίσους εὐθὺς ὀφθέντα ἄξιον ἐκεῖνον ἐλέγχει, ᾧπερ ἐνῴκησε.

Pretending to seek wisdom, they waste their life in empty words. But when wisdom is found in a person, it is seen by lighting up its possessor's face, just as shamelessness proves at first sight that the person in whom it dwells is worthy of hatred.

Chapter Eight began with two rhetorical questions: "Who is like the wise person? (מי כהחכם) and "Who knows the interpretation of a saying/thing?" (מי יודע פשר דבר). Coming after Koheleth's comments at the end of the previous chapter concerning how infinitesimally few wise people he was able to find in his search, the questions seem to imply that there are virtually no wise people in existence who can fathom the meaning of things. In the case of LXX, we find that the translator or a copyist has felt that the two rhetorical questions read better if the verb of the second question (οἶδα for ידע) is also employed in the first question; thus the Greek reader is asked, "Who knows the wise person?" (τίς οἶδεν σοφούς;) as well as "Who knows the interpretation of a saying/thing?" (τίς οἶδεν λύσιν ῥήματος;). The questions now seem to imply that the one who knows a wise person has an opportunity to learn wisdom.

The paraphrase links this matter very closely with what has just been said: human beings busy themselves with complex reasonings and endless questionings, but in all this are they really wise people, getting to the heart of things? No, Gregory says in answer to the rhetorical questions; their σοφία is merely a pretence (προσποιέομαι, "to pretend, simulate") and their ῥήματα are in reality ῥημάτια ("empty words, rubbish").

Gregory hastens to add, by way of introduction to Koheleth's next proverbial observation, that true σοφία can be found (ἐξετάζομαι) in a certain type of person, and it can easily be seen (φαίνομαι) in such a case. This is because, as Koheleth

noted, wisdom "brightens" (φωτίζω, as in LXX) the face of the
person who possesses it.

Koheleth's final phrase here — עז פניו ישנא — was less clear.
The Masoretes vocalise עז as a noun (with *cholem*) and dia-
criticise the verb as being ישנה with a *shin*, which yields the
meaning, "the strength of his face is changed" (i.e., a hard or
stern facial expression is softened by the possession of wisdom).
LXX, however, read עז as an adjective (with *patach*) and the verb
as being ישנא with a *sin*, and so offered the translation ἀναιδὴς
προσώπῳ αὐτοῦ μισηθήσεται, "a person of shameless countenance will be hated". Accordingly, Gregory's paraphrase employs
μῖσος, "hate", the cognate noun to LXX's verb; he further uses
the noun ἀναίδεια, "shamelessness, impudence", not because of
any critical judgment that LXX erred in reading עז as an adjective, but rather solely for reasons of balance with the noun σοφία
in what is now very clearly an antithetical clause. Koheleth may
well have intended both clauses to be a reference to the visible
effect of wisdom upon the person who possesses it, but his Greek
interpreters seem to be agreed that the two clauses present a
contrast between the wise person and his opposite — both of
these types, says Gregory, can be easily seen for what they are.

(2) Πάνυ δὲ χρὴ ἐπιμελῶς τοῖς τοῦ βασιλέως προσέχειν λόγοις,
ὅρκον δὲ ἐκ παντὸς τρόπου φεύγειν, μάλιστα τὸν εἰς Θεοῦ ὄνομα
γινόμενον.

**A person should certainly be careful to pay attention to the
words of the king and by all means to avoid an oath, especially
one made in God's name.**

Koheleth launched into some sound advice for aspiring
courtiers (and royal subjects in general) with an abrupt and
isolated אני. This may have been his short-hand way of saying "I
would give the following advice" or "my view is as follows", or
it may be a scribal error for את (although if Koheleth were a good
grammarian we would in such a case have expected to see the
definite article on the front of מלך). LXX (similarly Targum and
Peshitta) gave no sign — neither by an ἐγώ nor by a σύν — that
anything of either kind stood at this point in the Hebrew text on

which it is based, which perhaps suggests a later dittography arising from the immediately preceding יצוא. And since LXX takes no account of it, neither does Gregory. The actual advice given was to "watch the king's mouth" (LXX στόμα βασιλέως φύλαξον), which Gregory paraphrases in much better Greek as "to pay attention to the king's words" (τοῖς τοῦ βασιλέως προσέχειν λόγοις).

Gregory takes LXX's φυλάσσω as governing both clauses. This is the same interpretation as that made in the Targum of MT's שמר — in contrast to the consensus among modern commentators and translators who, taking the second clause as offering a supporting rationale for the advice given in the first clause, interpret καὶ περὶ λόγου ὅρκου θεοῦ (ועל דברת שבועת אלהים) as "and [the reason why one should do that is] on account of the oath of God" (which is to say, either that as a courtier/subject of the king one has sworn an oath before God to obey the king's commands, or that God himself has sworn an oath to uphold the divine right of the king to issue commands which courtiers/subjects must obey).[2] But the phrase can equally well be read as "and in regard to the matter of an oath of God", exactly as the Targum translates it,[3] and this is how Gregory interprets it: a person should not only be careful to pay attention to the words of the king, but he should also be careful to avoid swearing an oath in God's name. The advice given here is, in this interpretation, reminiscent of the advice Koheleth gave at the beginning of Chapter Five, where he counselled against the thoughtless making of vows. And Gregory's emphatic language here, χρὴ... δὲ ἐκ παντὸς τρόπου φεύγειν ("one must... by all means flee"), recalls his paraphrase of 5:5, δεῖ δὲ παντοίως φεύγειν. For even further emphasis, he warns his readers that, although any kind of oath is to be strenuously avoided, the kind which must "most of all" (μάλιστα) be avoided is the oath sworn in God's name.

(3) Ἐφίστασθαι δὲ ὅμως προσήκει λόγῳ πονηρῷ· ἀλλὰ φυλάσσεσθαι ἅπασαν τὴν εἰς τὸν Δεσπότην βλασφημίαν.

But although it is proper to give one's attention to an evil word, it is also proper to guard against any blasphemy against the Lord.

Gregory experiences some difficulty with this verse. He appears only to deal with the central thought concerning "an evil word/matter" — and he appears to be in something of a quandary as to how to deal with that, as we shall see presently. Koheleth's opening thought that a person should not leave the king's presence too quickly is not apparent in the paraphrase. Indeed the first words, "do not hasten" (LXX μὴ σπουδάσῃς), had been assigned by LXX to the previous verse, where they have probably contributed to the Church Father's understanding of the latter part of v. 2 as having to do with the same concern as was voiced at the beginning of Chapter Five (cf. LXX's μὴ σπεῦδε in the context of 5:1). If Gregory did read μὴ σπουδάσῃς with the καὶ περὶ λόγου ὅρκου θεοῦ of v. 2 (resulting in the sentence "and in regard to the matter of an oath of God, do not be hasty"),[4] he is left here in v. 3 with the phrase ἀπὸ προσώπου αὐτοῦ πορεύσῃ ("you will go [or: be driven] from his presence"), for which he has been unable to devise a suitable paraphrase. On the other hand it is perhaps possible that a reading of the two phrases as both constituting part of the verse now at hand (yielding, in a somewhat unwieldy way for Greek, the sentence "do not hasten from the king's presence") has contributed to Gregory's understanding of this verse as saying that a person must give his attention to an evil word/matter — the paraphrast's thinking may be: even if the king speaks evil, it is a courtier's duty to listen to him rather than rush away from him.

Koheleth's closing thought that a king can do whatever he wants (LXX πᾶν ὃ ἐὰν θελήσῃ ποιήσει) is similarly not apparent in the paraphrase. Perhaps it is this thought which has contributed to Gregory's idea that a person must give attention to evil things — his thinking may be: even if the king commands evil, he still has absolute power and so his will must be obeyed. On the other hand Gregory may feel that he is treating this matter adequately in his paraphrase of the next verse, where Koheleth's continuation of the thought, through the comment that the king speaks with absolute authority, leads Gregory to speak in effect of the heavenly King's right to do whatever he wants.

As for the central thought of the verse, which Gregory does

treat, we find that he is in two minds: the injunction concerning "an evil word" is interpreted first of all as advising the reader that he will have to have dealings with such evil, and then as counselling him not to become involved in a particular kind of evil word, namely the sin of blasphemy.

Koheleth said clearly enough, "**Do not** stand in an evil word/matter" (LXX μὴ στῇς ἐν λόγῳ πονηρῷ), while Gregory seems to be saying quite the opposite: "**It is proper** to stand in an evil word/matter" (ἐφίστασθαι... προσήκει λόγῳ πονηρῷ). Ἐφίσταμαι might, of course, be intended in the negative sense of "stand against, oppose", in which case Gregory is paraphrasing Koheleth's instructions perfectly; but the context in which the verb is utilised points strongly in the direction of the positive sense, "to stand by [or: near], to give one's attention to". Gregory has just said in the previous verse that "it is proper to give one's attention to the king's words" (χρὴ ἐπιμελῶς τοῖς τοῦ βασιλέως προσέχειν λόγοις), and now he sets up an antithesis between such a propriety and an even more important one: notwithstanding (ὅμως) the necessity of being attentive to such things, even if they are evil, yet (ἀλλά) there is the greater necessity of never blaspheming against God. If Gregory intended that his readers should here be instructed in the dual necessity of opposing evil words/matters and avoiding blasphemy, then we would expect not a ὅμως... ἀλλά but an ἀλλά... καί construction, or one without conjunctions at all (as indeed in the previous verse, where the paraphrase provides just such an "it is proper to do this, and especially this" formulation).

Gregory's second thought concerning this λόγος πονηρός is true to Koheleth's "do **not** stand": "guard against, avoid" (φυλάσσομαι) becoming a party to βλασφημία. As an equivalent to λόγος πονηρός, βλασφημία may be intended here to simply carry its general meaning of "evil talk", and hence in the context of δεσπότης to be referring to the highly dangerous practice of bad-mouthing the king. If this is the intended meaning, then the paraphrase is instructing the would-be courtier that, although a sovereign may say whatever he wants, a subject will be in big trouble if he says whatever he feels — those who are under the king must be able to take it, but must not dish it out!

However, a Christian reader can be expected to understand βλασφημία as a reference to the sin of blasphemy against the heavenly δεσπότης, an interpretation which is strengthened by the paraphrase of the next verse, where "the only Lord and King" (ὁ μόνος δυνάστης καὶ βασιλεύς) clearly refers to the One God and not to any earthly lord and king. (The present edition of Gregory's work places a capital *delta* on Δεσπότης in this verse, to ensure that the reader makes this association, but does not bother to style δυνάστης and βασιλεύς in the same way in v. 4, where there is no possible ambiguity of reference.) But further aspects of this interpretation of Koheleth's βασιλεύς (מלך) as the divine King may be properly raised in the comments to the following verse.

(4) Οὐ γὰρ δὴ ἐπάγοντός τι μέμφεσθαι ὑπάρξει, οὐδὲ ἀντιλέγειν τοῖς τοῦ μόνου δυνάστου καὶ βασιλέως δόγμασι.

For it will not be possible to bring forward any criticism or to dispute the decrees of the only Lord and King.

Koheleth continued his words of wisdom to those who have dealings in the royal court: they must remember that the king's word is law (MT דבר־מלך שלטון, "the king's word has power"; LXX λαλεῖ βασιλεὺς ἐξουσιάζων, "having power, the king speaks")[5] and no subject may question his will with impunity.

The rhetorical question concerning the questioning of the king's will, "Who will say to him, 'What are you doing?'" (LXX τίς ἐρεῖ αὐτῷ Τί ποιήσεις;) — was virtually identical with the rhetorical question of Job 9:12 (LXX τίς ἐρεῖ αὐτῷ Τί ἐποίησας;).[6] On the lips of Job the doings in question are those of God, and it may be for that Gregory interprets the present verse of Ecclesiastes as also referring to the doings of God. If Koheleth was here deliberately mimicking the words of Job, it was presumably to make the point that kings exercise authority in the same absolute fashion as does God — a similar point, perhaps, to the comment in v. 2 linking obedience to kings with an oath to God, given that ancient kings routinely used the state cult to back up their authority. But there can be little doubt that

Koheleth, although he may have been alluding to the heavenly Potentate, was meaning to refer to the earthly potentates with whom his earliest readers, probably for the most part trainees for administrative service, would have to deal. Nevertheless, Koheleth's words provided the opportunity for an interpreter who was not concerned with the training of young men for government careers to speak of the ultimate King who cannot be gainsaid by mere mortals. And such an idea was, after all, not foreign to Koheleth, who commented frequently enough about human powerlessness over against the will of God (e.g., 3:14; 7:13). Accordingly, the βασιλεύς here is nothing less for Gregory than "the only Lord and King" (ὁ μόνος δυνάστης καὶ βασιλεύς), a clear designation of God. To question this King about what he is doing would be a ludicrous thing for a human being to do, and Gregory well pictures the impossibility of mere mortals "censuring" (μέμφομαι) or "disputing" (ἀντιλέγω) — much more colourful words than LXX's tame "saying" (λέγω [i.e., ἐρῶ]) — the will of the Immortal.

So readers of the paraphrase are left in no doubt in this verse that the βασιλεύς who is beyond criticism is God. In the previous verse Gregory left unparaphrased the matter of the king who can do what he pleases, but it is quite likely that he has taken it, in concert with the present verse's contention that the king speaks with authority, as indicating the absolute unquestionability of whatever the heavenly King does. And, as already noted, for his second paraphrase of v. 3's talk of "an evil word" in the context of "the king's presence", Gregory speaks of "blasphemy against the Lord".

All this raises the question of whether in fact the reader of the paraphrase is meant to think of the heavenly King rather than an earthly king throughout this passage. Gregory unambiguously interprets the βασιλεύς of this verse as being God, and he was at least in half a mind that God was the one referred to in v. 3; perhaps the reader is also to take the advice of v. 2 as concerning "the words of the [only Lord and] King" who is here spelled out more fully in v. 4. If Gregory does not intend his readers to think of the λόγοι of an earthly king in v. 2, it is not so easy to understand what he means by the λόγος πονηρός

paralleled to βλασφημία in v. 3 — the Christian paraphrast
would hardly conceive of God speaking evil and blaspheming
against himself — but perhaps he could be taken as saying that a
person might regard certain actions of God as being apparently
evil or unjust, or might receive a "painful word [of judgment]"
from the Almighty, and in such a case it is necessary to guard
against the knee-jerk response of cursing the One who has
decreed as he wills. If this is a correct understanding of the
paraphrase, then that verse is presenting a contrast between the
supposed evil word of the divine Being against the human being
and the actual evil word of the human being against the divine
Being.

A consistent interpretation of βασιλεύς as the Βασιλεύς
(with a capital *beta*) throughout this passage might accordingly
read the Christian paraphrase as teaching:

> A person should certainly be careful to pay attention to the words of the
> [heavenly] King and by all means to avoid an oath, especially one made
> in God's name; it is proper to accept a harsh word [from the Lord] and to
> guard against any blasphemy against the Lord, for it will not be possible
> to bring forward any criticism or to dispute the decrees of the only Lord
> and King.

But if this were Gregory's intended meaning, he might have
expressed it much more clearly. It seems more natural to take
the πονηρός of v. 3 as denoting the kind of evil in which earthly
rulers are routinely involved (cf. 4:1, and Gregory's talk of
"blood-stained rulers" in 12:5) than as denoting the just decrees
of the heavenly Ruler, unless the paraphrast were to include a
rider such as "**supposed** evil" (cf. ἀγαθὸς δοκῶν in 3:8). And the
ὅμως... ἀλλά construction of v. 3 militates against an understanding of that verse as presenting the dual necessity of
receiving an evil word from God and not responding with an
evil word against him — a person cannot accept the Lord's will
and yet nevertheless curse him for it, but rather the avoidance of
impious speech against the Lord goes hand in hand with
acceptance of his will.

So it seems on the balance of probabilities that Gregory at
first in this passage is referring, as was Koheleth, to the earthly
office of rulership, but that the Christian version of Ecclesiastes
soon directs its readers' thoughts above to the ultimate Lord and

King.⁷ Given that the people to whom the paraphrase is directed are much less likely to be involved in courtly affairs than were the original readers of Koheleth's thoughts, this change in reference from mortal kings to the immortal King is a very understandable one.

(5) Βέλτιον δέ, καὶ λυσιτελέστερον ἐμμένοντα ταῖς ἱεραῖς ἐντολαῖς, λόγων τῶν πονηρῶν ἐκτὸς καθεστάναι. Σοφὸς γὰρ ἀνὴρ ἐπίσταται καὶ προγινώσκει τὴν εἰς καιρὸν κρίσιν, ὅτι δικαία ἔσται.

It is better and more useful to keep the holy commandments and to keep apart from the words of wicked people. A wise person knows and understands beforehand that the judgment, which will take place at the right time, will be just.

The "command[ment]" (LXX ἐντολή) to which Koheleth referred in this context was most likely the order of a king, and the "evil word/matter" (LXX ῥῆμα πονηρόν)⁸ experienced by the foolish person who does not obey the king's command would be the royal wrath. But for an interpreter wishing to redirect the advice of this passage to all mortals serving the Immortal, here is a perfect opportunity to speak of "the holy commandments" (αἱ ἱεραὶ ἐντολαί), the keeping of which involves the avoidance of the "words of the evil" (λόγοι τῶν πονηρῶν) in this world. The paraphrase provides another example of the way in which it customarily counter-balances clauses: keeping or standing steadfastly by (ἐμμένω) the holy words of God is matched by keeping away from or standing against (ἐκτὸς καθίστημι) the wicked words of human beings.

Koheleth then spoke of לב חכם — in the absence of an article on חכם, this looks like "a wise heart", but LXX nevertheless read it as "the heart of the wise" (καρδία σοφοῦ);⁹ Gregory dispenses with the unnecessary imagery of the καρδία, simply picturing "a wise person" (σοφὸς ἀνήρ). The wisdom concerns עת ומשפט — in the presence of a conjunction on משפט,¹⁰ this looks like "a time and a judgment", but LXX nevertheless read it as "the time of judgment" (καιρὸς κρίσεως);¹¹ Gregory terms it "the timely judgment" (ἡ εἰς καιρὸν κρίσις).

The original observation here on the part of the Wisdom

teacher would appear to have been that those who are skilled in
wisdom know when the correct or most opportune time at
which to act arrives, and are able to make the best decision about
how to act at that time. But for Gregory, what is in view here is
the wise example of the person of faith, who lives his life in the
awareness that there will surely come a time of judgment — and
he is concerned to add that the forthcoming judgment is a just
one (δίκαιος). It is at the time of judgment, he hints, that
keeping the holy commandments will be seen to be a highly
useful or profitable (λυσιτελής) policy to have pursued during
one's life.[12]

Simply "knowing" (LXX γιγνώσκω) that there will be a time
of judgment is too weak an expression to satisfy the Christian
paraphrast; a wise person both "knows/understands" (ἐπίσταμαι) and "knows/understands beforehand" (προγιγνώσκω)
what will certainly take place.

(6) Πάντα γὰρ τὰ ἐν τῷ βίῳ τῶν ἀνθρώπων πράγματα
περιμένει τὴν ἄνωθεν κόλασιν· πλὴν ὅ γε πονηρός, οὐ λίαν
γινώσκειν ἔοικεν, ὅτι πολλῆς ἐπ' αὐτῷ οὔσης προνοίας, οὐδὲν
ὁτιοῦν εἰς τὸ μετέπειτα λήσεται.

All things in the life of human beings await punishment
from above; but the wicked person does not seem to really
understand that since a mighty providence is over him, nothing
at all will be hidden in the time to come.

LXX had not seen a conjunction in Koheleth's עת ומשפט in
the previous verse, but on its second appearance now in the
present verse the Greek translation attested its presence: "a time
and a judgment" (LXX καιρὸς καὶ κρίσις).[13] Gregory acts as
though there is no discrepancy, in the form of this expression,
between the two verses — as indeed there is not in MT — by
speaking of the "punishment" (κόλασις, as a variation on LXX's
κρίσις which he copied in v. 5) which is coming at some future
time (εἰς τὸ μετέπειτα). "Awaiting punishment from above"
(περιμένω τὴν ἄνωθεν κόλασιν) is a notion of some importance to
the Church Father, for he will repeat the expression in 12:5,
where the text before him is silent concerning any κρίσις. The

text before him here in 8:6 does not specify any precise kind of
"thing" (LXX πρᾶγμα) which has a correct time and procedure,
but Gregory leaves his readers in no doubt that it is the
πράγματα which ἄνθρωποι do in their lives which will attract
the attention of the Judge.

In support (indicated by LXX's ὅτι) of the foregoing
contention, Koheleth mentioned a great רעה among human
beings. This might be interpreted either as the wickedness of
human beings (hence the Targum's חובת אינשין עבדי בישא, "the sin/
guilt of evildoers") or as the dreadfulness of the situation in
which they find themselves (hence Symmachus' κάκωσις τοῦ
ἀνθρώπου, "the suffering of human beings"), the latter interpretation being in agreement with the use of רעה רבה in 2:21. But
here in 8:6 LXX (and Theodotion) read דעת, and so spoke of the
great γνῶσις which a human being has. This reads as though a
person has considerable "knowledge" to bring to bear upon the
matter of correct times and procedures, although it might be
interpreted more in keeping with Koheleth's mood as indicating
human awareness of the complexity and impossibility of the
situation (taking πολύς... ἐπ᾽ αὐτόν literally as "great... upon/
against him", and interpreting in connection with the sentiment
concerning the increase of knowledge expressed in 1:18).

LXX's reference to human knowledge (γνῶσις τοῦ
ἀνθρώπου) does not make sense to Gregory in this context,
particularly in view of the following verse and if πολύς... ἐπ᾽
αὐτόν is indeed read literally. Instead the Christian interpreter
speaks of divine knowledge (πρόνοια) which is πολὺς ἐπ᾽ αὐτῷ
— and so πολύς that absolutely nothing (οὐδὲν ὁτιοῦν) can "be
unknown" (λανθάνω) to it. Far from approving LXX's talk of
human knowledge, the paraphrase actually specifically contrasts
its own talk of divine knowledge with human ignorance or lack
of understanding (οὐ γιγνώσκω), at least on the part of wicked
people; presumably the pious are well aware that there is a
forthcoming time of judgment, but neither that awareness nor
God's awareness of their piety could be regarded as being
disadvantageous to them (if ἐπί is taken in the above-mentioned
sense).

It is tempting to suppose that Gregory's reference to ὁ

πονηρός has arisen from Koheleth's רעה (cf. the Targumic para-phrase אינשין עבדי בישא) and represents an attempt to make sense of both the MT and LXX readings, but the reference could quite plausibly have arisen simply as the paraphrast's device for making a smooth transition between the preceding verse, where he has spoken of the wise person's knowledge of the judgment that is to come, and the following verse, where he will speak of general human ignorance concerning what is to come.

(7) Οὐ γὰρ οἶδε τὰ ἐπιόντα· οὐδὲν γὰρ αὐτῶν κατ' ἀξίαν τις ἀναγγείλαι δυνήσεται·

He does not know what things are in store for him, since no-one will be able to adequately report on them.

This is a relatively straightforward paraphrase of Koheleth's sentiments, but with a subtle shift following on from the paraphrase of the previous verse. Koheleth appears to have been referring to the ignorance of Everyman concerning the future, but Gregory is referring to the ignorance of the wicked person concerning the forthcoming punishment from above. Although the context itself points the reader of Gregory's version to that understanding, the paraphrast's choice of the more colourful ἐφίημι ("to send upon or against"), to replace his predecessor's simple εἰμί, gives a further indication that divine retribution is to be thought of here.

This is of course not the first time that the Christian inter-preter has limited the scope of Koheleth's observations to refer only to the ungodly (cf., e.g., comments under 2:17), and it will not be the last time that he implies that significant ignorance only afflicts wicked people (cf. 8:17 and 11:5). He concedes that no-one is able to "adequately report" (κατ' ἀξίαν ἀναγγέλλω) on what will be, echoing Koheleth's rhetorical question, but in Gregory's version it suggests nothing more than the inability of the pious to convince the impious that bad things are in store for them if they persist in their impiety; the implication is still there that the wise person is not ignorant concerning the events that are to come, and indeed Gregory's Solomon will provide some details on those events in the concluding chapter.

(8) ὅτι οὐχ οὕτως τις ἰσχυρὸς ὑπάρξει, ὡς τὸν ἀφαιρούμενον τὴν ψυχὴν αὐτοῦ ἄγγελον κωλῦσαι δύνασθαι, οὐδέ τις ὅλως μέθοδος εὑρεθείη ἂν τοῦ παραγράψασθαί πως τὸν καιρὸν τῆς τελευτῆς· ἀλλ' ὥσπερ ἐν πολέμῳ μέσῳ ληφθέντα, ἄφυκτα παντα- χόθεν ἔστιν ὁρᾶν, ἀσέβεια δὲ πᾶσα ἀνθρώπου συνεξόλλυται.

No-one will be strong enough to be able to hold back the angel who takes away his soul, and no method whatsoever will be discovered to cancel in any way the time of the end. Just as, when someone is captured in the middle of a battle, there is no escape to be seen on any side, so all human ungodliness is completely destroyed together.

The first example which Koheleth here presented of human powerlessness was the inability to "hold back" or "restrain" (LXX κωλύω) the πνεῦμα. If πνεῦμα (רוח) is interpreted here as denoting "wind" (as it evidently does in 1:6), then the matter under discussion is the impossibility of preventing the wind from blowing; if it is interpreted as denoting the "breath of life" (as it evidently does in 3:21 and 12:7), then the matter under discussion is the impossibility of putting off one's death, in parallel to the very next phrase which clearly talks of human powerlessness over the day of death.[14] Gregory makes the latter interpretation, expressing the idea by means of the word ψυχή (which is also his choice in 3:21 and 12:7 — on only one other occasion does he prefer this to LXX's πνεῦμα, viz. 2:26).

But the Christian paraphrase does not speak simply of an inability to hold back one's ψυχή, but of an inability to hold back ὁ ἀφαιρούμενος τὴν ψυχὴν αὐτοῦ ἄγγελος, "the angel who takes away one's ψυχή". In view of the close affinity in the paraphrase between 3:21 and 12:7, both of which are fashioned by Gregory as having to do with the human ψυχή "flying up" (ἀναπέτομαι), it might have been expected that he would be satisfied with such a notion here, rather than introducing the concept of the Angel of Death. But using the same formulation three times would not be in accordance with his policy of variation, and there is the further consideration that in those other two verses Gregory's idea of the soul's ascent is a rather positive thought, either in contrast to the alleged non-possession of an eternal soul on the part of animals (3:21) or in contrast to the alleged non-attainment of salvation on the part of ungodly people (12:7), whereas in the verse now at hand the paraphrast has in mind the death of precisely that kind of person, as the ἀσέβεια towards the end of the verse makes clear.

So the concept of the Angel of Death at this point deliberately sounds a more ominous note than is present in the other two verses which Gregory styles as having to do with the ψυχή's fate at death. But it also neatly takes account of Koheleth's repetition of πνεῦμα without being repetitious.

Gregory appears to have decided that two different kinds of πνεῦμα are here being referred to: the human ψυχή, and the superhuman ἄγγελος to whom power over the former kind of spiritual essence has been assigned. It may be that the Church Father was aware of the rabbinical midrash concerning this verse which speaks, in the light of Psalm 104:4's paralleling of רוח with מלאך (in LXX, Psalm 103:4's paralleling of πνεῦμα with ἄγγελος), of human powerlessness over against the Angel of Death (מלאך המות, Koheleth Rabbah 8:8).

Death itself (LXX θάνατος) was then itemised by Koheleth as the second thing over which human beings can exercise no power. Gregory prefers to speak ambiguously of the τελευτή, which might mean the "end" of an individual person's life when his time has come, or that great and terrible "end" of all things to which the paraphrast looks forward (cf. the same ambiguity with τέλος in 2:16 and 3:16). Retention of LXX's ἡμέρα, instead of its replacement by καιρός, might have been an appropriate hint to the readers if they are to think eschatological thoughts at this point, given the standard prophetic expression ἡμέρα κυρίου to which the paraphrase alludes in 12:1 (and possibly also in 11:2), but Gregory provides a different hint in the latter part of the verse that it is indeed a collective τελευτή rather than an individual one which he has in mind: he pictures all human ungodliness "being completely destroyed together [or: at the same time]" (συνεξόλλυμαι).

Koheleth's third example of powerlessness was drawn from the all too familiar human scene of war: there is no "leave" (LXX ἀποστολή) at the time of battle (LXX's formulation ἐν ἡμέρα πολέμου is probably a harmonisation with the preceding ἐν ἡμέρᾳ τοῦ θανάτου [ביום המות] rather than a genuine reading of ביום מלחמה where MT has simply מלחמה).[15] "Leave" might mean any way in which one is permitted to avoid a battle, such as a discharge before the battle commences or being sent on a safe non-combatant mission elsewhere while the battle rages (cf. the meanings of the verb ἀποστέλλω, and of שלח, the root of MT's משלחת).

Gregory well paraphrases the idea by contending that there is absolutely "no escape" (ἄφυκτος) from the scene of battle (although the possibility of being killed or wounded would be just as relevant in this context as the situation which he specifies, viz. being captured).[16]

As his final observation on powerlessness in this verse, Koheleth noted that there is no ultimately worthwhile or lasting power to be gained through "wickedness" (רשע; LXX says ἀσέβεια, "ungodliness"): the person who possesses it (LXX ὁ παρ' αὐτῆς) should not think that it can "save" (LXX διασώζω) him. For Koheleth, this doubtlessly meant that even becoming very skilful ("a master", so to speak: בעל) at evil-doing is not going to guarantee a person success in life or avoidance of death. For a pious interpreter, however, it just as surely means that evildoers will not be saved at "the time of the end" (ὁ καιρὸς τῆς τελευτῆς, as Gregory calls it earlier in the verse). Just as there is emphatically no escape for a person captured in battle, says the Christian version of Ecclesiastes, so (when the cosmic battle comes to its predestined conclusion) there will be a complete annihilation of all that is ungodly.

(9) Καὶ ἐκπέπληγμαι δέ, ὁπότ' ἂν ἀπίδω οἷα καὶ ὅσα εἰς βλάβην τῶν πέλας ἄνθρωποι ἐπιτετηδεύκασιν.

I am amazed, whenever I look at the manner and magnitude of things that human beings have practised to their neighbours' harm.

Gregory's talk of amazement or astonishment (ἐκπλήσσω) at what goes on in the world perhaps betrays a more pious outlook than Koheleth's seemingly resigned and detached talk of simply observing (LXX ὁράω) the ways of human beings, but he does re-employ his frequent expression "I applied my heart" (LXX ἔδωκα τὴν καρδίαν μου, cf. 1:13, etc.), which the paraphrase covers by ἀπίδω (ἀφοράω, "to look at, have in view"). His even more frequent expression "under the sun" (LXX ὑπὸ τὸν ἥλιον) is ignored by Gregory, who no doubt feels that the mention of ἄνθρωποι is a sufficient indicator of what is in view.

MT's reference to a particular time (עת) appears to have been transformed in LXX to a reference to a great number of times (ὅσος, "how many"). Perhaps LXX read את at this point,[17] in which case the rendering ὅσος makes a refreshing change from LXX Ecclesiastes' mechanical and frequently nonsensical σύν,[18] but if that is the case then it is only a momentary lapse into good Greek, for immediately afterwards we find another instance of LXX Ecclesiastes' mechanical — though on this occasion not exactly nonsensical[19] — rendering of ἐν for *beth*. Gregory is happy enough with ὅσος, which he pairs with οἷος ("what kind") to round out the paraphrase a little, but he prefers an expression with εἰς to one with ἐν in this context.

Εἰς βλάβην, "to [one's neighbour's] harm" is an excellent equivalent of what Koheleth expressed by means of לרע. The early versions appear to have read לרע as an infinitive verbal form, in that they translate by means of a verb meaning "to harm, afflict" (LXX κακόω, Peshitta ܠܒܐܫ aphel, Targum באש haphel), but since Gregory's work is a paraphrase we would be unwarranted in drawing the conclusion that his expression here supports the Masoretic reading against the other versions — which may in any case also be paraphrasing the Hebrew at this point.

There was in MT a possible ambiguity in the final לו: does this refer to the first אדם who exercises the power, or to the second אדם over whom the power is exercised? In view of the preceding verse, it is not impossible that Koheleth was thinking of some harm that the protagonist might bring upon himself through his wickedness (cf. Rashi's interpretation), but in view of such passages as 4:1, it is most likely that he has in mind the harm which is inevitably suffered by the oppressed rather than any harm which may or may not be suffered by the oppressor. The early versions, in employing an active or causative verbal form here, move in the direction of this latter interpretation (though Symmachus' version, with its ἑαυτοῦ for לו, moves in the opposite direction). Gregory leaves no room at all for ambiguity in his rendering: the damage is certainly done to the "neighbour" (πέλας) of the ἄνθρωπος in question and not to that ἄνθρωπος himself — but the Church Father will move quickly in the following verses to make it clear that there **are** dire consequences in store for the kind of person who pursues wicked practices to the harm of his fellow human beings.

(10) Ἐπίσταμαι δὲ προαναρπαζομένους ἐνθένδε τοὺς ἀσεβεῖς καὶ γινομένους ἐκ ποδῶν, ἀνθ᾽ ὧν ἑαυτοὺς ματαιότητι δεδώκεσαν.

But I know that ungodly people are snatched prematurely from this life and are put out of the way, because they have given themselves over to futility.

This verse presents several difficulties for an interpreter.

Koheleth undoubtedly began by talking about wicked people (MT רשעים, LXX ἀσεβεῖς), but was he still talking about such people towards the end of the verse? Symmachus understood אשר כן־עשו as "those who do right", τὰ δίκαια,[20] but LXX understood it as "that they [i.e., the afore-mentioned wicked people] had done thus", ὅτι οὕτως ἐποίησαν. Gregory's version runs ἀνθ᾽ ὧν ἑαυτοὺς... δεδώκεσαν, "because they have devoted themselves [to such wickedness]".

It is a sad thing when a good person is not remembered (cf. 9:15), but if it is indeed wicked people who are still in view at this point, how is it an example of ματαιότης for such people to "be forgotten" (שׁכח hithpael)? LXX saw the ματαιότης as lying in the fact that such people "are praised" (ἐπαινέομαι, reading — or emending to — שׁבח hithpael) when their wickedness ought to bring them condemnation. Gregory does not follow LXX in depicting any praise being given to the wicked; it may even be that his talk of such people being got "out of the way" (ἐκ ποδῶν) owes something to the non-LXX reading of שׁבח, although this paraphrastic expression looks like it is intended as Gregory's version of LXX's expression "out of the holy place" (ἐκ τόπου ἁγίου).

This "holy place" (MT מקום קדוש) is a further problem for interpreters. Is it a place of religious burial (a cemetery, where the wicked ought not to receive burial), or a place of religious services (the temple or a synagogue, where prayers are said for the righteous dead), or the holy city (Jerusalem, if Koheleth has a specific "city" [LXX πόλις] in mind)?[21] Gregory prefers to be quite unspecific and to make no mention of any "holy place" out of which the wicked come — they simply come ἐκ ποδῶν, as mentioned above. And similarly, the Christian paraphrase speaks somewhat vaguely of these people going "from here" (ἐνθένδε), which as a paraphrase of going "into the tombs" (LXX εἰς τάφους — MT has קברים, "being buried") is presumably meant to refer to a departing from this life, though a reader of Gregory's version alone might take this to mean that wicked people will be arrested before they can do too much of their planned mischief (προαναρπάζομαι, "to carry off beforehand" can carry such a meaning) and locked away in a prison by the authorities.

Gregory's rendering of this verse leaves him with the problem of having a situation which a pious interpreter would regard as just — ungodly people getting what they deserve — described as an example of ματαιότης. He overcomes this problem by placing the ματαιότης judgment not upon the situation that is described here but upon the activities to which these ungodly people have devoted themselves: they have given themselves over to futility, and so they receive their just recompense. This is some distance from what may well have been intended in the original version of Ecclesiastes to be a complaint that the wicked receive what they do not deserve — a proper burial with full religious honours and praise for what they have done!

(11) Ἐπειδὴ γὰρ οὐκ ἐφ' ἁπάντων μετέρχεται ἡ τοῦ Θεοῦ πρόνοια ὀξέως διὰ τὴν πολλὴν ἀνεξικακίαν, οὐδὲ παραυτίκα τιμωρεῖται ἐπὶ ταῖς πλημμελείαις, τούτου χάριν οἴεται δεῖν ὁ πονηρὸς ἀνὴρ ἁμαρτάνειν ἐπὶ πλεῖον, ὡς ἀθῶος ἀπαλλάξων·

Since divine providence does not attend to everyone swiftly, because of God's great patience with evil, and a person is not punished immediately over the committing of offences, for

this reason the wicked person thinks that he should sin even more, as if he will get off scot-free.

Koheleth now pointed to the basic problem in the traditional idea of a swift retribution for one's deeds: retribution simply does **not** come swiftly. In making this point, he employed the Persian loan-word פתגם, "decree" — in this context doubtlessly meaning a decision or judgment made and executed upon the perpetrator of a deed. The Targumist brings this meaning out clearly by expanding the expression to read "a decree of retribution/punishment" (פתגם פורענות);[22] the meaning is also well understood by the Syriac translator (ܕ‍ܝ‍ܢ‍ܐ, "judgment, punishment") and by Symmachus (ἀπόφασις, "decision, judgment"), but LXX got פתגם a little wrong, offering ἀντίρρησις, "controversy, counter-statement" as its translation.

Gregory is not misled by LXX. Disputation was not what Koheleth was talking about here, but punishment for evil, and so Gregory speaks clearly of "being punished" (τιμωρέομαι)[23] — in his second re-expressing of Koheleth's words, for at first he is less clear when he speaks of πρόνοια. If πρόνοια is meant to be taken as meaning God's providential care for those who are wronged, then Gregory could be attempting to extract some meaning from LXX's ἀντίρρησις, picturing God as the advocate of those who are falsely accused; Gregory has spoken of the συκοφαντία which some people have to endure (see 4:1), but he has also expressed his faith that God is a βοηθός for people who are treated unjustly (3:15), so it may be that here in 8:11 he is noting that God does not immediately intervene as the divine ἀντιρρήτωρ on behalf of those who are falsely accused, but allows evil to take its course for the time being. Alternatively, Gregory may well mean by πρόνοια God's all-knowing judgment upon those who do wrong, which is after all the way in which he used this same word in v. 6, and if this is his meaning again in v. 11, then the first of his two formulations here — like his second, with τιμωρέομαι — is quite independent of LXX's ἀντίρρησις.

But whatever it is precisely that Gregory has in mind with πρόνοια, there is no doubt that the agent he sees here is none other than ὁ Θεός. Although Koheleth was very likely thinking of a divine decree upon evildoing, he did not specify this, and so it is possible to interpret him as referring to human authorities who do not dispense prompt justice but are actually on the side of the evildoers (cf. 4:1); Gregory, however, names God as the ultimate purveyor of justice.

Having clearly identified God as the subject at this point, Gregory is confronted by the significant question, "Why does God not act swiftly to punish the wicked?" Koheleth could offer no explanation for this phenomenon — it was for him one of the most telling examples of the utter inscrutability of what God does in the world. But his Christian interpreter has an explanation, and he is quick to supply it for his readers: characteristic of God is his great ἀνεξικακία, "patience with evil, forbearance" (2 Peter 3:9 may be in the Church Father's mind).[24]

Gregory is in agreement with Koheleth on the result of this disjunction between the committing and punishing of evil — people are thereby encouraged to continue and even increase their evildoing — and, lest any of his readers entertain such an idea, he already in this same sentence introduces the subject-matter of the following two verses: people should not think that there are no consequences of evildoing.

(12) οὐ συνιείς, ὅτι καὶ μετὰ πάμπολυν χρόνον ἀδικήσας οὐ λήσεται· ἀγαθόν γε μὴν μέγιστον, εὐλαβεῖσθαι Θεόν·

He does not understand that even after a very long time an evildoer will not go undetected. Truly the greatest good is to reverence God.

Koheleth appears to have retained some regard for the traditional view that evildoing has its consequences, for he here put forward the thought that it is better to live a righteous life. This is the kind of verse that is close to a Church Father's heart, and Gregory paraphrases with glee: it is not simply that "it will be well" (LXX ἔσται ἀγαθόν) for the one who fears God, but fearing God is the veritable "greatest good" (ἀγαθὸν μέγιστον) that human beings can pursue. In phrasing the matter in this way, Gregory makes a deliberate link with v. 15, where he also speaks of "the greatest good" (τὸ μέγιστον τῶν ἀγαθῶν); it is in that latter verse that Koheleth expressed what he believed to be the only "good" for human beings — namely eating, drinking, and finding enjoyment in life — but in Gregory's view that belief is one which has been abandoned by a now wiser Solomon in favour of a God-fearing lifestyle. The Christian paraphrase fences v. 15 in with clear signposts of past wrong thinking (ἔδοξα at the front and ἡγησάμην at the back), while the thinking of v. 12 is given a small but sure sign of positive affirmation (μήν).

Koheleth spoke of a wicked person "doing evil a hundred-fold" (עשׂה רע מאת). LXX appears to have read or emended to מעת, and so spoke of a sinner "doing evil from that time" (ἐποίησεν τὸ πονηρὸν ἀπὸ τότε), though the reader might well wonder what τότε is being referred to — perhaps it was the time when the evildoer first realised that he would not immediately be struck down by God when he committed evil, so that he has continued in his wickedness ever since then. (The other Greek translations of the Hexapla — Aquila, Symmachus, and Theodotion — appear to have read or emended to מת or מית, and so speak of the sinner "dying" or "being put to death" [ἀπέθανεν], a line of interpretation which might be expected to appeal to a pious interpreter, but which is nevertheless not followed by Gregory; meanwhile Peshitta and Targum support the MT reading.) Having read the mem on מאת as the preposition מן, LXX did the same with מאריך לו, "lengthening him" — which is to say that the wicked person experiences a long life — translating this as ἀπὸ μακρότητος αὐτῷ, "from a long time before that" — which perhaps is to say that evildoers begin their wickedness at an early age, before they even reason that evil is not punished swiftly.

Gregory does not attempt to make precise sense out of LXX's ἀπὸ τότε and ἀπὸ μακρότητος αὐτῷ — the point is that a sinner may commit evil for "a very long time" (πάμπολυς χρόνος), while the important thing is not what happened beforehand but what is going to happen afterwards (μετά). And in this regard the significant matter for the Christian interpreter is not what "I know/understand" (LXX γιγνώσκω ἐγώ) — that the Godfearer fares well — but what "he [the sinner] does **not** know/ understand" (οὐ συνιείς) — that the evildoer comes undone in the long run. Koheleth repeated himself on the question of "fearing" God (LXX φοβέομαι twice), but Gregory is satisfied with a simple "being reverent" (εὐλαβέομαι).

(13) οὗπερ ἀσεβὴς ἐκπεσών, οὐ πολὺν χρόνον τῇ ἑαυτοῦ
μωρίᾳ καταχρήσεται.

**When an ungodly person falls away from that, he will not
have a free rein with his own foolishness for a long time.**

The reader of Ecclesiastes is now presented with the contrast
(to the Godfearer faring well) of the wicked person not faring
well — without apparent concern, on the part of either Koheleth
or Gregory, for the contradiction between the words of the previous verse, where it was said that a sinner may have a long life,
and the words of the present verse, where it is said that a sinner
will not have a long life. Koheleth's לֹא־יַאֲרִיךְ יָמִים (which LXX
correctly understands as οὐ μακρυνεῖ ἡμέρας, "he will not
lengthen [his] days") runs counter to his מַאֲרִיךְ לוֹ (which LXX had
mistakenly rendered as ἀπὸ μακρότητος αὐτῷ) in v. 12, as does
Gregory's οὐ πολὺς χρόνος to his earlier πάμπολυς χρόνος.
God's judgment may not come quickly (v. 11), but it seems that
— at least to the eye of faith — it does not come slowly, either.

"The one who is not a Godfearer" (LXX ὃς οὐκ ἔστιν
φοβούμενος ἀπὸ προσώπου τοῦ θεοῦ) is pictured by Gregory as
one "having fallen away" (ἐκπεσών). Since he has just
mentioned reverencing God, and this phrase in his version
follows on immediately from that reference to reverence,
Gregory sees no need to repeat the notion as such, despite
Koheleth's persistence in using the same phrase now for the
third time in as many lines. He does, however, feel that it is
appropriate to provide an antithesis to the fear of God, and that
is nothing other than sheer μωρία, "foolishness".

A fleeting life being compared to a shadow (MT כַּצֵּל, read by
LXX as בַּצֵּל and hence translated ἐν σκιᾷ) is a familiar biblical
image, but again — as in 6:12 — Gregory has no place for it in his
paraphrase.

(14) Χειρίστη δὲ καὶ ἐψευσμένη δόξα ἀνθρώπους ἐπινέμεται
πολλάκις, περί τε δικαίων καὶ ἀδίκων. Ὑπολαμβάνουσι γὰρ περὶ
ἑκατέρων τἀναντία· καὶ δίκαιός γε τὶς ὤν, οὐ τοιοῦτος ἔδοξε· καὶ

πάλιν ἀσεβής, ἔμφρων ἐνομίσθη. Ταύτην ἔγωγε τὴν πλάνην χαλεπὴν ἐν τοῖς μάλιστα τίθεμαι.

But a most base and false opinion is often spread among human beings regarding the righteous and the unrighteous. They form quite the reverse idea concerning these two: someone who is righteous is thought to be not so, while in turn an ungodly person is considered sensible. I regard this as an extremely serious error.

An occasional tendency on Gregory's part to interpret LXX's ματαιότης as denoting some kind of falsehood has already been seen (2:15; 4:16; 6:11). Now in 8:14 this line of interpretation is developed more fully. Koheleth both began and ended this verse with a declaration that what he was here describing is an example of ματαιότης (הבל), and in so doing left his readers in no doubt that the absence of just retribution in the world was keenly felt by him to be one of the most significant indicators of the futility of human life. Gregory begins and ends the verse with a declaration that what is here described is one of the worst possible falsehoods (ψεύδομαι, "to be false" is used in the opening phrase and πλάνη, "error" in the closing phrase) that are entertained by human beings, and in so doing leaves his readers in no doubt that only the "basest" (χείριστος) of people — and not the great Solomon, author of Ecclesiastes — would form the described opinion.

However, Koheleth and Gregory do not seem to be describing exactly the same opinion. Koheleth's opinion was that so often in this world what "happens" (LXX φθάνω, "overtakes") to the one type of person is "in accordance with the deed" (LXX ὡς ποίημα) of precisely the opposite type of person — a righteous person suffers or dies young, which is what ought to happen to an unrighteous person, while the latter enjoys what ought to be the lot of the former, namely good fortune and a long life. But Gregory depicts an opinion which he sees as being all too prevalent in this world: what "is thought" (δοκέω for the first phrase and νομίζω for the second, since Gregory does not wish to be as repetitious in his phraseology as Koheleth) concerning the one type of person is in accordance with the reality of precisely the opposite type of person — a righteous person is not regarded as such, while an unrighteous person is esteemed in the way in which the former ought to be esteemed. The sage of Jerusalem was accusing God of treating people unjustly, but the bishop of Neocaesarea is accusing people of appraising their fellows falsely.

"On the earth" (LXX ἐπὶ τῆς γῆς) is a variation on the more frequent "under the sun" (LXX ὑπὸ τὸν ἥλιον), which will appear again in the very next verse. As he is wont to do, Gregory substitutes a reference to ἄνθρωποι, indicating that what is in focus is the realm of human activity; nothing is said here, in his view, of divine activity. If there is a matter here which the Church Father can describe as "grievous in the extreme" (χαλεπὸς ἐν τοῖς μάλιστα), it is not that God fails to reward the good and punish the evil — which **was** extremely grievous to Koheleth — but that people fail to see the truth about righteousness and unrighteousness.

(15) Ἔδοξα δέ ποτε τὸ μέγιστον τῶν ἀγαθῶν βρῶσιν εἶναι καὶ πόσιν· κἀκεῖνον θεοφιλέστατον, ὃς ἂν τούτων ἀπολαύῃ παρὰ τὸν²⁵ βίον, ὡς οἷόν τε μάλιστα· καὶ παραμυθίαν τῆς ζωῆς, τὴν τοιαύτην εὐθυμίαν μόνην ἡγησάμην·

I once imagined eating and drinking to be the greatest good, and that the person most highly favoured by God was the one who could enjoy these things to the utmost throughout his life. Such cheerfulness was the only consolation in life, I thought.

The final occurrence of Koheleth's expression οὐκ ἔστιν ἀγαθὸν... εἰ μή (אֵין־טוֹב... כִּי אִם) is handled by Gregory in ways he has already practised: as he did in 2:24, he employs the neat pair of βρῶσις and πόσις for "eating" and "drinking" (LXX ἐσθίω and πίνω); as he did in 3:12, he speaks of "the greatest good" for human beings (here he phrases it τὸ μέγιστον τῶν ἀγαθῶν as a slight variation on the τὰ μέγιστα ἀγαθά of 3:12 — and the ἀγαθὸν μέγιστον he has worked in to 8:12); and as he did in 3:22, he prefaces his paraphrase of Koheleth's expression with the verb δοκέω in a past tense. Now, as if to bid good riddance to this un-Christian sentiment on its final appearance (although the same notion is yet to be put forward by Koheleth once more in 9:7 without the οὐκ ἔστιν ἀγαθόν [אין טוב] formulation), Gregory adds at the end of the verse the verb ἡγέομαι in a past tense. With these two signs fore and aft, plus the clear temporal marker ποτέ, "once", the reader is left in no doubt that what is here expressed is an example of the past wrong thinking of a now much wiser Solomon.

It is no surprise that the Church Father does not give approval to the advice contained in this verse, even though Koheleth himself "commends" it (LXX ἐπαινέω), since it sounds like an "eat, drink, and be merry" philosophy. But Gregory might also see in the aorist tense of ἐπήνεσα some textual support for his interpretation of this verse as having to do with a no longer current commendation of such a philosophy.

Characteristically, Koheleth underpinned his conclusion concerning the simple pleasures of life with a note to the effect that ὁ θεός (האלהים), as the One who has set up this sub-solar system, is in favour of the enjoyment that people can gain from eating and drinking. But for Gregory the idea that people are θεοφιλής ("highly favoured by God") in the highest degree when they are enjoying these pleasures to the greatest extent is not to be countenanced.

Koheleth, for that matter, did not approve of unrestrained pleasures. But in the simple enjoyment of life it seems that the creator of Ecclesiastes had found the only answer to that overwhelming הבל or ματαιότης of which he was so aware, and so he exclaimed: αὐτὸ συμπροσέσται αὐτῷ (הוא ילונו), "this will go with him", this is the thing that can sustain a person through his life of toil under the sun! His paraphrast captures this moving sentiment very well indeed by speaking of the only παραμυθία ("consolation, abatement, relief") that there is in life — but then comes the sharp ἡγησάμην, "I thought!" The point at which Koheleth arrived after his long journey to discover wisdom has become the point from which Solomon departed on that journey.

(16) καὶ τοίνυν προσεῖχον οὐδενὶ ἐτέρῳ, ἢ τῇ οἰήσει ταύτῃ, ὡς μήτε νύκτωρ μήτε μεθημέραν ἀπάντων, ὅσα πρὸς τρυφὴν ἀνθρώποις εὕρηται, ἐμαυτὸν ἀπάγειν.

Accordingly, I devoted myself to nothing other than this notion, so that neither by night nor by day did I withdraw myself from all the things which have been devised for human indulgence.

Whenever LXX had mentioned a "distraction" (περισπασμός), Gregory has always understood this to be a reference to the distress and anxiety which people suffer in life (see 1:13 and parallels), but on this occasion — following on as it does from the advice to "eat, drink, and be merry" of the previous verse — it suits Gregory's purposes to refer to human "indulgence" (τρυφή) in food, drink, and merriment. The verse actually reads very much as a parallel of 2:23, where Koheleth spoke of the troubles which assail a person day and night, so that he has no rest, and at that point Gregory paraphrased accordingly. But perhaps here in 8:16 he reasoned that it was not appropriate to talk about an inability to experience "sleep" (LXX ὕπνος, a reference which Gregory deletes) during the day (μεθημέραν for LXX's ἐν ἡμέρᾳ) as well as during the night (νύκτωρ for LXX's ἐν νυκτί), since only the night is a time for sleeping, whereas the young and foolish indulge themselves both then and in the daylight hours.

So the paraphrase pictures the young and foolish Solomon having given himself over to a wanton lifestyle, a picture with which Gregory's readers are now well familiar. Accordingly, there can be no suggestion that this was an "applying of the heart" (LXX δίδωμι τὴν καρδίαν) to σοφία! On the contrary, it was a "devoting of oneself" (προσέχω) to nothing other than a particularly foolish "self-conceit" (οἴησις).

(17) Ἔγνων τε τοσοῦτον, ὅτι ἐν ἐκείνοις τις²⁶ ἐμφύρων, οὐδαμῶς δυνήσεται, οὐδὲ πολλὰ μοχθήσας, εὑρεῖν τὸ ὄντως ἀγαθόν.

And I learned this much: that someone who involves himself in these things will be completely unable, no matter how much he strives, to find the real good.

So insistent was Koheleth that the human quest for ultimate truth is a fruitless quest, that he said no less than three times in this verse that it is just not possible to "find out" (LXX εὑρίσκω) what on earth is going on. Gregory, ever ready to rectify Koheleth's repetitiveness, is content with just one εὑρίσκω clause and so considerably shortens the verse. At the same time, he has considerably changed the impact of his predecessor's assertion: in the first two of these clauses Koheleth built up the contention that Everyman (LXX [ὁ][27] ἄνθρωπος) is quite incapable of comprehending what is going on, and then in the third clause delivered the *coup de grâce* that not even "the wise person" (LXX ὁ σοφός) — quite likely a reference to the professional Wisdom teacher whose business it was to understand these matters and instruct others in them — can comprehend it, but the paraphrase presents only the "one who involves himself in these things" (ἐὰν ἐκείνοις τις ἐμφύρων, "these things" being the eating, drinking, and merriment of the previous verses) as being unable to discover Truth.

Thus, while Koheleth clearly stated that a wise person is just as ignorant as anyone else, despite that type of person's claim (LXX εἶπον) to the contrary, Gregory clearly implies that a wise person — i.e., someone who does not involve himself in these self-indulgent pleasures — can discover Truth. Only the foolish type of person whom the Church Father has depicted in these verses is incapable of seeing what is "the **real** good" (τὸ ὄντως ἀγαθόν) — not the supposed τὸ μέγιστον τῶν ἀγαθόν of v. 15, on which the fool sets his eyes, but the real ἀγαθὸν μέγιστον of v. 12, on which the eyes of faith focus.

Chapter Nine

(1) Ὤμην γὰρ ἅπαντας τότε τῶν αὐτῶν ἀνθρώπους ἠξιῶσθαι· καὶ εἴ τέ τις σοφός, δικαιοσύνης μὲν ἐπεμελήθη, ἀδικίαν δὲ ἐξετράπη, καὶ ἔχθραν ἔφυγε πρὸς ἅπαντας δεξιὸς ὤν, ὅπερ ἐστὶν ἀρεστὸν Θεῷ, ...

At that time I thought that all people were regarded as worthy of the same things; and if a wise person practised righteousness, turned from unrighteousness, and avoided hatred, being courteous to everyone (which indeed is pleasing to God), ...

Having now firmly established the technique of marking off certain of Koheleth's ideas as being false thinking, Gregory employs this device with particular regularity throughout the first half of Chapter Nine. The tone is set in the very first word of the chapter, where the past tense of οἴομαι indicates that Solomon's previous (τότε) ideas are no longer acceptable now that he has regained wisdom.

The mistaken view which Koheleth put forward at first in this chapter (vv. 1-3), though not for the first time in this book (cf. 3:17-22), was that the same fate lies in store for all people, irrespective of whether they are good or evil. Koheleth did not actually state this explicitly until v. 2, but Gregory feels that it is best to let the reader know at the outset what this passage is getting at: the supposition that everyone is "considered worthy" (ἀξιόομαι) of the same things. Gregory, for his part, does not state explicitly in whose mind this consideration of worthiness takes place, such that one might interpret the former Solomonic reasoning here as follows: human beings treat all their fellows in exactly the same evil way, so it does a person no good to be a good person. But since Gregory is paraphrasing Koheleth's fatalistic contention that everything human beings are and do is "in the hand of God" (LXX ἐν χειρὶ τοῦ θεοῦ), it is best to interpret the depicted reasoning along those lines: God regards everyone as deserving of the same ignoble end, so there is nothing to be gained in striving for nobility of life. That it is indeed the way in which God views human beings and their actions that is the important thing, is asserted by Gregory at the end of the verse in his insistence that there is a way of life which is ἀρεστὸς Θεῷ, "pleasing to [or: approved by] God" — therein giving the lie to the earlier contention that God thinks all people deserve the same treatment at his hands.

Koheleth mentioned "the righteous" (LXX οἱ δίκαιοι) and "the wise" (LXX οἱ σοφοί) and what they do (LXX ἐργασίαι αὐτῶν, "their works"), so Gregory ties these concepts together by suggesting that a person who is σοφός "does" (ἐπιμελέομαι, "is engaged in, cultivates") δικαιοσύνη and studiously avoids its opposite, ἀδικία. Continuing in this vein, Gregory renders Koheleth's μῖσος οὐκ ἔστιν εἰδὼς ὁ ἄνθρωπος (שׂנאה אין יודע האדם), which could conceivably be translated as "this person does not know hate", as ἔχθραν ἔφυγε, which suggests that the wise person also studiously avoids hatred.

This makes for a neat paraphrase, but it conveniently ignores the fact that Koheleth had coupled μῖσος (שׂנאה) with ἀγάπη (אהבה). In fact Koheleth appears to have been saying that a person does not know whether he will experience love or hate in the future at God's hands; i.e., we have no idea whether God will act benevolently or malevolently towards us, and how we act — righteously or unrighteously — does not remove this uncertainty about how God will act. Gregory, of course, has no such doubts concerning the will of God; in his view God acts righteously and will reward those people on earth who act righteously, so there is no possibility of interpreting Koheleth as saying otherwise. What is being said here, according to the Christian paraphrase, is that the wise person avoids hatred.

But then what of the concomitant notion of love? To interpret consistently at this point would put Gregory in the uncomfortable position of suggesting that the wise person studiously avoids not only μῖσος, but ἀγάπη as well. There have been philosophers who are quite willing to make just such a suggestion, but it would hardly sit well with a Father of the Church. On the contrary, the Christian interpreter wants his readers to know that the God-pleasing approach is "to be courteous towards all" (πρὸς ἄπαντας δεξιὸς εἰμί),[1] a paraphrase which draws a moral lesson out of Koheleth's enigmatic final phrase "all [is] in front of them" (LXX τὰ πάντα πρὸ προσώπου αὐτῶν).[2] In all likelihood Koheleth's intention with that phrase was to depict the uncertainty of the future — people simply do not know what awaits them — but Gregory sees depicted here all the opportunities for good and wise service which God has placed before each individual in the form of one's fellow human beings. Koheleth complained about divine amorality, while Gregory encourages human morality.

(2) ... οὗτος ματαιοπονεῖν ἐφαίνετο. Τέλος δὲ ἓν ἐδόκει δικαίου τε καὶ ἀσεβοῦς, ἀγαθοῦ τε καὶ κακοῦ, καθαροῦ τε καὶ ἀκαθάρτου, καὶ Θεὸν ἱλασκομένου καὶ μή. Ὅτε γὰρ ἄδικος καὶ ὁ ἀγαθός, ὅτε ἐπίορκος, καὶ ὁ τέλεον ὅρκον ἐκτρεπόμενος, εἰς ταὐτὸ τέλος ἐλαύνειν ἠλπίζετο, ...

... he appeared to be toiling in vain. There seemed to be one end for both a righteous person and an ungodly person, a good person and an evil person, a pure person and an impure person, a person who worships God and a person who does not. And when it is anticipated that the unrighteous person and the good person, the person who swears falsely and the person who completely avoids swearing an oath, are heading towards the same end, ...

The Hebrew text which has come down to us introduces this verse by proclaiming הכל כאשר לכל מקרה אחד, "all as to all, one destiny", and then proceeds to illustrate this thesis by listing a number of opposite characters of people who nevertheless have exactly the same fate awaiting them, rounding the matter off with a restatement of the thesis in the following verse: מקרה לכל אחד, "one destiny to all". LXX, however, read this opening הכל as הבל (as did the Peshitta) — and the following *kaph* as *beth* — and so translated ματαιότης ἐν τοῖς πᾶσιν, "futility is in all". This reading also makes good sense in the context, particularly if taken as a conclusion to v. 1 with its talk of human ἐργασίαι,[3] so Gregory's resultant depiction here of the person of v. 1 "toiling in vain" (ματαιοπονέω) is eminently Kohelethine. The reader is immediately reminded, however, that Koheleth's perspective is only of things as they "appear to be" (φαίνομαι).

Gregory is persistent in giving his readers this reminder. At
both the beginning and the end of the lists of opposite characters
of people, where the idea is put forward that one and the same
"end" (τέλος, an appropriate paraphrase of Koheleth's single
συνάντημα [מִקְרֶה], "occurrence" at the outset of the list) awaits
both types of character alike, he inserts just such a caveat: this is
only what "seems" (δοκέω) to be the case, or, more significantly,
is what the sinner "hopes" (ἐλπίζω) will be the case — for that
type of person has most to lose if it is not.

The character types themselves are listed much as in LXX:
"righteous" (δίκαιος) versus "ungodly" (ἀσεβής), "good" (ἀγαθός) versus "evil" (κακός — where MT is silent, perhaps because
רע was inadvertently omitted by a scribe; the Targum attests to
MT as it stands, while the Peshitta agrees with LXX that טוב
stands in juxtaposition to an evil contrast), and "pure" (καθαρός) versus "impure" (ἀκάθαρτος). However, Gregory prefers
"worshipping" (ἱλάσκομαι) as a more relevant expression for his
contemporaries than the "sacrificing" (LXX θυσιάζω) which was
part and parcel of the cult in Jerusalem, and he also prefers to list
as reprehensible specifically an oath "sworn falsely" (ἐπίορκος)
rather than "oath-swearing" in general (LXX ὀμνύω); presumably there is less significance in his use of "unrighteous" (ἄδικος)
in preference to "sinner" (LXX ἁμαρτάνων). Koheleth had listed
the pairs of character types with the good in first place and the
bad in second, with the exception of the final pair, where it
seems that the better character came second;[4] Gregory structures
his list in two sentences, placing the good consistently in first
place in the first sentence and consistently in second place in the
second sentence.

(3) ... κατάγνωσίς τέ τις ὕπεισι τοῦ εἰς ὅμοια τελευτᾶν
ἅπαντας. Γινώσκω δὲ νῦν ὡς ἀφρόνων ταῦτα ἐνθυμήματα, καὶ
πλάναι καὶ ἐξαπάται. Καὶ πολλὰ λέγουσιν, ὡς ὁ ἀποθανὼν
οἴχεται τέλεον·

... a false opinion gradually arises, that all people do come to
the same end. I know now that these are fools' arguments —
errors and deceits! They strongly assert that the person who is
dead is completely gone, ...

The fact that there is "one destiny for all" (LXX συνάντημα ἓν τοῖς πᾶσιν) was profoundly disturbing to the sage of Jerusalem, who here labelled it an "evil" (LXX πονηρός). But the bishop of Neocaesarea does not believe that "all come to the same end" (εἰς ὅμοια τελευτᾶν ἅπαντας), and so he labels this view as a "low opinion" (κατάγνωσις, a word which normally denotes a contemptuous opinion which one holds concerning someone or something else,[5] but Gregory evidently means it to denote an opinion which is itself contemptible), the kind of opinion which "beguiles" a person or "comes upon [him] stealthily" (ὕπειμι) when he considers that death awaits the righteous person, just as it does the unrighteous.

But the person who succumbs to this sort of "reasoning" (ἐνθύμημα), Gregory now tells his readers plainly, is a fool (ἄφρων), the victim and/or purveyor of error (πλάνη) and deceit (ἐξαπάτη). In this Gregory takes his cue from Koheleth's contention that people's hearts are filled with evil (LXX πονηρόν) and "senselessness" (LXX περιφέρεια), but in all likelihood there is a significant difference between his version of affairs and that of Koheleth: the original probably meant that people set their minds on evil and senselessness because of the observable fact that in the end they will die and will have gained nothing by being good and sensible, but Gregory's paraphrase undoubtedly means that people's minds are full of evil and senselessness if they reason that death is the absolute end and nothing is to be gained by being good and sensible.

The depiction of death as the absolute end now follows. Koheleth expressed it in a rather abrupt and dramatic way — "afterwards [i.e., after this life of evil and madness], off to the dead!" (LXX ὀπίσω αὐτῶν πρὸς τοὺς νεκρούς)[6] — while Gregory expresses it in a way which is somewhat analogous to the modern English saying, "when you're dead, you're dead!" (ὁ ἀποθανὼν οἴχεται τέλεον). But it is only a saying, as Gregory's introductory λέγουσιν makes clear; those who express this kind of thinking are the very fools who have been deceived by appearances, and who do not see with the eyes of faith. Koheleth himself — who often enough gave expression to the view that death is the end, as he did once again in this passage —

stands condemned by his interpreter, even though that interpreter doubtlessly believed that he was condemning only what the writer of Ecclesiastes had himself come to reject and condemn by the time he had his thoughts committed to writing. Such are the ironies of pious paraphrases.

(4) καὶ προτιμητέον τὸν ζῶντα τοῦ τεθνηκότος, κἂν ἐν σκότῳ κείμενος ᾖ, κἂν κυνὸς τρόπον, τὸν βίον διαπορεύηται, παρὰ τὸν λέοντα τὸν τεθνηκότα.

... and that the living is to be preferred to the dead, even if he were to lie in darkness or spend his life in the manner of a dog, as compared with a dead lion.

The Masoretic scribes were apparently a little uncomfortable with בחר, "to prefer" in the context of this verse, and so they noted that חבר, "to be in the company of" should be read here instead.[7] LXX presented κοινωνέω, which attests to a reading of — or emendation to — MT's *Qere*. Gregory, however, employs προτιμάω, which seems to go back to the *Kethib* of the Hebrew text. While this might be put forward as evidence that Gregory could work with the Hebrew text, or was drawing on the insights of someone who could,[8] there are two other possible explanations. It may merely be a coincidence which has arisen through Gregory's paraphrastic endeavour: LXX told its readers that the person who is in the company of the living has hope[9] (as opposed to the person who is in the company of the dead, who has no hope), so Gregory paraphrases this by saying that the living is to be preferred to the dead. Or it may simply be that Gregory, guided by the second half of the verse, is employing προτιμάω as his equivalent to Koheleth's ἀγαθὸς "A" ὑπὲρ "B" (טוב "א" מן "ב") formula (cf. προτιμότερος in 7:3 and the use of αἱρέομαι in 4:6 and προκρίνω in 4:6,13 and 6:3), without any awareness of a Hebrew reading of בחר.

A comparison was now made between a "living dog" (LXX ὁ κύων ὁ ζῶν) and a "dead lion" (LXX ὁ λέων ὁ νεκρός); though most people would rather live as a king than as a cur, it is better to be still alive in a lowly state than to be dead and buried in splendour. Gregory waxes lyrical about "leading a dog's life" (κυνὸς τρόπον τὸν βίον διαπορεύω), even tossing in an additional image of "lying in darkness" (ἐν σκότῳ κεῖμαι, which recalls Koheleth's own talk in 2:14 and 5:16 of a life spent ἐν σκότει [חשׁך]); on the leonine side of the scale, however, inventiveness is set aside, and the Christian paraphrase ends the verse tamely with παρὰ τὸν λέοντα τὸν τεθνηκότα. This phrase is somewhat ambiguous, since it could be understood as depicting the dog lying beside the carcass of a dead lion, as a dog might be expected to act, but since Gregory's παρά stands where LXX's ἀγαθὸς ὑπέρ stands, the reader with an eye to what Gregory is paraphrasing must conclude that the dead lion is to be viewed in comparison with the living dog, the contemptibility of the latter being placed beside the dignity of the former.

(5) Οἱ μὲν γὰρ ζῶντες τοῦτο γοῦν ἐπίστανται, ὅτι τεθνήξονται· οἱ δὲ νεκροὶ οὐδ' ὁτιοῦν γινώσκουσιν. Ἀμοιβαὶ δὲ οὐδενὸς πρόκεινται μετὰ τὸ ἀποπληρῶσαι τὸ χρεών.

The living at least know this: that they are to die; but the dead know nothing at all. No rewards lie ahead of anyone after he has completed his appointed span.

Gregory adds some literary trimmings to the LXX pattern in v. 5's opening comparison between the respective cognisance of the living and the dead: the living know something at least (τοῦτο γοῦν), while the dead know nothing "whatsoever" (ὁτιοῦν). His approach at this point — after having clearly signalled that these ideas are the erroneous and deceitful arguments of fools (v. 3) — is to present the precise ideas which Koheleth himself had presented, and so the mistaken perception now put forward is that after death there are no "wages" (LXX μισθός, Gregory ἀμοιβαί) for what a person does in life.

Koheleth was here repeating an observation which he had previously recorded in 2:16, that the "remembrance" (LXX μνήμη) of everyone "is forgotten" (LXX ἐπιλανθάνομαι). In that earlier verse Gregory was representing Solomon as speaking true wisdom, and so he had him say quite the opposite of what Koheleth actually said: people are remembered, and what is more they do receive an appropriate ἀμοιβή from God for the kind of life — wise or foolish— they have lived. In 9:5 he is representing Solomon as quoting folly, and so he has no compunction about setting down what Koheleth actually meant: there is no ἀμοιβή for anyone after he has "completed" (ἀποπληρόω) what he has been "fated" (χρεών) to complete.

(6) Ἥ τε ἔχθρα καὶ ἡ φιλία ἡ πρὸς τοὺς τεθνηκότας, τέλος ἔχει. Ἐκείνων γάρ, εἴτε ζῆλος, ἐξέλιπεν· εἴτε βίος, ἠφάνισται. Μέτεστι δὲ οὐδενὸς τῷ ἅπαξ ἐντεῦθεν ἀπελθόντι.

Hatred and love are at an end for the dead. Their fervour for these things has ceased; their life has been blotted out. Once a person has gone from here, he has no share in anything.

Although the notion that the dead no longer experience the passions of life was commonly accepted in ancient Israel (cf., e.g., Psalm 115:17), it was not an acceptable notion to the Fathers of the Church. And so Gregory continues to present these pronouncements as being the mistaken thinking of the wicked (in this particular verse there is no actual sign to the reader that what he is reading is an erroneous notion, but such a reminder follows immediately at the beginning of v. 7).

Koheleth simply listed, one after the other, three passions which end at death: "love" (LXX ἀγάπη, Gregory φιλία), "hate" (LXX μῖσος, Gregory ἔχθρα), and "envy" (LXX and Gregory ζῆλος). The first two are obviously primary emotions in human life, and the third was seen by Koheleth as the fundamental factor behind much human activity (4:4), so placing these three together here in depicting the great end which is death is most appropriate. Ζῆλος, however, can be taken as denoting "passion" in general; hence Gregory, rather than simply listing it as third in a series of passions, uses it as a general term referring to the pair of emotions listed first: the dead no longer experience hatred and love, because they no longer have any "zest for those things" (ἐκείνων... ζῆλος) — or, putting it even more bluntly, they no longer have any "life" (βίος).[10] Gregory's formulation calls for no less than three verbs for the perishing of the human life-force — (τέλος) ἔχω, ἐκλείπω, and ἀφανίζω — to LXX's one — ἀπόλλυμαι.

LXX's μερίς, "portion" or "share" is on this occasion neatly paraphrased by the verb μέτειμι, "to have a share in something" — in this case, to have a share "in nothing" (οὐδενός), as Koheleth's negative (LXX οὐκ ἔστιν) made clear. Having no share "ever again" (LXX ἔτι εἰς αἰῶνα) in what goes on ὑπὸ τὸν ἥλιον prompts Gregory's fool to speak of a person going "from here" (ἐντεῦθεν); i.e., departing this realm ὑπὸ τὸν ἥλιον. Despite LXX's mention of εἰς αἰῶνα, the fool does not confess any hope in a future life ὑπὲρ τοῦ ἡλίου (indeed, v. 2 suggests that he is hoping desperately that no such future exists);[11] on the contrary, he will say in v. 9 that not only is there very little to be said for the life "here" (ἐνθάδε), but there is nothing to be said of a life "after death" (μετὰ θάνατον). The idea of an after-life is to be left for Solomon himself to express forthrightly, when he is speaking his own mind and not citing the ideas of wicked people.

(7) Ταῦτα ἡ πλάνη ἐπᾴδουσα ἔτι, καὶ τοιαῦτα συμβουλεύει· Τί πράττεις, ὦ οὗτος, καὶ οὐ τρυφᾷς, οὐδὲ ἐμφορῇ μὲν ἐδεσμάτων παντοίων, οἴνου δὲ ὑπερεμπίπλασαι; Οὐκ αἰσθάνῃ, ὡς ἐκ Θεοῦ ταυτὶ δέδοται πρὸς ἀπόλαυσιν ἀνεπικώλυτον;

Still singing this enchanting song, Deception also gives advice such as this: What are you doing, my friend, not living self-indulgently or stuffing yourself full with all kinds of food and filling yourself up with wine? Don't you realise that these things have been given by God for our unrestrained enjoyment?

Gregory felt that he could not present this fifth and final call for people to "eat and drink" (the previous calls coming at 2:24; 3:13; 5:17; and 8:15) without an explanatory introduction to protect the reader from the dangerous view that he may eat and drink to his heart's content in this life, since God has already given him *carte blanche* to do so.[12] The introduction makes it clear that what Solomon is presenting in this passage is not his own wise counsel, but the counsel of Deception (ἡ πλάνη). In v. 3 Gregory had labelled this passage as containing πλάναι (and ἐξαπάται and ἀφρόνων ἐνθυμήματα!), but since he has now been paraphrasing without such comment for several verses, he evidently feels it necessary to remind the reader that this is not

Truth which is being set forth. After all, Deception "sings an enchanting song" (ἐπᾴδω), and some readers may be in danger of succumbing to the enchantment if no warning sign is given at this crucial point where the call to "eat and drink" is made. The call was to "eat your bread with joy!" (LXX φάγε ἐν εὐφροσύνῃ ἄρτον σου) and "drink your wine with a cheerful heart!" (LXX πίε ἐν καρδίᾳ ἀγαθῇ οἶνόν σου). This strikes Gregory as being precisely the same endeavour as that which had been spoken of in Chapter Two, introduced in the first verse there with the same key words, εὐφροσύνη and ἀγαθός. He therefore paraphrases this advice here in Chapter Nine in an analogous way to his description of the unbridled lifestyle in the earlier passage: it is advice "to live self-indulgently" (τρυφάω — cf. τρυφή in 2:1,10) and "to take one's fill" (ἐμφορέω and ὑπερεμπίπλαμαι — cf. μεθύω and ῥέω in 2:3) of what life offers, in an orgy of "unrestrained enjoyment" (ἀπόλαυσις ἀνεπικώλυτον — cf. ἀκράτη ὁρμή in 2:10).

Gregory styles the call to eat and drink as a seductive question addressed to an imaginary victim (ὦ οὗτος, a device which he also employs in 11:9, though on that occasion it is Solomon himself who addresses the οὗτος and hopes to persuade him to his point of view; cf. ὦ φίλος in 10:4 and 12:12). The victim is asked what he is "doing" (πράττω, which might be taken as asking, in good Kohelethine fashion, what the person thinks he is "achieving") by not giving himself over to licentious living; and further, whether he does not "perceive" (αἰσθάνομαι) that a licentious lifestyle is all right with God. Here Gregory is dealing with one of Koheleth's crucial ideas, namely that human enjoyment of the simple pleasures of life has been "approved" by God (εὐδοκέω [רצה]) — in several parallel passages Koheleth used δίδωμι [נתן], which Gregory thinks is appropriate here, too), but the paraphrase has considerably distorted the original message. Koheleth offered a moving conclusion, on the basis of his observations of life, that the only thing of value which an inscrutable God has allowed human beings in their fleeting life is the enjoyment to be gained from the fruits of the earth; but Gregory presents the voice of the fool, calling on people to become gluttons and drunkards.

(8) Περιβαλοῦ ἐσθῆτα νεόπλυτον, καὶ μύρῳ τὴν κεφαλὴν χρισάμενος, ...

Put on freshly-washed clothes, and anoint your head with oil.

It is not often that a paraphrase is briefer than the text it paraphrases, but here is one such occasion. Gregory's brevity is achieved by deleting the temporal (LXX ἐν παντὶ καιρῷ) and pronominal (two instances of LXX's σου) references as unnecessary, and replacing the negative (LXX μή...) with a positive expression. Apart from that, he simply repeats the word-order of his predecessor, though he replaces LXX's word choices in all cases except κεφαλή. For the "clothes", he favours the word ἐσθής rather than LXX's ἱμάτια, and for the "oil" he prefers μύρον to ἔλαιον — in both cases his preference may be for a word which he regards as a more general term rather than terms which could be taken more specifically as referring to "cloaks" and "olive-oil". Perhaps because of a similar motivation — to avoid a term which may not be of general relevance, given that not everyone's best clothes are necessarily white garments — he thinks it more appropriate to speak of the clothes as being "newly-washed" (νεόπλυτος) rather than "white" (LXX λευκός). But the art of a paraphrast is best seen in Gregory's choice of verbs: instead of a prosaic "be" (LXX εἰμί) in the first phrase, he uses the appropriate verb for putting clothes on one's body (περιβάλλω), and he balances this in the second phrase with the appropriate verb for putting oil on one's head (χρίω), in place of his predecessor's ὑστερέω, "to be without" (which nevertheless in its context was an appropriate antonym to εἰμί).

(9) ... ὅρα τὴν γυναῖκα ταύτην, κἀκείνην δὲ ματαίως τὸν μάταιον πάρελθε βίον;[13] Ἕτερον γὰρ οὐδὲν ὑπολείπεταί σοι παρὰ ταῦτα, οὐκ ἐνθάδε, οὐδὲ μετὰ θάνατον.

See this woman and that, and pass your empty life in an empty way. There is nothing else left for you but this, neither here nor after death.

The text of Gregory's paraphrase presents two difficulties in this verse. The first problem arises with the appearance of the little particle δέ, and the second comes at the end of the same sentence, where editorial tradition has placed a question mark. If there were no δέ, there would be no difficulty in dividing the constituent clauses in the way suggested by the above translation, "See this woman and that, [and] pass your empty life in an empty way" (viz., ὅρα τὴν γυναῖκα ταύτην κἀκείνην, ματαίως τὸν μάταιον πάρελθε βίον), but δέ forces κἀκείνην into the role of beginning a new clause, with which it is not in declensional agreement — if it belongs to the second clause, then either it has been altered from an original form of κἀκεῖνον by a scribe influenced by the immediate proximity of ταύτην, or an even more careless scribe has written βίον where Gregory had chosen ζωήν (which LXX has). But even if this difficulty of grammatical gender is resolved, κἀκείνην δέ as the beginning of a new clause yields the meaning, "See this woman, and pass that empty life of yours in an empty way", a result which makes the first clause non-sensical, for just who is "this woman" who is to be the object of attention? But while ταύτην by itself as a qualifier of τὴν γυναῖκα does not make good sense in this context, in conjunction with κἀκείνην the meaning is evident: the voice of Deception, which has been urging its victim to pursue a licentious lifestyle, now calls for such an approach also in the area of sexual relations. Accordingly, δέ is best ignored at this point, on the assumption either that it has arisen here by mistake or that some other connective word between it and κἀκείνην has been dropped.

It is also best to ignore the appearance of the question mark at the end of the sentence, since Gregory's formulation here is hardly interrogative. Evidently an editor has nevertheless felt it appropriate to enclose the fool's counsel within an interrogative sign — if the fool is depicted as asking (in v. 7), "Why don't you live self-indulgently and have your fill of bread and wine?", then he can just as well be depicted as asking (in vv. 8 and 9), "Why not put on clean clothes and perfume, go from woman to woman, and so pass this empty life?" — but that is not the way Gregory has chosen to phrase the matter at this point.

He has chosen, however, to represent Koheleth's phrase "a

woman whom you love" (LXX γυνὴ ἣν ἠγάπησας) as referring to a sexually promiscuous situation. And who better than Solomon — legendary in respect to the numbers of women he had "seen" in his lifetime, but in Gregory's model a now wise elder looking back to the foolish ideas of his younger days — to "quote" the wicked counsel which had seduced him as a youth? All the young men who read Gregory's version of Ecclesiastes are thus warned of the evils of promiscuity. But at the same time they receive no word concerning the good state of marriage, which other pious interpreters have found in this verse.[14] "A man who has no wife lives without good, help, joy, blessing, and atonement", says the Midrash *Koheleth Rabbah* in response to what the Rabbis saw as Koheleth's advice to enjoy life with the wife you love. But the Church Father probably believes that it is better for a man to pursue a celibate lifestyle, judging from his treatment of 7:26-28; and if Gregory sees women as bringing no good or blessing, in contrast to the rabbinical view, then there is no motivation for him to paraphrase this verse as Solomon lauding the joy of living with a woman.

Koheleth did not abandon his usual perspective in presenting this matter of "seeing good" in a life shared with a woman; he remained insistent that the simple pleasures of life do not invalidate his basic judgment that life is ματαιότης. Perhaps because it is precisely in this area of life that men are prone to act unwisely (cf. his warning in 7:26), Koheleth felt compelled to speak here, not once, but twice of "all one's days [of a life] of futility" (LXX πάσας ἡμέρας [ζωῆς] ματαιότητός σου).[15] Gregory skilfully incorporates this reiterated insistence on ματαιότης into a neat paraphrase which does not simply repeat the one formula: ματαίως τὸν μάταιον πάρελθε βίον, "pass your empty life in an empty way". Of course the respective ματαιότης judgments of Koheleth and Gregory are not the same, for while the former was noting that even the good life which he advocated is fleeting and insubstantial, his paraphrast is noting that the hedonistic lifestyle which a wicked person advocates is unsatisfying and unrewarding; Gregory seems always able to limit Koheleth's stamp of disapproval to the sinful or foolish life, rather than to encompass life *per se*.

As in v. 6, Gregory handles LXX's μερίς well with a negated verb; this time the verb is ὑπολείπομαι, "to remain over and above", and to say that a person is left with "nothing beyond this" (οὐδὲν... παρὰ ταῦτα) is a good way of paraphrasing Koheleth's contention that "this" alone (LXX αὐτό) is a person's μερίς in life. The life ὑπὸ τὸν ἥλιον is the only real life of which Koheleth knew (Sheol of the next verse is only a shadowy, gloomy existence that can hardly be called "life"), so Gregory is quite correct — albeit unknowingly, since he apparently believes that in this passage Solomon is merely characterising another's opinion — in paraphrasing Koheleth as putting forward the idea that there is nothing further "after death" (μετὰ θάνατον).

(10) Ἀλλὰ πράττε τὰ προστυχόντα. Οὔτε γὰρ λογισμὸν σέ τις τούτων εἰσπράξεται· οὔθ' ὅλως γινώσκεται ἐκτὸς ἀνθρώπων τὰ ὑπ' ἀνθρώπων γινόμενα. Ἅδης δέ, ὅ τί ποτε καὶ ἔστιν, εἰς ὃν ἀπιέναι λεγόμεθα, σοφίας καὶ αἰσθήσεως ἀμοιρεῖ. Ταῦτα μὲν οἱ μάταιοι.

Occupy yourself with whatever comes your way. No-one will demand an accounting from you for these things; nor are the things which are done by human beings known at all outside the human sphere. Hades (whatever that is), to which we are said to depart, is without wisdom and perception. These are the things which hollow people say.

Koheleth urged a *carpe diem* approach to life, since death is a fast approaching inevitability. To encapsulate what this foolish philosophy teaches a person to "do" (LXX ποιέω), Gregory fittingly re-uses the verb he had put in Deception's mouth earlier in the piece when he had asked the person who does not act in this way what he thought he was "doing" (πράττω, v. 7). LXX's rather lengthy Semitism πάντα ὅσα ἂν εὕρῃ ἡ χείρ σου τοῦ ποιῆσαι ὡς ἡ δύναμίς σου (כל אשר תמצא ידך לעשות בכחך),[16] "all that your hand finds in your power to do" is then deftly taken care of by the short and simple Greek expression τὰ προστυχόντα, "whatever you encounter" (cf. τὰ παρόντα, "whatever is at hand" in the analogous context of 3:22).

Koheleth then listed four things which do not occur among the dead: physical activity (LXX ποίημα), mental activity (LXX

λογισμός), knowledge (LXX γνῶσις), and wisdom (LXX σοφία).
Gregory singles out the mental and physical activities for special
treatment: the fool alleges that after death no λογισμός will be
demanded of the person who follows his wicked advice in life
(evidently Gregory is interpreting the word in its stricter sense of
a "reckoning"), since no knowledge of human activities (τὰ ὑπ'
ἀνθρώπων γινόμενα) is possessed by any supposed superhuman
beings, be they angels who keep an account of people's deeds or a
divine Judge who will ask for an accounting at the end of days.
If anything at all awaits us after death — and even of this
Gregory's fool is highly sceptical, as is emphasised by the
parenthetical remark ὅ τί ποτε καὶ ἔστιν ("whatever that is") and
by the important addition at the end of the phrase εἰς ὃν ἀπιέναι
λεγόμεθα ("to which we **are said to** depart", a paraphrase of LXX's
ὅπου σὺ πορεύῃ ἐκεῖ) — then it is not Οὐρανός, where those who
refused to follow the fool's counsel might rejoice and sing, and
Γέεννα, where those who embraced the fool's philosophy might
weep and gnash their teeth, but merely Ἅδης (as in LXX, for
MT's שאול), where there is neither rejoicing nor weeping, since in
this shadowy realm of the dead there is, as Koheleth noted,
simply no knowledge (Gregory's αἴσθησις, which can mean
"sense-perception", is an improvement in this Hadesial context
on LXX's mechanical γνῶσις) and no wisdom (Gregory is satisfied
with LXX's standard σοφία).

But the fool has held the stage long enough. Gregory has
permitted him to speak his mind for much of this chapter
(though in a manner which leaves the reader in no doubt that it
is indeed folly which is speaking), and now there is an end to it.
The Church Father feels that it must be underlined that the
preceding words have been words of ματαιότης, even if Koheleth
did not reiterate his familiar judgment at this point. And so the
Christian version of Ecclesiastes closes this section (looking back
at least to v. 7's introductory τοιαῦτα συμβουλεύει, and probably
to v. 3's introductory λέγουσιν) with the concise statement ταῦτα
οἱ μάταιοι — the things which Solomon has been saying in this
section are thus unambiguously stamped as being not his own
full wisdom, but what he sees clearly as the products of hollow
minds. As a master rhetorician, having characterised in these

preceding verses the foolish thinking of lesser mortals, he will now proceed to counter the wicked ideas which such people propound.

(11) Ἐγὼ δὲ εὖ οἶδα, ὡς οὔτε οἱ κουφότατοι δοκοῦντες τὸν μέγαν δρόμον ἐκεῖνον ἀνύσουσιν, οὔτε οἱ δυνατοὶ καὶ φοβεροὶ παρὰ ἀνθρώποις δεδοξασμένοι, τὸν φοβερὸν πόλεμον νικήσουσιν. Ἀλλ᾽ οὐδὲ ἐν ἐδωδῆς πλήθει φρόνησις δοκιμάζεται, οὐδὲ σύνεσις πλούτῳ κοινωνεῖν εἴωθεν. Οὐδὲ συγχαίρω τοῖς οἰομένοις ἅπαντας τῶν ὁμοίων τεύξεσθαι.

But I know well that those who seem the swiftest will not win that great race, and those who are thought by human beings to be powerful and terrifying will not be victorious in the terrible battle. Prudence is not proved by a great amount of food, and intelligence is not usually accompanied by wealth. I do not congratulate the people who think that everyone will encounter the same things.

On a number of occasions when Koheleth turned his attention to some new or supporting observation, he said just that: "I turned and considered [such-and-such]" (here LXX ἐπέστρεψα καὶ εἶδον, almost identical with the formulation ἐπέστρεψα ἐγὼ καὶ εἶδον in 4:1,7 and very similar to ἐπέβλεψα ἐγὼ τοῦ ἰδεῖν in 2:12). On other occasions the verb ὁράω (ראה) was preceded, not by another verb, but by an adverb or particle (ἔτι [עוד], 3:16; τότε [בכן], 8:10; καί γε τοῦτο [גם־זה], 9:13), but in each instance it was evident that Koheleth was introducing a further observation in support of his overall case. In the present instance of 9:11, he had just demonstrated his case concerning the righteous receiving the same fate as the wicked (vv. 2-6, followed by a timely repetition of his overall conclusion from his observations in vv. 7-10), and now, since he had said in v. 1 that both the righteous and the wise are at the mercy of the same inscrutable, possibly malevolent Providence, he "turned" to demonstrate the same case in regard to the wise (vv. 11ff.).

But whenever Koheleth said that he "turned", Gregory is disposed to see a change of thinking (though not in 4:7, where the verb was preceded by what the Church Father felt to be correct thinking!). Thus, having given voice to false thinking in the preceding verses of this chapter, the paraphrase now has Solomon turn from these erroneous ideas with a decisive ἐγὼ δὲ εὖ οἶδα, "but I know well".

Now presenting Solomonic wisdom rather than the earlier voice of Deception, the paraphrase expands on Koheleth's short and sharp list of expected results which do not occur.

The first two protagonists on the list are the physically well-endowed: fast runners and strong fighters, whom one would expect to win their respective contests. Gregory tells us that the "swift" (he makes a superlative of LXX's κοῦφος) and the "strong" (δυνατός, as in LXX) only "seem" (δοκέω) to be so by common human standards, but since the "race" (LXX δρόμος) and "battle" (LXX πόλεμος) to which Solomon refers are not physical contests, but "that great race" (ὁ μέγας δρόμος ἐκεῖνος) for the victor's wreath of eternal life and "the terrible battle" (ὁ φοβερὸς πόλεμος) against the forces of evil, they are struggles in which the apparently swift and strong will not be successful (ἀνύω for the first-mentioned contest, νικάω for the second). Gregory's double use here of φοβερός, first in connection with the powerful people of this world who are feared by their fellow human beings (φοβεροὶ παρὰ ἀνθρώποις δεδοξασμένοι), and then in connection with the great battle which is truly fearful, recalls Jesus' double use of φοβέομαι in Matthew 10:28, "Do not fear those who kill the body but cannot kill the soul, but rather fear him who can destroy both soul and body in hell".

The second two protagonists on the list are the mentally well-endowed: the possessors of wisdom and intelligence, whom one would expect to achieve success in worldy affairs.[17] Gregory tells us that such success — measured in human terms by the possession of "much food" (ἐδωδῆς πλῆθος, for LXX's simple ἄρτος) and "wealth" (πλοῦτος, as in LXX) — does not indicate the possession of the said virtues (for LXX's σοφία in this context he prefers to speak of the more practical wisdom of φρόνησις, but in the second case he is content to take LXX's lead of συνετός and to speak of intelligence as σύνεσις). Indeed, not only does the accumulation of worldly goods not at all "prove" (δοκιμάζω) that one is wise, but it probably can be taken as proof

that one is **not** wise, since wisdom and wealth do not "go hand in hand" (κοινωνέω) — or at least not customarily (ἔθω), Gregory adds, perhaps in order not to offend those of his flock who have accumulated more worldy goods than others (cf. 6:8's ὡς ἐπὶ τὸ πλεῖστον).
Koheleth had a fifth item on his list: "favour" or "grace" (LXX χάρις) is not bestowed on "the knowledgeable" (LXX οἱ γινώσκοντες). Because this item was expressed in precisely the same pattern as the preceding four items, there can be no doubt that it was intended as an analogous case (as the Targumist understands it). Yet Gregory takes it as an introduction to the concluding clause which follows it: Solomon's favour is not bestowed on — i.e., he does not "congratulate" (συγχαίρω)[18] — the people who reach the sort of conclusion which Koheleth made here, that everyone is subject to the same arbitrary fate. Perhaps Gregory would argue that these two clauses should be so linked because Koheleth's ὅτι (כי) is to be read as "that" rather than "because",[19] but then the following ὅτι καί γε (כי גם) which began v. 12 should be read as "and also that", a reading which would yield a different approach to v. 12 than that which is taken by Gregory. There is indeed an evident continuity between the thought concluding v. 11, that a καιρός strikes everyone,[20] and the thought in v. 12, that no-one knows his καιρός and that it will fall upon him suddenly, but it suits Gregory's purposes to take the reference in this verse as being to foolish thinking, concerning the supposed identical fate of all people, which Solomon does not commend (after all, he had labelled it a κατάγνωσις in v. 3, and so now the people who hold to it are not to be labelled οἱ γινώσκοντες [LXX], but rather οἱ οἰόμενοι), and the reference in the next verse as being to Solomon's own wise thinking concerning the fate of the fools.

(12) Πάνυ δὲ ὑπνώττειν ἐοίκασιν οἱ τὰ τοιαῦτα ἐνθυμούμενοι, καὶ μὴ λογιζόμενοι, ὡς δίκην ἰχθύων καὶ ὀρνέων ἀναρπαστοὶ[21] γινόμενοι, ἐν κακοῖς κατατριβήσονται, ἄφνω τῆς ἀξίας λαχόντες ἐπιτιμίας.

Those who form such ideas seem to be quite asleep, not realising that in the same way that fish and birds become caught,

they will be worn down by evils and all of a sudden receive the
punishment they deserve.

LXX's ὁ ἄνθρωπος is, as so often for Gregory, not Everyman
but only the fool. While Koheleth lamented a universal
ignorance — no-one "knows" (LXX γιγνώσκω) when his time
will come, though an evil time will inevitably come upon
everyone at one time or another — his Christian interpreter
laments a specific foible: many people do not "take into
account" (λογίζομαι) what a wise person knows, that an evil
time will come upon a foolish person. So the ignorant are
specifically οἱ τὰ τοιαῦτα ἐνθυμούμενοι, "the ones who form such
ideas", namely v. 11's idea that there is no difference in the fates
that await different kinds of people; and to indulge in such
thinking, adds Gregory, is to "seem like" (ἔοικα) someone who is
"sleeping" (ὑπνώσσω), for it is as plain as day to the bishop of
Neocaesarea that a rather different fate awaits the unrighteous
than that which the righteous can anticipate.

The hapless fish and birds (ἰχθύες and ὄρνεα, as in LXX) do
make an appearance in the paraphrase, but Gregory does not
dwell upon them, considering it quite sufficient to cover both
cases with one reference to being caught (a single ἀναρπαστός for
LXX's double employment of θηρεύομαι), and quite unnecessary
to make any reference at all to the implements used in such
catching (LXX's ἀμφίβληστρον, "net" and παγίς, "trap" respectively). This brevity on the part of the paraphrase makes it a little
unclear as to what comprises the analogy between the fate of fish
and birds on the one hand and the fate of wicked human beings
on the other. In Koheleth's phrasing the analogy clearly lay in
the unexpectedness or suddenness (LXX ἄφνω) with which
fortunes change for both animals and humans as they are
trapped in their fate, and this aspect is also present for Gregory
(who likewise uses the adverb ἄφνω in this context), but he has
added the notion of the wicked person "being worn down"
(κατατρίβομαι) by the situation preceding the sudden or
unexpected *dénouement,* and, in the absence of any details about
the situation involving the fish and birds, this makes for a
somewhat cloudy analogy.

In the paraphrase, it is no longer self-evident that the

sudden springing of the trap is being described, as it was in the original Ecclesiastes (the fish suddenly caught in a net, the bird suddenly caught in a snare, the human suddenly caught in an evil time). Gregory seems to be depicting the exhausting, hopeless struggle of fish, bird, or human within the trap before an unexpected *dénouement* (perhaps being roasted, in all three cases — the third possibly metaphorically — but this development hardly seems so sudden or unexpected given the "wearing down" of the victim which precedes it). It may be that Gregory is thinking of the victims being "worn down" by their unthinking evil pursuits which make them vulnerable to sudden and unexpected entrapment (i.e., the fish and birds greedily gobble up whatever available food they can find, the result being that this single-minded pursuit of gratification for their instinctual desires eventually leads them into a trap; by analogy, the person who occupies himself with whatever comes his way [v. 10] wears himself out with such a lifestyle and is unable to see or prevent the inevitable consequences). Some extra details from Gregory would have made the analogy clearer.

But he does provide some extra details on what the foolish person ought to expect. The "evil time" (LXX καιρὸς πονηρός) of which Koheleth spoke is a time of "punishment" (ἐπιτιμία) awaiting those who have been involved in "evils" (κακά) leading up to that time, and moreover — a complete counterpoint to all that Koheleth had been saying in this passage concerning a person's fate not corresponding to his character or attributes — the fate that awaits them is entirely fitting (ἄξιος), the precise fate which people of their kind deserve.

(13)   Ἐγὼ δὲ σοφίαν οὕτω τι μέγα ἡγοῦμαι, ...

I regard wisdom so highly, ...

Gregory sensibly paraphrases this verse as simply introducing the case study which follows, a case study which he also sensibly paraphrases as a hypothetical example of what occurs in the real world. This interpretation itself stands as an example of wisdom which ought to have been heeded by all those subsequent interpreters who sought to locate in time and space an actual city and an actual poor wise person whose respective fates are here narrated.[22]

(14) ... ὡς καὶ πόλιν μικρὰν ὑπ' ὀλίγων μὲν οἰκουμένην, ὑπὸ δὲ μεγάλου πολιορκουμένην βασιλέως χειρί, πολλὴν καὶ μεγάλην ἡγοῦμαι, ...

... **that I would regard a small and underpopulated city, under the besieging hand of a powerful king, as being great and powerful,** ....

Gregory repeats the basic details of Koheleth's case study — a small city (LXX's πόλις μικρά) with few (LXX's ὀλίγος) inhabitants faces a mighty king (LXX's βασιλεὺς μέγας) — but cannot resist shaping a more literary Greek composition with two ὑπό clauses, the first concerning the city "being inhabited" (οἰκούμενος, replacing LXX's substantive ἄνδρες) and the second concerning the city "being besieged" (πολιορκούμενος, summarising LXX's tripartite description of the king's military campaign: first coming against the city [ἔρχομαι], then surrounding it [κυκλόω], and finally building siegeworks against it [οἰκοδομέω χάρακας]).

Koheleth said that the king involved in this episode is μέγας (גדול), and Gregory agrees with this description. Koheleth further said that the king's military constructions are μέγας, but Gregory has not found room in his reshaping of the text to mention these structures here (only in the following verse does he speak of χαρακώματα); instead, he uses the second μέγας to form part of a neat irony which he spells out in this verse: the city itself is μέγας and πολύς in Solomon's eyes, even though it is apparently μικρός and ὀλίγος. This is because there is wisdom in this city (v. 15), and on a true scale of values wisdom is μέγας (v. 13) more than weapons of war (v. 18). Since the wise Solomon regards (ἡγέομαι at the end of v. 13) wisdom as μέγας, in exactly the same way he regards (ἡγέομαι at the end of v. 14) this dwelling-place of wisdom as μέγας.

(15) ... εἰ καὶ ἕνα σοφὸν ἄνδρα πολίτην ἔχοι πένητα. Δύναιτο γὰρ ἂν οὗτος καὶ ἐκ τῶν πολεμίων, καὶ ἐκ τῶν χαρακωμάτων τὴν

ἑαυτοῦ διασῶσαι πόλιν. Καὶ ἄλλοι μὲν τὸν σοφὸν ἐκεῖνον οὐ
γινώσκουσι πένητα·

... if it had one wise person, though poor, as a citizen.
For that person would be able to save his city from enemies and
from entrenchments. Others are not aware of that wise person,
as he is poor; ....

Here then is the criterion for a city to be truly great: it need
have just one wise citizen, even if he is poor (and chances are he
will be, given the principle Gregory enunciates in v. 11 and again
in v. 16 that wisdom is normally to be found associated with
poverty). When Koheleth first mentioned this individual, he
referred to him as ἀνὴρ πένης σοφός (איש מסכן חכם), "a poor, wise
person". Perhaps the asyndetic juxtaposition of the two
adjectives was meant to emphasise the surprise here for
traditional Wisdom, which assumed that wise people are able to
avoid poverty, such that the expression should be read "a poor
person — but a wise one". Gregory achieves such an effect,
though with the adjectives in reverse order, by mentioning
σοφός together with ἀνήρ and leaving πένης until the end of the
sentence: "a wise person... — though a poor one". When
Koheleth mentioned this individual again, he referred only to
his being πένης (מסכן), but Gregory regards his own earlier device
as so effective that he employs it once more: σοφός makes an
appearance near the beginning of the sentence and πένης is
brought in at the very end, creating the impression of "a wise
person... — being a poor one". But although it is the same
device, a variation in effect is achieved, since in the first case
Gregory's positioning of πένης suggested that the fact that this
particular individual is poor is ancillary to the fact that he is
wise, the possession of wisdom being the important thing, while
in the second case the positioning of πένης suggests that this
poverty is the central reason for the wise person's fellow citizens
overlooking his wisdom, the state of poverty being the
dominant thing in their minds.

Koheleth talked of the poor, wise citizen "saving" his
community (LXX διασώζω) and of no-one "remembering" him
(LXX μιμνήσκομαι). There are two possible ways of interpreting

this idea: Koheleth meant either that the wise person actually did save his city, but was not remembered for his efforts, or that he might have saved the city, but no-one thought of him.²³ Gregory adopts the second interpretation, speaking of the one who could have saved his city (the optative of δύναμαι is operative here on διασώζω) but is not recognised (γιγνώσκω) by his fellow citizens as being a wise person.

Having been brief in his description of what the city faced in v. 14, Gregory now chooses to spell out the mighty forces which one poor, wise individual is able to overcome, if given the chance by the municipal authorities: both the human enemies themselves (οἱ πολέμιοι) and the entrenchments or fortifications they construct (τὰ χαρακώματα, recalling LXX's χάρακας of v. 14). And having said all this, Gregory feels that it cannot then exactly be said that no-one remembers that person (LXX ἄνθρωπος οὐκ ἐμνήσθη σὺν τοῦ ἀνδρός), for Solomon evidently acknowledges the wisdom of such an individual; hence Gregory's Solomon points the finger at other people (ἄλλοι) who do not know wisdom when they see it.

(16) ἐγὼ δὲ καὶ πάνυ προκρίνω τὴν ἐν σοφίᾳ ἰσχὺν ταύτης τῆς δημώδους δυνάμεως. Ἀλλ' ἐνθάδε μὲν ἀτιμάζεται σοφία πενίᾳ συνοικοῦσα·

... but I very much prefer the power that is in wisdom to this popular strength. Here, however, wisdom is not honoured, since it goes hand in hand with poverty; ....

In 4:13 Koheleth had used his ἀγαθὸς "A" ὑπὲρ "B" ("א" טוב "ב" מ) formula to introduce the thought that a poor person who is wise is better than a powerful person who is foolish, and Gregory had paraphrased with an emphatic ἐγὼ προκρίνω, "I prefer". Here in 9:16, where Koheleth was making essentially the same comparison and was using the same formula, Gregory repeats his tactic (also covering here LXX's introductory εἶπα ἐγώ, "I said") and even adds an asseverative πάνυ to the Solomonic stamp of approval. What is approved is "wisdom" (LXX σοφία) over "strength" (LXX δύναμις), which is expressed a little too briefly for a paraphrast's liking, so Gregory adds an explanatory note to each side of the scale: wisdom — even when possessed by just one, poor citizen (v. 15) — has its own strength (ἰσχύς), outweighing that other strength which is δημώδης, "popular, common, vulgar".

But while Solomon esteems wisdom highly, he must admit that it "is esteemed lightly" (ἀτιμάζω, for LXX's dual ἐξουδενόομαι, "to be despised" and οὐκ ἀκούομαι, "to be unheeded") in the popular mind. The reason for this was implied in Gregory's positioning of πένης at the end of the previous verse, but now he states it explicitly: people fail to honour wisdom because it "lives together" (συνοικέω) with poverty — a mirror image of his contention in v. 11 that wisdom does not "accompany" (κοινωνέω) wealth. Gregory does not mean to suggest that a poor person necessarily possesses wisdom, but that a wise person is almost invariably poor (cf. 6:8).

(17) ἀκουσθήσεται δὲ μετέπειτα ὑπερφωνοῦσα δυνάστας καὶ τυράννους κακῶν ὀρεγομένους.

... but hereafter it will be heard speaking above the rulers and tyrants who grasp for evil things.

Wisdom's dishonoured status is only the case here and now (ἐνθάδε, v. 16); in the future (μετέπειτα, in this verse) things will be different, Gregory now assures his readers, revealing again his optimism concerning a future divinely-enacted reversal of the sorry state of affairs which currently exists under the sun. Koheleth's work did not breathe the same optimism, but he did here present the idea that quiet words of wisdom can be heard above — or at least ought to be listened to more than — loud words of folly, and this provides the Christian paraphrast with the grounds for his contention. Gregory does not say by whom quiet wisdom "is heard" (ἀκούομαι, as in LXX) above the shouting of fools; perhaps he has God in mind as the one who listens to the former and closes his ears to the latter,[24] but it is more likely that he is thinking of the δῆμος who currently honour strength above wisdom (ἡ δημώδης δύναμις above ἡ ἐν σοφίᾳ ἰσχύς, v. 16) but who in the future will find the true priority of values clearly revealed. Solomon has bemoaned the fact that at present οἱ ἄλλοι are quite unaware of wisdom (v. 15); now he prophesies that there will come a time when its existence will be evident.

The paraphrast's art involves a little contraction at one place and a little expansion at another. On the one hand, LXX's depiction of the "quiet words" (λόγοι ἐν ἀναπαύσει) of the wise being heard "above" (ὑπέρ) the "shouting" (κραυγή) of the fools is encapsulated in Gregory's briefer depiction of wisdom being heard "speaking above" (ὑπερφωνέω) folly. On the other hand, LXX's concept of "foolish kings" (ἐξουσιάζοντες ἐν ἀφροσύναις, literally "the ones who rule in foolishness", where MT says "the king of fools" [מושל בכסילים, literally "the one who rules among fools"]),[25] is fleshed out into a picture of "rulers and tyrants who grasp for evil things" (δυνάσται καὶ τύραννοι κακῶν ὀρεγόμενοι).

(18) Σοφία γὰρ καὶ σιδήρου δυνατωτέρα· ἀφροσύνη[26] τε ἑνὸς πολλοῖς κίνδυνον ἐργάζεται, κἂν πολλοῖς[27] καταφρόνητος ᾖ.

Wisdom is stronger than iron, but the foolishness of one person causes danger to many people, even if he is held in contempt by them.

The final ἀγαθὸς "A" ὑπέρ "B" statement in Ecclesiastes elicits an appropriate paraphrastic technique which Gregory has employed on more than a third of the appearances of this statement, expressing the idea by means of a comparative adjective (δυνατώτερος, "stronger"; cf. αἱρετώτερος, 4:3 and 7:2; βελτίων, 4:9; ἀμείνων, 5:4 and 7:10). Here Gregory fashions the comparison as being between "wisdom" (σοφία, as in LXX) and "iron" (σίδηρος, the material out of which so many of LXX's σκεύη πολέμου, "implements of war" are fashioned).

The other side of the coin from the strength of wisdom is the powerful nature of "folly" (ἀφροσύνη, understanding correctly that a Wisdom teacher means an ἄφρων, "fool" when he speaks of a ἁμαρτάνων, "sinner"). Koheleth noted that a small amount of this bad quality is able to "destroy" (LXX ἀπόλλυμι) "much good" (LXX ἀγαθωσύνη πολλή); in Gregory's version the one who possesses this bad quality is able to "cause danger" (κίνδυνον ἐργάζομαι) to "many people" (πολλοί). In both versions the "much" that is — or the "many" who are — adversely affected is contrasted to the "one" (εἷς) who has such a wide-reaching effect, but Gregory adds a further pessimistic thought: this great impact occurs irrespective of the way in which the foolish individual is regarded by the "many". Even if his fellow citizens regard him as καταφρόνητος, "contemptible" — or, even more strongly still (if the reading of the Medicean Codex is accepted),[28] as εὐκαταφρόνητος, "highly contemptible" or "easily despised" — in which case they are presumably safe from being themselves won over to his foolish ways, they are still in grave danger of being harmed by the activities of this one foolish individual. This is an interesting contrast to the picture Gregory painted in v. 15, where it is suggested that a single wise individual cannot achieve good for his fellow citizens if they regard him as being beneath their station. Had they listened to his wisdom, it would have proved "stronger than iron" and they would have been saved from their enemies; but even when they do not listen to folly, its presence proves to be highly dangerous and they may be destroyed as a result of it. Foolishness thus appears to be stronger than wisdom in this world.

Chapter Ten

(1) Καὶ γὰρ μυῖαι ἐμπεσοῦσαι μύρῳ, καὶ ἐναποπνιγεῖσαι, ἀσχήμονα τοῦ ἡδέος ἐκείνου χρίσματος, τήν τε ὄψιν, καὶ τὴν χρίσιν[1] ἐργάζονται· σοφίας δὲ καὶ ἀφροσύνης οὐδὲν ἐν ταὐτῷ[2] μεμνῆσθαι προσῆκον.

Flies falling into perfume, and drowning, make the appearance and use of that pleasant oil unseemly; so, too, it is improper to have both wisdom and foolishness together in one's mind.

The Hebrew text presented its translators with a number of difficulties in this verse. First of all the subject was introduced in the plural (זבובי, "flies") and then the action was described in the singular (יבאיש, "he gives a bad smell" and יביע, "he causes to putrefy" [if understood as נבע hiphil], placed in an asyndetic relationship). LXX overcame this problem by accepting the plural subject — μυῖαι, "flies" — and recasting the action in a plural form — σαπριοῦσιν, "they befoul", the second Hebrew verb being then understood as a nominal object of the action.[3] Accordingly, Gregory's paraphrase has a plural verbal form (ἀσχήμονα ἐργάζονται, "they make unseemly") to agree with the subject, μυῖαι. Moreover, Gregory follows LXX's noun (σκευασία [ἐλαίου], "the preparation [of the oil]"), where MT has a second verb (יביע), by speaking both of the ὄψις, "appearance" and χρῆσις, "use" (or χρῖσις, "anointing") of the oil. In actual fact it may be that σκευασία was a scribal error in the Greek text for σκεῦος (cf. Peshitta ܡܐܢܐ), "vessel", which would attest to a reading of — or emendation to — גביע in the Hebrew text,[4] but Gregory is evidently paraphrasing the Greek text as we have it.

LXX further spoke of ἔλαιον ἡδύσματος, "sweetened oil" (cf. Peshitta ܡܫܚܐ ܒܣܝܡܐ), where MT cites שמן רוקח, "perfumer's oil"; so Gregory, having at first simply mentioned μύρον (which he had also preferred to LXX's ἔλαιον in 9:8, though not in 7:1), further defines the substance in question as ἡδὺ χρῖσμα, "a pleasant oil", to make a fitting contrast to the ἄσχημον χρῖσμα it becomes when infested with flies. As for these flies which effect so complete a change, Gregory explains their "dying" (LXX θανατόω) as being due to their initial "falling into" (ἐμπίπτω) and subsequent "drowning in" (ἐναποπνίγω) the oil.

Further difficulties emerge in the second half of the verse, where Koheleth mentioned that יקר מחכמה מכבוד סכלות מעט, "a little folly is weightier than wisdom [and] than honour". Apart from an instance now of nominal asyndeton with מחכמה מכבוד (following the instance of verbal asyndeton with יבאיש יביע in the first half of the verse), a matter easily "corrected" by Targum and Peshitta by inserting a conjunction (מן חוכמת חכימין ועותר עתירין, "more than the wisdom of the wise and the wealth of the wealthy"; ܡܢ ܚܟܡܬܐ ܣܓܝܐܬܐ ܘܡܢ ܐܝܩܪܐ ܣܓܝܐܐ, "more than wisdom and more than much honour"), this saying is not difficult to interpret: just as one sinner destroys much good (9:18), and just as a small fly can ruin a whole bottle of perfume, so a little foolishness can outweigh wisdom and honour. But it did prove difficult to LXX, which rendered τίμιον ὀλίγον σοφίας ὑπὲρ δόξαν ἀφροσύνης μεγάλης, "a little wisdom is more valuable than the honour of great folly". Μέγας — or, for that matter, Peshitta's ܣܓܝܐܐ — is not necessarily out of place in this verse, given the context of **much** good being outweighed by a **little** bad (indeed, in this very clause it is possible that Koheleth meant by מחכמה מכבוד "more than wisdom in abundance" as a contrast to סכלות מעט),[5] but it is definitely out of place on Koheleth's scale when it is applied to the σοφία side of the scale; through this sleight of hand, which includes the removal of ὑπέρ (מן) from in front of σοφία (חכמה) and the construction of a genitival relationship between δόξα (כבוד) and ἀφροσύνη (סכלות), LXX has completely reversed the equation: a little folly does not outweigh much wisdom, as MT would have us believe, but rather a little wisdom outweighs much folly.

The Septuagintal treatment of this clause, while presenting its readers with the reverse of MT, was nevertheless a rather clever solution to what evidently struck the Greek translator as something of a problem.[6] The cleverness lies in the neat *a-b-b-a* pattern it achieved for the clauses of 9:18 and 10:1 —

> Wisdom is better than weapons of war,
>   though one sinner destroys much good;
> dying flies befoul a preparation of sweetened oil,
>   but a little wisdom is more valuable than the honour of great folly.

This clever pattern is not appreciated by Gregory, however. In fact the debate between MT and LXX concerning whether wisdom outweighs folly or folly outweighs wisdom finds no direct parallel in his paraphrase; he simply mentions σοφία καὶ ἀφροσύνη together, with no mention of either one being "little" or its opposite being "great". What he does say about them, though, is that it is "not at all proper" (οὐδὲν... προσῆκον) to have them both together (ἐν ταὐτῷ, "in the same [place]" or "at the same [time]") in one's mind (μιμνήσκομαι, "to call to mind, give heed"), and in view of his presentation in the previous verse of the danger to a community of having even a little folly in its midst, it would seem that his warning here concerns the danger to an individual of giving any space at all in one's head to foolish thoughts. Viewed in this way, Gregory's paraphrase seems to agree with MT that folly can outweigh wisdom, but it might also be an inference drawn from LXX's formulation: it is better to have wisdom than to be honoured for one's foolishness, so one should not think that it is proper or possible to have both wisdom and honour in this world (cf. v. 6, where Gregory notes that the wise are humbled while the fools are honoured); a choice must be made between the two alternative courses, the way of wisdom and the way of folly, since a person cannot go in two different directions at once (v. 2), and clearly Gregory would agree with LXX that wisdom is more valuable than folly on a true scale of values.

(2) Ὁ μέν γε σοφὸς ἑαυτὸν ἐπὶ δεξιὰ τῶν πραγμάτων ὁδηγεῖ· ἄφρων δὲ εἰς ἀριστερὰ[7] ἀπονένευκεν, ...

The wise person guides himself along the right path in his actions, but the foolish person turns off to the left.

"Right" (LXX δεξιός) and "left" (LXX ἀριστερός) are such universally-understood symbols for right and wrong, good and bad, success and misfortune that Gregory sees no need to paraphrase widely.[8] The symbolism of the "heart" (LXX καρδία), however, is frequently re-expressed in Gregory's version of Ecclesiastes — out of 34 occurrences in the book, Gregory himself only says καρδία five times (2:10,23; 5:1; 7:22,26), often speaking instead of the ψυχή (2:3; 7:3,4,7; 11:9) or of thought-processes (λογίζομαι, 1:16; 2:3; 3:7; οἴομαι, 1:16; 8:11; 9:1; ἐνθυμήματα, 9:3; 10:3). So here, where Koheleth spoke of a person's heart being inclined either to the right or to the left, Gregory paraphrases in terms of the wise person "guiding" (ὁδηγέω) himself to the right and of the foolish person "turning off" or "inclining" (ἀπονεύω) towards the opposite direction. Lest it be thought that this is just a harmless thing that takes place in one's mind, Gregory adds that he is talking about the "deeds" (πράγματα) which flow from a person's attitude of mind.

(3) ... οὐδ᾽ ἔστιν ὅτε καλῶν ὁδηγῷ πραγμάτων ἀφροσύνῃ χρήσεται. Μάταια δὲ αὐτοῦ καὶ τὰ ἐνθυμήματα, ἀφροσύνης ἀναπεπλησμένα.

He will never use his foolishness as a guide to good actions; his thoughts are empty — full of foolishness!

Talk of a fool "going along [his] path" (LXX ἐν ὁδῷ... πορεύηται) suggests to Gregory persistence in a foolish course of action, and so he begins this verse by bemoaning the fact that the fool will never (οὐδ᾽ ἔστιν ὅτε, literally "there is no time when", reflecting on the negative side LXX's ὅταν, "whenever, every time") be inclined or able to deviate from his wicked ways. Mention of the fool's ὁδός prompts Gregory to picture foolishness as a ὁδηγός, "guide" which cannot be used to pilot a course along the path of "good deeds" (καλὰ πράγματα) — a clear contrast to the wise person Gregory had pictured in the previous verse, who is inclined and able to "be a guide" (ὁδηγέω) "along the right path of deeds" (ἐπὶ δεξιὰ τῶν πραγμάτων). Hence any reader who may not have grasped the point about δεξιός and ἀριστερός in v. 2 is now given a clear indication that the wise path to the right is the way of καλὰ πράγματα and (by implication) that the foolish path to the left is the way of κακὰ πράγματα. LXX's καρδία αὐτοῦ ὑστερήσει, "his heart [i.e., his mind, the seat of thought and understanding] is lacking" is well paraphrased, with an admirably Kohelethine choice of adjective, by μάταια αὐτοῦ τὰ ἐνθυμήματα, "his thoughts are empty". Koheleth's final comment on this matter was אמר לכל סכל הוא,

which either means "he says to all [that] he is a fool"[9] — i.e., he
clearly reveals to everybody through what he says (cf. vv. 12-14)
and does (cf. v. 15) that he is a fool, an understanding which may
lie behind the Targumist's free rendering כולא אמרין דשטיא הוא, "all
say that he is a fool" — or "he says concerning all, 'He is a fool'"[10]
— i.e., to a foolish person everyone who does not act as he does
appears to be a fool, an understanding reflected in Midrash
Koheleth Rabbah's paraphrase טפשא סבר דכל עמא טיפשין, "the fool
thinks that all people are fools" and in the Vulgate's *omnes
stultos aestimat*, "he regards all as fools".[11] This idea that אמר
referred to the thoughts inside the fool's לב was also adopted by
LXX (and Peshitta), though with a somewhat different rendering:
ἃ λογιεῖται πάντα ἀφροσύνη ἐστίν (ܕܡܢܐ ܟܠ ܕܡܬܚܫܒ ܗܘ ܫܛܝܘܬܐ), "all
that he thinks of is folly". So Gregory links this phrase with his
previous phrase concerning the fool's ἐνθυμήματα, now adding
that these thoughts are ἀφροσύνης ἀναπεπλησμένος, "full of
folly".

(4) Εἰ δὲ καὶ πνεῦμά σοί ποτε, ὦ φίλος, πολέμιον προσπέσοι,
ἔνστηθι ἐρρωμένως, γινώσκων ὡς καὶ πολλῶν ἁμαρτημάτων
πλῆθος Θεὸς ἱλάσασθαι δύναται.

**If at some stage, my friend, a hostile spirit comes upon you,
firmly resist it, knowing that God is able to forgive a great many
sins.**

Gregory did not read this verse as containing advice on how
a person should conduct himself in the presence of a despotic
ruler by remaining calm when the tyrant is greatly agitated (cf.
the similar advice given in 8:3, and the interpretation given
there by the paraphrast). To him "the spirit of the ruler" (LXX
πνεῦμα τοῦ ἐξουσιάζοντος) which "rises against you" (LXX
ἀναβῇ ἐπὶ σέ) suggests, not the hot-spirited anger of an earthly
ruler so frequently directed against his clerical underlings (at
whom is also directed much advice such as this in Wisdom
literature), but a spiritual entity which may rise against any
person within the faith community (to whom the bishop of
Neocaesarea naturally wishes to apply the sayings contained in
Ecclesiastes). So, rhetorically addressing his reader as ὦ φίλος (cf.

12:12), he speaks of the "hostile spirit" (πνεῦμα... πολέμιον) which "falls upon you" (σοι... προσπέσοι).[12] He says nothing about this spirit "ruling", but Koheleth's participle has no doubt contributed to Gregory's conviction that the πνεῦμα here is an evil one, judging by his paraphrasing of 1:14 and 3:11 (cf. 2:11; 4:4,6,16), which suggest that an evil spirit is in control of the present world.

If spiritual warfare is being pictured here, then Koheleth's advice "Do not abandon your place" (LXX τόπον σου μὴ ἀφῇς) must be a plea for the righteous reader to remain steadfast in righteousness and not to succumb to the attack of the evil spirit; hence the Gregorian call, "Stand against it steadfastly" (ἔνστηθι ἐρρωμένως, a rather poetically-executed paraphrase).[13]

Koheleth backed up his advice to stand one's ground with the note that "soothing lays to rest great offences" (LXX ἴαμα καταπαύσει ἁμαρτίας μεγάλας). An interpreter who has uncovered references to a spiritual battle in this verse is of course not going to see this last phrase as indicating a prudent approach to countering an earthly ruler's displeasure, but will naturally read ἁμαρτίαι as "sins", offences against the heavenly Ruler. The evil πνεῦμα might enjoy a certain "ruling" role in this world, but the paraphrast wants the reader to know that there is a more powerful spirit — Θεός — who is really in control: he has the power, Gregory tells us, "to forgive a great multitude of sins" (πολλῶν ἁμαρτημάτων πλῆθος... ἱλάσασθαι). By changing "great sins" to "a great multitude of sins", Gregory appears to be alluding to, and out-doing, a twice-used phrase in the New Testament, where it is said that a human being is able, through righteous activity, to "cover a multitude of sins" (καλύπτω πλῆθος ἁμαρτιῶν, James 5:20 and 1 Peter 4:8); how much more, Gregory's formulation suggests, is the all-righteous heavenly Being able to do so.

(5) Τυράννου δὲ ἔργα ταῦτα, καὶ πατρὸς πάσης πονηρίας·

These are the works of the prince and father of all wickedness: ....

As he had done in 6:1 (and in 5:12 with slight variation),

Koheleth here introduced a particularly irksome example of the way of the world with the phrase ἔστιν πονηρία ἣν εἶδον ὑπὸ τὸν ἥλιον (יש רעה ראיתי תחת השמש),[14] "there is an evil which I have seen under the sun". But Gregory is not one to repeat himself: in 6:1 he had spoken of human misfortune (and in 5:12 of the absurdity of a common human activity), but now in 10:5 he points to the one whom he sees as being responsible for all the misfortune and absurdity which characterises life under the sun.

As he had done in v. 4, Koheleth made mention here in v. 5 of a "ruler". He had used מושל for this figure in v. 4, but here employed שליט, which makes the Targumist think that a ruler of a different kind is meant, an actual human שולטן and not the evil spiritual power which could be detected in the previous verse. LXX realised that the two figures are actually one and the same, and so used ἐξουσιάζων in both instances (indeed in all instances; cf. שליט in 7:19 and 8:8 and מושל in 9:17), which aids Gregory's thinking that a ruler of the same kind is meant, a spiritual power in the same vein as the hostile spirit who was uncovered in the previous verse. There Gregory had mentioned both the spirit and God (in 3:11 he had more explicitly said how these two are opposing forces at work in this present age), and now he depicts that spirit as God's great opposite number, "the prince and father of all wickedness" (τύραννος... καὶ πατὴρ πάσης πονηρίας, recalling Jesus' talk of the devil in John 8:44 as ὁ πατὴρ ψεύδου,[15] "the father of falsehood"). Such a depiction arises from Koheleth's talk of "an error which comes from the ruler" (LXX ἀκούσιον ὃ ἐξῆλθεν ἀπὸ προσώπου τοῦ ἐξουσιάζοντος) when combined with the insight that the "ruler" who is the source of all errors or falsehood is none other than the devil — the one who rules "under the sun".

For the idea of this "error" on the part of a ruler, Koheleth used the word שגגה, which seems to imply that it is an "inadvertent error", something that the ruler may do unintentionally or unthinkingly rather than deliberately and premeditatedly. LXX's ἀκούσιον brings out strongly the idea of involuntariness, even of acting against one's true will under some kind of constraint. Gregory makes no mention of such an idea, but perhaps he has taken account of it: by speaking here of the devil's "deeds" (ἔργα) he is unlikely to be imagining that the father of all wickedness is acting against his true will (after all, John 8:44 says that the father of falsehood acts in accordance with his true nature, and it would probably be reading far too much into Gregory's paraphrase to suppose that he has understood the devil to be acting ἀκουσίως in that he cannot act other than in accordance with the nature given him by his creator), but Gregory may have in mind the thought that the people who carry out the devil's purposes in this world, as depicted in the following two verses, do so because their own will has been taken over and directed by the devil.

(6) τὸν μὲν ἄφρονα εἰς ὕψος αἴρεσθαι, τὸν πλούσιον δὲ φρονήσει ταπεινοῦσθαι·

... the foolish person is lifted on high, while the person rich in wisdom is lowered; ....

In accordance with the erroneous decisions that rulers are wont to make (v. 5) — in the Gregorian version, in accordance with the designs of the Wicked One — a person "is assigned" to (LXX δίδομαι), or has to "occupy" (LXX κάθημαι), the exact opposite position to what might have been expected to be properly his, be it "in high places" (LXX ἐν ὕψεσι) or "in a low place" (LXX ἐν ταπεινῷ) respectively. Gregory paraphrases these alternative assignations in terms of one type of person "being raised to a high place" (εἰς ὕψος αἴρομαι) while the other type of person "is lowered" (ταπεινόομαι). The first character-type, whom the devil causes to be exalted, is "the fool" (ὁ ἄφρων, as in LXX, which had vocalised סכל with a *qametz* in each syllable instead of MT's segholate vocalisation as "foolishness"), and his opposite number, whom the devil causes to be humbled, is "the one rich in wisdom" (ὁ πλούσιος φρονήσει, containing what Gregory evidently regards as a necessary gloss to LXX's πλούσιοι, "rich ones").

In so paraphrasing, Gregory has imposed numerical consistency on the verse: one person is pictured as being raised to a height (Koheleth had a plural object here, ὕψεις [מרומים], though a singular subject, ἄφρων [סכל]) and **one** person (where

Koheleth had a plural subject, πλούσιοι [עשירים], though a singular object, ταπεινόν [שפל]) is pictured as being lowered. He has also drawn an allusion to his paraphrase of 4:1, where he had spoken of those people who "are raised to a height — from which they will also fall" (εἰς ὕψος αἴρονται, ἐξ οὗ καὶ πεσοῦνται); so here, too, where Gregory again speaks of a person who "is raised to a height" (εἰς ὕψος αἴρεσθαι), the reader may draw comfort from the knowledge that this raising is the work of the devil (v. 5) and that a time is surely coming when God will retake control of affairs, bringing down the wicked fools and raising up the righteous wise. We need only wait until v. 8 for a reminder that in the future the wicked will fall.

(7) καὶ δούλους μὲν ἁμαρτιῶν ἐπὶ ἵππον φερομένους, ἄνδρας δὲ ἱεροὺς βαδίζοντας ἀτίμως ὁρᾶσθαι, τῶν πονηρῶν γαυρουμένων.

... and the slaves of sin are to be seen riding on horseback, while holy people are walking in dishonour — which brings joy to wicked people.

Just as Gregory felt it necessary to explain that "rich" (LXX πλούσιος) in v. 6 meant "rich in wisdom" (πλούσιος φρονήσει), so he feels it necessary to explain here in the analogous case of v. 7 that "slave" (LXX δοῦλος) means a "slave of sin" (δοῦλος ἁμαρτιῶν), the opposite of which is a "saint" (ἱερός, where LXX said ἄρχων, "ruler, prince"). Far be it from a biblical book to report simply on socio-economic reversals without any ethico-spiritual meaning — these are, after all, the works of the father of all wickedness (v. 5) which are here described.

As always, Gregory is keen to improve on Koheleth's habitual "go" (LXX πορεύομαι); these holy people are obviously "walking" (βαδίζω), while their counterparts on horseback are also supplied with a verb: φέρομαι, "to be carried". In case anyone does not realise what it means to have to walk on foot while others are able to ride on a horse, Gregory spells it out that such a person is having to go about ἀτίμως, "dishonourably, ignominiously" (presumably this arises from LXX's ὡς δούλους, "like slaves", though this second occurrence of "slaves" also gives rise to Gregory's πονηροί, "wicked people" as a parallel to his earlier δοῦλοι ἁμαρτιῶν for LXX's first citing of the δοῦλοι).

You do not have to be a Solomon to see what goes on in the world, according to Gregory; it is not a matter of "I saw" (LXX εἶδον) but of what is there "to be seen" (ὁρᾶσθαι). Moreover, he laments, when wicked people see these works of the prince and father of all wickedness, they "are exultant" (γαυρόομαι) about it. But he will now proceed to offer some reasons why their joy is misplaced and will not last.

(8) Εἰ δέ τις ἑτέρῳ ἐπιβουλεύει, λέληθεν αὐτὸν ὡς ἑαυτῷ πρώτῳ καὶ μόνῳ ἔνεδρον ἐργάζεται. Ὁ δὲ καθαιρῶν ἄλλου ἀσφάλειαν, περιπεσεῖται ὄφεως δήγματι.

But if someone plots against another person, he forgets that he is setting a trap firstly and only for himself. The person who destroys someone else's safety will be caught in a serpent's bite.

The various proverbial sayings collected in Chapter Ten of Ecclesiastes do not appear to be closely connected with each other,[16] but in the Paraphrase of Solomon's "Ecclesiastes" each verse is well linked to its neighbours, not just by means of Gregory's frequently-employed particle δέ (which appears in all but three verses in the chapter), but also in terms of the ideas expressed. Thus here in v. 8, where Koheleth may simply have been putting forward his pessimistic view that misfortune has a habit of suddenly striking people down (cf. in particular 9:12), Gregory has Solomon warn the wicked people of the previous verse — and at the same time comfort the righteous who presently suffer at the hands of the wicked — that the rejoicing on the part of the wicked is premature and transitory in the light of the just governance of the universe, wherein wickedness inevitably receives its own reward. Doubtlessly in this interpretation Gregory has an eye to Psalm 7:15-17 (English vv. 14-16), where the Psalmist sings of the wicked person who "conceives evil, and is pregnant with mischief, and brings forth lies: he makes a pit, digging it out, and falls into the hole which he has made; his mischief returns upon his own head, and on his own pate his violence descends."

So "digging a pit" (LXX ὀρύσσω βόθρον) here in Ecclesiastes

10:8 is a metaphor for conceiving evil, "plotting against" or
"laying a snare for" (ἐπιβουλεύω) someone else, but in reality
"setting a trap" (ἔνεδρον ἐργάζομαι) for oneself, because — as
Koheleth and the Psalmist (for Gregory, the prophet-kings
Solomon and his father David) both said — one "falls" (LXX
ἐμπίπτω) into the pit one has dug.

Indeed, says Gregory, not only
is the wicked person preparing a pit for himself first and
foremost (πρῶτος), but in fact he is the only one (μόνος) who will
be trapped; thus it is revealed that the wise and the holy, who
are pictured in hard times in vv. 6 and 7, ultimately are not
harmed by the devices of the fools and the sinners, whereas
those very fools and sinners who seek to do them harm are only
harming themselves in the long run.

Koheleth's second picture here is interpreted in the same
terms: "pulling down a wall/fence" (LXX καθαιρέω φραγμόν) is a
metaphor for "pulling down another's safety" (καθαιρέω ἄλλου
ἀσφάλειαν), the wall or fence being seen as a symbol of the
security it provides for those who live within its confines. In
saying that a "serpent" (LXX ὄφις) will "bite" (LXX δάκνω) the
person who pulls down the wall, Koheleth may simply have
been drawing attention to the very real possibility of a worker
inadvertently endangering himself and suddenly being
confronted with an unpleasant fate; in basically repeating this
picture of "a serpent's bite" (ὄφεως δῆγμα in the paraphrase, this
time leaving the imagery unexplained), Gregory believes the
concept can stand as a clear metaphor for the evils which
rebound upon the head of a person who devises evil against his
neighbour. The outcome for the evildoer is that he, and not his
intended victim, is the one who ultimately "is caught" or "falls"
(περιπίπτω, drawing an analogy to LXX's ἐμπίπτω of the first
picture in this verse, and applying a just reversal to Gregory's
own αἴρομαι of v. 6; cf. αἴρομαι followed by πίπτω in the
paraphrase of 4:1).

In picturing the sinner caught in a serpent's bite, the
Church Father doubtlessly wants his readers to think of that
"ancient serpent" (ὁ ὄφις ὁ ἀρχαῖος) of Revelation 12:9 and 20:2,
the devil, whom Gregory has just described as "the prince and
father of all wickedness" (v. 5). Describing the wicked as being

caught in this serpent's bite recalls Gregory's talk in 3:10,11 of "poisonous stings" (κέντρα ἰοβόλα) connected with an "evil observer of the times" (καιροσκόπος πονηρός) who "closes his jaws over" or "takes into his mouth" (περιχάσκω) this present age, and his talk in 4:4,5 of the "sting of an evil spirit" (οἶστρος πονηροῦ πνεύματος) connected with the "eating", "cutting", and "consuming" (διεσθίω, διαπρίω, and δαπανάω) of a person's ψυχή along with his σῶμα. Gregory's readers have been warned: the person who plots and practises evil against his neighbour is doing the devil's work, and will receive the devil's reward.

(9)   Ἀλλὰ μὴ[ν][17] ὁ λίθους ἐξαιρούμενος, ὑποίσει πόνον οὐ μικρόν· ἀλλὰ καὶ σχίζων ξύλα, ἐν αὐτῷ τῷ οἰκείῳ ὅπλῳ τὸν κίνδυνον οἴσει.

The person who removes stones certainly carries out no small task, and the person who splits logs carries danger in his own implement.

Although he completely rephrased "digging a pit" and "pulling down a wall" in the previous verse as metaphors for human beings doing unto others what will then justly be done unto them, Gregory is now content (at least for the moment, since he cannot resist adding two significant adjectives in v. 10) to simply reproduce Koheleth's next pair of labouring jobs: "removing stones" (LXX's ἐξαίρω λίθους) and "splitting logs" (LXX's σχίζω ξύλα), seemingly nothing more and nothing less.[18]

Gregory makes an analogy between the two activities by his use of ὑποφέρω, "carry out" or "endure" in the first case and φέρω, "carry" or "endure" in the second. The first activity, he says, is "no small task [or: trouble]" (πόνος οὐ μικρός, the noun arising from LXX's διαπονέομαι, "to be troubled"), while the second involves "danger" (κίνδυνος, a noun arising from LXX's verb κινδυνεύω, "to be endangered"). The only real change which Gregory has made is that he sees the danger as lying, not in the logs which the worker splits (LXX's ἐν αὐτοῖς, "in them"), but in the tool which he uses to split them (Gregory's ἐν αὐτῷ τῷ οἰκείῳ ὅπλῳ, "in his own implement"); in making this change he has an eye on the following verse.

(10) Ἐὰν δὲ συμβῇ τοῦ στελεοῦ¹⁹ τὸν πέλεκυν ἐκπηδῆσαι,
θορυβηθήσεται ὁ ταῦτα ἐργαζόμενος, οὐκ ἐπ᾽ ἀγαθῷ συγκομίζων,
καὶ ἐπαύξων αὐτὸς τὴν ἑαυτοῦ ἄδικον καὶ ὠκύμορον δύναμιν.

**If it were to happen that the axe sprang off the handle, the
person doing this work would be given trouble, getting a poor
return and exerting more of his wrongful and transitory
strength.**

The LXX translator stumbled over this verse, and
accordingly Gregory is led astray almost from the first word.
There were no problems with the introductory "if" (MT אם, LXX
and Gregory ἐάν), but then MT's קהה piel, "to be(come) blunt"
was inexplicably rendered in LXX by ἐκπίπτω, "to fall off", which
in turn is paraphrased by Gregory's ἐκπηδάω, "to leap out". This
has the effect of making the verse farcical, for it is difficult to
imagine even the most stupid of axemen continuing to chop
wood when there is no longer any axe-head on the handle he is
wielding — whereas Koheleth's picture of an axeman having to
put more effort into his work because of the bluntness of his
implement made perfect sense. קהה may be a rare verb, but the
Peshitta (with the Syriac ܟܗܐ) and the Vulgate (with retunsus
sit) are able to render it as "being blunt", so LXX might have been
expected to do so, too. Still, on the matter of an "iron" (MT ברזל),
LXX correctly took Koheleth's reference as being to an iron
implement (σιδήριον), which Gregory then narrows down with
even greater precision to an axe (πέλεκυς) which is — or was —
joined to an axe-handle (στελεός).

But Koheleth's second phrase proved to be another
stumbling-block. The pilpel of קלל, like קהה piel in the first
phrase, would also have been somewhat unfamiliar to a biblical
translator. Nevertheless, the Vulgate translation appears to be
based on a correct understanding of the verbal idea here, since
the concept of "sharpening" the axe (exacuo) appears in the
verse, though only after the concept of not being sharp (hebes sit)
has been reiterated (after the earlier retunsus sit). In post-biblical
Hebrew, however, קלקל quite commonly appears with a meaning
along the lines of "to upset" or "ruin"; hence LXX's ταράσσω,
"to disturb, trouble" (cf. Peshitta ܢܕܠ, neither LXX nor Peshitta

reading MT's לא in this phrase, though perhaps they did read the Oriental לו)[20] and accordingly Gregory's θορυβέομαι, "to be troubled/distressed". As for פנים, by which Koheleth may well have meant the "face" or "leading edge" of the axe, LXX's πρόσωπον (and Peshitta's ܐ̈ܦܐ) can only refer to the "face" or "countenance" of the human subject who is troubled, while Vulgate's *ut prius*, "as before" has defensibly taken it adverbially;[21] Gregory sees no point in pointing to the worker's face as such, but rather to the worker as a whole (ὁ ἐργαζόμενος), whose work (ταῦτα, presumably referring to the splitting of logs mentioned in the previous verse) is made considerably more difficult — impossible, really — by the fact of having no axe-head on his axe-handle.

Koheleth's next comment, that the person engaged in log-splitting with an implement unsuitable for the task has to "increase" (גבר piel) his "efforts" (חילים, literally "strengths") if he is to achieve what would have been achieved more easily with a good tool, is the only phrase in this verse which does not appear to have given LXX any difficulty. The worker has to "strengthen" (δυναμόω) his "strength" (δύναμις), said the Greek translation. Gregory remains unimpressed with such expressions involving cognate verb and noun,[22] and paraphrases this as "increasing" (ἐπαύξω) one's δύναμις — but a δύναμις which he describes as ἄδικος, "unrighteous" and ὠκύμορος, "transient". Until the addition of these two adjectives it had appeared that Gregory was reproducing Koheleth's talk of stone-removal and log-splitting as being simply and straightforwardly these two labouring jobs, unlike his metaphorical interpretations of pit-digging and wall-wrecking as being unrighteous activities aimed at causing harm to a person's neighbour; but now through ἄδικος he suggests that the reader also apply the log-splitting activity on the level of inter-personal morality (though the reader must make the application himself, since Gregory has not done it for him as he did in v. 8), and through ὠκύμορος he suggests again that the wicked cannot go on forever in their wickedness.[23]

While the penultimate phrase was not problematic for Koheleth's Greek successors, the closing expression יתרון הכשיר חכמה is a different matter. The Masoretes vocalise הכשיר as the hiphil infinitive, and accent it as being linked to יתרון,[24] thus yielding the meaning "wisdom has the advantage of bringing success" (assuming that Koheleth used כשר hiphil as "to bring success", in accordance with his apparent use of the qal in 11:6 as "be successful"),[25] which is to say that a wise person would chop with a sharp axe and achieve the desired results without having to expend excessive amounts of energy. But LXX vocalised הכשיר as the qal participle with the definite article, and — not being sure what to make of כשר here (cf. στοιχέω, "to correspond, be satisfactory" in 11:6) but having an eye to the preceding phrase concerning the expenditure of greater effort — translated the phrase now at hand as περισσεία τοῦ ἀνδρείου σοφία, "wisdom is the advantage of a strong [or: vigorous][26] person", which virtually runs counter to the idea that a wise person is able to avoid a situation in which more strength or vigour is required to complete a task.

Τοῦ ἀνδρείου for הכשיר was still not the end of the Septuagintal difficulties, however, for in Codex Vaticanus we find that the Greek expression has become τῷ ἀνδρὶ οὐ, which yields the meaning "wisdom is of no advantage to a person", a contention even less in keeping with a Wisdom perspective than the general LXX reading (though Koheleth himself did indeed canvas such an idea in 1:17; 2:15; and 6:8). Yet the reading found in Codex Vaticanus is the one which Gregory follows, judging by his paraphrase οὐκ ἐπ' ἀγαθῷ συγκομίζων, "not gathering to any good, bringing in a poor harvest". The paraphrast has made sense of the Greek phrase before him by interpreting as follows: the advantages of wisdom are not for the person pictured in this verse, namely the kind of person who attempts to split logs with no axe on his handle; it does such a fool no good at all to put more and more effort into his task, but precisely because nothing good is achieved by his efforts he tries even harder. Οὐκ ἐπ' ἀγαθῷ has a double meaning here, judging by Gregory's depiction of the fool's strength as ἄδικος and ὠκύμορος: the "axeman" is a wicked person who intends no good for his neighbour, but in fact achieves no good for himself (cf. the "digger" and the "demolisher" of v. 8, as contrasted with the good individual of v. 12, in Gregory's version of things).

(11) "Οφεως δὲ δῆγμα λαθραῖον· οὐδὲν παραμυθήσονται οἱ ἐπᾴδοντες· μάταιοι γάρ εἰσιν.

A serpent's bite is stealthy, and the charmers will not bring relief, since they are worthless.

The serpent bites again, as it did in v. 8. The lack of "whispering" (MT שׁחל, LXX ψιθυρισμός) is probably on the part of the professional charmer, who is supposed to be able to prevent such bites from occurring (so שׁחל in Jeremiah 8:17, where LXX uses ἐπᾴδω, "to sing so as to charm", which both Symmachus and Theodotion employ for שׁחל here in Ecclesiastes 10:11; cf. Peshitta's ܪܚܫܘܬܐ, "charm, incantation"), but Gregory takes it as being on the part of the serpent itself, which makes no sound and thus gives no warning before it bites (its bite is λαθραῖος, "secret, stealthy", an interpretation which the Vulgate also adopts with its *in silentio*). In any case, once a serpent has actually bitten, there is no value in a professional charmer — MT's בעל הלשון, "master of the tongue" could arguably have been referring to the snake, as v. 20's בעל הכנפים, "master of the wings" refers to the bird of that verse, but LXX was probably correct in now employing the participle of ἐπᾴδω (cf. Peshitta ܪܚܫܘܬܐ), which Gregory adopts in a plural form.[27] He spells out this lack of value (LXX περισσεία) as being an inability to "relieve" (παραμυθέομαι) the pain suffered by the one who has been bitten; in a Kohelethine word, the charmers are μάταιος.

The ὄφις Gregory has in mind is once again more than the common or garden-variety snake, which serves merely as a metaphor for that satanic creature who stealthily entraps people in sin and holds them tight (cf. his ὄφις in v. 8), bringing about their destruction (see v. 12); and the worthless ἐπᾴδοντες are probably to be associated with those fools who try to enchant people with the message that the way of wickedness is a painless and enjoyable road (cf. Gregory's use of ἐπᾴδω in the context of 9:7), whereas it is actually the path of ματαιότης (cf. 9:10).

(12) 'Αλλ' ὁ μὲν ἀγαθὸς ἀνὴρ ἀγαθὰ ἐργάζεται αὐτῷ τε καὶ τοῖς πλησίον· ὁ δὲ ἄφρων εἰς ὄλεθρον ἐμπεσεῖται διὰ τῆς αὑτοῦ φλυαρίας.

But the good person brings about good things both for himself and for his neighbours, while the foolish person will fall into destruction through his own silly talk.

The typical Wisdom contrast between the σοφός and the ἄφρων re-entered the scene at this point of Ecclesiastes, though for Gregory it has been in view all along. The activities cited in the preceding verses have been interpreted as the activities of fools and sinners doing the work of their father, the devil, and so now the good works of ὁ ἀγαθὸς ἀνήρ can be briefly contrasted. Wicked people were pictured as bringing about bad things for themselves and for their neighbours (v. 8, and note the οὐκ ἐπ᾽ ἀγαθῷ of v. 10); now the good person is said to do precisely the opposite: to "bring about good things both for himself and for his neighbours" (ἀγαθὰ ἐργάζεται αὐτῷ τε καὶ τοῖς πλησίον — on the basis of Koheleth's view that what the wise person achieves through his words is χάρις [חן], "grace" or "favour"). Meanwhile the ἄφρων, pictured by Koheleth as being "swallowed up" (MT בלע piel) or "drowned" (LXX καταποντίζω) by his own lips, is pictured by Gregory as "falling into destruction" (εἰς ὄλεθρον ἐμπίπτω) as a result of his own foolishness.

The paraphrase does not speak of "the words of the mouth" (LXX λόγοι στόματος) of the commendable character — Gregory prefers to have a reference to good things in general at that point — but, where LXX mentioned the χείλη, "lips", the paraphrase cites the "silly talk" (φλυαρία, which Gregory sees as a particular characteristic of fools; cf. 2:15; 6:11; 7:21) of the reprehensible character, to be further commented upon in the following verses. Gregory will also return later in his paraphrase to a depiction of the fate of the fool in terms of the direction εἰς ὄλεθρον (11:10).

(13) Καὶ ἅπαξ ἀνοίξας τὸ στόμα, ἄρχεται ἀφρόνως, καὶ παύεται ταχέως, ...

Once he opens his mouth, he begins foolishly and quickly stops, ...

Gregory did not wish to comment specifically on the λόγοι στόματος ("the words of the mouth") of the wise individual in the previous verse, but he is only too happy to comment on the λόγοι στόματος of the foolish individual in this verse, since the fool most clearly reveals himself for what he is by what comes out of his στόμα as soon as he "opens" it (ἀνοίγω). The paraphrase is brief and to the point, replacing LXX's nouns with verbs (ἀρχή, "beginning" and ἐσχάτη, "end" are transformed into ἄρχομαι, "to begin" and παύομαι, "to come to an end" respectively) and adverbs (ἀφροσύνη, "foolishness" becomes ἀφρόνως, "foolishly" and περιφέρεια, "senselessness" is replaced — perhaps on the basis of the Greek word's association with the idea of "turning around" or "revolving" — by ταχέως, "quickly"). It seems that at this point the paraphrast is careful not to "multiply words", lest he be thought to be thereby revealing himself to be a "fool" (see the beginning of the next verse)!

(14) ... διὰ παντὸς ἐνδεικνύμενος τὴν ἑαυτοῦ ἄνοιαν. Ἀνθρώπῳ δὲ ἀδύνατόν τι γνῶναι, καὶ παρὰ ἀνθρώπου μαθεῖν τὰ ἀπ᾽ ἀρχῆς, ἢ τὰ ἐπιόντα. Τίς γὰρ ἔσται ὁ μηνύσων;

... displaying his foolishness through it all. It is quite impossible for a person to know, or to learn from another person, the things which have been from the beginning or the things which will come to be. So who will be the revealer of these things?

LXX's ὁ ἄφρων πληθύνει λόγους, "the fool multiplies words" does not mean for Gregory that a foolish person goes on and on with his φλυαρία (so Symmachus: ἀνόητος πολλὰ λαλήσει, "an empty person prattles on a great deal"), since the Christian paraphrast has just said that it comes to a swift end, but that in absolutely "everything" (πᾶς)[28] the fool says he "demonstrates" (ἐνδείκνυμι) that he is a fool (which may have been Koheleth's point at the end of v. 3, though Gregory did not see it there). Gregory seems to suggest that even the fool himself is aware of his foolishness, in closing his mouth again so quickly after opening it (v. 13), presumably to prevent his folly from becoming more obvious to others — but to no avail, since this abrupt end to his words, no less than the foolish beginning of them, only helps draw attention to his "lack of sense" (ἄνοια).

Since Koheleth opened this verse with a mention of the fool, and then proceeded to speak of the ignorance of human beings, we might have anticipated that Gregory would now speak of the ignorance of fools (cf. 8:7,17 and 11:5, where he limits Koheleth's talk of ignorance to evil or foolish people, even though Koheleth himself made no mention of such people at those places; here in 10:14 the possibility of such a line of interpretation is offered by the opening ὁ ἄφρων).[29] But Gregory does not link the ἄφρων to the ἄνθρωπος of the rest of this verse, seeing that the former is more correctly connected to the ἄφρων of the previous verses, and accordingly paraphrasing the opening phrase of v. 14 as part of the same sentence as v. 13.

To the impossibility of "knowing" (γιγνώσκω, as in LXX), Gregory — anticipating the rhetorical question which rounded off the verse — adds the impossibility of "learning" (μανθάνω) from someone who does know, since absolutely no-one has this knowledge.   That was precisely the point of the rhetorical question itself: that no-one can "report" (LXX ἀναγγέλλω) or "reveal" (Gregory μηνύω) what is hidden from human beings.

And what is hidden? According to MT, it is a knowledge of "what will be" (מה־שיהיה) and "what will be after him/it" (אשר יהיה מאחריו), which may well mean what is going to happen during a person's lifetime and what is going to happen after his death (as the Targumist puts it, מה דעתיד למהוי ביומוהי ומה דעתיד למהוי מן סופיה, "what is destined to be in his days and what is destined to be after his end").   According to LXX, however, what is hidden from human knowledge is "what has been" (τί τὸ γενόμενον) on the one hand and "what will be after him/it" (τί τὸ ἐσόμενον ὀπίσω αὐτοῦ) on the other, attesting to a reading of — or emendation to — שהיה in the first case (cf. Peshitta's ܗܘܐ in the first instance and ܢܗܘܐ in the second).   Gregory's paraphrase builds on the Septuagintal model: it is impossible to know "the things [which have been] from the beginning" (τὰ ἀπ' ἀρχῆς), just as it is impossible to know "the things which will come to be" (τὰ ἐπιόντα). While the Hebrew text concentrated on human ignorance concerning the future, the Greek translation and its daughter version have the past in view as well.

(15) Ἄνθρωπος δὲ ὃς οὐκ οἶδεν εἰς τὴν ἀγαθὴν πορευθῆναι πόλιν, κάκωσιν ὑπομένει, τοῖς τε ὀφθαλμοῖς, καὶ τῷ παντὶ προσώπῳ.

A person who does not know to go to the good city, suffers distress both in the eyes and in the whole face.

"Not knowing to go to town" (LXX οὐ γιγνώσκω τοῦ πορευθῆναι εἰς πόλιν) is evidently an idiomatic expression concerning utter stupidity on the part of "the fools" (LXX οἱ ἄφρονες)[30] mentioned in the first part of this verse. Gregory explains to his readers that the πόλις that is meant here is "the good city" (ἡ ἀγαθὴ πόλις), so the person who does not go there is missing out on the chance to escape from distress.[31] By speaking of a πόλις which is ἀγαθός, the Christian paraphrast is referring to a well-governed city whose citizens enjoy a good life (cf. the γῆ of v. 17, which is ἀγαθός and whose inhabitants will enjoy ἀγαθά, as opposed to the πόλις of v. 16, whose inhabitants will experience κακά), but it is also quite possible that he wishes to suggest at the same time the idea which his mentor Origen expressed in his Jeremiah homilies: ἔστι γὰρ ἡ πόλις τοῦ Θεοῦ ἡ Ἐκκλησία,[32] "the Church is the city of God", and a sinner must go to this city if he is to be saved from the evils of the present world (cf. Hebrews 12:22's πόλις Θεοῦ ζῶντος, "the city of the living God").

Gregory now itemises evils which a person could have escaped, had he gone to the good city. Koheleth had begun the verse by referring to the "toil" or "distress" (LXX μόχθος) of a fool, which "wearies" him (יגע piel). The Hebrew verb was correctly represented by Codex Sinaiticus as κοπόω, "to weary", but was corrupted by Codex Vaticanus to κακόω, "to ill-treat" and by Codex Alexandrinus to σκοτόω, "to darken, blind" (this last is least representative of יגע, but might be understood as an attempt to explain matters here as concerning the damage done to a careless worker's eyesight such that he can no longer find his way back into town). Gregory's version appears to para-phrase first the Vatican reading — κάκωσιν ὑπομένω, "to suffer ill-treatment/distress" — and then the Alexandrian reading — τοῖς ὀφθαλμοῖς, "in the eyes", adding also the wider reference τῷ παντὶ προσώπῳ, "in the whole face". Gregory may be thinking

apocalyptically of the vision of Zechariah 14:12 — "This shall be
the plague with which the LORD will smite all the people that
wage war against Jerusalem [i.e., in Patristic vein, the Church]:[33]
their flesh shall rot while they are still on their feet, their eyes
shall rot in their sockets, and their tongues shall rot in their
mouths." But perhaps he is simply warning his readers that the
person who does not have the sense to go to the good city will
have to witness with his own eyes the κακά (v. 16) which take
place outside of that city, and which profoundly affect one's
countenance and general disposition.

In addition to the variations in treating the Hebrew text's
יגע, the LXX scribes were not agreed on how the plural noun
(הכסילים, "the fools") accompanied by a singular pronoun (תיגענו,
"she wearies **him**") should best be handled (grammarians might
be further troubled by the feminine verbal form accompanying
the masculine noun עמל, but this problem does not arise in
Greek, where there is no gender distinction in the equivalent
verbal form). The solution of Codex Vaticanus was to keep the
noun as a plural (οἱ ἄφρονες) and to recast the pronoun in a
correspondingly plural form (κακώσει αὐτούς, "it ill-treats
them"), while Codices Sinaiticus and Alexandrinus took the
alternative course of reshaping the noun as a singular (ὁ ἄφρων)
and then leaving the pronoun in its Masoretic number
(κοπώσει/σκοτώσει αὐτόν, "it wearies/blinds **him**").[34] Gregory
accepts the majority decision, and speaks of one representative
person (ἄνθρωπος) who is ignorant of the correct path and who
suffers the consequences, rather than of a class of people who
share in such ignorance and its consequences.

(16) Πόλει δὲ ἐκείνῃ κακὰ προλέγω, ἧς ὅ τε βασιλεὺς νέος, καὶ
οἱ ἄρχοντες γαστρίμαργοι.

**I predict bad things for that city whose king is young and
whose rulers are gluttons.**

In this and the following verse Koheleth referred to a
political entity which MT terms an ארץ, a "land". LXX gave the
literal Greek equivalent γῆ in v. 17, but here in v. 16 employed
πόλις, which had just appeared for עיר at the end of v. 15.

270 GREGORY'S ECCLESIASTES

Symmachus makes a "correction" to γῆ for אֶרֶץ in this present verse, but Gregory pays no heed to Symmachus, using πόλις here and γῆ in the following verse, just as LXX does. This facilitates the Gregorian interpretation which links the thought of v. 15 with that of vv. 16 and 17 (cf. the Targumist who, working from MT, sees just a city in v. 15 but אֶרֶץ יִשְׂרָאֵל in vv. 16 and 17): since v. 16 speaks of a city-state, and v. 17 of another city-state, but πόλις is used in one case and γῆ in the other, the terms must be interchangeable and so the πόλις of v. 15 can be equivalent to the γῆ of v. 17, a good city to which fools do not go and in which good things transpire, as contrasted with the other πόλις of v. 16 which is now in focus, where fools are much in evidence and bad things are in store.

The prophetic-sounding cry "woe unto you!" (LXX οὐαί σοι) means that the wisest of all prophets — as Gregory styles Solomon in 1:1 — is now "foretelling" (προλέγω) the "woes" (κακά) destined to befall a city which is ruled by wicked people. The problem of having a king who is a "youth" (LXX νεώτερος) is not explained by Gregory's νέος, "young", which leaves the reader to assume that the king is inexperienced and unwilling or unable to rule well,[35] but the problem of having rulers who "eat in the morning" (LXX ἐν πρωΐᾳ ἐσθίω) is well explained by Gregory's γαστρίμαργος, "gluttonous", in view of another prophet's words concerning this kind of activity (Isaiah 5:11).[36]

(17) Μακαρίζω δὲ γῆν τὴν ἀγαθήν, ἧς βασιλεύει ὁ τοῦ ἐλευθέρου υἱός· ἔνθα εὐκαίρως ἀπολαύσουσιν ἀγαθῶν, οἱ ἐκεῖσε ἄρχειν ἠξιωμένοι.

But I congratulate the good land whose king is the son of the free; in that land the people who have been deemed worthy of ruling will enjoy good things in due season.

The antithesis of predicting woe is to "pronounce blessed/fortunate" (μακαρίζω, from LXX's adjective μακάριος), and the antithesis of forthcoming κακά is forthcoming ἀγαθά. Though Gregory speaks only of this land's rulers receiving the good things, whereas in v. 16 it was the city as a whole which would receive bad things, it is the land as a whole which he calls blessed

— and ἀγαθός, though he did not call the antithetical city κακός.
Gregory again styles the chief ruler of the city-state as
βασιλεύς (so LXX in both verses) and again regards as
unnecessary any explanation of the king's character (it is enough
to say that the country is fortunate if he is ὁ τοῦ ἐλευθέρου υἱός
[LXX had a plural genitive, υἱὸς ἐλευθέρων], "the son of the
free"), but rather than simply repeat the styling of the lesser
rulers as ἄρχοντες (so LXX in both verses, and so Gregory in v.
16) he varies things a little by calling them οἱ ἄρχειν ἠξιωμένοι,
"the ones who have been deemed worthy of ruling", which
brings in the nuance that rulership is granted to certain people
in trust, for them to govern well so that good things may ensue
for all. "To eat at the [right] time" (LXX πρὸς καιρὸν ἐσθίω)
Gregory takes to mean "to enjoy [things] in due season"
(εὐκαίρως ἀπολαύω), but he does not appear to be sure about just
what is meant by "in strength and not feeling shame" (LXX's ἐν
δυνάμει καὶ οὐκ αἰσχυνθήσονται appears to have detected the
root בוש rather than שתה in בגבורה ולא בשתי, "in strength and not in
drinking" — i.e., for sustenance rather than for drunkenness),
which he leaves unexpressed.

(18) Ὀκνηρὸς δὲ καὶ ἀργός, οἶκον ἐλαττοῦσι χλευασταὶ
γενόμενοι·

**A sluggard and an idler bring down the house, as they are
born scoffers.**

Gregory changes the abstract nouns into concrete individuals, and brings them together at the beginning of the verse
as being two of a kind: the "sluggish" person (ὀκνηρός, from
LXX's ὀκνηρίαι, "sluggishness", a plural form mimicking the
intensive[37] dual עצלתים, "sloth") and the "idle" person (ἀργός,
from LXX's ἀργία χειρῶν, "idleness of hands", a good understanding of the expression שפלות ידים, "lowering of the hands").
Koheleth's parallel descriptions of "the roof-beam being brought
low" (LXX ταπεινόεται ἡ δόκωσις) and "the house dripping" (LXX
στάζει ἡ οἰκία, presumably a reference to rain-water dripping
through the unrepaired roof, but taken by the Targumist as a
euphemism for menstruation!) are accordingly conflated into

the single paraphrase οἶκον ἐλαττοῦσι, "they lower the house".
But having expressed the proverb so compactly, Gregory decides
to add a little further comment of his own on sluggards and
idlers, calling them "born scoffers" (χλευασταὶ γενόμενοι, perhaps
with an eye on the laughter [LXX γέλως] with which the next
verse begins), people who are always willing to mock the efforts
of others but are never willing to make any effort themselves —
except for base motives (see the paraphrase of the next verse, a
continuation of the sentence of this verse).

(19) καὶ εἰς τὴν ἑαυτῶν λαιμαργίαν, τοῖς πᾶσι καταχρώμενοι,
ἀργυρίῳ ἀγώγιμοι, ἕνεκα ὀλίγου τιμήματος πάντα αἰσχρῶς καὶ
ταπεινῶς πράσσειν ὑπομένοντες.

**Using everything up in their own gluttony, the dupes of
money dare to do every shameful and base thing for the sake of a
small payment.**

That familiar threesome of bread, wine, and merriment
(LXX ἄρτος, οἶνος, and εὐφραίνω)[38] have never been viewed
positively by Gregory. So also here, where Koheleth's thought
may have been an essentially positive one, that food and wine
are the necessary ingredients for a cheerful life,[39] the Church
Father's stance is firmly negative, that gluttony (λαιμαργία) or
over-indulgence (καταχράομαι, "to use up, misuse") are
common characteristics of a wicked lifestyle. The presence here
of "laughter" (LXX γέλως), which Koheleth himself had linked
with merriment (LXX εὐφροσύνη) in a negative reference in 2:2,
only serves to strengthen Gregory's opinion at this point.

The relationship between "money" (LXX ἀργύριον) and
"everything" (LXX τὰ πάντα) in the final clause is not clear. The
verb here — ענה — was used by Koheleth in all other instances
(1:13; 3:10; 5:19) in the sense of "being busy/occupied", which
LXX translated by means of περισπάομαι, "to be distracted". Such
a meaning did not easily fit the phrase now at hand, and it
seems that the Greek scribes were unsure what to do: the
translation ἐπακούω, "to obey" was offered, but Codices
Vaticanus and Sinaiticus also include ταπεινόω, "to humble"
(which in connection with ἐπακούω must be read as the noun

ταπείνωσις, "humility"), resulting in the expression ταπεινώσει ἐπακούσεται, "in humility it will obey". In this way two alternative renderings of the polyhomonymical ענה have been put forward (cf. Peshitta's ܡܟܟ ܘܡܛܥܐ, "it humbles and leads astray"), while at the same time ἀργύριον was made the object and τὰ πάντα the subject of the phrase, even though Codex Alexandrinus' σύν before τὰ πάντα is evidence that at least some Greek scribes were aware of MT's objective particle את on הכל. Thus הכסף יענה את-הכל, "money answers (?) everything" became τοῦ ἀργυρίου ταπεινώσει ἐπακούσεται τὰ πάντα,[40] "everything humbly obeys money"; each of these phrases in its own way may well have been saying that money is necessary for everything, that all eating of bread and drinking of wine is dependent upon one's having sufficient money to procure such enjoyable commodities, but Gregory is not disposed to see anything positive here in either the consumption of, or the ability to purchase, these commodities — at least not in great quantities.

The paraphrase takes account of both ἐπακούω and ταπεινόω. From the former, with its message of "they obey money" (even though "they" are τὰ πάντα and not οἱ πάντες, as the paraphrast acknowledges with his own use of πάντα later in the verse), Gregory gets the idea of "those who are easily led by money" (ἀργυρίῳ ἀγώγιμοι, a cleverly poetical expression); from the latter, with its possible meaning of "to abase", he draws out the idea of those people acting ταπεινῶς, "in a base manner", to which he adds for good measure the synonymous adverb αἰσχρῶς, "shamefully". The complete enslavement of such people to money is emphasised by Gregory's juxtaposition of the smallest of prices (ὀλίγον τίμημα) for which they are willing to work and the greatest possible range (πάντα) of wicked activities in which they are prepared to engage. To a Father of the Church, the love of money is the root of all evils (cf. 1 Timothy 6:10).

(20) Βασιλεῖ δέ, καὶ ἄρχουσιν, ἢ δυνάσταις ὑπακούειν προσήκει, καὶ οὐκ ἀπεχθάνεσθαι, οὐδ' ὅλως λυπηρόν τι εἰς αὐτοὺς ῥῆμα ἀπορρίπτειν. Δέος γάρ, μὴ τὸ καὶ τὸ καταμόνας εἰρημένον, εἰς φανερόν πως ἔλθῃ. Τῷ γὰρ μόνῳ καὶ πλουσίῳ καὶ μεγάλῳ βασιλεῖ ἄγγελοι ὀξεῖς καὶ ὑπόπτεροι ἅπαντα διακομίζουσι,

πνευματικὴν ὁμοῦ καὶ λογικὴν τελοῦντες ὑπηρεσίαν.
It is proper to obey kings and officials or rulers, and not to
become hateful to them or to utter any harmful word against
them. There is reason for caution, lest what is spoken in secret
somehow come out into the open. For swift and winged
messengers carry everything to the only rich and mighty King,
thus performing both a spiritual and a rational service.

When Koheleth gave expression in v. 6 to the idea that
people who are "rich" (LXX πλούσιος) ought rightfully to be in
high positions, Gregory had corrected him: people who are "rich
in wisdom" (πλούσιος φρονήσει) are the ones who should be
exalted. In the present verse, where Koheleth spoke of those
who are πλούσιος as being on a par with the "king" (LXX
βασιλεύς), Gregory again corrects him: the ones who ought to be
so compared are the same ones who were mentioned along with
the βασιλεύς in vv. 16 and 17, viz. the ἄρχοντες, who may also be
termed δυνάσται — that is to say, the various rulers and officials
who stand just under the king in the governmental hierarchy,
and who must be obeyed just as surely as the king himself must
be obeyed. In addition to expressing this necessity in a positive
form (ὑπακούω, "to obey", perhaps with a glance back at LXX's
ἐπακούω in v. 19 — i.e., obey the king and other rulers rather
than money or those who possess money!), the paraphrase
handles LXX's twofold use of the negated καταράομαι, "to curse"
by means of two different negated verbs: ἀπεχθάνομαι, "to incur
hatred" and (λυπηρὸν ῥῆμα) ἀπορρίπτω, "to utter (a harmful
word)"; the first of these encapsulates the feelings which play in
one's innermost thoughts (LXX ἐν συνειδήσει σου, "in your
consciousness", which Gregory does not directly paraphrase) and
which lead to the second phase of audibly cursing in one's
innermost chamber (LXX ἐν ταμιείοις κοιτώνων σου, "in your
bedroom", well paraphrased by καταμόνος, "alone, in secret" and
contrasted with the frightening possibility of such matters
becoming φανερός, "open, in public").

This ever-present danger of one's secret thoughts and
words becoming known to the authorities was so real to
Koheleth that he doubled his efforts in warning the citizen

against harbouring and expressing disloyal sentiments: πετεινὸν τοῦ οὐρανοῦ ἀποίσει σὺν τὴν φωνήν (עוף השמים יוליך את־הקול), "a bird of the air will carry one's voice", he cautioned, and then, paraphrasing his own words, he repeated the warning in the form ὁ ἔχων τὰς πτέρυγας ἀπαγγελεῖ λόγον (בעל הכנפים יגיד דבר), "the possessor of wings will report one's speech". To a pious interpreter, this kind of language carries more meaning than merely a comment on the mysterious ways in which secrets are quickly spread, in the vein of the common English saying, "a little bird told me about it". No, "a 'bird' of heaven" and "a possessor of wings"[41] — who, what is more, "reports" (LXX ἀπαγγέλλω) one's most secret opinions — is to Gregory's eye transparently symbolic language for a heavenly messenger or angel, an ἄγγελος (cf. Targum's מלאכא).

Because Koheleth said his piece in two ways, Gregory identifies two types of service which God's messengers perform ("spiritual" [πνευματικός] and "rational" [λογικός]),[42] as well as ascribing to them two characteristics ("swift" [ὀξύς] and "winged" [ὑπόπτερος]). Gregory further identifies in no uncertain terms for whom the said services are performed: ὁ μόνος καὶ πλούσιος καὶ μέγας βασιλεύς, "the only rich and mighty King", in contrast to the merely mortal βασιλεύς and πλούσιος of whom Koheleth was so afraid in this verse; the One to be truly feared, warns the Church Father, is the One from whom truly no secrets can be hidden (cf. his paraphrase of 8:4 and 12:13).

Chapter Eleven

(1) Κοινωνεῖν γε μὴν ἄρτου καὶ τῶν ἀναγκαίων, ἃ πρὸς τὸν βίον ἀνθρώποις, δίκαιον. Εἰ γὰρ καὶ παραυτίκα τισὶ δόξεις ἀπολλύναι, ὥσπερ ὕδατι τὸν ἄρτον παραδιδούς, ἀλλ᾽ οὖν προϊόντος τοῦ χρόνου, οὐκ ἀνόνητός σοι φανεῖται ἡ φιλανθρωπία.

It is right to share bread and the things which are necessary for human life. Even if it seems at the moment to be wasted on some people, as if the bread was thrown into water, it will be seen in the course of time that the act of kindness is not unprofitable for you.

"Send your bread upon the waters, for you will find it after many days" was probably intended by Koheleth as shrewd business advice: "Invest in overseas trade, for you will be rewarded with large profits after long voyages." This interpretation fits well with the context, for Koheleth proceeded to offer other business advice, and with the nature of maritime trade in the ancient world, for a ship could take a very long time to complete a commercial voyage.[1] But the traditional Jewish interpretation, seen in the Targum's "Give your bread of sustenance to the poor... [and] you will find its reward in the world to come", is that the verse is an exhortation to the practice of charity and a guarantee of eventual just recompense for such goodness. Gregory readily accepts this interpretation, naming the activity described as φιλανθρωπία and pronouncing this activity to be δίκαιος.

"Bread" is not literally ἄρτος, as in LXX, but also figuratively τὰ ἀναγκαῖα, the necessities of life. "Sending" this (LXX ἀποστέλλω) means "sharing" it (κοινωνέω) with other people, even though appearances may suggest that in doing so the philanthropist is "wasting" it (ἀπόλλυμι) by "throwing" it (παραδίδωμι) away — into ὕδωρ, as in LXX. And "finding" it again (LXX εὑρίσκω) after many days means finding it to be "not unprofitable" (οὐκ ἀνόνητος) in the course of time. Thus what eventually appears — i.e., comes to light: φαίνομαι — contrasts sharply with what appeared to be — i.e., was thought to be the case: δοκέω.

The eventual "profit" Gregory has in mind is probably in this life — Proverbs 22:9 promises that the person who shares his bread with the poor will be blessed — but it may be only in the life to come — Matthew 25:34ff. promises that the person who gives the necessities of life to those in need will inherit eternal life. Gregory may have intentionally left the reference open to both time and eternity, but on either count he is considerably more optimistic than was Koheleth.

(2) Δίδου δὲ ἀφειδῶς, καὶ μέριζε τὰ σαυτοῦ πλείοσιν· οὐ γὰρ ἐπίστασαι τί ποτε ἡ ἐπιοῦσα ἐποίησεν ἡμέρα.

Give freely, and distribute what you have to many people, because you do not know what the coming day will produce.

Koheleth's next piece of advice, "Give a portion to seven and also to eight, for you do not know what evil there will be on the earth", appears to have been an injunction to diversify one's business interests in view of the unpredictability of life — a disaster in one area could ruin a person completely if he had all his eggs in that one basket. Not surprisingly, however, Gregory continues with the interpretation of philanthropy he employed in the previous verse.[2]

LXX's δίδωμι reappeared, though now in the present — rather than the aorist — imperative form, and LXX's μερίς, "portion, share" gives rise to Gregory's μερίζω, "to distribute, divide". The expression "seven and also eight" is an example of a common Semitic literary device of using consecutive numbers; the enumeration was not meant precisely but indicated an indefinite numerical value: "several" or "many", the sense of which Gregory has captured with πλείων in the plural. LXX's γιγνώσκω is well paraphrased by ἐπίσταμαι.

Koheleth was concerned about the ever-present possibility of misfortune (LXX πονηρός) that waits around the corner in this earthly life (LXX ἐπὶ τὴν γῆν). Gregory speaks only vaguely of what ἡ ἐπιοῦσα ἡμέρα, "the coming day" might bring. The absence of the spatial reference leaves open what this day is — probably just another earthly day, but it might be taken by the reader as a reference to the day of judgment (and hence to the end of this earthly life). And the absense of any parallel to LXX's πονηρός leaves open what this day will bring — it seems as though Gregory will not allow it to be said that "the coming day" might produce evil for those who give freely and distribute what they have to many people, since this would contradict the οὐκ ἀνόνητος promise which he had just given in v. 1. But despite his reticence about including something corresponding to πονηρός here, Gregory's meaning might still be "Give to many people because misfortune may strike you some day and then your acts of kindness can be repaid"; in other words, the profitability of kindness will be seen in that others will treat you in the way in which you have treated them (cf. the so-called "golden rule" in Matthew 7:12 and Luke 6:31).

(3) Κατέχουσι δὲ οὐδὲ νεφέλαι τὸν ἑαυτῶν πολὺν ὑετόν, ἀλλὰ τὸν ὄμβρον ἐπὶ γῆν ἀφιᾶσι· καὶ οὐδὲ δένδρον εἰς ἀεὶ ἔστηκεν, ἀλλὰ κἂν ἄνδρες αὐτοῦ φείσωνται, ἀνέμῳ γοῦν ἀνατραπήσεται.

The clouds do not hold back their plentiful rain, but send the thunderstorm upon the earth; nor does a tree stand forever, but even if human beings leave it alone it will at any rate be overturned by wind.

To introduce his advice to farmers to get on with their labours and not wait around for conditions to be perfect, Koheleth noted that the processes of nature follow their natural laws irrespective of human actions or wishes. With respect to clouds (LXX's νέφος is lengthened to νεφέλη), the paraphrase is in accord with what Koheleth said: rain will eventually fall upon the earth. With respect to trees (LXX's ξύλον [for MT's עץ] is more accurately specified as δένδρον, as it is also by Symmachus), the paraphrase makes an analogous point: trees will eventually fall down — Koheleth did not exactly say that, but rather had made the point that if a tree falls down, it will inevitably lie in the place where it has fallen.

Gregory's alteration here may be due to his penchant for well-balanced composition, for in his formulation he has balanced the clouds' "holding fast" (κατέχω, the opposite of LXX's ἐκχέω) with the tree's "standing" (ἵστημι, the opposite of

LXX's πίπτω and possibly arising from εἰμί in the last clause), and the former's "sending forth" (ἀφίημι, the equivalent of LXX's ἐκχέω) with the latter's "being overturned" (ἀνατρέπομαι, the passive equivalent in this context of LXX's active πίπτω). Or the paraphrase may be due to Gregory's concern about a possible anomaly in the original, for trees do not necessarily lie where they fall, but may be dragged away and/or chopped up by people. Koheleth did not state in this verse what might cause a tree to fall, though the juxtaposition of "wind" with "clouds" in the following verse suggests that he had wind in mind in this second half of v. 3 (just as he had had clouds in mind in the first half of the verse). Hence Gregory cites wind as the force which is able to overturn trees, but since some trees are cut down by people before the wind has had a chance to blow them over, Gregory feels constrained — perhaps in the light of 10:9's reference to such activities — to mention the human agency as well. His resultant formulation, a kind of "If the humans don't get you, the wind will", sounds very Kohelethine (cf. 10:8, "If you get through a wall, a snake will bite you").

(4) Πολλοὶ δὲ βούλονται καὶ τὰ ἐκ τοῦ οὐρανοῦ ἐσόμενα προγινώσκειν, καί τις εἴς τε νεφέλας ἀφορῶν, καὶ περιμένων ἄνεμον, ἀμήτου ἢ λικμητοῦ ἀπέσχετο, ἐπὶ μηδενὶ πεπεισμένος, ...

Many people want to know beforehand what will come from heaven. Some, looking at the clouds and waiting for the wind, have held back from harvesting or winnowing, believing in nothing, ...

On this occasion LXX translated רוח by ἄνεμος rather than by πνεῦμα, so there is no prompting of a spiritualised interpretation in the paraphrase (see comments at 5:15). Also on this occasion νεφέλη agrees with its LXX counterpart (cf. v. 3). The clouds are still "watched" (ἀφοράω for LXX's βλέπω), but the wind is now "awaited" (περιμένω) rather than "observed" (LXX τηρέω). There is still talk of a delay to "harvesting" (ἄμητος for LXX's θερίζω), but now the delay is also to "winnowing" (λικμητός) rather than to "sowing" (LXX σπείρω). For some reason Gregory must have felt that "harvesting" was better accompanied by an activity carried out in the same season rather than by one carried out in an opposite season, and since winnowing required an adequate amount of wind to separate the grain from the chaff, the two alterations — περιμένω and λικμητός — fall into place.

Gregory has also made additions to the beginning and end of the verse. The beginning makes clear the reason for the watching and waiting: the desire "to know beforehand what will come from heaven" (τὰ ἐκ τοῦ οὐρανοῦ ἐσόμενα προγιγνώσκω) — a precise contrast to the reality expressed at the beginning of the following verse: the inability "to know what will come from God" (τὰ ἐκ Θεοῦ ἐσόμενα γιγνώσκω). The end makes clear Gregory's view as to the problem at the root of the behaviour of those people who postpone their labours out of concern that conditions will not be perfectly suitable: a lack of trust in God, and in the processes of nature which he has created.

(5) ... μηδὲ γινώσκων τὶ τῶν ἐκ Θεοῦ ἐσομένων· ὥσπερ οὐδὲ οἷον ἡ κυοφοροῦσα τέξεται.

... and not knowing what will come from God — just as it is not known what a pregnant woman will produce.

Human ignorance of "the way of the רוח (LXX πνεῦμα)" was cited by Koheleth at the beginning of the verse. If this phrase is connected to the preceding verse, which referred to people watching the wind, it can readily be interpreted as meaning that human beings do not know how or why the wind blows or does not blow in this direction or that (the implication being that it is silly to watch the wind and delay the sowing). If the phrase is connected to the succeeding phrase, which refers to the embryo in the womb of a pregnant woman, it can readily be interpreted as meaning that human beings do not know how the breath or spirit of life enters an embryo (this is precisely the interpretation of the Targum, with its רוח נשמתא דחיי, and the change in LXX — from ἄνεμος in the previous verse to πνεῦμα here — perhaps points in that direction, as opposed to Symmachus' retention of ἄνεμος in this phrase). Gregory seems to have connected the phrase to the expression at the end of the verse concerning human ignorance of "the work of God", and interpreted it as meaning that human beings do not know how the Spirit moves. He treats the two expressions, "the way of the Spirit" (LXX ἡ ὁδὸς τοῦ πνεύματος) and "the works of God" (LXX τὰ ποιήματα³ τοῦ θεοῦ), as parallels, and so offers just one paraphrase to cover both: people's inability to know "what will come from God" (τὰ ἐκ Θεοῦ ἐσόμενα, itself a parallel to his expression τὰ ἐκ τοῦ οὐρανοῦ ἐσόμενα in the previous verse).

Gregory's pronouncement of human ignorance does not seem as universal as Koheleth's. In the paraphrase this lack of knowledge about divine activity is part of a sentence concerning those people who hold back from their work because of a lack of faith, which leaves open the possibility that the person of faith does know "what will come from God" — at least in general terms that good things will come to those who step forward in faith. Gregory is not averse in his paraphrase to limiting to foolish people an ignorance which the original Ecclesiastes ascribed to all people, no matter how wise (e.g., 8:17).

Ignorance of "the bones in the womb of a pregnant woman" (LXX ὀστᾶ ἐν γαστρὶ τῆς κυοφορούσης) is not for Gregory a lack of knowledge about how life enters the embryo; the ὡς (which gives rise to his ὥσπερ) between πνεῦμα and this phrase prevents him from making that interpretation. It is instead an inability to know beforehand "what a pregnant woman will produce" (οἷον ἡ κυοφοροῦσα τέξεται) — i.e., whether the bones of the developing infant are growing perfectly or it will be born deformed in some way, or whether the child will be a boy or a girl.[4]

(6) Σπείρας δὲ ἐν καιρῷ, συγκόμιζε τοὺς καρπούς, ὁπότ' ἂν τούτου καιρὸς ἐνστῇ· ἄδηλον γάρ, ὁποῖα αὐτῶν ἔσται ἀμείνω τῶν φυέντων. Γένοιτο δὲ ἅπαντα εἰς ἀγαθόν.

But having sown in season, gather in the fruits when the season for that arises. It is unknown what kind of product will be better. If only everything would go well!

"In the morning sow your seed and until the evening do not let your hand rest" appears to have been an injunction to unremitting diligence in one's labours: "Work all day" — none of this holding back until conditions are just right (v. 4)! But

Gregory takes LXX's πρωΐα as a metaphor for the season of
sowing (σπείρω, as in LXX) and ἑσπέρα as a metaphor for the
season of gathering in the fruits (συγκομίζω τοὺς καρποὺς is
evidently intended as a paraphrase of LXX's μὴ ἀφέτω ἡ χείρ σου,
which Gregory has thus not taken as referring to the activity of
sowing but to its opposite activity of harvesting, just as evening
is the opposite of morning).[5]

Koheleth further encouraged a full day's work by noting
that we do not know whether the earlier sowing or the later
sowing will be successful or whether both will turn out equally
well. To avoid LXX's repetitiveness with οὐ γιγνώσκω, Gregory
employs here the adjective ἄδηλος, "unknown". He also avoids
the clumsiness of LXX's ἢ τοῦτο ἢ τοῦτο (a translator less concerned to follow MT's זֶה־אוֹ זֶה precisely might have employed
ἐκεῖνον in the second instance), but by offering no paraphrase of
it at all. This leaves Gregory's expression ὁποῖα αὐτῶν ἔσται
ἀμείνω τῶν φυέντων, "what kind of product will be better" (an
expansion of LXX's ποῖον στοιχήσει) something of a puzzle for
the reader, since it cannot now refer to the products of the earlier
sowing and the later sowing respectively. Perhaps Gregory's
meaning is: We do not know if the kind of products gathered in
spring (such as wheat) will do better in any given year than the
kind of products gathered in autumn (such as olives), so we
ought to just go ahead with sowing or planting in the appropriate seasons and trust that there will be an adequate harvest when
the seasons for harvesting come around. Another possible
meaning might be: We do not know of any products which turn
out better than those sown during the correct season, so it would
be silly to delay the sowing when that season has arrived.[6]

Γένοιτο δὲ ἄπαντα εἰς ἀγαθόν, taking up the desirable
possibility that both the earlier sowing and the later sowing may
be equally ἀγαθός, is the wish of Everyman.

(7) Λογιζόμενος δέ τις, ὡς καλὸς μὲν ὁ ἥλιος, ἡδὺς δὲ οὗτος ὁ
βίος, ...

**When someone considers that the sun is beautiful and this
life is sweet ....**

In contrast to 4:2, where in the light of oppression Koheleth had thought that being dead was better than being alive, he now seems to have thought that life may not be so bad after all — at least as long as one is young. "Light" (LXX φῶς) in this verse is an image for "life", as opposed to "darkness" (LXX σκότος) in the following verse as an image for "death"; Gregory dispenses with the imagery and speaks plainly of βίος here and θάνατος there. "To see the sun" (LXX τοῦ βλέπειν σὺν τὸν ἥλιον) is similarly an image for "to be alive", and hence a parallel to "light" in the first clause, but Gregory retains mention of the ἥλιος anyway.

The paraphrase does not simply state that the sun is "good" (καλός for LXX's ἀγαθός) and that life is "sweet" (ἡδύς for LXX's γλυκύς). Rather, it says that someone may "consider" (λογίζομαι) them to be so, and in the next verses Gregory demonstrates that in his view this kind of thinking leads to certain dangers. The little word οὗτος is very significant: the intention might well be to imply that those who do not think too highly of this life, and so are able to avoid its dangers, can look forward to another life which is truly sweet (Revelation 21:11,23 even pictures that life as having no sun but being truly beautiful!).

(8) ... ἀγαθὸν δὲ καὶ τὸ πολυχρόνιον γενέσθαι διαπαντὸς εὐφραινόμενον, καὶ ὡς φοβερὸν ὁ θάνατος, καὶ ἀΐδιον κακόν, καὶ εἰς τὸ μηδὲν ἄγων, οἴεται χρῆναι, πάντων μὲν ἀπολαύειν τῶν παρόντων καὶ δοκούντων ἡδέων.

... — that having a long life and enjoying oneself throughout it is good — and that death is a fearful thing, an endless evil leading to nothing, he thinks that he ought to enjoy all the things which are at hand and are supposed to be pleasures.

As LXX's φῶς in the preceding verse really meant βίος, so its σκότος in this verse really means θάνατος. But while Koheleth really meant that one should enjoy life while one can before death arrives to destroy any chance of enjoyment, Gregory brands such thinking as foolish. In the paraphrase all the sentiments of this verse stand under the λογίζομαι of v. 7, and are included under the ἀνόητος judgment of v. 9. Οἴομαι and δοκέω continue the implication of wrong thinking begun by λογίζομαι.

A life which "lasts for a long time" (πολυχρόνιος arises from LXX's ἔτη πολλά) is thought to be "good" (ἀγαθός is perhaps brought across from LXX's ἀγαθός in v. 7), while death, which lasts "for ever" (ἀίδιος paraphrases LXX's second πολλαί), is thought to be "an evil thing" (κακόν) and "a matter for fear" (φοβερόν).

There can be no doubt that in incorporating this idea of the fear of death, Gregory is depicting the sentiments of the ungodly, since he undoubtedly would have believed that for the godly death has no sting (1 Corinthians 15:55) and leads to eternal blessedness. The ungodly may think that death leads to "nothing" (τὸ μηδέν paraphrases the ματαιότης that Koheleth said is lying in store), but Gregory has other ideas of what awaits them: judgment (v. 9) and destruction (v. 10). Such is the future of those who think that life is simply for "enjoying" (εὐφραίνομαι is taken from LXX and ἀπολαύω is added for good measure), or who regard it as containing "pleasures" (τὰ ἡδέα) because it is "sweet" (ἡδύς, v. 7).

(9) Συμβουλεύει δὲ καὶ τοῖς νέοις, τῇ ἑαυτῶν ὥρᾳ καταχρῆσθαι ἀνέντας τὰς ἑαυτῶν ψυχὰς εἰς πᾶσαν ἡδονήν, καὶ χαρίζεσθαι μὲν ἐπιθυμίαις, πράττειν δὲ τὰ αὐτοῖς δοκοῦντα, καὶ βλέπειν τὰ τέρποντα, καὶ ἀποστρέφεσθαι τὰ μὴ οὕτως ἔχοντα. Πρὸς ὃν τοσοῦτον λέξω· Ὅτι ἀνοηταίνεις, ὦ οὗτος, μὴ προσδοκῶν τὴν ἐφ᾽ ἅπασι τούτοις ἐκ Θεοῦ κρίσιν ἐσομένην.

He also advises young people to make full use of their time of life, giving their minds up to every pleasure, and to indulge their passions, do what seems good to them, look at what delights, and turn away from things which are not like that. To that sort of person I would say: You are a fool, my friend, not anticipating the judgment which will come from God upon all these things.

Koheleth seems to have been speaking with a forked tongue in this verse, in one breath calling on young people to gratify their desires and in the next breath calling out that God will judge them for doing so. Many commentators have felt that the first message was that of the genuine Koheleth, while the second was an addition from the hand of a pious glossator.[7] Gregory, however, felt that the second of the two contradictory messages was genuinely that of the writer of Ecclesiastes, while the first was his representation of advice with which he did not agree.

As in 9:7, Gregory uses συμβουλεύω, "to advise" as an introduction to a piece of Kohelethine counsel which he regards as being wicked advice. There he stamped the advice as error even before revealing what it was; on this occasion he allows the advice to be given before stamping it as foolishness. Codex Vaticanus of LXX gives a completely different kind of advice, *viz.* περιπάτει ἐν ὁδοῖς καρδίας σου ἄμωμος, καὶ μὴ ἐν ὁράσει ὀφθαλμῶν σου, "walk in the ways of your heart **blameless**, and **not** in the sight of your eyes". The strategic insertion of ἄμωμος and μή, not found in other LXX manuscripts, results in a more orthodox flavour for an otherwise embarrassing passage,[8] but there is no indication that Gregory had that version of the text in front of him, for he sets down the advice without negation or talk of blamelessness, or any other attempt at turning it into orthodox counsel.

LXX's νεανίσκος, "youth" is shortened to νέος, but other matters are spelled out more fully: "to walk in the ways of one's heart" (LXX περιπατέω ἐν ὁδοῖς καρδίας) means "to indulge one's passions" and "to do what seems good" (χαρίζομαι ἐπιθυμίαις and πράσσω δοκοῦντα), and "to walk in the sight of one's eyes" (LXX περιπατέω... ἐν ὁράσει ὀφθαλμῶν) means "to look at what delights" and "to turn from what is not so" (βλέπω τὰ τέρποντα and ἀποστρέφομαι τὰ μὴ οὕτως ἔχοντα), while "letting one's heart be cheerful" (LXX ἀγαθύνω ἡ καρδία) involves "giving one's mind up to every pleasure" (ἀνίεμαι τὴν ψυχὴν εἰς πᾶσαν ἡδονήν).

The close of the verse now becomes Solomon's reply to the imaginary opponent (ὦ οὗτος) whose thinking he had depicted in vv. 7-9. Those thoughts were not the genuine view of the all-wise writer of Ecclesiastes, but in fact nothing more than the thoughts of a fool, for a wise person lives in expectation of the coming judgment.

(10) Πονηρὸν δὲ ἀσωτία καὶ ἀσέλγεια, καὶ ῥυπαρὰ σωμάτων ἡμετέρων ὕβρις ὀλέθριος. Νεότητι μὲν γὰρ ἄνοια παρέπεται· ἄνοια δὲ ἄγει εἰς ὄλεθρον.

Profligacy and indecency are evil, and a filthy lust for our bodies is destructive. Foolishness accompanies a youthful spirit, and foolishness leads to destruction.

The call to make life as enjoyable as possible becomes a highly moralistic observation about sinfulness and its inevitable results. According to MT, Koheleth enjoined the removal of כעס ("irritation" or "anger") from one's mind and of רעה (literally "evil", but in this context doubtless in its sense of "misery" or "trouble") from one's body. According to LXX, he recommended the removal of θυμός (literally "soul", and hence the seat of "sorrow" or "anger") from one's mind and πονηρία ("a bad condition", most straightforwardly taken in the moral sense of "wickedness") from one's body. Gregory takes his cue from πονηρία, and has Solomon bemoan several things which are πονηρός, and in which presumably young people are particularly likely to be involved: viz., ἀσωτία, "prodigality"; ἀσέλγεια, "licentiousness"; and ὕβρις, "wantonness". Gregory may have introduced these three evils here because of his own experiences as a young man or with young people, or he may have felt that Solomon was particularly knowledgeable about such matters from his experiences. This time Gregory concentrates on the body (σῶμα for LXX's σάρξ); the mind (actually LXX's καρδία) does not rate a mention.

The *hapax legomenon* שחרות, which stood in parallel to ילדות, "childhood" or "youth", may be connected with שחר, "dawn" (and hence mean something like "the dawn of youth" or "the prime of life"), or it may be an abstract noun from שחר, "to be black" (at least that is how the Targumist took the word, rendering "the days of black hair" [יומי אוכמות שער] — as opposed to the grey hair of old age), but LXX made no such connection, and instead proposed ἄνοια, "foolishness" (cf. Peshitta ܪܠܐ ܝܕܥܬܐ, "ignorance") as a suitable parallel to νεότης, "youth" or "youthful spirit".[9] Gregory is happy to make use of such a parallel. He had just described as foolish the kind of advice

which is often given to youth, and now he notes that youth are
ever susceptible to foolishness — the latter "flies alongside"
(παραπέτομαι) the former. But just as he had warned that
judgment is coming for those who give and follow wicked
advice, he now warns that foolishness leads to ὄλεθρος,
"destruction" (Gregory's equivalent here to LXX's ματαιότης,
since for him the futility of folly is demonstrated by its result at
the coming judgment). Only ἄνοια and not νεότης *per se* is to be
condemned, as also are the evils mentioned earlier — they are
ὀλέθριος, "destructive". This forthcoming destruction will be
graphically depicted by the paraphrast in the following chapter.

Chapter Twelve

(1) Χρὴ δὲ ἔτι νέον ὄντα φοβεῖσθαι Θεόν, πρὶν ἢ ἑαυτὸν παραδοῦναι κακοῖς, πρὶν ἐλθεῖν τὴν τοῦ Θεοῦ μεγάλην ἡμέραν καὶ φοβεράν, ...

You should fear God while you are still young, before you give yourself over to wicked things, and before the great and terrible day of God comes.

The first seven verses of Chapter Twelve of Ecclesiastes described the forthcoming "bad days" (LXX ἡμέραι τῆς κακίας). There is general agreement among commentators, both in ancient and in modern times, that these "bad days" are the days of advancing old age and approaching death, depicted by means of various allegorical descriptions of the state of an old person — although there is no agreement on the details of the allegory (images of the failing of specific organs of the body?; the approach of death pictured as an advancing storm?, or the fall of night?, or the decay of a wealthy estate?; or some combination of these metaphors?).[1]

Gregory takes a different line of interpretation, and a most interesting one: the hard time that lies ahead is "the great and terrible day of God" (ἡ τοῦ Θεοῦ μεγάλη ἡμέρα καὶ φοβερά), foretold by the prophets. To Gregory's mind Solomon, too, is a prophet (cf. 1:1), and so now he introduces an oracle in words closely paralleling those of Joel 3:4 (English 2:31) and Malachi 3:22 (English 4:5) in LXX, πρὶν ἐλθεῖν ἡμέραν κυρίου τὴν μεγάλην καὶ ἐπιφανῆ.[2] It is worth noting that Gregory does not reproduce κύριος, even though the Old Testament prophetic term is "the day of the LORD" and not "the day of God"; it is a characteristic of Koheleth that he never employed κύριος (יהוה) and Gregory, accordingly, consistently also avoids its use — unlike other ancient translators/paraphrasts such as the creators of the Targumic and Peshitta versions of Ecclesiastes, who frequently refer to יהוה and ܡܪܝܐ respectively.[3]

"Your Creator" (LXX ὁ κτίσας)[4] is of course "God" (Θεός), and to "remember" him (LXX μιμνήσκομαι) means to "fear" him (φοβέομαι, bringing this verse into line with 3:14; 5:6; 7:18;

8:12,13; and 12:13). Χρή with the infinitive replaces the imperative, and the simple πρίν replaces LXX's ἕως ὅτου μή. Typically,
Gregory again takes LXX's κακία in a moral sense of wicked
things people do rather than unfortunate things that happen to
them. His paraphrase fits well with a model of Solomon as a
man who feared God while he was still young but later gave
himself over to wicked things. Gregory's Solomon has returned
to the correct path, but his readers may not have the time or
ability to do so "before the great and terrible day of God comes"
upon them, so they had best learn to "fear God" while they can.

(2) ... ὁπότε ἥλιος μὲν οὐκέτι λάμψει, οὐδὲ σελήνη, οὐδὲ οἱ
λοιποὶ ἀστέρες, ...

**Then the sun will no longer shine, and neither will the
moon nor the rest of the stars.**

The Targum well illustrates the common allegorical interpretation of this passage, taking the sun as an image of the
brightness of the face, the moon as a picture of the cheeks, and
the stars as a reference to the pupils of the eye, all of which are
affected by the aging process. In contrast, Gregory's view of the
verse is one of straightforward references to literal ἥλιος, σελήνη,
and ἀστέρες, all of which will cease to give light. Joel 3:4
(English 2:31), which shaped his closure of the previous verse, is
evidently still in his mind here[5] — along with its New Testament parallels in the apocalyptic sayings of Jesus in Matthew
24:29 and Mark 13:24,25. By adding λοιπός before ἀστέρες,
Gregory is calling the moon, and possibly the sun as well, a star
— they all "give light" (λάμπω) until the Eschaton. "Light" itself
(LXX φῶς) is left out of Gregory's paraphrase as unnecessary (cf.
Peshitta's treatment of this word as being in a construct relationship to the following words: [6]ܟܘܟܒܐ ܕܣܗܪܐ ܕܢܘܗܪܐ, "the light
of the moon and the stars"), while the thought of "clouds" (LXX
νέφη) and "rain" (LXX ὑετός), which mean the eyelids and tears
to the Targumist, will be taken up by the idea of a "storm"
(χειμών) in the next verse.

(3) ... κινηθήσονται δὲ αἱ ὑπέρτεραι δυνάμεις, ἐν ἐκείνῳ τῷ τῶν ὅλων χειμῶνι καὶ ταράχῳ, οἱ κοσμοφύλακες ἄγγελοι· ὡς παύσασθαι μὲν ἄνδρας δυνάστας, παύσασθαι δὲ καὶ γυναῖκας ἐργαζομένας, φευγούσας εἰς τὰ σκοτεινὰ τῶν οἰκημάτων, ...

The powers above — the angels guarding the universe — will be put into action in that storm and tumult of all things, so that powerful men will stop, and labouring women will also stop and will flee into the dark places of their houses.

The common allegorical interpretation is again well illustrated by the Targum: the "keepers of the house" who now tremble are the old person's knees, the "mighty men" who now become bent are the arms, the "grinding women" who become few and cease grinding are the teeth, and the "women who look out of the windows" are the eyes. These last three Gregory takes quite literally as being references to "powerful men" (ἄνδρες δυνάσται is virtually identical to LXX's ἄνδρες τῆς δυνάμεως), "labouring women" (γυναῖκες ἐργαζόμεναι is a general term which includes LXX's specific αἱ ἀλήθουσαι), and these same women[7] having fled into their houses, from where they might furtively peep out of a window (the reason why these people have become dark — LXX σκοτάζω — is that they have shrunk back into places which are σκοτεινός).

But Gregory, too, resorts to an allegorical interpretation of the "keepers of the house" (LXX φύλακες τῆς οἰκίας). This οἰκία is to him an image of the κόσμος, and so when Koheleth spoke of an οἰκοφύλαξ he was actually referring to a κοσμοφύλαξ, an ἄγγελος who guards the universe. These angelic guardians will "tremble" (LXX σαλεύομαι) in that they will be "stirred into motion" (κινέομαι). It is easy to trace the connection in Gregory's mind between this verse and the preceding one, in the prophecy of Matthew 24:29 and Mark 13:24,25 (where "the powers of the heavens will be shaken" follows the description of darkness in the heavenly bodies); the vision of the Sixth Seal in Revelation 6:12-17 also has much in common with Gregory's version of this Kohelethine passage (a tumult of all things, and people fleeing and hiding themselves); and perhaps he has in mind, too, the saying of Amos 5:18,19 (where "going into the house" is framed by "the day of the LORD is darkness"). Gregory again balances things in a deft contrast: the heavenly powers (αἱ ὑπέρτεραι δυνάμεις) begin activity (κινέομαι), with the result that the human powers (ἄνδρες δυνάσται) cease activity (παύομαι).

It might be said that Gregory has let slip by an excellent opportunity to make another connection with Jesus' apocalyptic sayings. Koheleth's "the grinding women cease because they are few" could lend itself to the prophetic saying of Matthew 24:41, "two women will be grinding at the mill; one is taken and one is left", if an eschatological interpretation is to be made as full as possible in this section of Ecclesiastes. But Gregory leaves "grinding" out of the picture here, probably because it is mentioned in the very next verse and he wants to give a more all-inclusive picture of working women in this verse, as a scene-setter.

(4) ... κεκλεισμένων ἁπασῶν τῶν θυρῶν· καί τις γυνὴ τοῦ ἀλήθειν ἀποσχομένη διὰ τὸ δέος, ἰσχνοτάτη φωνῇ χρήσεται ὥσπερ λεπτότατον ὄρνεον· ἅπασαι δὲ ἄναγνοι γυναῖκες εἰς γῆν πεσοῦνται, ...

All the doors will have been shut. A woman will be held back from grinding by fear, and will speak in the weakest voice — like the tiniest bird. All impure women will fall into the earth.

Gregory continues to take Koheleth's expressions quite literally. If Solomon spoke prophetically of the doors (LXX θύραι) being shut (LXX κλείω), he meant precisely that, and not — à la Targum — that the elderly person will be prevented from going into the street. So Gregory employs the same terms as LXX, although he employs a passive form of the verb.[8]

הטחנה is very likely to be vocalised as the noun "mill", as it is in MT. But it might be vocalised as the feminine participle of טחן (cf. הטחנות in the previous verse) and rendered "the grinding woman", which is the rendering of LXX (ἡ ἀλήθουσα) and then of Gregory, who speaks of τις γυνὴ τοῦ ἀλήθειν ἀποσχομένη, "a woman kept away from [her work of] grinding". Hence the φωνή in question is not the "sound" of the grinding of the mill but the "voice" of the woman who does the grinding. Her voice, says Gregory, is most "meagre, withered" (ἰσχνός, his adjectival equivalent to LXX's ἀσθένεια, "weakness", which in turn has construed as a noun MT's infinitive construct of שפל, "to be low", as has Peshitta's ܡܟܝܟܘܬܐ, "lowliness"), and he adds the explanation that she is afraid, like all the labouring women of v. 3. ("Grinding" both in v. 3 and in this verse means chewing food to the Targumist and countless other interpreters.)

"He arises (LXX ἀνίσταμαι) at (LXX εἰς) the sound of the bird" is commonly taken, as it is by the Targum, to mean that the old person sleeps so lightly that even the sound of a bird will disturb his slumber. But it can be read as "it [i.e., the voice of the grinding woman just mentioned] gets up to [i.e., approaches, becomes like — admittedly a rather unlikely nuance of the phrase] the voice of the bird", and such is the understanding of the phrase which Gregory presents in his "like (ὥσπερ) the tiniest [or: quietest] (λεπτότατος) bird". LXX particularised with στρουθίον, "sparrow" (a rendering which Symmachus accepts) for MT's general צפור, "bird", when Gregory's ὄρνεον, or ὄρνις, would have been a more accurate equivalent; while it might be thought that Gregory is here showing some awareness of the original Hebrew version of Ecclesiastes by rendering "bird" rather than "sparrow", it is more likely that he is offering "tiniest bird" as a paraphrase of στρουθίον (the diminutive of στρουθός).

Who are "the daughters of song" (LXX αἱ θυγατέρες τοῦ ᾄσματος) who "are brought low" (LXX ταπεινόομαι)? To the Targumist they are the lips which, being aged, are no longer able to sing as they did when they were young. To Gregory they are "impure women" (ἄναγνοι γυναῖκες) who will "fall" (πίπτω [cf. Aquila κλίνομαι]) εἰς γῆν. By this last expression he may mean no more than that they will fall "onto the ground", just as everyone who is struck by the mighty blow of v. 6 is pictured in v. 7 as being ἐπὶ γῆς, "on the ground"; but since this would be saying no more about impure women than what happens to everything else as well (whether pure or impure) on the great and terrible day of God, and in view of Gregory's use of εἰς τὴν γῆν πίπτω in 5:14 (cf. 3:20) to depict a person's body returning to the earth from which it came, it seems quite likely that he means that they will fall "into the earth" — i.e., their bodies will return to dust (cf. εἰς τὴν γῆν and εἰς γῆν in LXX Genesis 3:19), or perhaps he is even picturing the earth opening up for all such unholy women to fall into hell.

But whatever the precise meaning of this expression, the Church Father reveals, in paraphrasing "the daughters of song" by "impure women", that he regards female singers as quintessential sinners. Presumably he has in mind the singers of bawdy songs in the secular world, but, given the controversy in the early Church regarding the use of choirs of women and girls in worship,[9] it is not impossible that a personal opposition to such choirs has helped to shape his interpretation of this verse. In 2:8 mention was made of male and female singers as part of Solomon's licentious lifestyle, and in 7:26-28 Gregory's Solomon had spoken from personal experience of the large number of impure women in the world, by whose wiles many men are led astray; now he prophetically disposes of these temptresses.

(5) ... καὶ πόλεις καὶ αἱ τούτων ἀρχαὶ αἱ μιαιφόνοι, περιμένουσαι τὴν ἄνωθεν κόλασιν, ἐνστάντος καιροῦ πικροτάτου καὶ αἱματώδους, ὥσπερ ἀνθοῦντος ἀμυγδάλου καὶ συνεχῶν ἐπικειμένων κολάσεων, ὥσπερ πλήθους ἐφιπταμένων ἀκρίδων, καὶ ἐκποδῶν ῥιπτουμένων τῶν παρανόμων, ὥσπερ μελαίνης καὶ εὐκαταφρονήτου καππάρεως. Καὶ ὁ μὲν ἀγαθὸς ἀνὴρ εἰς αἰώνιον οἶκον τὸν ἑαυτοῦ χαίρων πορεύσεται· οἱ δέ γε φαῦλοι, πάντα τὰ αὐτῶν ἐμπλήσουσι κοπτόμενοι, ...

Cities and their blood-stained leaders will wait for punishment from above. A most bitter and bloody time will arise like a blossoming almond-tree, continuous punishments will be imposed like a swarm of flying locusts, and lawbreakers will be thrown out of the way like a black and contemptible caper-plant. The good person will enter into his eternal home with rejoicing, but the bad people will fill all their homes with mourning.

Virtually all interpreters take the opening of this verse as indicating an old person's fear of heights and of journeys, but

Gregory has no problems reading it eschatologically, for what
Koheleth literally said was: "From on high (MT מגבה, LXX ἀπὸ
ὕψους) they will be afraid (or: they will look [LXX's ὁράω reading
ראה rather than ירא]) and terrors (LXX θάμβοι) in the way." Those
who are on high, in Gregory's mind, are the inhabitants of cities
generally (perhaps because a πόλις often occupied high ground),
and in particular their authorities (αἱ ἀρχαί, the holders of high
office), and the terror which awaits them is "punishment"
(κόλασις) from a higher authority. One is reminded of Isaiah
5:14,15's depictions of the citizens of Jerusalem and their
"haughty ones" (MT גבהים, LXX μετέωροι) being brought low.
The Bible often spoke of the city as a place of wickedness, an
opinion which Gregory endorses here, perhaps influenced by his
experiences during the Decian persecution when he withdrew
into the mountains with a large part of his flock.

Of all the phrases in this famous passage (vv. 1-7),
Koheleth's references to the "almond-tree" (LXX ἀμύγδαλον),
the "locust" (LXX ἀκρίς), and the "caper-berry" (LXX κάππαρις)
provide the most difficulty for interpreters, including Gregory —
who is forced to treat them as metaphors. The difficulty of
interpretation may be due to the nature of the topic, for it is
possible that Koheleth was here depicting the failing of sexual
powers, a prominent characteristic of old age and precisely the
one that would be expressed in veiled and figurative form.[10]
Gregory continues his eschatological interpretation, but this time
he employs three ὥσπερ phrases to link the Kolelethine
metaphors to their prophetic meanings: the blossoming (LXX
ἀνθέω) of the ἀμύγδαλον is an image of the arising (ἐνίσταμαι) of
the End Times, to which may possibly be associated Jesus' saying,
"From the fig tree learn its lesson...", in Matthew 24:32,33;[11] the
increase (LXX παχύνομαι [MT, with סבל hithpael, speaks of a
burdening]) of the ἀκρίς is an image of the imposing (ἐπίκειμαι)
of punishments, to which may possibly be associated the vision
of the locusts in Revelation 9:1-11; and the scattering (LXX
διασκεδάννυμαι [MT, with פרר hiphil, speaks of a failure]) of the
κάππαρις is an image of the casting away (ῥίπτομαι) of
lawbreakers, to which may possibly be associated Jesus' sayings
concerning the harvest of wheat and fish in Matthew 13.

The last two phrases of this verse presented no need for inventive analogies. Koheleth spoke of a man going "to his eternal home" (LXX εἰς οἶκον αἰῶνος αὐτοῦ) and of those who remain behind and "mourn" (LXX κόπτομαι), and Gregory reproduces this (εἰς αἰώνιον οἶκον τὸν ἑαυτοῦ and κόπτομαι). But for Gregory the expression "eternal home" is a synonym of "heaven" (cf. v. 7) rather than a euphemism for "grave" (cf. Targum בית קבורתא, "house of burial"),[12] and so the one who goes there is not Everyman (LXX ὁ ἄνθρωπος), but only the worthy (ὁ ἀγαθὸς ἀνήρ), from which it follows that the ones who do not go there are not the hired mourners merely going about their professional routine,[13] but the unworthy (οἱ φαῦλοι) weeping and gnashing their teeth at the perception of their own personal plight, so starkly contrasted with the joyful (χαίρω) fate of the righteous. The eschatological picture would not have been complete without reference to the separation of the sheep and the goats (cf. Matthew 25:31-46), and the message of judgment between ἀγαθός and φαῦλος will be reiterated before the paraphrase of Ecclesiastes is complete (v. 14).

(6) ... καὶ οὔτε ἀργύριον ἀποτεθησαυρισμένον, οὔτε χρυσίον δόκιμον ἐπωφελὲς ἔτι. Μεγάλη γὰρ ἅπαντα καθέξει πληγή,[14] καὶ μέχρις ὑδρίας ἑστώσης πρός τινι κρήνῃ, καὶ τροχοῦ ὀχήματος, ὃν ἂν τύχῃ καταλελεῖφθαι ἐν τῷ κοιλώματι[15] παυσαμένης,[16] χρόνον[17] τε περιδρομῆς, καὶ τῆς δι' ὕδατος ζωῆς παροδεύσαντος τοῦ λουτροφόρου αἰῶνος.

Neither stored silver nor tested gold will be of any further use. A mighty blow will strike everything, right down to a water-pot standing next to a well, and to a carriage-wheel which happens to have been left in the ditch, its time of revolving ceased, and to the life that, by water, has passed through the age of washing.

A "cord" (LXX σχοινίον) of silver suggests to Gregory silver which "is stored" (ἀποθησαυρίζομαι), and a "flower" (LXX ἀνθέμιον [MT has גלה, "bowl"]) of gold — a Greek expression denoting the choicest or costliest gold[18] — suggests to him gold which is "tested, approved, esteemed" (δόκιμος). To speak of these being "overturned" (LXX ἀνατρέπω [MT, with הרס niphal, speaks of them being "removed"]) and "crushed" (LXX συν- θλίβω) is to picture a time when they can no longer "aid" or "help" anyone (ἐπωφελέω, a term which fits well in this book — cf. Gregory's ὄφελος for Koheleth's favourite περισσεία [יתרון] in 1:3 and ὠφελέω for περισσόν [יתר] in 6:11; Gregory's ὄφελος will appear again in the context of LXX's περισσόν in 12:12).

Most commentators see in the expressions in this verse metaphors for the advent of death (cf. the Targum's rather graphic portrayal of bodily deterioration culminating in the קבר, "grave"), but again Gregory is able to take them relatively literally, and to see them as a description of the actual state of affairs on the great and terrible day of God. The scene of a "water-pot" (ὑδρία, as in LXX) at the "well" (κρήνη, for LXX's πηγή) and a "wheel" (τροχός, as in LXX) in the "hollow" (κοίλωμα, for LXX's λάκκος, "cistern") seems to show how everything on the earth, no matter how small or seemingly inconsequential, is affected by this "storm and tumult of all things" (v. 3). Such things are "broken" (LXX συντρίβω) and "run together" (LXX συντροχάζω [MT has רצץ niphal, "crushed", but LXX apparently took the Hebrew as רוץ — cf. Targum and Peshitta רהט/ܪܗܛ, "run"]) because they are "struck" (κατέχω) by "a mighty blow" (μεγάλη πληγή).

Gregory seems to feel that the "wheel" requires some explanation. Koheleth probably had in mind the wheel by which the water-pot is raised from the well on a rope, but Gregory has in mind the wheel of an ὄχημα, "carriage". Hence the paraphrase κοίλωμα as a more likely place for a carriage-wheel to have come to a stop than in a λάκκος, and for good measure an additional note to make it clear that being there involves a cessation of "running round" (περιδρομή, perhaps prompted by LXX's συντροχάζω).[19] This addition may also be meant to imply that all the various cycles of which Koheleth has spoken (the ceaseless rounds of nature in Chapter One, the constant turning of the times in Chapter Three) will finally come to an end, when the "time" (χρόνος) of revolving ceases.[20]

Gregory now adds a puzzling clause on this matter of the end of time as we know it: the "age" (αἰών) of "bringing water for washing" (λουτροφόρος) has passed. This thought, which might have arisen from the idea of the water-pot being broken, may be intended to indicate that once the great and terrible day of God arrives it is too late to repent and be baptised[21] (cf. the frequent use of λουτρόν, "washing" by patristic writers as an equivalent to βάπτισμα, the rite of "baptism").[22] If the life which has come through that age δι' ὕδατος, "by water" is the life which has been through baptism, then Gregory is saying that the mighty blow strikes absolutely everything on the Last Day, even (μέχρις) the physical life of the believer — only the souls (ψυχαί) of the believers can be saved, as will be stated in the next verse. Gregory may well intend here an allusion to 1 Peter 3:20,21, which speaks of the ψυχαί which were saved δι' ὕδατος in the time of Noah and of the saving βάπτισμα which now corresponds to this; certainly the drawing (even in rather veiled terms) of an analogy with the Flood would be very fitting in a depiction of the final destruction of all life on earth.

(7)   Ἀνθρώπων δὲ ἐπὶ γῆς κειμένων μία σωτηρία, εἰ ἐπιγνοῖεν αὐτῶν αἱ ψυχαί, καὶ πρὸς αὐτὸν ἀναπταῖεν ὑφ' οὗ καὶ γεγέννηνται.

For people lying on earth there is one salvation, if their souls acknowledge and fly up to the One by whom they were brought into being.

In speaking of the "dust" (LXX χοῦς) returning to the earth and the "breath of life" (LXX πνεῦμα) returning to God who gave it, Koheleth pictured death in terms obviously based on the creation story (Genesis 2:7; 3:19). Gregory's paraphrase strengthens this allusion to Creation by employing the word ψυχή rather than πνεῦμα (cf. LXX Genesis 2:7 ψυχὴ ζῶσα, "living soul"); he also uses γῆ in preference to χοῦς (as LXX does in Genesis 3:19 and as Gregory also does in Ecclesiastes 3:20), and he replaces Koheleth's "give" (LXX δίδωμι) with "come into being" (γίγνομαι, used by LXX in Genesis 2:7). Such allusions to the First Days are most apt in a description of the Last Days.

Κεῖμαι in Gregory's version may simply refer to people "being" on this earth, but its usual sense of "lying outstretched or still" — asleep, sick, or dead — suggests, particularly in view of its paraphrasing the return of the dust to the earth, that Gregory has in mind the people who have been struck down by the "mighty blow" mentioned in the previous verse. Although the physical lives of all who are still living on that great and terrible day will then be brought to an end, there is still the possibility of "salvation" or "preservation" (σωτηρία) for the ψυχή.

For Gregory it is not every πνεῦμα which "returns" (LXX ἐπιστρέφω) to its Maker, but only the ψυχή which "acknowledges" (ἐπιγιγνώσκω) and "flies up" (ἀναπέτομαι) to that Maker; ἐπιστρέφω in the sense of "repent" lends itself to such an alteration of Koheleth's thought. The soul which wings its way to God presumably belongs to the life which has been through the water of repentance and baptism (cf. v. 6) while the opportunity to do so — the age of λουτροφόρος — existed.

Thus Gregory is able to close his depiction of the Last Day with a note of hope for his readers. To have interpreted this whole passage (vv. 1-7) as a depiction of the Last Day is a unique treatment of what is generally regarded as an allegory of old age. The Targum mentions angels who seek the judgment of the individual in v. 5, and now in this verse speaks of the individual soul returning to the LORD for judgment, but Gregory speaks of the approaching Judgment Day for all people. The Syriac Apocalypse of Baruch utilises the picture of the pitcher at the well in v. 6 and the idea of the passing of youth to describe the decay of the world (2 Baruch 85:10),[23] but Gregory fashions each of Koheleth's phrases into an apocalyptic vision. A passage which has struck virtually all interpreters as an allegorical description of the end of each life has been ingeniously paraphrased by Gregory as a literal prophecy of the end of the world.[24]

(8) Λέγω τοίνυν αὖθις ἃ καὶ πρότερον εἴρηκα, πάνυ ματαίως ἀνθρώπους διακεῖσθαι, καὶ μήτε ὑπερβολὴν ὅλως ἐνδέχεσθαι τῶν ἐπινοουμένων πραγμάτων τὴν ματαιότητα.

So I say again what I said before: Human beings are in an utterly empty state; in short, nothing can exceed the emptiness of all the things they think about.

Koheleth (or his editor) repeated the formulae of the opening declaration (1:2), doubtlessly intending to give the feeling that the thesis "all is futility" had been sufficiently demonstrated by what had been presented between these two occurrences of the statement. Gregory notes that what is said here is a repetition of what has been said before, and his τοίνυν, "therefore, accordingly" gives the feeling that the reiteration is justified by what has preceded this current verse.

Gregory does not simply reproduce 1:2, since as a paraphrast he has studiously avoided repetitiveness. This time he is content to employ cognates of μάταιος, having used many synonyms for variation throughout the work. But he is careful to once again limit the scope of the judgment that unreservedly "all is ματαιότης" to the realm of human πράγματα: the common person, who concerns himself with empty things, is in a state of emptiness; there can be no suggestion that the system which the Creator has set up is μάταιος.

(9) Περιττὸς δέ μοι ὁ κάματος ἐκκλησιάζοντι σοφῶς, ὅτι διδάσκειν ἐπιχειρῶν τὸν λαὸν τοῦτον ἀδιδάκτως καὶ ἀνιάτως ἔχοντα. Δεῖ δὲ ἀνδρὸς γενναίου, πρὸς τὸ συνιέναι λόγους σοφίας δυνηθῆναι.

My labour of speaking wisely to the assembly has been a great one, because I am trying to teach these people, who are ignorant and incorrigible. A noble person is needed, so that words of wisdom can be understood.

Only in this and the following verse of Ecclesiastes was Koheleth spoken of in the third person.[25] Up to this point all had been presented as being the first-person words of Koheleth himself, apart from the superscription to the book (1:1) and the words "says Koheleth" in the thematic statement (1:2 and 12:8) and in one other saying (7:27). But in Gregory's version Solomon, after being introduced as the speaker at the very beginning, has never had his flow of words interrupted with a "says Solomon", and now here in the closing verses of Chapter Twelve that same Solomon continues to speak in the first person, describing his own activities as naturally as he had done

in Chapter Two and finally presenting his concluding remarks.
The title ἐκκλησιαστής again gives rise in Gregory's paraphrase, as in 1:12, to the verb ἐκκλησιάζω, "to address the assembly" — or "to preach in the Church" in the mind of the Christian reader. He performs this task "wisely" (σοφῶς) because he is "wise" (LXX σοφός, a straightforward translation of MT's חכם, which might in fact designate Koheleth's office as one of the Wise and hence be better rendered as σοφιστής). LXX's περισσόν, evidently meaning "moreover, besides", prompts in Gregory the observation that Solomon's task has been περιττός, "prodigious, extraordinary, beyond the normal", because the people he is attempting to teach are so ἀδίδακτος, "ignorant" and ἀνίατος, "incorrigible". LXX mentioned Koheleth's role of "teaching (διδάσκω) the people (ὁ λαός)",[26] but the value-judgment about those people is Gregory's own. Perhaps he has in mind the continual back-sliding of the Israelite people, or perhaps he is writing from personal experience of frustration in his own teaching ministry, but it might well be a note of annoyance about people who have misunderstood what Koheleth has said in his book, thus making it necessary for Gregory to write a paraphrase making its correct interpretation clear.

The Hebrew text gave an indication of how Koheleth operated: "he pondered (אזן piel) and searched out (חקר piel) and set in order (תקן piel) many proverbs." LXX did not latch onto this meaning and, taking אזן and תקן as nouns, put forward an indication of how Koheleth's listeners are to operate: "the ear (οὖς) will trace out (ἐξιχνιάζω) the order (κόσμιον) of the parables."[27] Aquila showed a better understanding of the Hebrew in his rendering "he gave ear to (ἐνωτίζομαι) and searched out (ἐρευνάω) and arranged [or: constructed] (κατασκευάζω) proverbs",[28] but Gregory takes his cue from LXX. Having just referred to the ignorance and incorrigibility of the people, however, he is not at all confident of the ability of the average ear to make the right sense of proverbial sayings. Thus he notes that a "noble" (γενναῖος) person is necessary, in order that the people might be able to "understand" (συνίημι) words of wisdom; this is the role of the noble Solomon,[29] who taught the people wisdom, but it is also the precise role in which Gregory has cast himself in undertaking to paraphrase Solomon's wise words in a more understandable form.

(10) Ἐγὼ δὲ ἤδη πρεσβύτης ὤν, καὶ μακρὸν βίου διελθὼν χρόνον, ἔκαμον εἰς τὸ ἀνευρεῖν τὰ τῷ Θεῷ ἀρεστὰ διὰ τῶν τῆς ἀληθείας μυστηρίων.

Already an old man — having passed through a long lifetime — I laboured through the mysteries of the truth to find out what is pleasing to God.

Gregory begins this verse by working in a reference to the advanced age of Solomon at the time of giving this address. That it is an older and wiser man who speaks in these pages may have been implicit in some of the earlier passages of the paraphrase, but now it is explicitly stated that he is a πρεσβύτης, "old man, elder" who has lived a long life. He had earlier told his audience how he had strayed from the path which is pleasing to God (e.g., 7:23), and now he relates that he came back to that path in his old age.

Koheleth was represented as seeking to find "words of pleasure" (MT דברי־חפץ) or "words of desire" (LXX λόγοι θελήματος),[30] which doubtlessly meant that he strove to express Wisdom in a pleasant or attractive form. Gregory's Solomon represents himself as being concerned not with things that are pleasing to human beings but with "the things that are pleasing to God" (τὰ τῷ Θεῷ ἀρεστά). In order to "find out" (ἀνευρίσκω, from LXX's εὑρίσκω, "find") what it is that God approves of, Solomon had to "labour through" (κάμνω... διά, for LXX's ζητέω, "search out", reiterates Gregory's κάματος of the previous verse) "the mysteries of the truth" (τὰ τῆς ἀληθείας μυστήρια, for LXX's λόγοι ἀληθείας, "words of truth"). Gregory does not mention "writing" (LXX γράφω) as the activity of the author of Ecclesiastes, since he has styled the book as a speech delivered orally to the assembly rather than as a collection of thoughts set down in writing. He also has no direct parallel to "uprightness" (LXX εὐθύτης), but the word may have helped to prompt his interpretation of this verse as having to do with God-pleasing things.

(11)   Ἐπίσταμαί τε ὡς ἐπεγείρει ψυχάς, καὶ νύττει οὐχ ἧττον
τὰ τῶν σοφῶν παραγγέλματα, ἢ διατίθεται σώματα³¹ βουκέντρῳ, ἢ
ἥλῳ ἐμπερονηθέντα. Δώσουσι δέ τινες τὰ σοφὰ ἐκεῖνα διδάγματα,
παρ' ἑνὸς ἀγαθοῦ λαβόντες ποιμένος καὶ διδασκάλου, ὥσπερ ἐξ
ἑνὸς στόματος ἅπαντες αὐτοῖς συμφώνως δαψιλέστερον τὰ
πιστευθέντα διηγούμενοι.

I know that the mind is roused and spurred by the
instructions of wise people just as much as the body is by an ox-
goad being applied or a nail being driven in. Some people will
pass on those wise lessons which they have received from one
good shepherd and teacher, just as if everybody with one voice
described in unison and in greater detail what was entrusted to
them.

The analogy between "the instructions of the wise"
(Gregory's formulation, τὰ τῶν σοφῶν παραγγέλματα, for LXX's
λόγοι σοφῶν, "the words of the wise") on the one hand and an
"ox-goad" (βούκεντρον, as in LXX) and a "nail" (ἧλος, as in LXX)
on the other,³² is explained in the paraphrase: the former has
the same kind of effect upon the mind (ψυχή) as the two latter
objects would have upon the body (σῶμα). In the work Gregory
is paraphrasing only ἧλος was supplied with a verb — φυτεύω,
literally "to plant" but here evidently meaning "to drive in a
nail", which Gregory handles more precisely by ἐμπερονάω³³ —
but he then balances things out by supplying βούκεντρον with
the verb διατίθημι, "to arrange, inflict upon",³⁴ and adding two
verbs on the ψυχή side of the analogy which describe the effects
of the activities verbalised on the σῶμα side: ἐπεγείρω, "to
awaken, rouse up" is the achievement of applying a goad, and
νύσσω, "to prick, spur" is the achievement of driving in a nail.

The reference to בעלי אספות, "masters of assemblies" was
rather puzzling, being perhaps an allusion to schools or councils
of wise men, or a reference to wise sayings which have been
assembled into collections.³⁵ LXX took the latter view: wisdom
is given παρὰ τῶν συναγμάτων, "from the collections".³⁶ Gregory
presents the idea of people who pass on wisdom as if they spoke
ἐξ ἑνὸς στόματος, "with one voice" and σύμφωνος, "in unison/
harmony".   Perhaps this idea arose from the "masters of

assemblies" (if Gregory was aware of more than the Septuagintal understanding of the expression here) being thought of as the people who publicly teach the assembly of believers; or it may have arisen from σύναγμα being thought of as "agreement" or "harmony" (cf. συναγορεύω).[37]

It is interesting that Gregory does not style these wise lessons as simply being given, as does the original (LXX δίδωμι), but as being first received (λαμβάνω) and then given (δίδωμι); this is the very way in which Paul styled the transmission of traditional teaching in 1 Corinthians 11:23 and again in 15:3 (παραλαμβάνω and παραδίδωμι). In paraphrasing Ecclesiastes, Gregory himself is passing on what has come down to him as part of the tradition; moreover, he is "describing more fully" or "setting out in greater detail" (δαψιλέστερον... διηγέομαι) what has been "entrusted" or "committed" (πιστεύομαι) to him.

The one who originally gave the wise lessons is a "shepherd" (ποιμήν, as in LXX, for MT's רעה) and a "teacher" (διδάσκαλος, a Gregorian addition). Neither in the original nor in the paraphrase is the identity of this individual self-evident. He is either the author of Ecclesiastes (i.e., in Gregory's mind, King Solomon) or the divine source of all wisdom (i.e., God, who is often designated רעה in the Old Testament, or perhaps in Gregory's mind Christ, who is designated both ποιμήν and διδάσκαλος in the New Testament).[38] A divine source is more likely the intended reference both in Ecclesiastes and in Gregory's paraphrase.

(12) Λόγων δὲ πολλῶν οὐδὲν ὄφελος· οὐδέ σοι συμβουλεύω, ὦ φίλος, ἀνόνητα καταγράφειν τὰ περὶ τὸ προσῆκον, ἐν οἷς τοῦ κάμνειν εἰκῆ ἐστιν οὐδὲν πλέον.

There is no use in many words. Nor do I advise you, my friend, to write down useless things about what is proper — that is nothing more than toil without purpose.

The reader was now warned (LXX φυλάσσομαι, "be on one's guard" [MT has זהר niphal, "be warned"]) that there is no "end" (LXX περασμός) to the making of many "books" (LXX βιβλία) and that the study of them is a great "weariness" (LXX κόπωσις).

Gregory's reader is "advised" (συμβουλεύω) that there is no "use" (ὄφελος, probably arising from LXX's περισσόν — cf. ὄφελος for LXX's περισσεία in 1:3) in many "words" (λόγοι) and the writing down of useless things is purposeless "toiling" (κάμνω, the same word as that used in v. 10 for Solomon's purposeful labours). This verse of Ecclesiastes seemed to register a concern that readers may be harmed if the book they had just read prompted them to read too widely and indulge in study of heterodox books. Gregory, as a pupil of Origen, is not opposed to the reading and study of a wide range of material, including non-Judaeo-Christian works, but is concerned only that what is true and useful should be picked out and what is erroneous should be rejected;[39] hence he does not proscribe books or study as such, but the transmission of "useless things" (ἀνόνητα).

The formulation "useless things about (περί) what is proper" seems somewhat strange. Perhaps the text should read "contrary to (παρά) what is proper",[40] which makes it clear that anything written down beyond fitting things is to be condemned. But it may be that Gregory wants to particularly advise against writing improper things about what ought to be treated in a proper manner; as a Christian bishop he no doubt often had occasion to rue the use made of the scriptures and teachings of the Church by heretics and pagans. It is possible that here he particularly has in mind what he would regard as an improper use of the biblical book of Ecclesiastes on the part of people who have interpreted it falsely or treated it as non-scriptural.

"My son" (LXX υἱέ μου) was a common form of address in Wisdom literature, when a writer employed a term of endearment used by a teacher to his disciple. Gregory naturally employs the common Greek form of address of a speaker/writer to a listener/reader: ὦ φίλος, "O friend". The reader of Ecclesiastes was referred to as υἱέ μου only here in 12:12,[41] but Gregory has earlier used ὦ φίλος at 10:4 as a useful device for referring to the reader in amongst some general observations on wise and foolish people (cf. ὦ οὗτος in 9:7 and 11:9).

(13) Ἀλλά μοι λοιπὸν ἐπιλόγου δεήσει τοιοῦδέ τινος, ὅτι· Ὦ ἄνθρωποι, ἰδοὺ διαρρήδην ὑμῖν καὶ συντόμως προαγορεύω,

φοβεῖσθαι μὲν Θεὸν τὸν πάντων δεσπότην τε ὁμοῦ καὶ ἐπόπτην,
τηρεῖν δὲ αὐτοῦ καὶ τὰ παραγγέλματα·

It only remains necessary for me to give a conclusion such
as follows: Listen, my people; I tell you, clearly and concisely, to
fear God, who is both the Lord and Guardian of all, and to keep
his commandments.

The "end" (LXX τέλος) of the matter is a "conclusion"
(ἐπίλογος) which may or may not have been in keeping with the
book as a whole but which has done much to reconcile pious
souls to the existence of Ecclesiastes in the canon, and which
Gregory is happy to reproduce as a perfectly fitting conclusion to
his version of the book: "Fear (φοβέομαι, as in LXX) God, and
keep (τηρέω, for LXX's φυλάσσω) his commandments." In the
conclusion of his own *Panegyric to Origen*, Gregory had
expressed similar sentiments, praying that God "may guide us in
the future also, standing by us in all things, instilling his
commandments into our minds, implanting within us his godly
fear, which will be our best guide."[42]   And now, for this
conclusion to his paraphrase of Ecclesiastes, Gregory provides a
sizeable build-up to it as the summary thought which the reader
should take with him from Ecclesiastes, by noting first the need
for a conclusion to be given, then addressing the people formally
(ὦ ἄνθρωποι) and calling for their attention (ἰδού)[43] while
promising to deliver a proclamation (προαγορεύω) in clear and
concise form (διαρρήδην, συντόμως), before actually giving the
conclusion.   This kind of language reiterates at the end of the
book what Gregory had indicated at the beginning, that Solomon
is speaking to a public assembly.

זה כל־האדם, "this is the whole of man" meant either that a
person's entire efforts should be spent on fearing God and
obeying his commandments as the only thing worthy of one's
attention, or that the injunction to fear God and obey his
commandments is directed towards everybody without exception (the Targum paraphrases כדין חזי למהוי אורח כל אינש, "this is
the proper path for every human being"). Gregory seems to
stand with the latter interpretation, for LXX's τοῦτο πᾶς ὁ
ἄνθρωπος is reflected in his addressing the proclamation to the

ἄνθρωποι and in his note that this God who is to be feared is Lord and Guardian "of all" (πάντων). Gregory apparently likes the title δεσπότης πάντων, since he has already employed it in 2:26 as a synonym of θεός, and here he adds ἐπόπτης — perhaps by way of suggesting that God "watches over" (cf. ἐποπτεύω) the people and thus knows who "watches over" (τηρέω) his commandments and who does not, which sets the scene for the note of judgment in the next verse.

(14) πείθεσθαι δέ, πάντα τινὰ μετέπειτα καὶ κριθήσεσθαι, καὶ κατ᾽ ἀξίαν ἀπολήψεσθαι ἕκαστον τῶν αὐτοῦ ἔργων τὴν ἀμοιβὴν ἀγαθῶν τε ὁμοῦ καὶ φαύλων.

You should also believe that everything will be judged in the future, and everyone will receive the payment he deserves for his deeds, both good and bad.

Orthodoxy had the final say in Ecclesiastes, so Gregory is content to paraphrase this verse quite straightforwardly: God is going to "judge" (κρίνω, from LXX's κρίσις) every "deed" (ἔργον, for LXX's ποίημα), whether "good" (ἀγαθός, as in LXX) or "bad" (φαῦλος, for LXX's πονηρός). He notes in addition that this judgment means that everyone will receive ἀμοιβή, "recompense, payment" in accordance with what they deserve — v. 5 in the paraphrase had indicated what that recompense would be: a joyful eternal home for the people whose deeds are ἀγαθός but a home of mourning for those whose deeds are φαῦλος. Gregory styles v. 14 as part of Solomon's final clear and concise proclamation to the people (as introduced in v. 13), and so he has the great king and prophet (1:1) now close his address or sermon by charging his flock to be firmly convinced that there is a coming judgment and to act accordingly.

Gregory has overlooked the phrase concerning things which have been overlooked (LXX παροράομαι) or hidden (MT עלם niphal), presumably a reference to those deeds which are known only to the perpetrator himself and not to his fellows (cf. the Targum's פתגם דאתכסי מן בני אנשא, "a thing which was concealed from people"), but which cannot be overlooked by or kept hidden from the all-seeing divine Judge. Gregory must have felt that πάντα, "everything" was sufficiently ominous for his readers (cf. Vulgate's frightening *pro omni errato*, "for every error"), without having to spell out that this includes their most secret sins. The final word of this biblical book was πονηρός (רע), "evil". Such a harsh ending has been upsetting to some, and so Jewish tradition has ordained that the penultimate verse be repeated after the final verse in order to conclude on a more positive note, a custom which was also instituted in the cases of Isaiah, Malachi, and Lamentations.[44] A paraphrast could easily arrange his material in such a way that the ultimate word or thought is a positive one, but Gregory is not concerned with such niceties.[45] In keeping with the text before him, he closes his version with a "bad" word: φαῦλος.

CONCLUSION

The Linguistic Transformation

As an exercise in rephrasing the book of Ecclesiastes in proper, readily-understandable Greek, Gregory's work is something of a masterpiece. Here for the first time Koheleth is presented as speaking in a fluent Greek voice. Gregory's paraphrastic enterprise frees him from the Semitic forms to which the earlier Greek translator — whose work was incorporated in the Septuagint — had felt himself bound, so all foreign stylistic elements (such as the mechanical σύν wherever there was a Hebrew את and the persistent ἐν for the prepositional *beth*) can be swept aside. Superlatives are now formed in the standard Greek way, rather than in the "futility of futilities" style, people can be referred to as "people" rather than as "the sons of man", and actual adverbs are employed in the place of nominal phrases.[1] A full range of common Greek literary particles, such as μέν and δέ, ἀλλά and γάρ, conspicuously rare or absent in LXX Ecclesiastes, are now brought into frequent play to make for a smoother progression of thought.[2]

In fact each verse now appears to flow on harmoniously from the preceding verse, no matter how disjointed some of the transitions may seem to be in the original Ecclesiastes — Koheleth typically placed contrasting thoughts side by side, or abruptly changed from one topic to another, but Gregory just as typically is able to present each new idea as being closely linked with what has come before.[3] If it is necessary on occasion to rearrange the order in which Koheleth put forward his thoughts, so that a more logical sequence of thought might be achieved, then Gregory is not afraid to do so.[4] Nor is he reluctant to introduce additional concepts into the text, matching or contrasting the concepts actually expressed, in order to create a more finely-balanced composition of ideas — in fact the frequency with which he couples a word or expression with a synthetical or antithetical word or expression suggests that such a feature is a favourite compositional device of his.[5] He has also put his mind to overcoming the repetitiousness of the original

work, in which certain key words and phrases frequently recur,
almost to the point of monotony — Gregory is very inventive
with the number of variations he can produce for Koheleth's
stock expressions, such as "futility" ("emptiness, uselessness,
absurdity, deceitfulness, wretchedness, wickedness, folly, falsehood, ...") and "under the sun" ("on the earth, among human
beings, down here, in the lower regions, ...").[6] And if the
language of the original appears to be too prosaic or un-
imaginative, Gregory is happy to come forward with a more
descriptive or colourful way of saying things.[7]

In this paraphrastic exercise, Gregory is not concerned to
establish with accuracy what Koheleth originally said. It might
be expected that a person who was trained in the academy of
Origen would have some interest — even when engaged in
"paraphrasing" and not "translating" — in making his
rendering of a biblical book as faithful to the original as possible,
without sacrificing a good Greek style. But there is no clear
indication that Gregory took account of the Hebrew text, or drew
on the insights of someone who could, in producing his version
of Ecclesiastes: time after time he takes up ideas which are
suggested by LXX but which are not supported by MT,[8] whereas
on those few occasions where it seems possible that he might be
taking up an idea suggested by MT rather than LXX, an
alternative explanation for the phenomenon can readily be
given.[9]

More significantly, when the non-LXX Greek translations of
Origen's Hexapla (Aquila, Symmachus, and Theodotion) point
to an inaccuracy in the LXX translation, Gregory appears to be
unaware of, or uninterested in, their efforts.[10] Neither is he at
all distracted by their insistence that LXX has pointed in the
wrong direction with its rendering of certain key words: they
claim that הבל has to do with ἀτμός rather than ματαιότης and
that רוח has to do with ἄνεμος rather than πνεῦμα, but Gregory
consistently follows LXX's lead.[11] Occasionally in his quest to re-
express Ecclesiastes in good and non-repetitive Greek, Gregory
does employ words which are also to be found in Symmachus'
version, but examples of this are not frequent enough to be
clearly more than coincidental.[12]

Thus it appears that Gregory was working from LXX alone — although the text in front of him may have included some variant readings[13] — and had set himself the task of independently transforming this "rough" Greek document into a "smooth" Greek work.

The Theological Transformation

This characterisation of Gregory's enterprise, as essentially a smoothing out of whatever struck the paraphrast as rough in the original work, is true also on the level of the ideas presented in the book: whatever ideas seemed heterodox have been made orthodox. Any suggestion that God might be to blame for the human predicament, or that he might act arbitrarily and unjustly, is not to be countenanced;[14] there is no doubt that it is human sinfulness,[15] under the influence of a certain "evil spirit" at work in the world,[16] which is to blame for the problematic nature of life, just as there is no doubt that a loving and just God oversees all that happens in this world and comes to the aid of those in need.[17] The recurrent conclusion that there is nothing better for a person to do in life than to eat and drink and find enjoyment for himself sounds suspiciously like a certain well-known but un-Christian philosophy of life; Gregory tells his readers bluntly that the perfect good does **not** lie in eating and drinking, and that enjoyment is only granted by God to those people who act righteously.[18] Frequently the paraphrase invests the original words of Koheleth with a moral flavour which they do not appear to have actually carried: for example, it seems that Koheleth employed the word "good" in particular contexts to speak of good fortune or worldly goods, but Gregory is inclined to treat such passages as instructions in standard Christian ethics.[19] And no matter that the original book of Ecclesiastes gave little or no credence to the theory that there is life after death — Gregory is able to find many occasions on which to direct the reader's thoughts beyond this mortal life.[20]

But just as surely as the paraphrase enlarges the vision of Ecclesiastes to take into view another — heavenly — life in addition to this life "under the sun", so it carefully limits the scope of the book's critique of life. No longer is it unreservedly said that "all is futility". Koheleth might have thought that the ceaseless cycles of nature are an example of tedium and pointlessness, but Gregory sees them as a fine example to human beings of how we ought to act in accordance with the divinely-ordained rules of behaviour; the works of God can never be described as empty or fleeting, as so many human activities are.[21] But neither is all human endeavour without meaning. Koheleth might have thought that life is ultimately futile, but Gregory does not see this conclusion as applying to Everyman; only the life of the unrighteous can be said to be a futile life.[22] Koheleth might even have said that life is to be despised because of its utter futility, but what he was really saying was that the lifestyle of a sinner is to be rejected on account of its evident wickedness.[23] And when he complained about our human inability to discern the meaning of life or to understand God's dealings with his creation, what he was actually lamenting was the shortsightedness of foolish people, who refuse to acknow-ledge the truths of the faith.[24] Those who have eyes to see know that not all is futility.[25]

They also know that they will receive a just reward for all that they do in this world. True, the doctrine of appropriate requital for the righteous and the unrighteous appears to have been under particular attack in the original book of Ecclesiastes, but in Gregory Thaumaturgos' version it is firmly reasserted. Koheleth had lamented that ultimately it seemed to make little difference whether you were wise or foolish, for in either case you had exactly the same end: death. But Gregory asserts that a wise person never shares the same fate as a foolish person: in this life the blessings of God are enjoyed by those who live a righteous life, while those who live an unrighteous life are afflicted with various distresses of body and mind arising from their wicked lifestyle[26] — and in the life to come there is a pit of punishment awaiting the ungodly, but quite a different place set apart for the godly.[27] Koheleth had been particularly disturbed by his observation that all too often the life of a good person is unjustly cut short, while a wicked person lives on in his wicked-

ness. Gregory, however, is confident that it is unrighteous
people who are snatched prematurely from this life, while
righteous people live on in their righteousness;[28] the godly may
suffer some ill-treatment at the hands of the ungodly, but the
perpetrators of such evil will surely be brought down.[29] If
judgment appears to be delayed, the Christian version of
Ecclesiastes assures us (as does the New Testament) that this is
only because of the great forbearance of the heavenly judge,[30] but
there will certainly come a time when those who are good will
enter into their eternal home with rejoicing and those who are
evil will be sent away, mourning.[31]

    In order to make this book speak with so Christian a voice,
the paraphrase occasionally seems to bluntly contradict the
original text: for example, the original text might appear to have
been saying that "the wise person dies, just like the fool", while
the paraphrase very clearly says that "the wise person never
shares the same fate as the fool".[32] But more often a clever twist
in the phrasing removes the suggestion of heresy: for example,
if the original text appears to have been blaming God for the
human plight, the simple removal of the word "God" in favour
of an impersonal construction allows the pious reader to make
his own assumption as to where the blame lies[33] — and in the
context of the paraphrase he will doubtlessly assume that the
fault lies with human beings themselves, or with that
superhuman Being who has opposed himself to God. It is
interesting to note that the same phrase in the original text can
be paraphrased in two opposite ways, depending on whether
Gregory does or does not find himself in agreement with the
opinions Koheleth was expressing: for example, the expression
"I turned [to this further matter]" is rendered as "I also know
[this additional matter]" when the pious interpreter approves of
the ideas which were put forward, but as "I turned away [from
such thoughts]" when he disapproves of what was said.[34]

    In fact this latter method — noting that certain thoughts
which have been expressed are to be rejected as false or
dangerous ideas — is a favourite device of Gregory's for coping
with the many heterodox statements sprinkled throughout
Ecclesiastes. It is not possible or necessary to refashion every

statement into an orthodox sentiment;   particular cases of erroneous ideas can be clearly marked off as the mistaken attitudes of the writer in his younger, more foolish days — "I once thought that such and such was the case, but now I know that such thinking is wrong"[35] — or as the sinister opinions of wicked people — "a person might think that he ought to do such and such, but I say that he is a fool for thinking in such a way".[36] Occasionally Gregory allows Koheleth to speak his mind relatively freely, with only an expression like "it seemed to me that this was so" hinting that the writer no longer held to this mistaken view at the time of writing,[37] but often he places immediately before or after a dangerous idea a clear note to the effect that he is here citing a false or foolish opinion.[38]

Gregory also makes it clear that the work he is paraphrasing stems from none other than Solomon, whose words deserve a hearing because he was the most honoured of all kings and the wisest of all prophets.[39] The book is called "Ecclesiastes" because it is an address which Solomon "speaks to the whole assembly (ἐκκλησία) of God"[40] — note "speaks" (present tense) and "ἐκκλησία" (read: "church"), assuring the Christian reader that this address is directed to him. Far from being the somewhat unorthodox thoughts once expressed by an unknown Hebrew sage, or even a superseded Old Testament address once given by a famous Israelite king, Ecclesiastes is to be understood as an abidingly-relevant sermon being preached to God's congregation by the wisest of his chosen messengers.

This presumption of Solomonic authorship gives rise to certain motifs in Gregory's interpretation. One idea referred to throughout the paraphrase is that Solomon lost and subsequently regained wisdom — he had received wisdom from God but had afterwards rejected it, and so he had gone through a long period of foolishness before he came to his senses and was able, as an old man, to give the wise counsel contained in this book.[41] And since Gregory sees Solomon as being not only a king but also a prophet, a number of statements are treated as speaking in a somewhat visionary way of the cosmic battle between the forces of good and evil and of the final separation of good and evil human beings; this apocalyptic motif reaches its climax in an ingenious paraphrase of the final chapter's "Allegory of Old Age" as a prophecy of the end of the world.[42]

In his paraphrase of the closing verses of the book, Gregory gives some indication of how he saw his role as a paraphrast. He speaks of the ordinary people needing someone to teach them how to understand words of wisdom, and of the responsibility of the ones who do the teaching to "pass on those wise lessons which they have received from one good shepherd and teacher, just as if everybody with one voice described in unison and in greater detail what was entrusted to them" — in paraphrasing Ecclesiastes, Gregory himself is passing on in a more understandable form the wise lessons which he has read in its pages and in which he has been instructed by his teachers; moreover, he is setting these lessons out in greater detail than they were in the form in which they had been entrusted to him, and he has presented the voice of this particular biblical book as being in unison with the general Christian tradition.

In doing so, Gregory is performing for the Church essentially the same service as that which the Aramaic paraphrase was to perform in the Jewish community when it presented the words of Koheleth as being in harmony with the general Jewish tradition. Though the Targum to Ecclesiastes was produced some centuries after Gregory's work,[43] it is no surprise that the two paraphrases handle this biblical book in broadly similar ways, since Gregory — at least through the instruction of Origen in Caesarea, if not also through direct contact with Jews in Neocaesarea — could not have been completely ignorant of the Jewish approach to Ecclesiastes which came in time to be codified in midrashic and targumic texts. Thus Gregory shares with the Targumist the decisive conviction that Solomon, as king and prophet,[44] is speaking of life "under the sun" not as the only perspective open to human beings, but as the prelude to a life to come in which everything will fall into place for the person who lives wisely and faithfully in this present life.[45] To be sure, the Greek Christian paraphrase is consistently less periphrastic and allegorical than its Aramaic Jewish counterpart, and it is naturally uninterested in linking Solomon's observations with various matters of Jewish tradition,[46] but the agenda of the two interpreters is quite analogous: just as the Targumist presented Koheleth's words in a form with which the pious Jew could live, so Gregory presented those words in a form with which the pious Christian could live.

And so it is that the Christian tradition was able gradually to embrace Ecclesiastes as a pious book of the Church. A little over a century after Gregory Thaumaturgos wrote his paraphrase, Jerome produced a commentary on Ecclesiastes which became something of a standard in the ongoing tradition of Christian interpretation of this book. Jerome refers to and directly quotes from Gregory's work,[47] and he makes considerable use of the method of reading certain statements in the book as being what Solomon had erroneously thought before he came to a correct understanding of things. Jerome moves on from Gregory in offering many allegorical interpretations, such as the eating and drinking in which the reader is advised to engage being properly understood as a feeding on Christ's body and blood in the eucharist,[48] and once this process had begun there was no holding back the inventiveness of the allegorists — Ambrose, for example, uncovered the doctrine of the Trinity in the saying, "the threefold cord is not quickly broken".[49]

Indeed, it might have been expected that Gregory himself, being a pupil of Origen, would have treated many of the enigmatical sayings of Koheleth in an allegorical or mystical way, even though his work is presented as a "paraphrase" rather than a full-scale "commentary". Gregory's interpretation of Ecclesiastes is considerably more restrained than that of many of the Fathers and later interpreters — unlike them he does not, for example, unearth references to Christ in this book, despite the prophetic abilities he ascribes to Solomon. Nevertheless, in representing the book as a sermon on the futility of the unregenerate life and the certainty of appropriate requital for the righteous and the unrighteous in the life to come, Gregory can be said to have "Christianised" the seemingly heretical words of Koheleth.

In presenting the Church with this smooth paraphrase of a formerly uncomfortable work, Gregory Thaumaturgos stands firmly at the beginning of a long tradition of seeking to remould Ecclesiastes into a more ecclesiastical book.

NOTES

Introduction

1. This depends on precisely what is meant by "withdraw" (גנז) in the discussions: exclude from the canon, or completely withdraw from circulation? The meaning is investigated by Sid Z. Leiman, *The Canonization of Hebrew Scripture: the talmudic and midrashic evidence* (Hamden, Connecticut: Archon Books, 1976), pp. 72-86; Solomon Zeitlin, *An Historical Study of the Canonization of the Hebrew Scriptures* (Philadelphia: Jewish Publication Society of America, 1933), pp. 1-8; and Roger Beckwith, *The Old Testament Canon of the New Testament Church and its Background in Early Judaism* (London: SPCK, 1985), pp. 281-283.

2. The first formulation is that of the talmudic tractate *Shabbath* (30b), the second of the Midrashim to Ecclesiastes (1:3 and 11:9) and Leviticus (23:10). The *Aboth* of Rabbi Nathan (1:4) actually claims that "Proverbs, Song of Songs, and Ecclesiastes were withdrawn, for they presented mere parables and were not part of Scripture", but since in context this claim is merely an inference from Proverbs 25:1 ("These also are proverbs of Solomon") and based on the understanding that Solomon was the author of these three books, it can have little if any historical validity (see Leiman, p. 80, who shows that this claim was an attempt to explain why Hezekiah's men copied out Solomon's proverbs: to make them available to the public). Cf. Frants Buhl, *Canon and Text of the Old Testament* (Edinburgh: T. & T. Clark, 1892), p. 30.

3. This is recorded in the mishnaic tractate *Yadayim* — "Hands" — (3:5). Rabbinic regulations decreed that a priest must ritually wash his hands after touching a sacred book, so to say that a particular book defiled or did not defile the hands — i.e., necessitated or did not necessitate a ritual washing — was tantamount to saying that that book did or did not belong to the Sacred Scriptures (for a fuller discussion of the meaning of "defile the hands", see Leiman, pp. 102-120; Zeitlin, pp. 15-21; Beckwith, pp. 278-283).

4. Leiman, pp. 120-124; Buhl, p. 27; Beckwith, pp. 316-317, 320-321; Herbert Edward Ryle, *The Canon of the Old Testament: an essay on the gradual growth and formation of the Hebrew Canon of Scripture* (London: Macmillan & Co., 1895), p. 189. Zeitlin, pp. 11,37, thinks that *Yadayim* can be used to show that Ecclesiastes was not in the canon at the time of the destruction of the temple but was added to the canon at the council of Jamnia.

5. *Tosephta Yadayim* 2:14.

6. *Corpus Christianorum*, Series Latina, vol. 72 (Turnholt: Brepols, 1959), pp. 360,361 (comments on 12:13,14).

7. Cf. the case of Ecclesiasticus (Ben Sira), which was kept out of the canon, despite its orthodoxy, because it was known to have been written after "the Holy Spirit ceased out of Israel" (see Beckwith, p. 288).

8. For example, if Solomon seemed to be saying that there was no value in anything under the sun, then he meant that there was value in the study of the Torah (which was created before the sun); if he seemed to be talking about eating and drinking, then he was picturing Torah and good deeds; and if he stated that "there is one alone and not a second" (4:8), then he was dogmatising about the Oneness of God.

9. In addition to the two decisive factors just mentioned (the ascription of

authorship to Solomon and the way in which the book was interpreted), yet a
third factor, operating on a subconscious level, might be supposed to have
played a part in the process by which Ecclesiastes came to be acknowledged as
sacred literature: an undeniable fascination with and a genuine affection for
this little scroll.

It can perhaps already be seen in the epilogue to the book
itself (12:9-14), where the writer of the epilogue seems to be captured by the
stimulating sayings that have been assembled in Ecclesiastes as well as
troubled by the possible danger to faith that they present.   The book was
problematic, but was also simply too attractive to be surrendered.

10. Song of Songs, Esther, and Ezra as well as Ecclesiastes, and it is
doubtful whether there are any quotations or reminiscences from Judges,
Ezekiel, Nahum, Zephaniah, Ruth, Lamentations, Nehemiah, and Chronicles.
Cf. Leiman, p. 40; Buhl, p. 17; Ryle, p. 162.

11. *The Apostolic Fathers*, tr.   Kirsopp Lake (The Loeb Classical
Library), vol. 2 (London: Heinemann, 1913), p. 100.   Some other possible
allusions to Ecclesiastes are listed in J. Allenbach *et al.*, eds., *Biblia Patristica:
Index des citations et allusions bibliques dans la littérature patristique*, vol. 1
(Des origenes à Clement d'Alexandrie et Tertullien) (Paris: Centre National de
la Recherche Scientifique, 1975), p. 210.

12. The occurrences are listed in *Biblia Patristica*, vol. 2 (Le troisième
siècle [Origène excepté] (1977), pp. 208-210.

13. The occurrences are listed in *Biblia Patristica*, vol. 3 (Origène) (1980),
pp. 213,214.

14. It has recently been claimed by Joseph Wilson Trigg, *Origen: The
Bible and Philosophy in the Third-century Church* (London: SCM Press, 1985),
p. 167, that "in all probability" Gregory Thaumaturgos did not study under
Origen and did not even know him, the basis for this claim being that the
Panegyric to Origen was delivered by a man named Theodore.   But Trigg's
assertion requires that we assume that Eusebius of Caesarea, the disciple of
Origen's disciple Pamphilus, was making a scarcely-conceivable error in
reporting that among the foreign pupils of Origen "as especially distinguished
we know to have been Theodore, who was the selfsame person as that renowned
bishop in our day, Gregory, and his brother Athenodore.... Five whole years
they continued with him, and made such progress in divine things that while
still young both of them were deemed worthy of the episcopate in the churches
of Pontus" (ὧν ἐπιστήμους μάλιστα ἔγνωμεν Θεόδωρον, ὃς ἦν αὐτὸς οὗτος ὁ καθ᾽
ἡμᾶς ἐπισκόπων διαβόητος Γρηγόριος· τόν τε αὐτοῦ ἀδελφὸν Ἀθηνόδωρον·....
Πέντε δὲ ὅλοις ἔτεσιν αὐτῷ συγγενόμενοι, τοσαύτην ἀπηνέγκαντο περὶ τὰ θεῖα
λόγια βελτίωσιν, ὡς ἔτι νέους ἄμφω ἐπισκοπῆς τῶν κατὰ Πόντον Ἐκκλησιῶν
ἀξιωθῆναι — *Ecclesiastical History* VI.30, quoted in Jacques-Paul Migne, ed.
Patrologia Graeca, vol. 10 [Turnholt: Brepols, 1978 (a reprint of the Paris
edition of 1857}], col. 973; cf. the testimony of Jerome in cols. 977,978 and of
Socrates in col. 980).   See further below, Chapter Seven, n. 36.

15. They are printed in Migne, cols. 1577-1588.   Charles Lett Feltoe, ed.,
The Letters and Other Remains of Dionysius of Alexandria (Cambridge
University Press, 1904), pp. 208-227, includes some additional fragments.

16. For this reason it is surprising that Gregory's paraphrase has been
largely overlooked by scholars.   Svend Holm-Nielsen, "The Book of
Ecclesiastes and the Interpretation of it in Jewish and Christian Theology", in
Annual of the Swedish Theological Institute 10 (1976), pp. 38-96, does not give
it a mention.   Roland E. Murphy, "Qohelet Interpreted: The Bearing of the Past

on the Present", in *Vetus Testamentum* 32 (1982), pp. 331-337, offers (on p. 332) a paragraph on Gregory's paraphrase as "the first extant work" on Ecclesiastes. The only studies devoted to it are the recent and brief treatments of K.W. Noakes, "The Metaphrase on Ecclesiastes of Gregory Thaumaturgus", in *Studia Patristica*, vol. 15 (Texte und Untersuchungen zur Geschichte der altchristlichen Literatur 128; Berlin: Akademie-Verlag, 1984), pp. 196-199; and Françoise Vinel, "La *Metaphrasis in Ecclesiasten* de Grégoire le Thaumaturge: entre traduction et interprétation, une explication de texte", in *Cahiers de Biblia Patristica* 1 (1987), pp. 191-215.

17. For an outline of what little we know about the life of Gregory Thaumaturgos, see the introduction in S.D.F. Salmond, tr., *The Works of Gregory Thaumaturgus, Dionysius of Alexandria, and Archelaus* (Ante-Nicene Christian Library 20; Edinburgh: T. & T. Clark, 1882), pp. 1-4. The traditional picture of Gregory's career is given in Herbert Thurston and Donald Attwater, eds., *Butler's Lives of the Saints* (Westminster: Christian Classics, 1956), vol. 4, pp. 362-364; an interesting recent examination is presented by Robin Lane Fox, *Pagans and Christians* (New York: Alfred A. Knopf, 1987), pp. 516-542. The various early references to Gregory are quoted in Migne, cols. 973-982, after some *notitia* on his life and works, cols. 963-972. On the legendary material, see William Telfer, "The Latin *Life* of St. Gregory Thaumaturgus" (in *Journal of Theological Studies* 31 [1930], pp. 142-155,354-362) and "The Cultus of St. Gregory Thaumaturgus" (in *Harvard Theological Review* 29 [1936], pp. 225-344). The *Vita* of Gregory by Gregory of Nyssa is found in Migne, vol. 46, cols. 893-958.

18. William Metcalfe's translation of the Panegyric in his *Origen the Teacher* (London: SPCK, 1907), p. 81. The Greek text in Migne, vol. 10, col. 1093, reads: αὐτὸς ὑποφητεύων καὶ σαφηνίζων, ὅ τί ποτε σκοτεινὸν καὶ αἰνιγματῶδες ἢ (οἷα πολλὰ ἐν ταῖς ἱεραῖς ἐστι Φωναῖς· ἤτοι οὕτω φίλον ὂν τῷ Θεῷ προσομιλεῖν ἀνθρώποις, ὡς μὴ καὶ ἀναξίαν ψυχήν, οἷαι αἱ πολλαί, γυμνὸς καὶ ἀσκεπὴς ὁ θεῖος εἰσίη λόγος· ἢ καὶ τῇ φύσει μὲν σαφέστατον καὶ ἁπλούστατον πᾶν τὸ θεῖον λόγιον ὄν, ἡμῖν δὲ ἀποστᾶσι Θεοῦ, καὶ ἀπομεμαθηκόσιν ἀκροᾶσθαι ὑπὸ χρόνου καὶ παλαιότητος, ἀσαφὲς καὶ σκοτεινὸν καταφαινόμενον, οὐκ ἔχω λέγειν).

19. Metcalfe, p. 87 (Migne, col. 1101: φέροντες ἐκ τῶν σπερμάτων καὶ τοὺς καρποὺς καὶ τὰς δραγμίδας).

20. Indeed, shortly after Gregory had left Origen's academy, the master had written a letter to his graduate, in which he admonished him to seek to uncover the meaning of the Scriptures: "Do you then, my son, diligently apply yourself to the reading of the sacred Scriptures. Apply yourself, I say. For we who read the things of God need much application, lest we should say or think anything too rashly about them. And applying yourself thus to the study of the things of God, with faithful prejudgments such as are well pleasing to God, knock on its locked door, and it will be opened to you by the porter, of whom Jesus says, 'To him the porter opens' [John 10:3]. And applying yourself thus to the divine study, seek aright, and with unwavering trust in God, the meaning of the holy Scriptures, which so many have missed" (Frederick Crombie's translation of the letter in his *The Writings of Origen*, vol. 1 [Ante-Nicene Christian Library, vol. 10; Edinburgh: T. & T. Clark, 1869], p. 390; the Greek text in Migne, vol. 11, col. 92, reads: Σὺ οὖν, κύριε υἱέ, προηγουμένως πρόσεχε τῇ τῶν θείων Γραφῶν ἀναγνώσει· ἀλλὰ πρόσεχε· πολλῆς γὰρ προσοχῆς ἀναγινώσκοντες τὰ θεῖα δεόμεθα· ἵνα μὴ προπετέστερον εἴπωμέν τινα, ἢ νομίσωμεν περὶ αὐτῶν· καὶ προσέχων τῇ τῶν θείων ἀναγνώσει μετὰ πιστῆς καὶ Θεῷ ἀρεσκούσης προλήψεως, κροῦε τὰ κεκλεισμένα αὐτῆς, καὶ ἀνοιγήσεταί σοι

ὑπὸ τοῦ θυρωροῦ, περὶ οὗ εἶπεν ὁ Ἰησοῦς· «Τούτῳ ὁ θυρωρὸς ἀνοίγει.» Καὶ προσέχων τῇ θείᾳ ἀναγνώσει, ὀρθῶς ζήτει καὶ μετὰ πίστεως τῆς εἰς Θεὸν ἀκλινοῦς τὸν κεκρυμμένον τοῖς πολλοῖς νοῦν τῶν θείων γραμμάτων).

21. Robert B. Salters, "The Book of Ecclesiastes: Studies in the Versions and the History of Exegesis" (Ph.D. dissertation, University of St. Andrews, 1973), pp. 18,19, lists a number of other features of Aquila's translation of the Hebrew Bible which show up in Ecclesiastes: lamed with the infinitive represented by τοῦ with the infinitive, lamed with a noun by article and noun wherever εἰς would be out of place, and אם by καί γε to distinguish it from ו/καί. [All subsequent references to Salters, unless otherwise specified, are to this dissertation.] Beckwith, p. 331, n. 109, however, notes that LXX Ecclesiastes lacks some other marks of Aquila's translation-technique: it does not render את by καὶ καίγε or אך by καίπερ, it has a few loose renderings, and it translates nine Hebrew expressions in more than one way. Further non-Aquilan characteristics are raised by Kyösti Hyvärinen, Die Übersetzung von Aquila (Coniectanea Biblica, Old Testament Series, no. 10; Lund: CWK Gleerup, 1977), in his chapter "Die LXX-Übersetzung des Ecclesiastes", pp. 88-99.

22. Cf. Richard R. Ottley, A Handbook to the Septuagint (London: Methuen, 1920), p. 24. Beckwith, in his Appendix "The Four Greek Versions of Ecclesiastes in Origen's 'Hexapla'" (pp. 472-477), argues that the version listed as "Aquila" in the Hexapla is in reality the original Septuagint version, which has been displaced from the Septuagint by the actual version of Aquila (or "proto-Aquila"); while Dominique Barthélemy, in his section "La 'Septante' de L'Ecclésiaste" (pp. 21-30 of his Les Devanciers d'Aquila [Supplements to Vetus Testamentum, vol. 10; Leiden: E.J. Brill, 1963]), argues that the version cited as "Aquila" is from another hand, displaying certain characteristics of Symmachus. But see the counter-arguments in Hyvärinen, pp. 88-99, and in John Jarick, "Aquila's Koheleth", forthcoming in Textus 16 (1990), which suggest that the renderings which have come down to us under the name of Aquila are indeed from an Aquilan version.

23. This is the view of Barthélemy, pp. 32,33, cited with approval by Salters, p. 21, and by Sidney Jellicoe, The Septuagint and Modern Study (Oxford: Clarendon Press, 1968), p. 82.

24. This is the view of Holm-Nielsen, ASTI, p. 58; and of Beckwith, pp. 302-304, who notes that Theodotion's version of Daniel ousted the original Septuagint as a preferable version of that book.

25. Cf. Jean Danielou, Origen, tr. Walter Mitchell (New York: Sheed and Ward, 1955), p. 133.

26. Metcalfe, pp. 42,43 (Migne, cols. 1052,1053).

27. On Origen's knowledge of Hebrew, see the discussion in Jellicoe, op. cit., pp. 104-106 — and on the possible ancillary use of the Hexapla as an aid in learning Hebrew, see pp. 108,109 (the full text of the Orlinsky article there discussed has since been conveniently reprinted in Jellicoe's Studies in the Septuagint: Origins, Recensions, and Interpretations [New York: KTAV Publishing House, 1974], pp. 369-381).

28. The Hexapla was apparently begun in Alexandria and completed in Caesarea (Jellicoe, Septuagint & Modern Study, p. 101; Henry Barclay Swete, An Introduction to the Old Testament in Greek [Cambridge University Press, 1914], p. 73, places its completion between the years 240 and 245). It is quite possible that the Hexapla of Ecclesiastes had been completed by, or was completed during, the time of Gregory's studies (in the late 230s), and it is

equally possible that Gregory's interest in paraphrasing this particular book was kindled at that time.

29. Even if Gregory was not able to make use of the Hexapla when he came to produce his paraphrase, it is conceivable that he may have had access to the translation of Symmachus, since it appears that this Greek version of the Hebrew Bible was in circulation in Cappadocia (see Jellicoe, *op. cit.*, pp. 94-99). Of the three non-LXX Greek translations of the Hexapla of Ecclesiastes, Symmachus' version, having the greatest paraphrastic tendency, would be perhaps the most useful to someone engaged in Gregory's task.

30. This is the form given in Migne, cols. 987,988. Johannes Quasten, *Patrology* (Westminster: Newman Press, 1964), vol. 2, p. 127, has Σολομῶνος instead of τοῦ Σολομῶντος.

31. Quasten, p. 127; Migne, cols. 977 and 979.

32. The text in Migne is divided into chapters, but not verses (though the accompanying Latin translation includes verse numbering). For the purposes of this study, I have divided the paraphrase into verses, in accordance with the versification of the Hebrew Bible.

33. The editions of the Septuagint (LXX) and the Hebrew Bible (MT) used for comparative purposes in the following study are Alfred Rahlfs, ed., *Septuaginta* (Stuttgart: Privilegierte Württembergische Bibelanstalt, 1950), and Kurt Elliger and Wilhelm Rudolph, eds., *Biblia Hebraica Stuttgartensia* (Stuttgart: Deutsche Bibelstiftung, 1967/77). On occasion it proved worthwhile to consult the earlier editions of Henry Barclay Swete (*The Old Testament in Greek according to the Septuagint* [Cambridge University Press, [3]1907]), Robert Holmes and James Parsons, *Vetus Testamentum Graecum cum variis lectionibus*, vol. 3 [Oxford: Clarendon Press, 1823]), and Rudolf Kittel (*Biblia Hebraica* [Stuttgart: Privilegierte Württembergische Bibelanstalt, [4]1949).

34. I have consulted Field's edition of the Hexapla (Frederick Field, ed., *Origenis Hexaplorum*, vol. 2 [Oxford: Clarendon Press, 1867]), Lane's edition of the Peshitta (in *The Old Testament in Syriac, according to the Peshitta Version*, edited on behalf of the International Organization for the Study of the Old Testament by the Peshitta Institute, Leiden [Leiden: E.J. Brill, 1979], part 2, fascicle 5, pp. 1-20), and Weber's edition of the Vulgate (Robert Weber, ed., *Biblia Sacra Iuxta Vulgatam Versionem* [Stuttgart: Württembergische Bibelanstalt, 1969]). For the Targum, I have generally preferred the edition of Paul de Lagarde, *Hagiographa Chaldaice* (Osnabrück: Otto Zeller, 1967 [a reprint of the 1873 edition]), but I have taken account of certain interesting differences in the edition of Alexander Sperber, *The Bible in Aramaic*, vol. 4A (Leiden: E.J. Brill, 1968).

Chapter One

1. Preferring an acute accent before a comma, I have throughout the text, wherever Migne's edition has a grave accent in such a position (as here on Σαλομών), changed this to acute.

2. It may be noted that the Jewish Aramaic paraphrase of Ecclesiastes (the Targum) begins with a similar opening to the Christian Greek paraphrase: these are פתגמי נבואה דאתנבא, "the words of prophecy which he [King Solomon] prophesied". The Targumist finds considerably more words of prophecy in this book than does Gregory (though interestingly he does not share the latter's

prophetic interpretation of 12:1-7), but they are agreed that the one who speaks here is more than a simple king.

3. Indeed, in the published text the technical term appears with a capital *epsilon*, and although this tells us nothing about Gregory's intention (since the distinction between upper and lower cases is a development considerably later than his time), it does indicate that at least some of his readers have understood ἐκκλησία here in the sense of "Church".

4. Svend Holm-Nielsen, "On the Interpretation of Qoheleth in Early Christianity" (in *Vetus Testamentum* 24 [1974], pp. 168-177), p. 170, claims that ματαιότης twists the meaning of הבל in an ethical direction. Salters, p. 72, shows that ματαιότης, "purposelessness", which has no physical reference, rather than ἀτμός, "steam, vapour", which has no figurative reference, is quite appropriate in this context.

5. In his panegyric over Origen, Gregory had used this term in an explicit contrast to divine matters (*Panegyric*, ch. 5: Migne, col. 1065, line 31 — the case is cited in G.W.H. Lampe, *A Patristic Greek Lexicon* [Oxford: Clarendon Press, 1961], p. 139); he may well intend an implicit such contrast here.

6. Codex Thuan. has κατά instead of περί (Migne, column 989, n. 86-87).

7. The introduction of this higher perspective to Koheleth's harsh picture seems to be the basic way in which a pious interpreter can reclaim Ecclesiastes as a scriptural book. The Targumist uses precisely the same device in saying that a person's worldly labours under the sun bring him no advantage — but he can receive a good reward in the world to come if he studies Torah in this world! Cf. Rashi's interpretation of תחת השמש as "instead of the sun", "the sun" referring to the light of the Torah; i.e., whatever labour is undertaken in place of Torah-study is of no avail and yields no reward.

8. This might be called a *hapax legomenon*. It is not found in Henry George Liddell and Robert Scott, *A Greek-English Lexicon*, revised Henry Stuart Jones and Roderick McKenzie (Oxford: Clarendon Press, ⁹1940), and Lampe, p. 1434, cites only this passage.

9. Graham Ogden has recently proposed (*Qoheleth* [Sheffield: JSOT Press, 1987], p. 30, following a fuller treatment in "The Interpretation of דור in Ecclesiastes 1.4", in *Journal for the Study of the Old Testament* 34 [1986], pp. 91-92) that דור in this verse did not refer to human generations but to the circular movement within nature. This suggestion has some attractiveness, but it is most natural in view of the human scene just mentioned in v. 3 and in view of the general meaning of דור throughout the Hebrew Bible to understand the word in the way in which the ancient interpreters understood it: LXX γενεά, Targum דרא (the paraphrastic context making it evident that human generations are in view), and Gregory ὁ τῶν ἀνθρώπων βίος. [All subsequent references to Ogden, unless otherwise specified, are to his *Qoheleth*.]

10. The translation of this verse by Edwin M. Good ("The Unfilled Sea: Style and Meaning in Ecclesiastes 1:2-11", in *Israelite Wisdom: Theological and Literary Essays in Honor of Samuel Terrien*, ed. John G. Gammie *et al.* [Missoula: Scholars Press, 1978], pp. 59-73), p. 67 — "Goes to the south, circles to the north, circles, circles, goes the wind, and on its circles turns the wind" — well captures the effective style of Koheleth. Gregory's "It is the same with the winds" is very poor in comparison, though he has his own excellence of style in other verses (see his rounding-off of this section in v. 8); clearly Gregory is at pains to avoid conveying the "air of oppressiveness" (Good, p. 69) in nature which Koheleth was seeking to convey (see comments below on v. 7).

11. Migne, cols. 989 and 990, n. 88.

12. Codices Reg. and Thuan. place a καί before τί (Migne, col. 990, n. 89).

13. Salters, p. 103, and Robert Gordis, *Koheleth — The Man and his World: A study of Ecclesiastes* (New York: Schocken Books, [3]1968) p. 207, both make this point. The full form of this and the following parallel sentence in LXX was: τί τὸ γεγονός; αὐτὸ τὸ γενησόμενον· καὶ τί τὸ πεποιημένον; αὐτὸ τὸ ποιηθησόμενον. Swete, p. 481, has the question marks shown here, while Rahlfs, p. 329, prefers commas — in Koine Greek τί could be used as a substitute for the indefinite relative pronoun (cf. Walter Bauer, *A Greek-English Lexicon of the New Testament and Other Early Christian Literature*, tr. & ed. William F. Arndt & F. Wilbur Gingrich [Chicago University Press, [2]1979], p. 819), in which case the LXX clauses should probably be understood as indirect questions.

14. LXX Jeremiah 38:31 (MT 31:31), quoted in Hebrews 8:8. Cf. καινὴ κτίσις, 2 Corinthians 5:17 and Galatians 6:15.

15. Codex Medic. has ἔπη τις, "one could understand/take [as being...]" instead of ὅ τι δ' ἂν εἴπη, "which one could say [is...]" (Migne, col. 990, n. 90).

16. MT and LXX did not introduce these facts in quite the same way, MT vocalising דבר as a noun and LXX representing it as a verb (λαλήσει — cf. Peshitta ܢܡܠܠ), but this has no reflection in Gregory's paraphrase, unless we are to suppose that λαλέω has prompted the idea of introducing this verse with οἴομαι.

17. Cf. τὸ πάλαι, "the past"; τὸ (or τὰ) νῦν, "the present".

18. So LXX. MT has the future in both clauses.

19. Holm-Nielsen, *VT*, p. 171, accepts LXX's invitation to make such an interpretation. Gregory's failure to take up the possibility here is in contrast to his interpretation of 2:16; 3:11,16; 4:2; 11:2; 12:1-7.

20. Λήθη was the name of the river of oblivion in the lower world in Greek mythology and as such might be considered a most appropriate word to use in a paraphrase of Ecclesiastes, in which the shadow of ᾅδης (שאול) was continually present (cf. particularly 9:10, where ᾅδης appeared explicitly, with οὐ... γνῶσις covering the idea which λήθη carries here in Gregory's paraphrase).

21. The Targumist's solution is to suppose that the LORD, through the agency of a demon, had driven Solomon from the throne on account of his great sins in amassing wealth and foreign women, so that the deposed ruler wandered about the countryside lamenting "I am Koheleth, whose name was formerly called Solomon, who was king over Israel in Jerusalem". Needless to say there is no support in the biblical account of Solomon's life for this inventive fable, and — if indeed he knew of it — it does not appeal to Gregory, who has his own extra-biblical theory on the course of Solomon's career (see comments on 7:23).

22. An emendation in LXX Codex Sinaiticus places ἥλιος at this point, and a Cairo Geniza Hebrew fragment has שמש rather than שמים.

23. This is the conclusion, after a review of various possibilities, of George Aaron Barton, *A Critical and Exegetical Commentary on the Book of Ecclesiastes* (Edinburgh: T. & T. Clark, 1908), pp. 85,86; Michael A. Eaton, *Ecclesiastes* (Leicester: Inter-Varsity Press, 1983), p. 63; and J. Lloyd, *An Analysis of the Book of Ecclesiastes* (London: Samuel Bagster & Sons, 1874), p. 16. The occurrences of the expression רעות רוח/רעיון רוח in Ecclesiastes are 1:14,17; 2:11,17,26; 4:4,6,16; 6:9.

24. Gregory's interpretation is also in contrast to that of his "colleague" Dionysius, who says that this πνεῦμα is the human ψυχή (Migne, col. 1581).

25. Lampe, pp. 107,108 (ἀνακτάομαι and its cognate noun ἀνάκτησις).

26. Translating the Hebrew expression דברתי אני עם־לבי. LXX's ἐν may indicate a reading of בלבי here, as in the analogous expression in 2:1,3,15; 3:17,18.

27. On the question of the frequent use of the separate personal pronoun אני in the book of Ecclesiastes, see the comments of Takamitsu Muraoka, *Emphatic Words and Structures in Biblical Hebrew* (Jerusalem: Magnes Press, 1985), pp. 48,49; and Bo Isaksson, *Studies in the Language of Qoheleth, with special emphasis on the verbal system* (Acta Universitatis Upsaliensis: Studia Semitica Upsaliensia 10; Uppsala University Press, 1987), pp. 163-171.

28. Cf. the Targum's "all the wise who were before me in [ב] Jerusalem".

29. Gordis, p. 212, notes that it would be an especially easy error in the uncials, ΠΑΡΑΒΟΛΑΣ for ΠΑΡΑΦΟΡΑΣ. Salters, p. 123, speculates that a copyist may have deliberately changed παραφοράς to παραβολάς here, thinking the former a mistake.

30. Περιφορά in 2:12 and 7:25; περιφέρεια in 9:3 and 10:13. Theodotion has παραφορά here in 1:17 (Field, p. 382) and some LXX manuscripts have it in 2:12 and 7:25 (Rahlfs, pp. 241,252).

31. MT סכלות in 2:3,12,13; 7:25; 10:1,13. In 7:25 LXX rendered it ὀχληρία, "troublesomeness" (or in some manuscripts σκληρία, "stubbornness" — see ch. 7, n. 30), because ἀφροσύνη had just been employed for כסל.

32. Cf. the Targum's "complexities and intelligence" (תולחלתא... וסוכלתנו), and the Peshitta's "proverbs and understanding" (ܡܬ̈ܠܐ ܘܣܘܟܠܐ).

33. LXX has taken the second דעת of MT as a noun (as do the Targum's מנדעא and the Peshitta's ܝܕܥܬܐ) rather than as an infinitive.

34. Cf. Peshitta ܪܘܓܙܐ, "wrath" and Targum רגו, "wrath (of the LORD!)". LXX rendered כעס as θυμός in all later occurrences (2:23; 7:3,9; 11:10).

Chapter Two

1. The *iota* subscript is missing in Migne, col. 992.

2. As indeed it is here too in two Hebrew manuscripts; cf. the Peshitta's ܬܚܝܬ ܫܡܫܐ and the Vulgate's *sub sole*, but note the Targum's תחות שמיא.

3. This may be compared with the approach of the Targumist, who makes room in his treatment of these verses for quite a number of intrusive elements, such as the Rabbis of the Sanhedrin in Jamnia in this verse and various kinds of demons from India in the next verse!

4. 2 Kings 18:17; Nehemiah 2:14; 3:15,16; Isaiah 7:3; 22:9,11; 36:2; Nahum 2:9. Κρήνη, "well, spring" was employed at 2 Samuel 2:13; 4:12; 1 Kings 22:38; 2 Kings 20:20; and λίμνη, "pool" at Song of Songs 7:5.

5. Codex Medic. has γενέσθαι (Migne, col. 991, n. 91).

6. LXX's approach is in keeping with MT, which also has two etymologically-unrelated words, עבד and שפחה (perfectly balanced titles might have been provided by נער and נערה, although these would not have meant exactly the same thing). So also Targum (עבדין ואמהן), Peshitta (ܥܒ̈ܕܐ ܘܐܡ̈ܗܬܐ), and Vulgate (*servi et ancillae*).

7. A בן־בית, "child of the house" in this context is undoubtedly a house-born slave (cf. Genesis 15:3), and so was well rendered by LXX's οἰκογενής. Less commendable is the Targumic interpretation, which makes a distinction not between bought and house-born slaves but between "the children of Ham" (בניהון

חזק, who can be bought as slaves) and "the people of my house" (אינשי ביתי, who are freemen, to be served by those of the former category).

8. Francis Brown, S.R. Driver, and Charles A. Briggs, *A Hebrew and English Lexicon of the Old Testament* (Oxford: Clarendon Press, 1972), p. 889, cite Ecclesiastes 2:7 thus under מקנה, 2.

9. Codex Medic. deletes δέ (Migne, col. 992, n. 93).

10. In LXX, this appears in the "miscellanies" of Chapter Three (3:46b in Rahlf's versification), while in the Vulgate, and in English Bibles, it is 4:21.

11. It is presumably this last passage which is referred to in Migne col. 992, n. 92, as "III Reg. IX,24: *Et omnes reges terrae quaerebant faciem Salomonis, et ferebant dona*", which looks like a translation of part of LXX's 3 Kings 10:24,25: καὶ πάντες βασιλεῖς τῆς γῆς ἐζήτουν τὸ πρόσωπον Σαλωμών.... καὶ αὐτοὶ ἔφερον ἕκαστος τὰ δῶρα αὐτοῦ (Vulgate reads *Et universa terra desiderabat vultum Salomonis.... et singuli deferebant ei munera*).

12. Eaton, p. 67, n. 2, raises the possibility that MT's masculine and feminine sequence (שרים ושרות) is an example of the idiom found later in the same verse (שדה ושדות, discussed below) and should be translated "many singers, male and female". If this is so, Gregory's παμπληθής, "very numerous" is very fitting.

13. Cf. Gordis, pp. 218,219; Wesley J. Fuerst, *The Books of Ruth, Esther, Ecclesiastes, The Song of Songs, Lamentations: The Five Scrolls* (Cambridge University Press, 1975), p. 107; Victor E. Reichert and A. Cohen, "Ecclesiastes", in *The Five Megilloth*, ed. A. Cohen (London: Soncino Press, 1946), p. 117; Christian D. Ginsburg, *Coheleth* (London, 1861; reprint New York: KTAV Publishing House, 1970), pp. 285,286.

14. The plural is the reading of Codex Alexandrinus and a "correction" in Codex Sinaiticus; Codex Vaticanus has the singular (cf. Aquila's κυλίκιον καὶ κυλίκια, "a wine-cup and wine-cups"). The other ancient versions also interpret in terms of Aramaic שדי: thus Peshitta ܐ‍ܒ‍ܢ‍ܐ‍ ܐ‍ܒ‍ܘ‍ܐ‍, while the Targumist speaks of "pipes which pour out cold water and pipes which pour out hot water".

15. In contrast to this interpretation, the Targumist has no problem in saying that wisdom stayed with Solomon, since he has managed to interpret the entire exercise as being the good works which the great king did in Jerusalem.

16. If this clause (οὐδ' ἂν καταλέγειν ἔχοιμι) is taken as referring to the "wine stewards" of v. 8, as it is by Salmond, p. 9, it may be an exceptionally fine rendering of a Hebrew nuance on the part of Gregory (cf. n. 12 above).

17. Gregory's parallel to LXX's μεγαλύνω is ὑπερβάλλω, "to excel"; ἐλασσόω is his rejoinder to LXX's ἵστημι.

18. Codex Anglicus has δείλαιος, and a manuscript of Codex Medic. has μοχθηρά τε ὁμοῦ (Migne, col. 992, n. 94).

19. Manuscripts of Codices Reg. and Thuan. have τοῦτον (Migne, col. 993, n. 95).

20. Codex Medic. has ἐπιστρέψῃ (Migne, col. 993, n. 95).

21. Gordis, pp. 219,220, contends that MT means "I saw that wisdom is madness and folly". Note that LXX has understood הוללות and סכלות correctly here, unlike in 1:17 (cf. Salters, p. 143).

22. The first view is taken by O.S. Rankin, "Ecclesiastes", in *The Interpreter's Bible*, ed. George Arthur Buttrick (Nashville: Abingdon Press, 1956), vol. 5, pp. 37,38; the second view is taken by Gordis, pp. 220,221, and by Reichert and Cohen, p. 118; the third view is taken by Eaton, pp. 68,69. The

Targumist has yet a different interpretation: there is no use in petitioning a king after judgment has been passed and executed (צלי pael, strictly speaking "to pray", suggests that the "king" here is the heavenly King).

23. Rahlfs, p. 241, inserts ὁ at this point, though none of the three major codices has the article; he supplies it from Codex Venetus.

24. Salters, pp. 145,146, notes that the Aramaic derivation is more likely than an original translation of τοῦ βασιλέως having been changed by a copyist's error into τῆς βουλῆς.

25. Syriac ܡܠܟܐ is ambiguous, in that it could mean "king" or "counsel", but Peshitta's ܡܠܟܐ ܕܒܗ looks like a kind of parallel to Targum's גזירת מלכא, "the decree of the king", and so is to be rendered "the king in [his] judgment".

26. Cf. Targum נהור יומא and חשוך ליליא, "the light of day" and "the darkness of night" for MT אור and חשך.

27. Migne, cols. 993,994, n. 96, proposes that this καί and its preceding comma be placed before τὴν πρόσοψιν rather than after it; I am happy to follow this suggestion in my translation.

28. Ἀφαιροῦμαι has been proposed (Migne, col. 994, n. 96).

29. This verse, along with Ecclesiastes 8:1, is cited in Migne, col. 993, n. 1 (to the Latin translation).

30. Just as the Targumist was quick in this verse to indicate to his readers that a righteous person **can** avoid the fate of the wicked.

31. Actually our LXX editions place the question mark before περισσός, which is then part of the next sentence and not part of the rhetorical question (ἵνα τί puts the question by itself); see the following paragraph in my comments.

32. Cf. Targum's negating addition of לית.

33. LXX μνήμη δικαίων μετ᾽ ἐγκωμίων, ὄνομα δὲ ἀσεβοῦς σβέννυται, "the memory of the righteous will be a blessing, but the name of the wicked will rot".

34. The same nuance is carried by MT's אין. The Targumist understands that this is a complaint (איכדין), but changes it into a complaint that "people say" (יימרון בני אינשא) that the same end awaits righteous and wicked alike, when in fact it does not!

35. Cf. Targum's limitation to כל חיין בישין, "all evil life" of wicked people.

36. The Targum applies this prophetically to Solomon's son Rehoboam.

37. Cf. Symmachus γοργότης, "vigour"; Peshitta ܚܝܠܬܢܘܬܐ, "skill, success, vigour"; Targum צדקו, "righteousness".

38. Gordis, p. 225, mentions two other possibilities: to read the clause interrogatively ("Is it not good...?"), or to assume the absence of an excluding particle like אך or רק.

39. Targum and Peshitta, however, sensibly insert אילהין/ ܐܠܐ in the phrase here. The Targumist, too, is happy to bring this verse into line with the other אך טוב verses (because he interprets them as having to do with good works and rejoicing in the Torah).

40. So, too, Peshitta ܚܠܐ. Two other possibilities are "to worry" (thus Targum חששא, "anxiety") and "to enjoy" (the meaning arrived at after a lengthy survey of possibilities by J. de Waard, "The Translator and Textual Criticism [with particular reference to Eccl 2,25]", in Biblica 60 [1979], pp. 509-529 — see especially pp. 526,527).

41. The Targumist says that Solomon alone seems to be concerned with matters of Torah and the coming judgment — a common complaint on the part of

prophets (cf. Elijah's complaint in 1 Kings 19:10,14), and for the Targumist (as for Gregory), Solomon is a prophet.
    42. Again the conclusion of de Waard (see especially pp. 519,520).
    43. Cf. Rankin, pp. 41,42; Gordis, pp. 227,228.

Chapter Three

    1. Codex Anglicus has ἐναντιωτάτων (Migne, col. 995, n. 97).
    2. Gerhard von Rad, *Wisdom in Israel*, tr. James D. Martin (London: SCM Press, 1972), p. 139, n. 3.
    3. Cf. Heinz Zahrnt, *What Kind of God?* (Minneapolis: Augsburg Publishing House, 1972), p. 152. Alexander Maclaren, *The Books of Esther, Job, Proverbs, and Ecclesiastes* (London: Hodder and Stoughton, 1907), p. 323, captures the feeling well in pointing out that the disparate events and activities appear to be "as purposeless as the play of the wind on the desert sands, which it sometimes piles into huge mounds and then scatters."
    4. The Targum interprets the passage at hand as saying that everyone is granted the opportune time for various activities, and conveys throughout a positive feeling of appropriate human action in accordance with the particular times for action.   Dionysius of Alexandria, who (like Gregory) studied under Origen, stands with the Targumist and against Gregory in viewing the times positively as each having its appropriate activity.   For example (though not one which would appeal to the Targumist), Dionysius comments on v. 6 that "before the Incarnation it was a time to keep the letter of the law, but it was a time to cast it away when the Truth came in its flower" (τὸ νομικὸν γράμμα πρὸ τῆς Ἐπιδημίας, καιρὸς ὑπῆρχε φυλάττεσθαι· ἐκβληθῆναι δέ, ἡνίκα ἤνθησεν ἡ Ἀλήθεια — Migne, col. 1588).
    5. The Targumist does just the opposite.   He does not vary the basic formula from one verse to the next ("a select time for..., and a select time for..."), but he expands his description of many of the activities enumerated, since his concern is to provide a justification for the various times which God has appointed.   For example, he expands the death-clause in this opening couplet into a reference to the death penalty justly imposed upon wicked and disobedient children; or again, in the following verse, the killing is specified as taking place during war and hence may be just, for a man is permitted — even duty-bound — to kill during a just war, the appropriate or select time for killing, in the Targumist's view. Thus he consistently makes small additions to justify as ἀγαθός what Gregory sees as activities to be judged as κακός.   For the Targumist, all is right with the world, while for Gregory, it is a sad fact that bad things are part and parcel of this present age.
    6. E.H. Plumptre, *Ecclesiastes* (Cambridge University Press, 1881), p. 127, would like to think that gathering in the fruits of the earth "and not a wanton destruction, which would be a violation of the natural order, is clearly meant"; but he admits that where עקר occurs elsewhere in the Hebrew Bible, it "is used figuratively of the destruction of cities" (cf. Zephaniah 2:4).
    7. Barton, p. 100; G. Currie Martin, *Proverbs, Ecclesiastes, Song of Songs* (London: T.C. & E.C. Jack, 1908), p. 236; and Franz Delitzsch, *Commentary on the Song of Songs and Ecclesiastes*, tr. M.G. Easton (Edinburgh: T. & T. Clark, 1877), p. 257, all opt for this interpretation.
    8. Leviticus 14:40-42 described the cleansing of tainted houses by

throwing away the unclean stones and replacing them with clean stones. Midrash *Koheleth Rabbah* holds that "scattering stones" is used to symbolise sexual intercourse and "gathering stones" abstinence, and thus links this first half of the verse with the second half concerning "a time to embrace and a time to refrain from embracing". Gordis, p. 230, quotes the Midrash with approval, and cites Exodus 1:16, Jeremiah 2:27, and Matthew 3:9 as offering support for this understanding. These biblical citations are unconvincing, however, since none of them actually links stones with sexual intercourse; they can be quite naturally explained as references to objects used by midwives in their work, pagans in their idolatry, and God in his power without any metaphorical meaning. Ludwig Levy, *Das Buch Qoheleth: Ein Beitrag zur Geschichte des Sadduzäismus* (Leipzig: J.C. Hinrichs'sche Buchhandlung, 1912), devotes a considerable Appendix ("Das 'Steinewerfen' in Qoheleth 3:5, in der Deukalionsage und im Hermeskult", pp. 144-152) to the sexual symbolism of stonethrowing.

9. The reversal is required because Gregory has interpreted the scattering of stones as the negative action and the gathering of stones as the positive action. But J.A. Loader ("Qohelet 3:2-8 — a 'Sonnet' in the Old Testament", in *Zeitschrift für die alttestamentliche Wissenschaft* 81 [1969], pp. 240-242) argues attractively, on the basis of the chiasmic structure of the Catalogue, that the scattering of stones must have a "desirable" meaning and the gathering of stones an "undesirable" meaning (see especially p. 242).

10. Barton, p. 100, and Plumptre, p. 129, are concerned to show that the two halves of the verse are not exactly synonymous.

11. Cf. especially the use of ῥάπτω with the objects φόνος, "murder"; θάνατος, "death"; and μόρος, "doom" in Homer's *Odyssey* 16.379,422 (cited by Liddell and Scott, p. 1565).

12. Barton, pp.104,105; Plumptre, p.130; Delitzsch, p.259; Martin, p.236.

13. Eaton, pp. 78,79, suggests that the pairing of varying aspects of human life in Ecclesiastes 3:2-8 simply indicates totality, like "man and woman" or "great and small" is used to say emphatically "everybody". But this misses the point, which Gregory did not miss, that the activities mentioned by Koheleth are not value-neutral, but are ἀγαθός and κακός respectively in each case.

14. As it is called by Ogden, p. 54 (cf. p. 28). Barton, pp. 101,105 calls it "the crying question", "a refrain which well expresses [Koheleth's] mood".

15. Given the meaning of περισπασμός (and given that in MT ענין signifies an occupation which causes trouble or costs effort), there is no real necessity for such an adjective.

16. The Targum styles 3:10 as having to do with the LORD afflicting evil people.

17. Various possibilities of interpretation are reviewed by Barton, p. 105; Rankin, pp. 46-49; Gordis, p. 231; and Oswald Loretz, *Qohelet und der Alte Orient: Untersuchungen zu Stil und theologischer Thematik des Buches Qohelet* (Freiburg: Herder, 1964), pp. 281,282 (n. 277). MT's vocalisation of עלם with *cholem* and *qametz*, which is supported by LXX's αἰών, gives "eternity, the world", or some aspect of "eternity" — such as the future, hidden time, or permanence. A vocalisation of עלם as a segholate noun gives "ignorance" or "mystery", and a consonantal rearrangement to עמל with double *qametz* gives "toil". Although these latter proposals would make good sense in the light of v. 10, MT/LXX's reading is quite acceptable in the context of v. 11 (as explained

in the commentary above) and so should be retained.

18. See the conclusions of Samuel Cox, *The Book of Ecclesiastes* (London: Hodder and Stoughton, 1899), p. 81; Walther Zimmerli, *Old Testament Theology in Outline*, tr. David E. Green (Atlanta: John Knox Press, 1978), p. 162; Derek Kidner, *A Time to Mourn and a Time to Dance: Ecclesiastes and the way of the world* (London: Inter-Varsity Press, 1976), p.39; and Graham S. Ogden, "Qoheleth's Use of the 'Nothing is Better' Form" (in *Journal of Biblical Literature* 98 [1979], pp. 339-350), p. 345. In his commentary, p. 55, Ogden accepts the meaning "a consciousness of the eternal". James L. Crenshaw, "The Eternal Gospel (Eccl. 3:11)" (in *Essays in Old Testament Ethics*, ed. James L. Crenshaw and John T. Willis [New York: KTAV Publishing House, 1974], pp. 23-55), p. 42, speaks of the human quest to search out "the divine mysteries hidden in the world". Isaksson, p. 183, translates העלם as "the eternal work [of God]", and explains this as "the work that has been done from the outset of creation and will be done to the end of time".

19. Barton, pp. 102,106; Martin, p. 237.

20. A Medicean manuscript has πραγμάτων (Migne, col. 995, n. 98 [the matter concerning a reading ἐναντιοτήτων should presumably be part of n. 97 rather than n. 98]).

21. Ogden, p. 341.

22. Fuerst, p. 115.

23. Rankin, p. 49; Martin Hengel, *Judaism and Hellenism: studies in their encounter in Palestine during the early Hellenistic Period* (London: SCM Press, 1974), pp. 121,126. Gordis, p. 233, suggests that Koheleth's depiction of God keeping human beings in their place reflects the widely-held primitive religious concept of "the jealousy of the gods" (cf. Genesis 3:22; 11:6).

24. Levy, p. 84: *Gott erstrebt das schon einmal von ihm Erstrebte wieder.*

25. Gordis, p. 234, and Barton, pp. 102,103, both opt for this interpretation. Cf. the New English Bible's translation, "God summons each event back in its turn", or the Good News Bible's "God makes the same thing happen again and again".

26. Salters (in his article, "A Note on the Exegesis of Ecclesiastes 3:15b", in *Zeitschrift für die alttestamentliche Wissenschaft* 88 [1986], pp. 419-422), pp. 420,421, and Delitzsch, p. 264, both cite the Vulgate translation approvingly. Cf. Salters' dissertation, p. 160, where he says that of the ancient translators only the Vulgate has obtained a satisfactory sense for the passage in context.

27. Midrash *Koheleth Rabbah* agrees, offering a long list of biblical examples of "God seeking the pursued" in precisely this sense, such as helping Jacob who is pursued by Esau, or David who is pursued by Saul, and so on.

28. Reichert and Cohen, p. 128, hold the former view; Barton, p. 108, following Graetz, holds the latter view.

29. Gordis, p. 234.

30. Rahlfs, p. 244, seems to be so sure that εὐσεβής is a mere slip of the pen for ἀσεβής that he places ἀσεβής in the text and relegates εὐσεβής to the critical apparatus.

31. Equally unsurprisingly, the Targumist's paraphrase is in keeping with MT. He laments that, in the place of judgment, the wickedness of condemning the innocent and acquitting the guilty is taking place, and in the place of righteousness, the wickedness of an evil generation oppressing the righteous is taking place.

32. This is precisely the tack followed by the Targumist, who notes that on "the day of the great judgment" everyone will be judged for everything they have done in this world.

33. So Rahlfs' edition, p. 244. The edition of Holmes and Parsons, *ad loc.*, places ἐκεῖ at the end of v. 17.

34. The Targumist, in contrast, baulks at reproducing heresy even for a moment, and so styles this verse as drawing a comparison between "the wicked person" (אנשא חייבא) and "the unclean animal" (בעירא מסאבא), who will share the same fate unless the wicked person repents before his death.

35. Cf. Symmachus σύμβαμα, "happening". Gregory also has ὅμοιος and πλέον in his paraphrase of this verse, two words which Symmachus uses here but LXX did not; they are, however, perfectly natural paraphrases of LXX. If Gregory were consulting Symmachus' version, it might be expected that he would grasp the word ἀναπνοή, "breath" in preference to πνεῦμα, given his concern in v. 21 to differentiate between the πνεῦμα of human beings and the πνεῦμα of animals.

36. MT presented a statement, "the human has no advantage over the animal" (מותר האדם מן־הבהמה אין), and LXX, reading מותר as מה יתר (this is more likely than Barton's suggestion, p. 112, of מי יתר), took the clause as a question with אין as its answer: "what advantage has the human over the animal? — none!" (τί ἐπερίσσευσεν ὁ ἄνθρωπος παρὰ τὸ κτῆνος; οὐδέν). Gregory, wittingly or unwittingly, restores the statement to a straight assertion: "there is nothing more in a human [than in an animal]" (πλέον ὑπάρχειν ἐν ἀνθρώποις μηδέν).

37. Codices Regii and Thuan. have ἀναστήσονται instead of ἀναπτήσονται (Migne, col. 997, n. 1).

Chapter Four

1. See Thurston and Attwater, p. 363; and Salmond, p. 3.

2. *A la* Barton, p. 116; and Gordis, p. 238. Ginsburg, p. 321, on the other hand, argues that it is glaringly inconsistent to take the same expression in the same verse in two different senses.

3. Elsewhere in LXX more general words for "oppression" were employed, such as ἀδικία, "injustice" (Ezekiel 22:29) and καταδυναστεία, "exercise of power over another" (Jeremiah 6:6) — this latter was also employed for the form at hand, עשקים, in Amos 3:9. Συκοφαντία did, however, make an appearance in the place of the noun עשק at one place outside of Ecclesiastes, *viz.* Psalm 119 (LXX 118):134, and συκοφαντέω, "to slander" did service for the verb עשק on occasion (e.g., Proverbs 22:16) and also for the one other occurrence of עשקים as an abstract noun in MT (although again arguably a passive participle), in Job 35:9. In Syriac usage, ܛܠܡ means "to slander" more often than it means "to oppress", but it is interesting to note that the Peshitta version of Ecclesiastes only uses this root in 7:7 (where an interpretation of "slander" perhaps makes most sense), preferring to employ here in 4:1 the root ܥܠܒ, "to oppress" and then in 5:7 the root ܓܠܙ, "to defraud", while the Targumist adopts the root אנס, "to oppress, rob" as suitable for all three occasions. Gregory's persistent following of LXX's συκοφαντία is particularly surprising in view of his ἀδικέομαι, "to be wronged, done an injustice" (cf. LXX's ἀδικία mentioned above) for LXX's συκοφαντέω later in the verse, and the very general ἀπορία, "difficulty, straits" towards the end.

4. This word appears under the category ἄλλος in Field, p. 386. It seems that the translator of the Peshitta also wishes to avoid repetitiveness here, translating מנחם first as ܡܒܝܐܢܐ, "comforter" and then as ܡܥܕܪܢܐ, "helper".

5. As Salmond, p. 14, also notes (cf. Migne, col. 997, n. 2).

6. The Targumist's approach to this verse is somewhat similar to that of Gregory. He too makes the point, and explicitly (unlike Gregory, who leaves us to draw the implication) that the dead are better off, not because they are blissfully unaware of all the oppression that is being perpetrated in the world, but because they will not personally experience the punishment which comes into the world after they have died. But for the Targumist, as for Koheleth, it is all the dead who are to be praised for their better state of being, and not just the unrighteous dead. Gregory, on the other hand, never seems comfortable with the idea that the respective futures of good people and evil people should have anything in common (cf., e.g., 2:16).

7. Codex Medic. has καί before μηδέπω rather than δέ after it (Migne, col. 997, n. 3).

8. Eaton, p. 92, mentions Herodotus, Theognis, Sophocles, and Cicero (cf. Barton, p. 114), and Buddhism (cf. Plumptre, p. 139).

9. "They... took a vote and decided that it were better for man not to have been created than to have been created" — 'Erubin 13b ('Erubin, tr. Israel W. Slotki [London: Soncino Press, 1938], p. 87).

10. See Albrecht Stumpff, "ζῆλος", in Theological Dictionary of the New Testament, ed. Gerhard Kittel, tr. & ed. Geoffrey W. Bromiley (Grand Rapids: William B. Eerdmans Publishing Company, 1964), vol. 2, pp. 877-882.

11. Codex Medic. has τιθέμενος (Migne, col. 998, n. 4).

12. This is the way in which the Targum clearly understands it, as evidenced by the parallel phrase there, "and he does not want to toil".

13. Again, this is the Targum's understanding, as evidenced by the note that the fool soon "eats all that he has".

14. Field, p. 387, gives μετὰ ἀναπαύσεως in the first clause, but the second clause is incomplete and he can only give a bracketed κόπου.

15. MT Kethib עיניו, but LXX followed the Qere עינו.

16. The first interpretation is that of Frank Zimmermann, The Inner World of Qohelet (New York: KTAV Publishing House, 1973), pp. 52,145, who feels that although the writer tried to objectify himself as if he were talking of another, this passionate outburst in the first person reveals he is talking of himself; since Zimmermann is attempting a highly problematic psychological analysis of Koheleth, his view need not be taken too seriously. However, Morris Jastrow, A Gentle Cynic (Philadelphia: Lippincott, 1919), p. 214; Barton, p. 115; and Delitzsch, p. 276, all feel that there may be an auto-biographical touch here. The second interpretation, that the question is the hypothetical one which the other person ought to ask himself, is taken by Eaton, p. 93; Gordis, p. 242; Reichert and Cohen, p. 133; Plumptre, p. 141; and Kidner, p. 46.

17. The Targum manages to include both meanings, by implying that a person ought to both "be joyful" (חדי) and "do righteous/charitable works" (עבד צדקתא).

18. This is the suggestion of Migne, col. 998, n. 4*.

19. Salmond's translation, p. 14, gives no evidence of taking a question mark into account at this point.

20. This is in contrast to the Targumic approach, which takes this

opportunity to comment on the effectiveness of the prayer and merit of the righteous. Already in the previous verse the Targumist gave evidence that his understanding of Koheleth's examples, as referring to the good which two (vv. 10,11) or at best three (v. 12) righteous people can achieve in this world and, specifically in v. 9, to the reward which the righteous will receive in the world to come, is some distance from Gregory's more accurate understanding of these examples, as referring quite straightforwardly to the physical and social benefits of companionship, irrespective of whether or not the participants in the lifestyle are to be numbered among the righteous (although Gregory does add his ὀρθῶς qualification).

21. This seems to be the scholarly consensus. Cf., e.g., Barton, p. 118; Gordis, p. 242; Eaton, p. 94.

22. Thus the Targumist reproduces this in his paraphrase here.

23. The text in Migne, col. 1000, reads φαιδρότητι σεμνύνεσθαι, which n. 5 (col. 999) says is based on the edition of Basil and supported by Codices Reg. and Thuan. The note also lists σεμνότητι σεμνύνεσθαι, the reading of Codex Medic., supported by Codex Vaquerius, and Billius' emendation to σεμνότητι φαιδρύνεσθαι.

24. "A man should get a companion for himself, to eat with him, drink with him, study Scripture with him, study Mishnah with him, sleep with him, and reveal to him all his secrets, the secrets of the Torah and the secrets of worldly things" (*The Fathers according to Rabbi Nathan*, tr. Judah Goldin [Yale Judaica Series 10; New Haven: Yale University Press, 1955], p. 50). Some commentators have tried to supply biblical support for the view that Koheleth is referring to travelling companions sleeping together, but without startling success. Eaton, p. 94, cites Jeremiah 36:22,30, but this only proves — if biblical proof were needed — that the land of Israel has cold winter nights. Plumptre, p. 142, cites Exodus 22:6, evidently meaning v. 26 (a typographical error?), but this only proves that people in early times commonly used their mantle as a covering at night.

25. Codex Medic., supported by Codex Vaquerius, reads a future tense here (βουλεύσεται), but Billius considers this suspect, marking it with an obelus in his edition (Migne, col. 999, n. 6).

26. In paraphrasing as he does, Gregory is obviously retaining Koheleth's sense of the physical, material benefits to be gained in companionship, an approach which is in contrast to that of the Targumist, who returns in this verse — after an as-brief-as-possible aside on the physical utility of marriage in v. 11 — to a homily on the place of righteous people in the spiritual scheme of things.

27. The Targum paraphrases the proverb along those lines: if two righteous people in a generation are useful, how much more useful are three righteous people in a generation!

28. Plumptre, p. 143. See also below: Conclusion, n. 49.

29. The Targumist here at v. 13 treats the reader to a somewhat lengthy account of the legendary interplay between Nimrod (who is revealed as the foolish old king that Koheleth/Solomon is talking about) and Abraham (who turns out to have been a poor youth whose wisdom consisted in knowing the LORD and having the spirit of prophecy from him when only three years old), the latter being thrown into a burning furnace by the former for not worshipping an idol; but their fortunes are reversed in v. 14, when Abraham reigns over the land of Canaan and Nimrod becomes poor. Midrash *Koheleth Rabbah* on v. 14

mentions this Targumic interpretation, and offers in addition an interpretation which sees the passage as an account of the interplay between Potiphar and Joseph. Among modern commentators, Barton, p. 119, lists many theories, including Joash and Amaziah, Cyrus and Astages, the high priest Onias and his nephew Joseph, and Herod the Great and his son Alexander; then, p. 120, he gives his view that they are Ptolemy IV and his five-year-old successor Ptolemy V! The comment of Ginsburg, p. 331, is worth quoting: "these expositors [who try to determine whom Koheleth meant by the old and young kings] might, with equal propriety, endeavour to fix the name of the solitary miser in verse 8, or try to identify the two social individuals mentioned in verse 9." An analogous criticism/challenge might be directed towards Charles C. Torrey ("The Problem of Ecclesiastes iv 13-16", in *Vetus Testamentum* 2 [1952], pp. 175-177), who attempts to overcome certain perceived problems with this passage, such as an "awkward transition" from v. 13 to v. 14, by inserting 10:16,17 into this passage, claiming that these "two isolated verses" in Chapter Ten "fell out by some accident from [their] original place" in Chapter Four (p. 177); there are countless supposedly "awkward transitions" in Ecclesiastes which could no doubt benefit from such a method of reinserting "misplaced fragments"!

30. The others are Origen, Apollinarius, Victorianus of Pettau, and Lactantius (J.N.D. Kelly, *Jerome: His Life, Writings, and Controversies* [London: Duckworth, 1975], p. 150).

31. Quoted in Migne, cols. 977,978.

32. *Corpus Christianorum*, Series Latina, vol. 72 (Turnholt: Brepols, 1959), p. 289, on the other hand, prefers a manuscript which has them in the same order as Gregory's γέρων and βασιλεύς.

33. MT has בית הסורים, but with a *qametz* under the *he* indicating the furtive existence of an *aleph* (cf. Gordis, p. 224; and Ginsburg, p. 331; but Charles F. Whitley, *Koheleth: His Language and Thought* [Beihefte zur Zeitschrift für die alttestamentliche Wissenschaft 148; Berlin: Walter de Gruyter, 1979], pp. 45,46, reads בית הסורים [without *aleph*] as "womb" — as did Rashbam, against Ibn Ezra and the other ancients).

34. Rahlfs' text excludes this possibility by having ἐγεννήθη rather than ἐγενήθη (i.e., γεννάω rather than γίγνομαι), on the basis of Codex Venetus.

35. The Targum appears to take it both ways, because it abandons the story it was telling concerning the youthful Abraham and launches into an even longer account concerning a different young man: Rehoboam, the successor of Solomon (תנין למלכותי, "second [in line] to my throne") — not the first occasion in the Targum of Ecclesiastes on which the prophet Solomon has been remarkably well informed on events involving his successor after Solomon's own death (already in 1:2 he had foreseen a great deal). Barton, p. 120, continuing his imaginative interpretation (see n. 29), thinks that if "successor" is meant, the reference is to Ptolemy V, but if a "second" youth is meant, the reference is to Antiochus III!

36. As quoted in Migne, col. 978. Salmond, p. 15, n. 3, quotes it without the *ante*, and with *senex* preceding *rex*, while *Corpus Christianorum*, p. 289, prefers a manuscript which also has *senex* before *rex*, but includes the *ante*.

37. English 5:1.

38. The temple-goer to whom Koheleth referred is pictured by the Targumist as listening to the priests and sages, rather than as being a priest or sage addressing the assembled people.

39. MT *Kethib* רגליך, but LXX followed the *Qere* רגלך (cf. Targum רגלך and Peshitta ܪܓܠܟ).

40. The LXX reading of Koheleth's מתת הכסילים זבח took מתת as a noun and assumed — unless it was actually there in the text before the LXX translator — that a prepositional *mem* had dropped out (due to haplography). The Masoretic vocalisation of מתת as the infinitive of נתן with the preposition *mem* gives the reading "rather than to offer the fools' sacrifice".

41. It may be, too, that Gregory has Jesus' parable of the pharisee and the tax-collector (Luke 18:9-14) in mind when he says here that the preacher — or church-goer generally — ought to be careful to pray for the foolish; in the parable the pharisee prays about sinners but not at all for them.

42. Cf. the Targum's "they do not know whether they are thereby doing good or evil".

Chapter Five

1. English v. 2. (This one-verse discrepancy between the Hebrew and English versification continues throughout Chapter Five.)

2. Lampe, p. 184, defines ἀπεριπτώτως in this instance alone as "not haphazard, thoughtfully", and says that the reference is to prayer, but this is not necessarily so. Gregory is referring not only to prayer, but to preaching as well (4:17), and probably to speaking in general.

3. Gordis, p. 248, and Barton, p. 123, seem to support the former interpretation; Eaton, p. 98, and Reichert & Cohen, p. 138, clearly support the latter interpretation.

4. So, too, the Targumist parallels the LORD's "sitting upon his throne of glory in the high heavens" with his "ruling over all the earth", which serves to forcefully remind the reader of his place in the universal scheme of things: God is far above human beings, but that does not mean that he is not keeping an active eye on what is going on down here.

5. This is an emendation, on the basis of Billius and Codex Medic., from the nominative forms (Migne, cols. 999,1000, n. 9).

6. Cf. Symmachus' ὄνειρος in this verse; he has ὄνειρος again in v. 6, but there Gregory reproduces LXX's ἐνύπνιον.

7. In contrast to the Targum, which is careful to keep God in the picture by stating clearly that "there is no pleasure for the LORD in fools". In the first part of the verse, where Koheleth had spoken clearly of vows made "to God" (MT לאלהים), the Targum followed suit with "before the LORD" (קדם יהוה).

8. The text in Migne, col. 1001, is indistinct at this point, but the indecipherable letters before καλός, "good" must be a negation, as is indicated both by the context and by the Latin parallel *turpis*, "foul".

9. Salters (in his dissertation, pp. 176ff., and in his article "Notes on the History of Interpretation of Koh 5.5", in *Zeitschrift für die alttestamentliche Wissenschaft* 90 [1978], pp. 95-101), while noting that LXX takes מלאך as referring to God, feels that it is probably a reference to the priest. Barton, p. 124, however, thinks that the LXX interpretation is probably right; but Eaton, p. 100, thinks that it is almost certainly incorrect. Cf. Meir Zlotowitz, *Koheles/Ecclesiastes: A New Translation with a Commentary anthologized from Talmudic, Midrashic and Rabbinic sources* (New York: Mesorah Publications, ²1977), pp. 110,111, on rabbinic opinions.

10. The Targumist, in contrast, takes up this matter with some enthusiasm, warming to his task of warning the sinners in plain terms that the anger of the LORD will be kindled against them.

11. Eaton, p. 100, cites a number of alternative ways of rendering this verse, but none of the alternatives alter the point of the verse.

12. The Targumist shares this understanding of the verse, although he cannot resist giving specific examples — the "many dreams and futilities and many words" to which Koheleth refers become in the Aramaic paraphrase specifically "the many dreams of false prophets", "the futilities of sorcerers", and "the many words of the wicked" respectively — and he cannot resist adding some extra advice to the idea of fearing God — *viz.*, paying attention to wise and righteous human beings as well.

13. Codices Vaticanus and Sinaiticus, as well as many other manuscripts — see Joseph Ziegler, "Die Wiedergabe der nota accusativi *'et, 'aet-* mit σύν" (in *Zeitschrift für die alttestamentliche Wissenschaft* 100 [1988], Supplement, pp. 222-233), p. 226 — have σύ instead of σύν, either because אֶת has been read as the second person pronoun rather than in accordance with MT's vocalisation of it as the accusative particle, or because an early copyist deliberately or inadvertently created better Greek by dropping the *nu*, but this variation makes no real difference to the meaning.

14. Salmond, p. 3; Thurston & Attwater, p. 363.

15. Migne, col. 1001, places οὐ within square brackets, but provides no explanatory footnote. The context requires a negation here.

16. The Targumist is unhappy to leave the system unchecked in the hands of sinful human beings, and so he pictures the one who is at the very top of the hierarchy as "the mighty God", who watches over all that the humans are doing and who allows certain powerful persons to exercise authority over others; at the same time, the Targumist implies that the reason God allows these powerful people to exercise their power wickedly is that those who are ruled over are likewise wicked and so deserve such rulers.

17. The first of these two possible interpretations is essentially that of Eaton, p. 101; Delitzsch, p. 294; and Barton, p. 127. The second is essentially that for which Reichert & Cohen, p. 141, opt (it also seems at least in part to have been in the minds of the translators of the New International Version). Gordis, p. 250, approves of the earlier-mentioned rendering of the Targum. Cf. Zlotowitz, pp. 113,114, on rabbinic opinions.

18. An emendation from ἐγγίνεται (Migne, col. 1001, n. 10).

19. *Koheleth Rabbah*, following on from the idea that everyone is dependent on the land (v. 8), asks rhetorically: if someone is greedy with money but has no land, what benefit does he derive? The Targumist moves right away from the notion of earthly produce, and warns that there is no profit in the world to come for the person who heaps up great wealth in this world, unless he uses that wealth for charitable works.

20. LXX also took מִי as invariably interrogative and accordingly styled the second stich as a question.

21. 12 times in MT Ecclesiastes, since in 2:1 MT has הוא instead of זה. The other occurrences are 2:15,19,21,23,26; 4:4,8,16; 6:9; 7:6; 8:10,14.

22. LXX Ecclesiastes always translated טוב by ἀγαθός, and on three occasions (7:11; 9:16,18) it translated טובה by ἀγαθός.

23. Putting this into the singular brings it into line with the pronoun on ὀφθαλμοὶ αὐτοῦ (עיניו). Similarly v. 12, with the pronoun on κακία αὐτοῦ (רעתו).

24. The Targumist plays on the double meaning of טיבותא (as ambiguous as Koheleth's טובה), since the "it" in "its owner who gathers it" and "do good with it" must be worldly goods, whereas the "good" one does with it must be a moral good — a person has to perform good deeds with his earthly goods if they are to be of any heavenly use, a re-expression of what the Targumist already said in the previous verse. (Instead of טיבותא in the second phrase, some manuscripts have צדקתא [literally "righteousness"; i.e., charitable deeds], as in the previous verse — cf. the texts of Lagarde, p. 188, and Sperber, p. 157.)

25. In contrast to the Targumist, who discovers at this point yet another opportunity to incorporate into his paraphrase the notions of occupying oneself with God's Torah in this world and of receiving for oneself a reward from God in the world to come.

26. Symmachus, however, has νόσος κακή, "an evil sickness".

27. The Targumist opts for the latter understanding, although he pictures the loss of wealth as occurring in the second generation rather than in the first (i.e., the child does inherit his father's ill-gotten riches, but precisely because they are ill-gotten they do not last in the child's hands and eventually there is nothing whatsoever of that wealth left).

28. Migne, col. 1001, has a grave accent on this word.

29. The Targum, on the other hand, elaborates on the matter by suggesting that "naked" (MT ערום) is to be understood both in a physical sense of "without clothing" and "without any good thing", and in a spiritual sense of "without merit".

30. Which the Targumist explains as living (or: sitting down [to eat] — שרי) in darkness in order that he might eat his food by himself.

31. MT vocalises כעס as a verb, "to be irritated/angry".

32. LXX ignored the pronominal suffix on MT's חליו.

33. Migne, col. 1001, has καματῶν.

34. Codex Medic. has ἁρπακτά (Migne, cols. 1001,1002, n. 11). See n. 35 below.

35. If the reading of Codex Medic. is accepted. The normative text's reading of ἁρπακτικός would make better sense applied to a noun denoting a "possessor" rather than to one denoting a "possession". The Targumist also felt it necessary to counsel against such a matter (אניסא, "ill-gotten wealth", v. 17) in this passage — and in the parallel passage of 8:15.

Chapter Six

1. Rashi interprets MT's רב in the former manner, and Ibn Ezra in the latter. The Targum, in using רב in an Aramaic context, points in the latter direction.

2. Codices Medic. and Thuan. have the present tense (ταμιεύεται), which is probably preferable (Migne, col. 1003, n. 12).

3. Migne (col. 1003, n. 12) suggests that such an editorial emendation should be made.

4. This view is argued by Gordis, p. 257 (without of course reference to Gregory Thaumaturgos' paraphrase of this verse); it is countered by Robert B. Salters, "Notes on the Interpretation of Qoh 6.2" (in Zeitschrift für die alttestamentliche Wissenschaft 91 [1979], pp. 282-289), pp. 286-289.

5. We should probably read a genitive (θανάτου) here, as noted by both

Migne, col. 1003, n. 12*, and Salmond, p. 18, n. 1.

6. See Gordis, p. 258; Barton, p. 129; Plumptre, p. 155. The Targumist appears to take this line of interpretation by offering the paraphrase "a grave was not prepared for him".

7. This is, incidentally, the way in which Reichert & Cohen, p. 146, interpret Koheleth's קבורה לא־היתה לו. Gordis, p. 258, cites other commentators who agree with such an interpretation.

8. Sforno's interpretation (in the 16th century) of Koheleth's phrase is along these lines (see Zlotowitz, pp. 121,122). Cf. Ginsburg, p. 361, who argues that the phrase means "the grave is not waiting for him", another way of saying that he has a very long life.

9. This is Alshich's interpretation (also in the 16th century) of Koheleth's phrase (see Zlotowitz, p. 122, n. 1).

10. LXX Codex Vaticanus has πίμπλεμαι.

11. A meaning which in fact is carried by MT's נפל (from the verb נפל, "to fall") though not by LXX's ἔκτρωμα (from the verb τείρω, "to suffer distress").

12. Because the subject is unexplained in the biblical text, there is a possible ambiguity. Given v. 5's talk of "not seeing the sun", the individual depicted is most likely the foetus, but perhaps Koheleth was thinking of the man of vv. 3 and 6 (cf. 5:16's talk of a person "living in darkness"), or intended that both types of individual — the man and the foetus — might be depicted in this manner.

13. Cf. the Targum, where the word "know" is expanded into an allusion to the Fall story of Genesis: the stillborn child does not "know good and evil" (cf. Genesis 2:9,17; 3:5) — from which it can be inferred that it does not participate in the sinfulness of human beings.

14. Salmond, p. 18, translates οὐχ ἀψάμενον κακῶν as "without having tasted the ills of life".

15. Gordis, p. 259, claims that "rest" cannot be what Koheleth was talking about, because to assert "that the still-born has more rest than a living human being is obvious to the point of banality"; but it would seem to be quite in keeping with Koheleth's agenda for him to have expressly pointed out that the foetus does not partake of the toil, pain, and lack of rest which afflict all who live under the sun (cf., e.g., 2:23; 4:3; 5:17). Gordis offers the Mishnaic meaning of "joy, pleasure" for נחת רוח; but it would seem reasonable to take נחת here in 6:5 in the same sense in which Koheleth used it elsewhere (4:6; 9:17).

16. Migne, cols. 1003,1004, n. 13, and Salmond, p. 18, n. 2, agree that we should read ἐπιγνῶναι here, or else (less preferably) ἀναμετρησάμενος earlier in the sentence.

17. Peter R. Ackroyd, "Two Hebrew Notes", in *Annual of the Swedish Theological Institute* 5 (1967), pp. 82-86, makes the interesting suggestion (p. 85) that the pronoun on לפיהו (εἰς στόμα αὐτοῦ) refers not to האדם (ὁ ἄνθρωπος) but to the מקום (τόπος) just mentioned in v. 6; the "mouth" is thus to be seen, in his view, as that great swallower, Sheol (cf. Isaiah 5:14; Habakkuk 2:5).

18. Gregory's interpretation of the phrase is also made by Gordis, p. 263, in contrast to many modern commentators. He translates (p. 172): "it is known that man cannot argue" etc.

19. Codex Sinaiticus has the comparative ἰσχυρότερος, which would make for better Greek, were it not for the retention of ὑπέρ. In the Hebrew text the full *Kethib* form, שהתקיף, appears to be undecided on whether the adjective תקיף ought to be preceded by the article *he* or by the particle *shin*, although the

meaning is essentially the same with either choice. The Masoretes finally
decided on *shin*, as evidenced by the *Qere* form שֶׁקְּיוֹ.

20. Hence the Targumist names him explicitly here as the LORD.

21. Migne, col. 1004, ends Chapter Six at this point, and begins Chapter
Seven with μηδαμῶς. Salmond's translation, pp. 18,19, takes its cue from this.
If Gregory himself made such a chapter division here, it must have been
because the LXX version in front of him did so. Though Rahlfs' edition, p. 250,
gives no hint of any LXX manuscript doing so, Swete's edition, p. 493 (as also
the edition of Holmes and Parsons *ad loc.*), does indeed end Chapter Six with
ματαιότητα, and begin Chapter Seven with τί περισσόν. Swete gives Rahlfs'
versification of Chapter Seven (which is in keeping with MT) as a variant. Cf.
Field, p. 391, where Chapter Seven begins with τί περισσόν, and the MT
versification is given in brackets. The same kind of discrepancy occurs also at
the end of the chapter (see 8:1 [n. 1]).

22. Gordis, p. 263, among others, assumes that the meaning here is
"words" rather than "things". But Rashi's interpretation is equally plausible:
there are many activities in which human beings involve themselves which
are in reality futile (see Zlotowitz, pp. 126,127). Reichert & Cohen, p. 148, are
more even-handed than Gordis, allowing for both possibilities of meaning.

23. See n. 21 above.

24. Codex Savilius does not have γάρ (Migne, col. 1004, n. 14).

25. Cf. the agenda of the pious interpreter also in the Targum, where the
reader is again advised to study the Torah.

Chapter Seven

1. In the same vein the Targumist here at Ecclesiastes 7:1 simply adds
another טבא after the שמא to avoid any possible confusion on the part of his
readers.

2. Barton, p. 139, and Eaton, p. 110, support the former interpretation;
Gordis, p. 269, and Reichert & Cohen, p. 150, support the latter interpretation.

3. Barton, p. 138, however, manages to imitate the word-play in his
English rendering, "as the crackling of nettles under kettles" (cf. Ginsburg, p.
372, "as the noise of nettles under the kettle", which he has modelled on
Knobel's *wie das Geräusch der Nessel unter dem Kessel*.

4. Some scholars do connect הבל זה וגם with v. 7 rather than v. 6 (e.g., J.A.
Loader, *Ecclesiastes: A Practical Commentary*, tr. John Vriend [Grand Rapids:
William B. Eerdmans Publishing Company, 1986], pp. 78-79), while others see
no connection whatsoever (e.g., Barton, p. 140); still others see connections both
ways (see, e.g., Gordis, pp. 269-271).

5. This interpretation remains valid if עשק is taken in its other common
sense of "extortion", which is, after all, a particular form of oppression or
corruption. There is no need for emendation or other strained interpretations (*à
la* Gordis, p. 270) to create a parallelism between the two halves of the verse.
Nor is Eaton, p. 111, convincing in his comment that vv. 1-14 deal with the
suffering of oppression and therefore that this verse is not to be understood as
dealing with the exercise of oppression.

6. Codex Medic. has λόγον, which would yield the sense, "it is proper to
applaud a speech at its end, not its beginning" (Migne, col. 1005, n. 15; Salmond,
p. 19, n. 2).

NOTES   339

7. דבר is translated by ῥῆμα in LXX Ecclesiastes 1:1; 8:1,5; and (on the basis of a non-Masoretic vocalisation) by λαλέω in 1:10; 8:4; but in the twenty other occurrences in this book by λόγος. As regards LXX's plural rendering here at 7:8 (which Symmachus "corrected" to a singular rendering), Gordis' suggestion, p. 272, that the *mem* of מראשיתו may have been read with דבר, seems to overlook the fact that LXX translates the *mem* by ὑπέρ, but Barton's suggestion, p. 142, that the final *mem* of דברים may have been accidentally dropped before the following *mem*, is perhaps more plausible. As regards Gregory's copying of LXX's plural form, this can only be said if the reading of Codex Medic. (see n. 6 above) is not accepted as the original form in the paraphrase.

8. Cf. the interpretation of the Targumist, who employs עסקא, "affair, matter" as his equivalent to דבר in this context, in contrast to his choice of the more ambiguous פתגמא, "word" or "affair" in 6:11.

9. Unlike the construction of MT, with ארך־רוח and גבה־רוח, LXX did not actually have πνεύματι in the prescribed alternative, but from its position at the end of the clause it is to be understood as being governed by both μακρόθυμος and ὑψηλός.

10. Migne, col. 1005, has an acute accent on this word.

11. MT has מחכמה, "out of wisdom", but LXX may have read *beth* rather than *mem*.

12. Billius proposes φανοτέρα (Migne, cols. 1005,1006, n. 16; Salmond, p. 20, n. 1), and I follow this proposal in my translation, since "brighter" makes better sense than "more conspicuous" in this context.

13. See n. 12 above.

14. Symmachus has ὡς... ὁμοίως, and the Peshitta ܐ... ܕ ܡܝܠ, which might suggest a reading of כ... כ, but these translations may again be for the sake of intelligibility with no Hebrew textual warrant. Cf. the remarks of Gordis, pp. 273,274, and Eaton, p. 112, n. 3.

15. The Targumist expresses this well: "Just as a person finds shelter in the shade of wisdom, so he finds shelter in the shade of silver" (he cannot, however, resist adding the rider that this applies only in the case of someone who puts his silver/money to righteous purposes).

16. In MT there is a pause after דעת, such that the advantage is said to lie with knowledge as such, but this "knowledge" is presumably a parallel of the "wisdom" mentioned immediately thereafter (ויתרון דעת החכמה תחיה בעליה), "and the advantage of knowledge is that wisdom preserves the life of those who have it"). LXX read דעת as being in a construct relationship to החכמה, and so translated the phrase καὶ περισσεία γνώσεως τῆς σοφίας ζωοποιήσει τὸν παρ' αὐτῆς, "and the advantage of the knowledge of wisdom gives life to the one who has it".

17. Apparently reading the plural מעשי instead of MT's מעשה.

18. Since in MT ארך hiphil is used, we should probably supply ימים and translate "prolong his days" (cf. MT יאריך ימים, LXX μακρυνεῖ ἡμέρας in 8:13), as the Targumist does with מאריך יומין.

19. Rashi interprets the phrase somewhat similarly: even if his death is imminent, the righteous person will maintain his righteousness up to the last moment.

20. R.N. Whybray argues in favour of such a meaning in his article "Qoheleth the Immoralist? (Qoh. 7:16-17)", in *Israelite Wisdom: Theological and Literary Essays in honor of Samuel Terrien*, ed. John G. Gammie *et al.* (Missoula: Scholars Press, 1978), pp. 191-204. On p. 196 Whybray cites שרר hithpael (Numbers 16:13), "to imagine/set oneself up to be a prince" and חלה

hithpael (2 Samuel 13:5), "to pretend to be ill"; while this establishes the possibility of interpreting חכם hithpael (Ecclesiastes 7:16) in the same way, such that אל-תתחכם יותר could be understood as "do not pretend to be absolutely wise", it does not establish that the only meaning of חכם hithpael attested elsewhere in the Hebrew Bible (Exodus 1:10's "to behave wisely/cleverly") "can hardly be what is intended" here — on the contrary, אל-תתחכם יותר understood as "do not behave excessively wisely/cleverly" makes excellent sense here. Whybray is also unconvincing in his argument that אל-תהי צדיק הרבה means "do not be a self-styled צדיק", advice to the reader not to claim to be or see himself as being exceptionally righteous, expressed in this way by Koheleth "in order to give a special meaning to the word [צדיק] which could not be conveyed by the use of the verb" (p. 195); yet in accordance with Whybray's thesis concerning חכם hithpael, where אל-תתחכם יותר is said to mean "do not pretend to be absolutely wise" (despite Exodus 1:10), there is no reason why Koheleth should not use צדק hithpael, for אל-תצטדק הרבה could equally well be said to mean "do not pretend to be absolutely righteous" (despite Genesis 44:16, where in any case מה-נצטדק might be interpreted as "how could we pretend to be innocent?" if the interpreter were keen to follow this line of interpretation of hithpaels). No reason, that is, except for the stylistic consideration of chiasm in verses 16 and 17: אל-תהי צדיק of v. 16a corresponds to אל-תהי כסל of v. 17b, and אל-תתחכם of v. 16b corresponds to אל-תרשע of v. 17a. And here is the real difficulty for Whybray's understanding of v. 16, as it is for Gregory's understanding: the parallel expressions of v. 17 can hardly mean "do not be a self-styled כסל", advice to the reader not to claim to be or see himself as being exceptionally foolish, and "do not pretend to be absolutely wicked"; if Koheleth's expressions in v. 17 are telling the reader not to be too wicked or foolish for one's own good, then his expressions in v. 16 are telling the reader not to be too righteous/pious or wise/clever for one's own good. Perhaps Gregory could have been cited in support of Whybray's interpretation of this verse, but there is a disagreement between the two interpreters: Whybray, p. 200, says that "the self-styled [צדיק] is basically unrighteous just as the self-styled wise man is a fool", but Gregory presents the verse as referring to a basically righteous person who should not style himself as being more righteous and wise than he really is.

21. Aquila's πρὸ τοῦ here is an improvement on LXX's ἐν οὐ, a mechanical translation of בלא in MT's תמות בלא עתך.

22. Rahlfs, p. 251, is so confident of this that he has ἀνῆς in the text, although his footnote shows that Codices Vaticanus, Sinaiticus, and Alexandrinus are unanimously agreed on μιάνῃς. To support his reading Rahlfs cites the Latin version of Jerome, which reads ne dimittas. See also Field, p. 393; Salters, p. 26.

23. The Vulgate's interpretation is somewhat similar, though on a human rather than divine level, and with the flow of assistance going in the opposite direction — i.e., Gregory urges the reader to take hold of God in order that the reader may thereby be sustained by God and kept from everything that is contrary, while the Vulgate urges the reader to reach out to a righteous person who is in need of the reader's help: bonum est te sustentare iustum sed et ab illo ne subtrahas manum tuam, "it is good for you to sustain the just, and not to withdraw your hand from him".

24. Gordis, p. 279, makes this suggestion, citing Josephus' Vita 13 & 57 and Antiquities XX:8:11. The indefinite "many, any number" is the view of Ibn Ezra, and is followed by many interpreters. In the view of the Targumist,

however, the reference is to ten very definite men: the ten sons of Jacob, who killed all the males of Shechem and sold their brother Joseph for twenty pieces of silver (these details are present in Sperber's edition, p. 160, but are absent from Lagarde's edition, p. 192), while this same Joseph is the wise man referred to in the opening phrase of the verse.

25. Codex Alexandrinus does not have ἀσεβεῖς (Rahlfs, p. 251). The Peshitta has ܪܫܝܥܐ and the Targum רשיעיא, "wicked people".

26. These views are only two of many rabbinical interpretations which arose from reading the expression שיר השירים, "[Solomon's] Song of Songs" as denoting three songs or phases (the fuller discussion is recorded in *Shir Hashirim Rabbah* 1:1).

27. The Peshitta saw the phrase as a superlative, as though reading or postulating עמק עמקים.

28. Codices Reg. and Thuan. have τέλεον (Migne, col. 1006, n. 17).

29. This view is put forward by Plumptre, p. 170, who points out that, although the expression "I and my heart" has no exact parallel in Old Testament language, it harmonises with a common mode of speech familiar enough in the poetry of all times and countries. Delitzsch, pp. 330,331, proposes breaking the clause between אני and ולבי, and thus reading the expression as "I turned myself, and my heart was there to discern...." Rahlfs' edition of LXX, p. 252, makes the same proposal by placing a comma between ἐγώ and καὶ ἡ καρδία μου.

30. A few manuscripts have σκληρία, "stubbornness" (cf. σκληρός for סכל in v. 17), and Rahlfs, p. 252, places that in the text; however, Codices Vaticanus, Sinaiticus, and Alexandrinus all agree on ὀχληρία.

31. One manuscript has δηνέχθην (Migne, col. 1006, n. 18).

32. For γῆν, read σαγήνην or πάγην (Migne, cols. 1006,1007, n. 19; Salmond, p. 21, n. 1). See fuller comments below in the commentary to this verse.

33. One manuscript swaps the cases around: χεῖρα δὲ χειρί (Migne, col. 1006, n. 18).

34. See, for example, Eaton, p. 116; Zlotowitz, p. 144; Reichert & Cohen, p. 158. The Living Bible particularises the reference more than most other interpreters by translating as "prostitute" rather than "woman": "A prostitute (literally, [says a footnote,] 'the woman whose heart is snares and nets') is more bitter than death. May it please God that you escape from her, but sinners don't evade her snares." Roland E. Murphy, "A Form-Critical Consideration of Ecclesiastes VII" (in *Society of Biblical Literature 1974 Seminar Papers*, ed. George MacRae [Cambridge, Mass.: Society of Biblical Literature, 1974], vol. 1, pp. 77-85), p. 85, speaks of "the harlot stereotype in v. 26". The Targumist spoke specifically of the type of woman who causes so much trouble for her husband that it is better for him to divorce her than to remain with her.

35. Norbert Lohfink, *Kohelet* (Die Neue Echter Bibel 19; Würzburg: Echter Verlag, 1980), p. 57, translates מר ממות את־האשה as *stärker als der Tod sei die Frau*, "woman is stronger than death", an analogous saying to Song of Songs 8:6, "love is strong as death (עזה כמות אהבה) — an interpretation which he had presented in his article "War Kohelet ein Frauenfeind? Ein Versuch, die Logik und den Gegenstand von Koh. 7,23–8,1a herauszufinden" (in *La Sagesse de l'Ancien Testament*, ed. M. Gilbert [Leuven University Press, 1979], pp. 259-292), pp. 281,282, and which has been supported by Klaus Baltzer, "Women and War in Qohelet 7:23–8:1a" (in *Harvard Theological Review* 80 [1987], pp. 127-132), p. 128. For modern readers who are uncomfortable with the possibility of

Frauenfeindlichkeit in the Scriptures, this is indeed a very attractive interpretation; but the ancient interpreters, and certainly Gregory, had no hesitation in understanding מר (LXX πικρός) as "bitter".

36. The *Biblia Hebraica Stuttgartensia* editor disagrees with this linkage, and places a poetic line-break between מצודים and חרמים, despite the accent sign.

37. Σαγήνη is the suggestion of Cotelerius, while πάγη is Bengel's suggestion (Migne, cols. 1006,1007, n. 19; Salmond, p. 21, n. 1).

38. This clause appears near the middle of Chapter Six of the *Panegyric* (Migne, col. 1072). Migne and Salmond both cite the passage in a footnote to the *Paraphrase* at Ecclesiastes 7:26 (see n. 37 below).

39. Actually Gregorian authorship of the *Panegyric* has been recently disputed (see Introduction, n. 14), but the other contender for author of the *Paraphrase*, Gregory of Nazianzus, being a Father of the fourth century, could not have delivered the oration over Origen. Hence this shared use of ἤ εἰ between the two writings can work in both directions as support for the ascription of each of the writings to Gregory Thaumaturgos.

40. This is noted both by Migne, cols. 1007,1008, n. 20; and by Salmond, p. 21, n. 2. Salmond, however, notes only the second instance in the paraphrase of this verse, whereas the first instance offers a better parallel to the instance in the *Panegyric*.

41. MT actually has אמרה קהלת here, with a feminine verb (corresponding to the seemingly feminine noun), but the presence of the article in LXX's εἶπεν ὁ Ἐκκλησιαστής may suggest a reading of אמר הקהלת, as in 12:8 (although LXX also has the article in 1:2, where MT has אמר קהלת). The Targumic scribes appear to be in two minds, some apparently unwilling to tamper with the Hebrew form of אמרה (not even substituting the Aramaic feminine form, אמרת), while others evidently feel more comfortable with the masculine form, אמר (Lagarde's edition, p. 192, has אמרה קהלת, while Sperber's edition, p. 161, has קהלת אמר; the Peshitta has ܐܡܪ ܩܗܠܬ).

42. Cf. the interpretation of the Targum, where MT's אדם is taken as a reference to the first Adam, created upright and righteous by God but seduced by the serpent and Eve, whose many devices have brought death and misery to all the inhabitants of the earth.

Chapter Eight

1. Migne, col. 1008, ends Chapter Seven at this point, and begins Chapter Eight with σοφία. Salmond's translation, p. 21, takes its cue from this. If Gregory himself made such a chapter division here — as seems likely from the fact that what precedes this point of the verse has been paraphrased as part of a continuous sentence beginning with the previous verse — it must have been because the LXX version in front of him did so. Though Rahlfs' edition, p. 252, gives no hint of any LXX manuscript doing so, Swete's edition, p. 496 (as also the edition of Holmes and Parsons *ad loc.*), does indeed end Chapter Seven with ῥήματος and begin Chapter Eight with σοφία. Swete gives Rahlfs' chapter-division between πολλούς and τίς (which is in keeping with MT's division between רבים and מי) as a variant. Cf. Field, p. 395, where Chapter Seven ends with ῥήματος, but the beginning of a new chapter with τίς is given in brackets. The same kind of discrepancy has already been noted as occurring at

the beginning of the chapter (see 6:11 [n. 21]).

2. See, e.g., Gordis, p. 288; Reichert & Cohen, p. 160; Barton, p. 149; Eaton, p. 118.

3. ועל עיסק מומתא דיהוה, characteristically replacing "God" with "the LORD". The verse is then saying, in the Targumic interpretation, that one should not only be on one's guard against disobeying the king's commands, but one should also be on one's guard against swearing in vain by the LORD's name.

4. In fact the Jewish Publication Society of America's *New Translation of the Holy Scriptures according to the Masoretic Text*, despite the verse-division of MT, reads אל־תבהל with the ועל דברת שבועת אלהים of v. 2 (resulting in the sentence "and don't rush into uttering an oath by God").

5. In addition to λαλεῖ indicating a vocalisation of דבר as a verb, LXX's introductory καθώς indicates a reading of *kaph* rather than MT's *beth* on the beginning of אשר. Cf. Peshitta גמתגל ‎ܡܬܓܠ, but Symmachus διὰ τὸ λόγον and Targum מימרא ...ב.

6. In MT, מי יאמר־לו מה־תעשה (Eccles. 8:4) and מי־יאמר אליו מה־תעשה (Job 9:12).

7. A much stronger case can be made in respect to the Targum, which arguably has God in mind throughout the entire passage, even in the first instance at the beginning of v. 2 (although that מלכא is the one ambiguous instance).

8. Symmachus regards πρᾶγμα as a more appropriate translation than ῥῆμα here, but Gregory (λόγος) does not agree.

9. A reading with which the Targum concurs (לב חכימא [so Sperber, p. 161; Lagarde, p. 193, has the plural, חכימיא]).

10. Some manuscripts do not have the conjunction at this point, although all are agreed that it is present in the identical expression in the following verse (where LXX's καί attests to its presence). But even with the conjunction, it might still be legitimate to translate the Hebrew expression as a hendiadys: "a time of judgment" (so Ginsburg, p. 395; cf. JPSA's *New Translation*, "a time of doom").

11. A reading with which the Targum again concurs (עידן... דין). דין actually does have a conjunction, but this is because the Targumist has prefaced it with the additional thought that that time is also a time for prayer (צלותא).

12. The Targumist is also concerned to add that the forthcoming judgment is a just one (קשוט), and that keeping the commandments of the LORD will prove to be profitable (in the world to come).

13. The Targum, which agreed with LXX's reading of no conjunction in the previous verse, here agrees with its reading of a conjunction: עידן... ו... דין.

14. The former interpretation is preferred by, e.g., Barton, pp. 150,151; Reichert & Cohen, p. 162; and Loader, p.96. The latter interpretation is preferred by, e.g., Gordis, p. 290; and Eaton, p. 120 — and by the Targumist, who paraphrases it clearly as "the breath of life" (רוח נשמתא, as he had in 3:21 and 12:7, for the first occurrence, and then נשמתא דחיי for the second occurrence).

15. See Salters, p. 27. Rahlfs, p. 253, is so sure that the ἡμέρᾳ in this latter phrase is simply a device of the LXX translator to bring it into line with the former phrase that he places the word in question in the apparatus rather than in the text. Barton, p. 152, on the other hand, feels that LXX read יום in this latter phrase, and that that is possibly the correct reading.

16. The Targum's general apparent interpretation of this phrase as having to do with Everyman's battle against death is an attractive and arguably correct treatment of Koheleth's thought here: it is possible that this

was an intentional metaphor of death as that battle which everyone is destined to lose. Eaton, p. 120, interprets the Hebrew this way; he says: "As the indicates (in the Hebrew), the war in mind is death." It is doubtful, however, whether the presence or absence of a definite article can be taken as such a clear indicator in Ecclesiastes, and in this case we have only the Masoretic vocalisation to indicate the presence of an article (plus LXX's agreement that an article should be read here).

17. Gordis, p. 292, offers this explanation, but does not comment that this would be an exceptional translation in LXX Ecclesiastes, which normally renders את by σύν.

18. I mean, of course, nonsensical to the Greek reader unconcerned with having every jot and tittle of the Hebrew text taken account of in a Greek rendering. It has recently been claimed that this Aquilan use of σύν may be imitating the Homeric use of σύν as an adverb (cf. Jellicoe, *Septuagint & Modern Study*, p. 81; Emil Schürer, *The History of the Jewish People in the Age of Jesus Christ*, rev. & ed. Geza Vermes and Fergus Millar [Edinburgh: T. & T. Clark, 1973-1987], vol. III.1, p. 495), but even understood adverbially, the σύν in LXX Ecclesiastes is still frequently nonsensical to the Greek reader.

19. Salters, p. 20, regards this instance in 8:9 as an example of ἐν being used for *beth* regardless of the sense of the passage, but in fact ἐν can be used in Greek with the meaning "over" after verbs of ruling (see Liddell & Scott, p. 551, ἐν A.I.5).

20. JPSA's *New Translation* agrees: "such as had acted righteously". This line of interpretation is taken by Delitzsch, p. 345 ("such as acted justly"), and Reichert & Cohen, p. 163 ("they that had done right"). Cf. Zlotowitz, p. 151; Ginsburg, pp. 399,400.

21. "Cemetery" is preferred (marginally) by Gordis, p. 295 (and by Ch.W. Reines, "Koheleth VIII,10", in *Journal of Jewish Studies* 5 [1954], pp. 86-87); "temple" by Barton, p. 153 (and by J.J. Serrano, "I Saw the Wicked Buried [Eccl 8,10]", in *Catholic Biblical Quarterly* 16 [1954], pp. 168-170); and "Jerusalem" by Eaton, p. 122. For the Targumist, it is "the holy place where the righteous dwell", from which sinners are removed to a far different place, *viz.* Gehenna.

22. Both Lagarde, p. 183, and Sperber, p. 162, have פתגם ביש פורעגוות, but the ביש being unvocalised in Sperber's edition indicates that, although it is present in Jacob ben Chayim's Bible, it is not present in manuscript Or. 2375 of the British Museum.

23. Τιμωρέομαι might arguably mean "being helped" were it not for the context here of πλημμελείαι, "offences".

24. 2 Peter 3:9 reads, "The Lord is not slow about his promise as some count slowness, but is forbearing (μακροθυμέω) toward you, not wishing that any should perish, but that all should reach repentance." Note that Gregory, in the very next verse of his paraphrase, counsels transgressors to become reverent towards God. (The Targumist adds a similar explanation in the following verse of Ecclesiastes: the reason why the Almighty allows the sinner extra time before punishment is so that he may repent.)

25. Codex Medic. adds ἑαυτοῦ (Migne, col. 1009, n. 22).

26. Migne, col. 1009, has an acute accent on this word.

27. MT has האדם. None of the three LXX codices have ὁ with the first appearance of ἄνθρωπος, and only Codex Sinaiticus has it with the second appearance.

Chapter Nine

1. Although δεξιός commonly means "dexterous, clever", such that Salmond's translation (p. 23) of ἔχθραν φεύγω πρὸς ἅπαντας δεξιὸς εἰμί as "being sagacious, avoid hatred with all" is very defensible, I believe my understanding of the phrase makes good sense in itself, as well as in view of what Gregory is paraphrasing, as outlined in my comments to this verse.

2. MT הכל לפניהם. One possibility of making this phrase less enigmatic is that given in n. 3 below.

3. *Biblia Hebraica Stuttgartensia* suggests that הבל is the correct reading, to be read as part of v. 1. This yields the sentence הכל לפניהם הבל, "all before them is futility", a reading supported by Peshitta's ܣ̇ܟܠܐ ܕܡܬܡܐ ܗܠ (and perhaps also by Symmachus' τὰ πάντα ἔμπροσθεν αὐτοῦ ἄδηλα, "all before them is uncertain"). A number of commentators adopt the same reading (e.g., Barton, p. 158; Fuerst, p. 138). But MT as it now stands is not non-sensical.

4. This is so whether "fearing an oath" (MT שבועה ירא, LXX τὸν ὅρκον φοβέομαι) is taken as meaning "being afraid to take an oath" (R.B.Y. Scott, *Proverbs, Ecclesiastes* [The Anchor Bible 18; New York: Doubleday & Company, 1965], p. 244) or "observing one's oath" (Barton, p. 159), as long as 5:4 — "better not to vow than to vow and not observe one's oath" — is kept in view. Barton does not improve his case here by referring to "the analogy of the series, in which the bad character uniformly comes first"; it is quite the reverse in this series, with δίκαιος (צדיק) coming before ἀσεβής (רשע), ἀγαθός (טוב) before κακός (presumably רע, were it to be in the Hebrew text), καθαρός (טהור) before ἀκάθαρτος (טמא), θυσιάζων (זבח) before μὴ θυσιάζων (אין זבח), and ἀγαθός (טוב) before ἁμαρτάνων (חטא).

5. Liddell and Scott, p. 887; Lampe, p. 706.

6. MT אחריו אל־המתים, LXX changing to a plural pronoun because this comes after ζωὴ αὐτῶν (חייהם).

7. The Targumic scribes were apparently in two minds, some writing בחר and others חבר (Sperber's text, p. 163, has יתמחר, while Lagarde's text, p. 195, has אתחבר).

8. The only interpretation which the Midrash *Koheleth Rabbah* offers is one based on the *Kethib*, which may indicate that early Jewish interpreters were keen to make sense of what stood in the text (on the other hand, transposing consonants was a favourite device of rabbinical eisegesis). Among more modern interpreters, making sense of what stands in the text is the concern of Levy, p. 118, who maintains that the *Kethib* is correct; he translates כי־מי אשר יבחר as *denn wer wird vorgezogen* [or: *auserwählt*]?

9. ὋΟτι τίς ὃς κοινωνεῖ πρὸς πάντας τοὺς ζῶντας; ἔστιν ἐλπίς, "For who is in the company of [or: is joined to] all the living? There is hope [for him]."

10. There is an ambiguity in the Greek versions. LXX's ἀγάπη αὐτῶν, μῖσος αὐτῶν, and ζῆλος αὐτῶν could indicate either the love, hate, and envy which the dead formerly felt towards other people, or the feelings which other people formerly had towards those who are now dead. Similarly, Gregory's ἐκείνων... ζῆλος might be translated "envy of those people" — i.e., others may have envied them in life, but they are no longer envied once they have died. So, too, πρός can be understood as exclusively indicating the hatred and love which were formerly directed "towards" those who are now dead. However, in view of the following μέτειμι, "to have a share in", it is probably

best to understand πρός in the sense of "with" or "in reference to", such that hatred and love may be seen as passions in which the departed were participants and not merely recipients.

11. MT's עוד לעולם and תחת השמש directed the Targumist's thoughts to the dual spheres of the world to come (עלמא דאתי) and this present world (עלמא הדין). Ἔτι εἰς αἰῶνα, however, does not prompt Gregory to say anything about a life to come, because he is presenting the views of the fool, who does not believe that there is a life to come; having just had the fool say that he thinks life is blotted out at death, Gregory can hardly now have him say that he thinks this is not so.

12. The Targumist also feels that such an introduction is necessary at this point, and so he explains that Solomon is speaking by the spirit of prophecy from the LORD, and is setting down what God himself is going to say to the righteous when they enter into their reward; the interpretation then follows that in the next life the righteous will be able to eat and drink with a joyful heart because they gave bread and wine to the hungry and thirsty in this life, a good work of which God approves.

13. Migne, col. 1012, has this question mark, but questions its appropriateness by placing sic in brackets after it. See comments below.

14. A recent example of this interpretation of אשה אשר־אהבת is Harold I. Leiman, Koheleth: Life and its meaning (Jerusalem: Feldheim Publishers, 1980), p. 133: "Koheleth sees in wife and family the greatest source of joy for man in his sojourn under the sun.... Because of the frustrations and afflictions that every man is subject to, there is a need for the strength and security that only a wife and family can provide." The midrash quoted in the comments below shows that this line of interpretation is very old, and there is no doubt that the Targum, too, understands the reference here as being to a wife. Yet Ginsburg, pp. 416,417, would have us believe that all interpreters, except for a couple of bishops, have recognised that amor vulgivagus and not "the enjoyments of the matrimonial state" was here being urged! Gordis, p. 306, says on this verse that Koheleth "was certainly no apologist for the marriage institution" — but he has second thoughts, and adds in his third augmented edition (p. 410) that neither was Koheleth "an advocate of promiscuity".

15. Some MT manuscripts (and the Targum) do not have the phrase twice. Some LXX manuscripts (and the Peshitta) do not repeat it either, but Gregory has not followed such a manuscript.

16. This is the clause as defined by the Masoretes, who place a tiphcha on בכחך. Others would prefer the pause to be placed on לעשות, thus linking בכחך to the עשה which follows it (so Barton, p. 167, and Gordis, p. 307, the latter citing Biblia Hebraica, which cites some manuscripts which do so place the pause — Biblia Hebraica Stuttgartensia, however, does not include this matter in its critical apparatus); similarly, it may be thought preferable in the Greek text to end the clause at ποιῆσαι and to link ὡς ἡ δύναμίς σου to the ποίησον which follows it (so Rahlfs, p. 255). Hence many translate in the vein of the Revised Standard Version: "Whatever your hand finds to do, do it with your might." But Ginsburg, p. 417, feels that the verse should not be construed against the accents, and translates in this vein: "Whatever your hand finds to do while you are able [i.e., while you are in your strength], do it." Incidentally, LXX's ὡς suggests a reading of kaph rather than beth, which would yield a meaning of "as your power permits" or "as you are able".

17. The Wisdom teachers generally held that wealth was the result of

intelligence and hard work, and poverty the result of their opposites. See J. David Pleins, "Poverty in the Social World of the Wise", in *Journal for the Study of the Old Testament* 37 (1987), pp. 61-78. On p. 68, Pleins says, "Herein lies a major point of contention between the prophets and the wise", to which we may add: and a major point of contention between Koheleth and the tradition of the wise, for here in 9:11 he sees no necessary connection between wisdom and wealth. Ch.W. Reines, "Koheleth on Wisdom and Wealth", in *Journal of Jewish Studies* 5 (1954), pp. 80-84, even speculates that Koheleth was a member or an observer of a class of impoverished Wisdom teachers.

18. Perhaps this is a scribal error for συγχωρέω, "to agree". "To congratulate" seems a little strange here.

19. A less charitable explanation for Gregory's handling of Koheleth's "Favour is not to the knowledgeable" might suggest that he does not wish to interpret Solomon as contradicting his own words in Proverbs 13:15, "Good sense wins favour".

20. The expression used here is καιρὸς καὶ ἀπάντημα (עת ופגע), "time and chance". It is interesting to note that in 8:5, MT's עת ומשפט, "time and judgment" was rendered by LXX as καιρὸς κρίσεως, "time of judgment", but the same approach is not followed here. So also the Targum renders עידן... דין in 8:5, but עידן וערעיתא here. The Jewish Publication Society of America's *New Translation*, however, is consistent in what its notes call these "synonymous" expressions, rendering "time of doom" in 8:5 and "time of mischance" here.

21. Migne, col. 1012, has ἀνάρπαστοι.

22. Gordis, p. 309, and Barton, pp. 164,165, give some examples of these enterprising interpretations. Barton is all but won over to one of the contenders (the siege of Abel-Beth-Maacah), but Gordis is more prudent in saying that "most probably Koheleth is inventing a typical case (or generalizing) in order to illustrate his point, rather than invoking a specific historical incident". There can be little doubt that Koheleth would more highly regard Gregory's interpretation of this passage than that found in the Targum, where every effort is made to remove the narrative from the real world and to paint a scene in which the *yetzer ha-ra* (יצרא בישא, the evil spirit or inclination, v. 14) and the *yetzer ha-tov* (יצרא טבא, the good spirit or inclination, v. 15) fight within a person's body in order to have him either committed to or saved from the fires of hell. The irony is that here at the outset in v. 13 the Targumist takes explicit note of Koheleth's customary reference to the real world תחת השמש (ὑπὸ τὸν ἥλιον), paraphrasing this in his equally customary way as בעלמא הדין תחות שמשא, while Gregory's paraphrase ostensibly ignores it.

23. Gordis, pp. 311,312, interprets in the first way; Scott, p. 247, in the second. The Targumist takes the first line, speaking of the one who actually saves his city but is afterwards not remembered by his fellow citizens — although this event is used only as an analogy to the situation with which the Targumist is really dealing, wherein a person is actually saved from the machinations of the *yetzer ha-ra* by the wisdom of the *yetzer ha-tov*, but forgets this and regards himself as being an innocent person.

24. In the Targum it is asserted that the quiet words of prayer offered by wise people are "listened to" or "accepted" (קבל ithpaal) over the entreaties of a wicked person, the one who hears them being no-one less than the Lord himself (מרי עלמא).

25. LXX rendered the participle as a plural perhaps in order to parallel σοφοί (חכמים) in the first clause, and perhaps read the noun as כסילות. (The first of

these surmises is that of Gordis, p. 312; on the rendering of כסילים as ἀφροσύναι, however, he surmises that the noun was rendered abstractly on the basis of other abstract nouns that appear as plural in form.)

26. Migne's text, col. 1012, places a capital *alpha* on this word, even though it is preceded not by a full-stop but by a colon.

27. Some manuscripts have πολύ, which would yield the meaning "even if he were greatly contemptible" (Migne, col. 1011, n. 23; Salmond, p. 25, n. 1). With πολλαῖς the meaning is "even if he were contemptible to many people" (which I believe is better expressed in English in this context in the way in which I have translated below).

28. Migne, col. 1011, n. 23.

Chapter Ten

1. Codex Medic. has χρῆσιν, "use" (Migne, col. 1011, n. 24), which I have used in my translation. The meaning is hardly affected either way.

2. The breathing is lacking in Migne, col. 1012.

3. The Targum followed the opposite but equally logical course of recasting the subject as a single fly (דיבבא), which is then in agreement with the singular verbal forms (the participles מסרי, "spoiling" and מחבל, "destroying", placed in a more conventional relationship by means of a conjunction) — though the fly is only an analogy for the real subject of the Targumist's thoughts here, that ubiquitous *yetzer ha-ra*. The Peshitta took LXX's approach, with plural subject (ܕܒ̈ܒܐ), in agreement with plural verbal form (ܡܣܪܝܢ [the plural form of the Targum's מסרי], "causing to stink").

4. This explanation is proffered in *Biblia Hebraica Stuttgartensia*, along with the suggestion that יביע should be deleted from MT on the basis of Symmachus, Targum, and Vulgate. It is true that Symmachus and Vulgate render only יבאיש (or conflate the two verbs into one), but the Targum clearly renders both verbs, as shown above (n. 3).

5. So Gordis, p. 315.

6. Koheleth's scale also troubled the Targumist, who offers his own clever solution: it is a more wonderful thing for an ordinary person, who might be expected to be riddled with folly, to be only slightly and triflingly foolish, than it is for a wise person to be wise, since that is only what is rightly expected of him.

7. Codices Reg. and Savil. have ἀριστεράν (Migne, column 1012, n. 25).

8. Unlike the Targumist, who speaks of the acquisition of Torah on the one hand and of worldly riches on the other.

9. This interpretation is adopted by Scott, p. 249, and Gordis, p. 318.

10. This line of interpretation is adopted by Barton, pp. 166,169, and Ginsburg, p. 426. Whitley, p. 84, and Edgar Jones, *Proverbs and Ecclesiastes* (London: SCM Press, 1961), p. 334, do not commit themselves, but appear to lean in this direction.

11. Symmachus apparently also took this line (Field, p. 399, quotes Jerome's citation of Symmachus as *suspicatur* [ὑπολαμβάνει] *de omnibus quia stulti sunt*, "he supposes that all are fools").

12. The Targumist also sees in Koheleth's expression "the spirit of the ruler" (MT רוח המושל) a spiritual entity, *viz.* "the evil spirit" רוחא דיצרא בישא, literally "the spirit of [*or:* which is] the *yetzer ha-ra*") which "rules" (מתל)

over a person and strives to overcome him. (It would appear that מחל "to rule" is very unusual in Aramaic, since Marcus Jastrow, ed., *A Dictionary of the Targumim, the Talmud Babli and Yerushalmi, and the Midrashic Literature* [New York: G.P. Putnam's Sons, 1903], p. 862, gives only מחל "to compare"; cf. p. 855, where the two Hebrew verbs משל "to rule" and משל "to compare" are both given.)

13. So too the Targumic call, "Do not abandon your good place, in which you have been accustomed to stand", the טב nature of the reader's current position standing in clear contrast to the ביש nature of the spirit which seeks to change this situation.

14. In 5:12 חולה was added to רעה, which prompted LXX to speak of ἀρρωστία rather than πονηρία. In 6:1 Koheleth used better grammar by placing אשר before ראיתי, but LXX has ἥν before εἶδον in all three verses.

15. The actual text is ὅταν λαλῆ τὸ ψεῦδος, ἐκ τῶν ἰδίων λαλεῖ, ὅτι ψεύστης ἐστὶν καὶ ὁ πατὴρ αὐτοῦ, "whenever he speaks falsehood, he speaks according to his nature, for he is a liar and the father of it".

16. Gordis, p. 192, calls them "a collection of maxims dealing with the practical virtues, but with little organic connection among them"; and Jones, p. 334, speaks of "sundry maxims without logical sequence of thought". Barton, pp. 169ff., regards most of them as interpolations! Ginsburg, however, attempts to demonstrate a close and logical connection between them; in his comments to v. 8, for example, he says (p. 429): "The twelfth verse, which concludes with the counsel given in verse 4, *viz.*, the advantage of submitting patiently to and of conciliating the anger of the ruler, shews, beyond doubt, that the intervening adages in vv. 8-11, are designed to set forth the dangers to which the opposite conduct might expose the suffering subjects."

17. The text in Migne, col. 1013, has μή, and then in brackets ἴσ. μήν.

18. In contrast to the Targumist, who allegorises these labours as Solomonic prophesies concerning Manasseh's replacement of the stone tables of the Torah with stone idols, and Rabshakeh's replacement of the wooden ark with wooden idols, for which they will receive appropriate punishments.

19. Codices Reg. and Medic. have στελέχους (Migne, column 1013, n. 26).

20. They show no direct sign of having even read לו here, though Gordis, p. 321, says that the Peshitta "reproduces" the Oriental reading — in fact Peshitta's ܘܗܘ is clearly reproducing MT's הוא — and so "perhaps" does LXX "if αὐτῷ fell out after αὐτός" — for which we have no manuscript support, or at least none that is taken account of in Rahlfs' edition, p. 17 (and if there is any manuscript support for Gordis' contention with regard to the Peshitta, it has not been taken account of in Lane's edition, p. 17).

21. "Edge" is approved by Barton, p. 177; "before" is approved by Gins-burg, p. 433, followed by Gordis, p. 322. קלקל and פנים give rise to the Targumic message that the world can "be ruined" (קלל ithpalpel) by famine when a sinful generation of Israel does not pray "before" (קדם) the LORD (perhaps a similarity between the words פנים, "face" and כפנא, "famine" has played some role in the Targumist's talk about famine here).

22. He never reproduces such expressions: cf. μοχθέω and μόχθος (עמל and עמל), 1:3; 2:18,22; 5:17; 9:9; περισπάω and περισπασμός (ענה and ענין), 1:13; 3:10; ποιέω and ποίημα (עשה and מעשה), 4:3; 11:5; εὔχομαι and εὐχή (נדר and נדר), 5:3; θυμόω and θυμός (כעס and כעס), 7:9; σπείρω and σπέρμα (זרע and זרע), 11:6.

23. But even with these additions, Gregory's treatment of this verse is a model of constraint when compared with the Targumic picture of the people of Israel gathered together in strength and thus able to overcome their *yetzer*,

presumably the *yetzer ha-ra* who has led them into the sin for which the world is afflicted with famine.

24. Anthony Frendo ("The 'Broken Construct Chain' in Qoh 10, 10b", in *Biblica* 62 [1981], 544-545) offers the attractive suggestion that the phrase is really a "broken construct chain" in which יתרן stands in a construct relationship with חכמה, the two nouns being separated by the verbal element of the phrase; accordingly, he translates: "the advantage of wisdom is success". Frendo is not very charitable to the New International Version's translation "skill will bring success", which he accuses (p. 545) of being "in reality only a paraphrase". In reality NIV's understanding of the phrase appears to be very close to Frendo's own understanding of it, except that NIV legitimately treats הכשיר as an indicative rather than an infinitive, and (less defensibly) dispenses with a direct equivalent to יתרן, presumably because the phrasing "the advantage of skill is that it brings success" seems to verge on tautology. But Frendo might be accused of leaving the causative sense of the hiphil verb out of his own translation, presumably for the same reason.

25. Whitley, p. 86, suggests that the sense of 11:6 should be overlooked here; he prefers the meaning of כשר aphel, "to improve" (cf. Jastrow's dictionary, p. 677), and renders the phrase (against the Masoretic accents) as "the development of skill is an advantage". Gordis, pp. 322,323, has a similar view, rendering it as "it is an advantage to prepare one's skill in advance".

26. Cf. Symmachus ὁ γοργευσάμενος. The Peshitta's ܟܫܝܪܐ might mean "successful people" or "vigorous people". Aramaic כשר yields yet another meaning, as we see in the Targum: מותר אכשרות חוכמתהון, "the abundance of the *kosher* [i.e., true or proper] nature of their wisdom", the assembled wisdom of the people of Israel.

27. The Targumist interprets בעל הלשון metaphorically as גבר אכיל קורצין דמשתעי לישן תליתי, "a master of destructive backbiting, who talks with a forked [literally, 'threefold'] tongue" (so Lagarde, p. 198; Sperber, p. 165, has לישן ביש, "an evil tongue", which gets the point across more clearly, though it loses the imagery of a snake's forked tongue). Why a "threefold" tongue, when snakes are known for a two-pointed tongue? As suggested by Etan Levine, *The Aramaic Version of Qohelet* (New York: Sepher-Hermon Press, 1978), p. 61, the term "threefold tongue" means "talk about a third person" — i.e., gossiping about someone who is not present.

28. Alternatively, διὰ παντός might be translated as "always".

29. As Ginsburg shows, pp. 438, 439, a number of later interpreters took up this possibility. This makes Gregory's failure to do so all the more striking.

30. Cf. Isaiah 1:3, "The ox knows its owner, and the ass its master's crib; but Israel does not know, my people does not understand." On a plural reading of "fools" versus a singular reading of "fool" here in Ecclesiastes 10:15, see comments below.

31. In a somewhat similar vein, the Targumist explains to his readers that the עיר that is meant here is the city where the wise live, so the fool who does not go there is missing out on the chance to become wise under their instruction.

32. Migne, vol. 13, col. 349 (Homily 9:2).

33. Cf. Lampe, p. 671: Ἱεροσόλυμα, 4.

34. The Targum adopts singular forms — שטיא... ליה — while the Peshitta adopts plural forms — ܡ̈ܗܘܢ... ܣܟ̈ܠܐ — as their respective solutions to the problem.

35. The argument of Ogden, *Qoheleth,* p. 176, that נער, being the opposite of v. 17's בן־חורים ("a son of freemen"), here means "servant", the equivalent of v. 7's עבד, has merit. LXX's νεώτερος might even carry some such meaning as "usurper", or someone who has come to the throne by revolution (cf. νεωτερίζω) rather than by right.

36. Ginsburg, pp. 440,441 (copied by Barton, p. 174, and by Gordis, p. 325), also cites Acts 2:15 and the classical writers Cicero, Catullus, and Juvenal in support of just such an interpretation.

37. Barton, p. 178, and Gordis, p. 327, both opt for interpreting the dual as an intensive, though both admit the alternative understanding of it as being induced by ידים in the following parallel phrase.

38. LXX Codices Vaticanus and Sinaiticus add ἔλαιον (= שמן; cf. Peshitta ܡܫܚܐ), "oil", but this is probably due to the influence of such texts as Psalm 104:15 on the translators, rather than an indication that Koheleth originally had such a word here.

39. See the discussion of Robert Salters, "Text and Exegesis in Koh.10:19", in *Zeitschrift für die alttestamentliche Wissenschaft* 89 (1977), pp. 423-426.

40. As is evident from the comments above, Codex Alexandrinus (which is adopted by Rahlfs, p. 17) reads τοῦ ἀργυρίου ἐπακούσεται σὺν τὰ πάντα (cf. Vulgate's *pecuniae oboedient omnia*).

41. The Targum translates MT's בעל הכנפים literally as מרי גפין, "the lord of wings", and applies this as a title of נשרא, the "eagle", the most majestic of winged creatures — but the real object of this second version of Koheleth's warning becomes, in the Targumic version, none other than the heavenly Elijah, who is pictured as hovering in the air "like an eagle" (כנשרא), from which vantage point he is able to see all that is done in secret on the earth below. Thus he is virtually equivalent to the מלאכא which the Targumist sees in the עוף השמים of the first version of Koheleth's warning.

42. Λογικός is often used in New Testament and Patristic Greek to mean the same thing as πνευματικός (see Bauer, p. 476; Lampe, p. 805; note 1 Peter 2:2,5), so Gregory may not be intending a contrast between these two "types" of service performed by the heavenly beings, but two synonymous terms for essentially one spiritual service. Πνευματικός is possibly suggested to him by οὐρανός in LXX's first version of the warning and λογικός probably arises from the λόγος in LXX's second version. Similarly, Gregory's "winged" (ὑπόπτερος) evidently arises from LXX's ὁ ἔχων τὰς πτέρυγας in the second version, while "swift" (ὀξύς) is suggested by the image of the bird in the first version of the warning.

Chapter Eleven

1. Cf. Gordis, p. 330; Reichert & Cohen, p. 181. Indeed, Today's English Version paraphrases as follows: "Invest your money in foreign trade, and one of these days you will make a profit."

2. It is interesting to note that the Targum, which shared Gregory's interpretation of v. 1, takes v. 2 as a reference to the sowing of seed in the seventh and eighth months (Lagarde's edition, p. 198, has תשרי and כסליו, the latter being the ninth month, but Sperber's edition, p. 166, has תשרי and מרחשון).

3. LXX appears to have read the plural מעש (cf. Peshitta ܥܒܕܐ) instead of MT's singular מעשה.

4. Cf. the Targum's "you do not know whether it is a male or a female until the time when it is born", an interpretation which perhaps arises here in the context of "bones" (MT עצמים) in the womb because of the notion, based on the creation story in Genesis 2:21ff., that males have one bone less than females.

5. Typically, Gregory's interpretation is less metaphorical than that of the Targumist, who takes this verse as enjoining the fathering of children in one's youth and in one's old age.

6. Salmond's translation, p. 27, suggests the second possibility: "For it is not manifest what shall be better than those among all natural things."

7. For example, Barton, p. 185.

8. The Targumist also found it offensive and so changed the advice to counselling humility and carefulness. Cf. Salters, pp. 222-224.

9. Cf. Salters, pp. 233,234; Holm-Nielsen, p. 172.

Chapter Twelve

1. An overview of these various interpretations may be consulted in Gordis, pp. 338,339, and Barton, p. 186. More recently, John F.A. Sawyer ("The Ruined House in Ecclesiastes 12: A Reconstruction of the Original Parable", in *Journal of Biblical Literature* 94 [1975], pp. 519-531) has argued that the passage is not an allegory but a depiction of an estate falling into ruin as a parable on the fate of human efforts in this world; Graham S. Ogden ("Qoheleth xi 7–xii 8: Qoheleth's Summons to Enjoyment and Reflection", in *Vetus Testamentum* 34 [1984], pp. 27-38) has argued that the passage alludes not to what leads up to death — the declining powers of old age — but to what follows death — the diminished vitality of "life" in Sheol; and Michael V. Fox (see n. 24 below) has argued that the passage carries three types of meaning — literal, symbolic, and figurative. Professor Sawyer kindly read my manuscript of Chapter Twelve and made a number of helpful comments, for which I am grateful.

2. MT (in which the latter passage is v. 23) reads לפני בוא יום יהוה הגדול והנורא. Here in Ecclesiastes 12:1, where MT reads עד אשר לא־יבאו ימי הרעה and LXX translated ἕως ὅτου μὴ ἔλθωσιν ἡμέραι τῆς κακίας, Symmachus rendered πρὶν ἐλθεῖν τὰς ἡμέρας τῆς κακώσεώς σου, which has the effect of bringing the opening into line with the oracular expression found in the Septuagintal translation of the Prophets.

3. R.B. Salters, "The Word for 'God' in the Peshitta of Koheleth", in *Vetus Testamentum* 21 (1971), pp. 251-254, notes that an attempt seems to be made with the Syriac ܡܪܝܐ to identify the אלהים of Ecclesiastes with the יהוה of Jewish tradition.

4. MT's בוראיך may be construed as a plural of majesty.

5. Cf. also Joel 2:10 and 3:15, which include reference to the stars as well as to sun and moon. Isaiah 13:9,10 has the same ideas.

6. Quite a number of manuscripts have ܣܢܓܒܒܐ (Lane, p. 19).

7. Ginsburg, p. 459, makes the convincing point that Koheleth referred not to the same women but to two very different classes of women, the "ladies of the house" and "the grinding maids".

8. MT vocalises סגרו as a passive (pual), while LXX read the verb as an active (qal) and rendered κλείσουσιν, but Gregory prefers to paraphrase LXX's verb in a passive construction: κεκλεισμένων.

9. Cf. Christian Hannick, "Music of the Early Christian Church", in *The New Grove Dictionary of Music and Musicians*, ed. Stanley Sadie (London: Macmillan, 1980), vol. 4, pp. 363-371, especially p. 368 on "Women and Chant". 10. For a full discussion of this view, cf. Gordis, pp. 344-347. Barton, pp. 189-191, outlines a number of further interpretations. Sawyer, p. 529, in accordance with his interpretation of an estate falling into ruins, sees these three references as being to common features of a neglected garden. The Targumic interpretation is: "the top of your hipbone will come out [*or:* break] from leanness like the almond, the ankles of your feet will be swelled, and you will be hindered from rest (משכנא)." For משכנא (Lagarde, p. 200), Sperber, p. 167, has משכבא, which suggests a possible meaning of "you will shrink from the grave" — i.e., you will live in growing fear of your impending death — or "you will cease from sexual intercourse" (Gordis' translation, p. 346). The Syriac scribes found it too difficult to decide on just one line of interpretation, and so the Peshitta offers us the following possibilities: "sleeplessness will come upon him and the almond will sprout" for the first clause, just "the locust will grow fat" for the second clause, and then "the caper-berry will be scattered and the beshani-fruit will cease" for the third clause. Ginsburg, p. 464, translates the final Syriac phrase as "desire shall cease" (and the first as "the watch shall rush upon him", p. 462). Neither in Koheleth's words nor in the early versions, it seems, can we be completely certain just what is meant in this verse.

11. Cf. also Jeremiah's "rod of almond" (Jeremiah 1:11) and the almonds on the "rod of Aaron" (Numbers 17:8 [MT v. 23]). An exhaustive treatment of the subject of trees in biblical prophecy may be found in William R. Telford, *The Barren Temple and the Withered Tree* (Sheffield: JSOT Press, 1980); see especially p. 213 on the sign of impending judgment. John F.A. Sawyer, "Hebrew Words for the Resurrection of the Dead" (in *Vetus Testamentum* 23 [1973], pp. 218-234), p. 225, notes that the Midrash *Koheleth Rabbah* sees in this phrase a reference to the way in which human resurrection will take place.

12. Peshitta has ܒܝܬ ܚܝܠܐ, "house of labour", having swapped *lamed* and *mem*. It is interesting to note the similarity between Gregory's expression εἰς αἰώνιον οἶκον here in v. 5 and εἰς γῆν in v. 4; the two phrases could be synonyms, yet Gregory has two very different destinations in mind.

13. The Targumist sees them as "angels" (מלאכיא), who walk about "like mourners" (כספדיא), putting the finishing touches to their account of the departed's life.

14. Oecolampadius renders *fons*, "fountain", evidently reading πηγή rather than πληγή (Migne, cols. 1015ff., n. 27; Salmond, p. 28, n. 1), but LXX's πηγή is paraphrased by Gregory's κρήνη. The Latin translation in Migne, col. 1018, correctly renders *plaga* for Gregory's πληγή and *fons* for κρήνη.

15. It has been proposed that the comma should be placed here rather than after the following word (Migne, col. 1017, n. 28; Salmond, p. 28, n. 2); my translation follows this proposal.

16. Some have apparently emended παυσαμένης to δεξαμενῆς (δεξαμεναί are mentioned as water-storages in 2:6), presumably as a parallel to LXX's λάκκος (Migne, col. 1018, n. 28; Salmond, p. 28, n. 2), but κοίλωμα is Gregory's equivalent concept to λάκκος in this context.

17. Χρόνων has been proposed (Migne, col. 1017, n.28; Salmond, p. 28, n.2).

18. So explain Liddell and Scott, p. 139: "the purest quality (of gold)", citing this LXX text. J. Edgar Bruns, "The Imagery of Eccles. 12:6a", in *Journal of Biblical Literature* 84 (1965), pp. 428-430, prefers a more literal meaning:

"(gold) with a floral pattern" or "artificial flowers (made of gold)".

19. In the earlier clause concerning the golden bowl, Symmachus had used the word περιφερής, "revolving, circumference" for the bowl, and Aquila had spoken of the "running" (δραμάω [τρέχω]) of the bowl, but Gregory's περιδρομή comes in the clause concerning the wheel.

20. In Gregory's introduction to the Catalogue of Times in 3:1, he might be taken as speaking of this age (χρόνος) of revolving things.

21. This is the interpretation of Billius (Migne, col. 1018, n. 29; Salmond, p. 28, n. 3). If this is Gregory's meaning, then he has here provided a Christian balance to his picture of this age (αἰών) in 3:11 — it is a time of great activity by Satan, but God has provided in the waters of baptism a means for Satan's efforts to be overcome; Satan will strive until the end of time, but also until then the chance of salvation will be kept open.

22. See Lampe, p. 812.

23. In A.F.J. Klijn's translation (*The Old Testament Pseudepigrapha*, ed. James H. Charlesworth [London: Darton, Longman & Todd, 1983], vol. 1, p. 651): "For the youth of this world has passed away, and the power of creation is already exhausted, and the coming of the times is very near and has passed by; and the pitcher is near the well, and the ship to the harbour, and the journey to the city, and life to its end." Midrash *Koheleth Rabbah* to 12:1 notes that Rabbi Hiyya ben Nehemiah's interpretation of "the years draw nigh" is that "it refers to the days of the Messiah in which is neither merit nor guilt", but this interpretation is not further developed.

24. Gregory's interpretation did find echoes in the commentaries of Didymus and Jerome in the 4th century, Olympiodorus in the 6th century, Rupert of Deutz and Richard of St.-Victor in the 12th century, Hugh of St.-Cher and Bonaventure in the 13th century, and Nicholas of Lyra in the 15th century — see Sandro Leanza, "Eccl 12,1-7: L'interpretazione escatologica dei Patri e degli esegeti medievali", in *Augustinianum* 18 (1978), pp. 191-207. A modern commentator, Michael V. Fox, has recognised a "manifest but restrained" eschatological symbolism (together with literal and figurative meanings) in Koheleth's poem — see his "Aging and Death in Qohelet 12" (in *Journal for the Study of the Old Testament* 42 [1988], pp. 55-77), pp. 63-77, restated in his *Qohelet and his Contradictions* (Bible and Literature Series 18; Sheffield: Almond Press, 1989), pp. 289-294.

25. Because of this change from the first to the third person, and because of the tenor of these closing verses coming after the repetition of the הבל הבלים theme, modern commentators generally hold that vv. 9-14 stem from a later hand, who wished to set Koheleth's work within its proper context, or at least what this later writer believed to be its proper context (see, e.g., Gordis, pp. 200-201,349-351; Ogden, pp. 207-208; but for an interesting alternative view, see Michael V. Fox, "Frame-Narrative and Composition in the Book of Qohelet", in *Hebrew Union College Annual* 48 [1977], pp. 83-106, and his *Qohelet and his Contradictions* [Bible and Literature Series 18; Sheffield: Almond Press, 1989], pp.310-321). Some interpreters even see the epilogue as the work of a "canonical editor": Gerald Wilson, "'The Words of the Wise': The Intent and Significance of Qohelet 12:9-14", in *Journal of Biblical Literature* 103 (1984), pp. 175-192; Gerald T. Sheppard, "The Epilogue to Qoheleth as Theological Commentary", in *Catholic Biblical Quarterly* 39 (1977), pp. 182-189. If the epilogue is the work of a later, more orthodox hand, we may be seeing already within the book of Ecclesiastes itself the process which is fully fledged in the

paraphrases of Gregory and the Targumist, namely the interpretation of Koheleth's words as being completely in keeping with traditional piety. "Fear God and keep his commandments" (v. 14) is presented as a summation of the book's essential teaching; while there may be some question as to how comfortably this sits in the original Ecclesiastes, there is no doubt that it is an appropriate summary of the versions of the work produced by Koheleth's paraphrasts.

And as in Gregory's paraphrase, so also in the Targum there is no element of surprise concerning a change of person at this point of the book, though in quite the reverse way: while Gregory remains constantly in the first person, the Targumist found it necessary to insert the reminder "says Solomon", or words to that effect, in several places throughout the book (1:3; 3:11,12; 4:15; 9:7,11; 10:7,9) in addition to MT's occurrences of "says Koheleth", and even lapsed into a lengthy third-person narrative about Solomon at one point (1:12), so the reader of the Targum would not be surprised to find Solomon spoken about, rather than speaking, in the closing verses of the book.

26. Λαός is found in Rahlfs' text, p. 260, on the basis of Codex Venetus; other manuscripts have ἄνθρωπος. MT has העם.

27. LXX used παραβολή as its equivalent to משל here (cf. Aquila παροιμία).

28. The Targumist also understands MT, while making some typical additions to it: "he listened (צות aphel) to the voice of the wise and searched (בלש) in the books of wisdom and, by the spirit of prophecy from the LORD, prepared (תקן pael) books of wisdom and a great many wise proverbs". So, too, the Peshitta, but without the paraphrastic additions, employs ܐܨܬ, ܒܨܐ, and ܬܩܢ aphel.

29. Γενναῖος in the concrete sense of "of noble birth" fits in well with the Wisdom tradition, where much instruction was represented as coming from the king (cf. Ecclesiastes 1:1; Proverbs 1:1; the Egyptian "Instruction of King Amen-emhet"), but Gregory doubtlessly also intends the metaphorical sense of "noble" in mind".

30. LXX also employed θέλημα, literally "will", for חפץ at 5:3 and 12:1. Symmachus used χρεία, "want, need" or a cognate thereof in these places. The Targumist gets it right with "pleasure" (רעוא) in the first two cases, but here in 12:10 decides to talk about Solomon seeking to do without "witnesses" (סהדין) and having to be reminded by the LORD of the Torah's teaching on this matter.

31. Codex Medic. has τά before σώματα (Migne, col. 1018, n. 30).

32. In MT משמר is linked with בעלי אספות, but LXX links both βούκεντρον and ἧλος with λόγοι σοφῶν.

33. Migne, col. 1018, n. 31 (cf. Salmond, p. 29, n. 1), notes that instead of LXX's πεφυτευμένοι, "planted" some have read πεπυρωμένοι, "set on fire". He does not mention that Symmachus has πεπηγότες, "fixed in", but he cites the Vulgate's quasi clavi in altum defixi, "like nails driven in upwards" (or "on high").

34. The latter meaning is cited by Lampe, p. 361.

35. Reichert and Cohen, p. 190, opt for the former interpretation and Barton, p. 198, for the latter. The Targum takes the former view, seeing here "the Rabbis of the Sanhedrin, masters of legal and textual interpretations (halakoth and midrashim)".

36. Παρά suggests an original מן, absent from MT because of a haplographic error: נטועים מבעלי אספות inadvertently became נטועים בעלי אספות.

37. The idea may, however, have arisen without any particular textual support, but because of a frustration on Gregory's part that Christians were not

speaking "with one voice" and "in harmony" on various matters of faith, perhaps including the "wise lessons" given in the book of Ecclesiastes.

38. Διδάσκαλος seems to be a Christian extension of the title ποιμήν as applied to Christ, since it cannot be derived directly from ποιμήν as applied to God in the Old Testament. The Old Testament notion of God as רעה has the connotation of "guide" in a broad sense, but not the specific connotation of "teacher". But compare the Targumist's reference in this verse to Moses as the shepherd (and teacher, though neither noun is stated) of Israel.

39. On Origen's attitude to pagan learning and philosophy, see Danielou, pp. 16-18. Cf. Gregory's depiction of Origen's attitude in his Panegyric to him, chapters 13 and 14 (Metcalfe, pp. 75-81; Salmond, pp. 68-73; Migne, cols. 1088-1093); note especially the comment that "everything in each of the philosophers that was useful and true he used to pick out and set before us, and sift out what was false" (Metcalfe, p. 81; Migne, col. 1093: πᾶν μὲν ὅ τι χρήσιμον φιλοσόφων ἑκάστων καὶ ἀληθὲς ἦν, ἀναλέγων, καὶ παρατιθέμενος ἡμῖν· ὅσα δὲ ψευδῆ, ἐκκρίνων).

40. Cf. Migne, col. 1018, n. 31*; Salmond, p. 29, n. 2.

41. This is a further reason why many scholars believe the final verses of Ecclesiastes to be from another hand than the rest of the book (see, e.g., Gordis, p. 349; Ogden, p. 211; Wilson, pp. 175,176). The book as a whole does, however, follow certain conventions of the royal instruction literature (of which the "my son" form of address is one), and the reader is addressed νεανίσκε (בחור), "O young man" in 11:9 (cf. Sawyer, pp. 523,530).

42. Metcalfe, p. 88 (Migne, col. 1014: παρακαλῶν δὲ χειραγωγεῖν καὶ ἐν τοῖς μέλλουσι, διὰ παντὸς ἐφεστῶτα, ὑπηχοῦντα τῷ νῷ ἡμῶν τὰ αὐτοῦ προστάγματα, ἐμβάλλοντα ἡμῖν τὸν θεῖον φόβον αὐτοῦ, παιδαγωγὸν ἄριστον ἐσόμενον).

43. Ὦ ἄνθρωποι ἰδού seems to interpret LXX's τὸ πᾶν ἄκουε (reading שמע instead of נשמע in MT's הכל נשמע; cf. Peshitta ܫܡܥ ܟܠ) as "listen, everyone", despite the neuter form of πᾶς here — cf. Vulgate pariter omnes audiamus, "let us all listen together". (Rahlfs, p. 260, has corrected the LXX text to ἀκούεται, on the basis of Codex Venetus, but Gregory probably had ἄκουε in the text before him.)

44. Cf. Reichert and Cohen, p. 191; Gordis, p. 355.

45. Nor, apparently, is the Targumist, whose final word is ביש, "evil" (but the manuscript — Codex Urbinates Ebr. 1 — reproduced in Levine, p. 117, follows the custom referred to above, and repeats the Hebrew v. 13 after the Aramaic paraphrase of v. 14).

Conclusion

1. Some examples of such de-semitisation are ὡς κενὰ καὶ ἀνόνητα... and πάνυ ματαίως for ματαιότης ματαιοτήτων in 1:2 and 12:8 respectively; ἄνθρωποι for οἱ υἱοὶ τοῦ ἀνθρώπου, 2:3 et al.; ἔργον for τὰ ποιήματα χειρῶν σου, 5:5; ματαίως for ἐν ματαιότητι, 6:4; τὰ προστυχόντα for πάντα ὅσα ἂν εὕρῃ ἡ χείρ σου τοῦ ποιῆσαι ὡς ἡ δύναμίς σου, 9:10. Note also the use of comparative adjectives for ἀγαθὸς "A" ὑπὲρ "B" statements (αἱρετώτερος, 4:3; 7:2; βελτίων, 4:9; ἀμείνων, 5:4; 7:10; δυνατώτερος, 9:18), and the expression "the greatest good" for οὐκ ἔστιν ἀγαθὸν εἰ μή statements (τὰ μέγιστα ἀγαθά, 3:12; τὸ μέγιστον τῶν ἀγαθῶν, 8:15; cf. τὸ τέλειον ἀγαθόν, 2:24).

2. An excellent example of Gregory's Greek style in this regard can be seen in his handling of the terse Catalogue of Times in 3:1-8. Where LXX repeated the simple καί, Gregory has εἶτα (vv. 2,7,8), καί (vv. 3,4), τε... καί (v. 3), νῦν μὲν... νῦν δέ (vv. 5,6), ποτὲ μὲν... ποτὲ δέ (v. 5), ἄλλοτε... ἄλλοτε (v. 7), and ποτὲ μὲν... ἄλλοτε δέ (v. 8).

3. See, e.g., comments on 4:5,16; 5:6; 10:8; 12:9.

4. The Catalogue of Times (3:1-8) is made to conform to a pattern of good times being replaced by bad times (although this careful structuring breaks down in v. 4; cf. the structuring of good and bad in 9:2). In 5:16 the two halves of the verse are inverted in order that the line of thought of the previous verse can be smoothly continued. In 7:6 the matter already familiar to the reader is placed first, with the new matter being introduced after it.

5. For example, θεράπων and θεράπαινα, 2:7; δασμοφόροι and δορυφόροι, 2:8; σοφίας γνῶσις and κτῆσις ἀνδρείας, 2:21; εὐθυμία and εὐποιΐα, 3:12; λαβόντα τὴν σύστασιν and ἔξοντα τὴν ἀνάλυσιν, 3:20; μῆκος ἄπειρον and βάθος ἀμέτρητον, 7:24; οἷα καὶ ὅσα, 8:9. A good example of Gregory's love for counter-balanced expressions is found in 4:11, where an increase in good fortune is juxtaposed with a decrease in bad fortune, and what is noticeable by day is balanced by what is noticeable by night; or in 12:3, where the beginning of activity on the part of heavenly powers is contrasted with the ceasing of activity on the part of earthly powers.

6. For the concept of "futility", Gregory does sometimes employ μάταιος (e.g., 2:1,17; 3:19), but he also utilises such words as κενός, ἀνόνητος, 1:2; ἀτοπία, 1:15; ἄχρηστος, δολερός, ἄθλιος, 2:26; πονηρία, 6:2; ἄνοια, 6:11; πλάνη, 8:14. He never reproduces the expression ὑπὸ τὸν ἥλιον, preferring such ways of speaking as περὶ γῆν, 1:3; 2:17; πρὸς ἀνθρώπων, 1:9 (cf. ὑπ᾽ ἀνθρώπων, 2:11; ἐν ἀνθρώποις, 4:1; κατὰ ἀνθρώπους, 4:3); κάτω, 1:14; ἐν τοῖς κάτω μέρεσι, 3:16. When he tires of a repetitious Kohelethine expression (e.g., ὑπὸ τὸν ἥλιον in 2:18,19,20,22), he simply ignores it altogether. When σοφία and γνῶσις appeared together three times in quick succession in 1:16-18, Gregory employs them only once (v. 18); similarly, when εὑρίσκω was found three times in one verse (8:17), Gregory is content with just one occurrence. On the other hand, when δίδωμι occurred three times within the one verse (2:26), he offers τυγχάνω, θεήλατος, πλεονεξία, and δῶρον. When Koheleth said "more than all who were before me in Jerusalem" twice (2:7,9), Gregory first says "more than people in earlier times" (v. 7) before speaking of "outdoing all the men who had ruled over Jerusalem before me" (v. 9); and when Koheleth said "they have no comforter" twice (4:1), Gregory speaks of "those who ought to help them, or on the whole ought to comfort them in all the troubles that press down upon them from every side". Koheleth's repetition of the concept "all your days of futility" in 9:9 is skilfully handled by Gregory's "pass your empty life in an empty way" (ματαίως τὸν μάταιον πάρελθε βίον).

7. Thus the prosaic πορεύομαι, for example, can be rendered by ὑπαπαίρω, ἐμπίπτω, ἄπειμι, 1:4; ἐκδίδωμι, 1:7; πλανάομαι, 2:14; ἐκκλησιάζω, 4:17; ἀπέρχομαι, 5:14; ἐρεθίζω, ἐξίστημι, ἕλκω, 6:9; βαδίζω, φέρομαι, 10:7; or even by ἀνάλυσις, 3:20; τέλος, 6:6; and εὐθύτης, 6:8. Note the more graphic ἐπιμαίνομαι and ἀποστυγέω for περιλαμβάνω and μακρύνομαι in 3:5; the stronger μέμφομαι and ἀντιλέγω for the tame ἐρῶ in 8:4; or the greater rhetorical flair of παρέξομαι δὲ τῷ λόγῳ for the simple εἶδον in 6:1. And while the "conclusion" of Ecclesiastes was introduced with the short and sharp "The end of the matter; all has been heard", Gregory provides his readers with a much more sizeable

build-up to this all-important matter (see translation and comments, 12:13).

8. For example, παραβολαί, 1:17; πολλοὶ λόγοι, 2:15; εὐσεβής, 3:16; πένθος, 5:16; μιαίνω, 7:18; μάταιος and κακός, 9:2; τὰ ἀπ' ἀρχῆς, 10:14.

9. For example, ἀνανήφω, 2:11; οὔθ', 5:9; πονηρός, 8:6; προτιμάω, 9:4.

10. For example, γνῶσις corrected to θυμός (Aquila and Theodotion) or ὀργή (Symmachus), 1:18; θεός corrected to ἄγγελος (all three), 5:5; γνῶσις corrected to κάκωσις (Symmachus), 8:6; ἀπὸ τότε replaced by ἀπέθανεν (all three), 8:12; πόλις corrected to γῆ (Symmachus), 10:16.

11. On the rendering of הבל, see comments under 1:2; and on the rendering of רוח, see comments under 1:14 (cf. 5:15; 11:4,5).

12. For example, ποταμός, 1:7; δεξαμενή, 2:6; γῆ, 3:20; ἀμφότερος, 4:6; ὀργή, 7:9; δένδρον, 11:13. Cf. συμβαίνω, ὅμοιος, πλέον, 3:19; and πρὶν ἐλθεῖν, 12:1.

13. Note κάκωσιν… τοῖς ὀφθαλμοῖς, 10:15, which seems to paraphrase both the Vatican and Alexandrian readings. Vatican readings appear to lie behind γενναῖος, 7:7; οὐκ ἐπ' ἀγαθῷ, 10:10; and ταπεινῶς (also Sinaitic), 10:19; but there is no sign of the significant ἄμωμος and μή in 11:9. 4:1's παραμυθέομαι is found under the category ἄλλος in Field's Hexapla edition, while 12:9's λαός is equivalent to the Venetian reading.

14. Note the removal of θεός from 1:13 in favour of the impersonal δίδοται and from 3:10 in favour of ἐτέθη, or the distancing effect of θεήλατος rather than θεός in 6:2. 7:13 is made to declare the greatness and kindness of God, who cannot be said to have done anything "crookedly".

15. Cf., e.g., the application of ἀρρωστία πονηρά in 6:2.

16. Note Gregory's interpretation of the προαίρεσις πνεύματος refrain in 1:14; 2:11; 4:4,6,16 (though his approach is different in 1:17; 2:17,26; 6:9); and his talk of a καιροσκόπος πονηρός in 3:11, a πνεῦμα πολέμιον in 10:4, and the τύραννος καὶ πατὴρ πάσης πονηρίας in 10:5.

17. God is described as "a gracious and watchful God" (7:26), "the only Lord and King" (8:4; cf. 10:20), "the Lord and Guardian of all" (12: 13). His πρόνοια is both loving (2:25) and just (8:6), as 8:11 notes. Judgment will come from him upon all that we do (11:9), but he "is able to forgive a great many sins" (10:4) and will save those who fear him (5:6; 12:7); meanwhile a God-fearing lifestyle is rewarded already in this life (7:8), and "the person who is wronged has a helper in God" (3:15).

18. 2:24; 3:12-13; 8:15-17 (cf. 3:22).

19. See, e.g., comments on ἀγαθωσύνη at 5:10 and ὁράω ἀγαθωσύνην at 6:6. 4:14 provides an example of Koheleth's failure to ascribe a moral judgment being "rectified" by his paraphrast, and 5:18 an example of Gregory ensuring that Solomon cannot be taken as giving his approval to amorality.

20. He speaks of ὁ αἰὼν οὗτος (3:11), hinting that there is an αἰὼν μέλλων, and so he contrasts the way things are ἐνθάδε (9: 16) with the way things will be μετέπειτα (9:17). He alludes to "the things that will happen after everyone's death" (6:12), and prophetically sees "in the lower regions a pit of punishment awaiting the ungodly, but a different place set apart for the godly" (3:16); "the good person will enter into his eternal home with rejoicing, but the bad people will fill all their homes with mourning" (12:5). Only fools think that there is nothing after death (9:3-10; 11:7-9). People should look beyond this life under the sun (1:3; 2:14), and seek salvation (5:6; 12:7).

21. See particularly comments at 1:2,7,8.

22. See comments at 2:17,23; 7:15; 9:9.

23. Note Gregory's treatment of 2:17-26.

24. See comments at 7:24; 8:7,17; 9:12; 11:5; and cf. 5:10's "ability to perceive all things".

25. Most people, Gregory complains, "have given themselves over to transitory things, not wanting to look — with the soul's noble eye — at anything higher than the stars" (1:3); but "the person who has chosen goodness is like someone who sees everything — including what is above — clearly" (2:14).

26. 2:22,23,26; 4:4-6; 5:16,19.

27. The prophetic vision of 3:16.

28. Note Gregory's treatment of 7:15 and 8:10.

29. See 4:1,14; 12:5 (cf. 5:8; 10:8,12; 11:10).

30. "Divine providence does not attend to everyone swiftly, because of God's great patience with evil" (8:11; cf. 8:5, "the judgment... will take place at the right time").

31. The apocalyptic vision of 12:5.

32. See Gregory's treatment of 2:16 (cf. 2:9, where Koheleth spoke of wisdom remaining, but Gregory speaks of wisdom diminishing; or 7:25, where Koheleth spoke of seeking wisdom, but Gregory speaks of abstaining altogether from seeking it).

33. Δίδοται, 1:13; ἐτέθη, 3:10.

34. Cf. the treatment of καὶ ἐπέστρεψα ἐγώ in 4:1 and 4:7.

35. 1:16–2:1; 2:10-11; 8:15-17; 9:1-3.

36. 9:7-11; 11:7-9.

37. This is his approach in the passage 3:17-22.

38. Thus he introduces 8:14 as "a most base and false opinion [which] is often spread among human beings"; and in the passage 9:3-10 he tells the reader that "these are fool's arguments — errors and deceits" (v. 3), gives a reminder that it is the voice of Deception which offers this kind of advice (v. 7), and finally underlines that "these are the things which hollow people say" (v. 10).

39. Παρὰ πάντας ἀνθρώπους βασιλεὺς ἐντιμότατος καὶ προφήτης σοφώτατος, 1:1.

40. Λέγει... ἁπάσῃ τῇ τοῦ Θεοῦ Ἐκκλησίᾳ, 1:1 (cf. ἐκκλησιάζω in 1:12 and 12:9).

41. See 2:9-12,17-21; 7:15,23; 8:15-17; 12:10.

42. See especially 3:11; 12:1-7 (cf. 2:16; 3:16; 4:2; 8:8; 10:8,11; 11:2).

43. Levine, p. 68, places the terminus a quo of the Targum to Ecclesiastes at about the year 500, the date of the completion of the Babylonian Talmud (cf. Holm-Nielsen, ASTI, p. 63).

44. See comments above on 1:1 (n. 2).

45. See, e.g., comments on 1:3 (n. 6).

46. See, e.g., my comments on 2:4 (n. 3); 3:2 (n. 5); 4:13 (n. 29) & 15 (n. 35); 9:13 (n. 22) & 15 (n. 23); 10:9 (n. 18) & 10 (n. 23); and 12:1 (the Targumist's יהוה). Cf. Levine's comment, p. 70, that the Targum to Ecclesiastes' "primary function is allegorization and the incorporation of alien concepts", and his list on pp. 68,69 of its folkloric/legendary material.

47. See comments on 4:13-16.

48. See Jerome's comments on 2:24 (Corpus Christianorum, vol. 72, pp. 271,272).

49. Ecclesiastes 4:12 (see Jacques-Paul Migne, ed., Patrologia Latina, vol. 16 [Paris: Migne, 1845], col. 1274; Mary Melchior Beyenka, tr., Saint Ambrose:

Letters [The Fathers of the Church: A New Translation, vol. 26; Washington: Catholic University of America Press, 1954], p. 319. So also Ambrose saw Christ as the one who lifts up his companion (v. 10) and warms him (v. 11), and the one who went from the house of bondsman to be king (v. 13). Jerome had also seen the Trinity in Koheleth's saying concerning the threefold cord (see *Corpus Christianorum*, vol. 72, p. 287).

BIBLIOGRAPHY

Primary Sources

Allenbach, J., *et al.*, eds. *Biblia Patristica: Index des citations et allusions bibliques dans la littérature patristique.* Paris: Centre National de la Recherche Scientifique.
1 (1975): *Des origenes à Clement d'Alexandrie et Tertullien.*
2 (1977): *Le troisième siècle (Origène excepté).*
3 (1980): *Origène.*

Bauer, Walter. *A Greek-English Lexicon of the New Testament and Other Early Christian Literature.* Tr. & ed. William F. Arndt and F. Wilbur Gingrich. Chicago University Press, ²1979.

Brown, Francis, S.R. Driver, and Charles A. Briggs. *A Hebrew and English Lexicon of the Old Testament.* Oxford: Clarendon Press, 1972.

Corpus Christianorum, Series Latina, vol. 72: *S. Hieronymi Presbyteri Opera*, Pars I (Opera Exegetica), 1. Turnholt: Brepols, 1959.

Elliger, Kurt, and Wilhelm Rudolph, eds. *Biblia Hebraica Stuttgartensia.* Stuttgart: Deutsche Bibelstiftung, 1967/77.

Feltoe, Charles Lett, ed. *The Letters and Other Remains of Dionysius of Alexandria.* Cambridge University Press, 1904.

Field, Frederick, ed. *Origenis Hexaplorum*, vol. 2: *Libri Poetici et Prophetici.* Oxford: Clarendon Press, 1867.

Holmes, Robert, and James Parsons. *Vetus Testamentum Graecum cum variis lectionibus*, vol. 3. Oxford: Clarendon Press, 1823.

Jastrow, Marcus. *A Dictionary of the Targumim, the Talmud Babli and Yerushalmi, and the Midrashic Literature.* New York: G.P. Putnam's Sons, 1903.

Kittel, Rudolf, ed. *Biblia Hebraica.* Stuttgart: Privilegierte Württembergische Bibelanstalt, ⁴1949.

Lagarde, Paul de, ed. *Hagiographa Chaldaice.* Osnabrück: Otto Zeller, 1967 (a reprint of the 1873 edition).

Lampe, G.W.H., ed. *A Patristic Greek Lexicon.* Oxford: Clarendon Press, 1961.

Lane, D.J., ed. "Qoheleth." In *The Old Testament in Syriac, according to the Peshitta Version*, Part 2, fascicle 5, pp. 1-20. Edited on behalf of the International Organization for the Study of the Old Testament by the Peshitta Institute, Leiden. Leiden: E.J. Brill, 1979.

Liddell, Henry George, and Robert Scott, eds. *A Greek-English Lexicon.* Revised Henry Stuart Jones and Roderick McKenzie. Oxford: Clarendon Press, ⁹1940.

Midrash Rabbah, vol. 5 (Deuteronomy, Ecclesiastes, and Lamentations). Warsaw: Drukarni H.N. Schriftgisser, 1850.

Migne, Jacques-Paul, ed. *Patrologia Graeca*, vol. 10. Turnholt: Brepols, 1978 (a reprint of the Paris edition of 1857).

Rahlfs, Alfred, ed. *Septuaginta.* Stuttgart: Privilegierte Württembergische Bibelanstalt, 1950.

Sperber, Alexander, ed. *The Bible in Aramaic*, vol. 4A: *The Hagiographa: Transition from Translation to Midrash*. Leiden: E.J. Brill, 1968.

Swete, Henry Barclay, ed. *The Old Testament in Greek according to the Septuagint*. Cambridge University Press, ³1907.

Weber, Robert, ed. *Biblia Sacra Iuxta Vulgatam Versionem*. Stuttgart: Württembergische Bibelanstalt, 1969.

Secondary Sources

Ackroyd, Peter R. "Two Hebrew Notes." In *Annual of the Swedish Theological Institute* 5 (1967), pp. 82-86.

Balzer, Klaus. "Women and War in Qohelet 7:23–8:1a." In *Harvard Theological Review* 80 (1987), pp. 127-132.

Barthélemy, Dominique. *Les Devanciers d'Aquila* (Supplements to *Vetus Testamentum*, vol. 10). Leiden: E.J. Brill, 1963.

Barton, George Aaron. *A Critical and Exegetical Commentary on the Book of Ecclesiastes*. Edinburgh: T. & T. Clark, 1908.

Barucq, André. *Ecclésiaste* (Verbum Salutis, Ancien Testament 3). Paris: Beauchesne, 1968.

Beckwith, Roger. *The Old Testament Canon of the New Testament Church and its Background in Early Judaism*. London: SPCK, 1985.

Bertram, Georg. "Hebräischer und griechischer Qohelet: Ein Beitrag zur Theologie der hellenistischen Bibel." In *Zeitschrift für die alttestamentliche Wissenschaft* 64 (1952), pp. 26-49.

Beyenka, Mary Melchoir, tr. *Saint Ambrose: Letters* (The Fathers of the Church: A New Translation, vol. 26). Washington: Catholic University of America Press, 1954.

Bruns, J. Edgar. "The Imagery of Eccles 12:6a." In *Journal of Biblical Literature* 84 (1965), pp. 428-430.

Buhl, Frants. *Canon and Text of the Old Testament*. Edinburgh: T. & T. Clark, 1892.

Charlesworth, James H., ed. *The Old Testament Pseudepigrapha*. London: Darton, Longman & Todd, 1983.

Cohen, A., tr. "Ecclesiastes." In *Midrash Rabbah*. Ed. H. Freedman and Maurice Simon. London: Soncino Press, 1939. Vol. 8, pp. 1-318.

Cox, Samuel. *The Book of Ecclesiastes*. London: Hodder and Stoughton, 1899.

Crenshaw, James L. *Ecclesiastes: a commentary* (Old Testament Library). London: SCM Press, 1988.

— — "The Eternal Gospel (Eccl. 3:11)." In *Essays in Old Testament Ethics*. Ed. James L. Crenshaw and John T. Willis. New York: KTAV Publishing House, 1974. Pp. 23-55.

— — "The Shadow of Death in Qoheleth." In *Israelite Wisdom: Theological and Literary Essays in honor of Samuel Terrien*. Ed. John G. Gammie *et al.* Missoula: Scholars Press, 1978. Pp. 205-216.

— — "Youth and Old Age in Qoheleth." In *Hebrew Annual Review* 10 (1986), pp. 1-13.

Crombie, Frederick, tr. *The Writings of Origen*, vol. 1 (Ante-Nicene Christian Library, vol. 10). Edinburgh: T. & T. Clark, 1869.

Danielou, Jean. *Origen*. Tr. Walter Mitchell. New York: Sheed and Ward, 1955.

Delitzsch, Franz. *Commentary on the Song of Songs and Ecclesiastes*. Tr. M.G. Easton. Edinburgh: T. & T. Clark, 1877.

De Waard, J. "The Translator and Textual Criticism (with particular reference to Eccl 2,25)." In *Biblica* 60 (1979), pp. 509-529.

Eaton, Michael A. *Ecclesiastes*. Leicester: Inter-Varsity Press, 1983.

Fox, Michael V. "Aging and Death in Qohelet 12." In *Journal for the Study of the Old Testament* 42 (1988), pp. 55-77.

-- "Frame-Narrative and Composition in the Book of Qohelet." In *Hebrew Union College Annual* 48 (1977), pp. 83-106.

-- "The Meaning of *Hebel* for Qohelet." In *Journal of Biblical Literature* 105 (1986), pp. 409-427.

-- *Qohelet and his Contradictions* (Bible and Literature Series 18). Sheffield: Almond Press, 1989.

Frendo, Anthony. "The 'Broken Construct Chain' in Qoh 10,10b." In *Biblica* 62 (1981), pp. 544-545.

Fuerst, Wesley J. *The Books of Ruth, Esther, Ecclesiastes, The Song of Songs, Lamentations: The Five Scrolls*. Cambridge University Press, 1975.

Galling, Kurt. "Der Prediger." In *Die Fünf Megilloth* (Handbuch zum Alten Testament, vol. 18). Tübingen: J.C.B. Mohr (Paul Siebeck), ²1969. Pp.73-125.

Ginsburg, Christian D. *Coheleth*. London, 1861; reprint New York: KTAV Publishing House, 1970.

Goldin, Judah, tr. *The Fathers according to Rabbi Nathan* (Yale Judaica Series 10). New Haven: Yale University Press, 1955.

Good, Edwin M. "The Unfilled Sea: Style and Meaning in Ecclesiastes 1:2-11." In *Israelite Wisdom: Theological and Literary Essays in honor of Samuel Terrien*. Ed. John G. Gammie *et al.* Missoula: Scholars Press, 1978. Pp. 59-73.

Gordis, Robert. *Koheleth — The Man and his World: A Study of Ecclesiastes*. New York: Schocken Books, ³1968.

Hannick, Christian. "Music of the Early Christian Church." In *The New Grove Dictionary of Music and Musicians*. Ed. Stanley Sadie. London: Macmillan, 1980. Vol. 4, pp. 363-371.

Hengel, Martin. *Judaism and Hellenism: Studies in their Encounter in Palestine during the early Hellenistic Period*. London: SCM Press, 1974.

Hertzberg, Hans Wilhelm. *Der Prediger* (Kommentar zum Alten Testament 17/4). Gütersloh: Gütersloher Verlagshaus Gerd Mohn, 1963.

Hirshman, Marc. "The Greek Fathers and the Aggada on Ecclesiastes: Formats of Exegesis in Late Antiquity." In *Hebrew Union College Annual* 59 (1988), pp. 137-165.

Holm-Nielsen, Svend. "The Book of Ecclesiastes and the Interpretation of it in Jewish and Christian Theology." In *Annual of the Swedish Theological Institute* 10 (1976), pp. 38-96.

-- "On the Interpretation of Qoheleth in Early Christianity." In *Vetus Testamentum* 24 (1974), pp. 168-177.

Hyvärinen, Kyösti. *Die Übersetzung von Aquila* (Coniectanea Biblica, Old Testament Series, no. 10). Lund: CWK Gleerup, 1977.

Isaksson, Bo. *Studies in the Language of Qoheleth, with special emphasis on the verbal system* (Acta Universitatis Upsaliensis: Studia Semitica Upsaliensia 10). Uppsala University Press, 1987.

Jastrow, Morris. *A Gentle Cynic.* Philadelphia: Lippincott, 1919.

Jellicoe, Sidney. *The Septuagint and Modern Study.* Oxford: Clarendon, 1968.

-- Ed. *Studies in the Septuagint: Origins, Recensions, and Interpretations.* New York: KTAV Publishing House, 1974.

Jones, Edgar. *Proverbs and Ecclesiastes.* London: SCM Press, 1961.

Kelly, J.N.D. *Jerome: His Life, Writings, and Controversies.* London: Duckworth, 1975.

Kidner, Derek. *A Time to Mourn and a Time to Dance: Ecclesiastes and the way of the world.* London: Inter-Varsity Press, 1976.

Lake, Kirsopp, tr. *The Apostolic Fathers* (Loeb Classical Library, vol. 2). London: Heinemann, 1913.

Lane Fox, Robin. *Pagans and Christians.* New York: Alfred A. Knopf, 1987.

Lauha, Aarre. *Kohelet* (Biblischer Kommentar, Altes Testament 11). Neukirchen-Vluyn: Neukirchener Verlag, 1978.

Leanza, Sandro. "Eccl 12,1-7: L'interpretazione escatologica dei Patri e degli esegeti medievali." In *Augustinianum* 18 (1978), pp. 191-207.

Leiman, Harold. *Koheleth: Life and its meaning.* Jerusalem: Feldheim Publishers, 1980.

Leiman, Sid Z. *The Canonization of Hebrew Scripture: the talmudic and midrashic evidence.* Hamden, Connecticut: Archon Books, 1976.

Levine, Etan. *The Aramaic Version of Qohelet.* New York: Sepher-Hermon Press, 1978.

Levy, Ludwig. *Das Buch Qoheleth: Ein Beitrag zur Geschichte des Sadduzäismus.* Leipzig: J.C. Hinrichs'sche Buchhandlung, 1912.

Lloyd, J. *An Analysis of the Book of Ecclesiastes.* London: Samuel Bagster & Sons, 1874.

Loader, J.A. *Ecclesiastes: A Practical Commentary.* Tr. John Vriend. Grand Rapids: William B. Eerdmans Publishing Company, 1986.

-- *Polar Structures in the Book of Qohelet* (Beihefte zur Zeitschrift für die alttestamentliche Wissenschaft 152). Berlin: Walter de Gruyter, 1979.

-- "Qohelet 3.2-8 — A 'Sonnet' in the Old Testament." In *Zeitschrift für die alttestamentliche Wissenschaft* 81 (1969), pp. 240-242.

Lohfink, Norbert. *Kohelet* (Die Neuer Echter Bibel 19). Würzburg: Echter Verlag, 1980.

-- "War Kohelet ein Frauenfeind? Ein Versuch, die Logik und den Gegenstand von Koh. 7,23–8,1a herauszufinden." In *La Sagesse de l'Ancien Testament.* Ed. M. Gilbert. Leuven University Press, 1979. Pp. 259-292.

Loretz, Oswald. *Qohelet und der Alte Orient: Untersuchungen zu Stil und theologischer Thematik des Buches Qohelet.* Freiburg: Herder, 1964.

Lys, Daniel. *L'Ecclésiaste, ou Que Vaut la Vie?* Paris: Letouzey et Ané, 1977.

Maclaren, Alexander. *The Books of Esther, Job, Proverbs, and Ecclesiastes.* London: Hodder and Stoughton, 1907.

Martin, G. Currie. *Proverbs, Ecclesiastes, Song of Songs.* London: T.C. & E.C. Jack, 1908.

Metcalfe, William. *Origen the Teacher.* London: SPCK, 1907.

Muraoka, Takamitsu. *Emphatic Words and Structures in Biblical Hebrew.* Jerusalem: Magnes Press, 1985.

–– "On Septuagint Lexicography and Patristics." In *Journal of Theological Studies* 35 (1984), pp. 441-448.

Murphy, Roland E. "A Form-Critical Consideration of Ecclesiastes VII." In *Society of Biblical Literature 1974 Seminar Papers.* Ed. George MacRae. Cambridge, Mass.: Society of Biblical Literature, 1974. Vol. 1, pp. 77-85.

–– "Qohelet Interpreted: The Bearing of the Past on the Present." In *Vetus Testamentum* 32 (1982), pp. 331-337.

Noakes, K.W. "The Metaphrase on Ecclesiastes of Gregory Thaumaturgus." In *Studia Patristica,* vol. 15 (Texte und Untersuchungen zur Geschichte der altchristlichen Literatur 128). Ed. Elizabeth A. Livingstone. Berlin: Akademie-Verlag, 1984. Pp. 196-199.

Ogden, Graham S. "The 'Better'-Proverb (*Tôb-Spruch*), Rhetorical Criticism, and Qoheleth." In *Journal of Biblical Literature* 96 (1977), pp. 489-505.

–– "Historical Allusion in Qoheleth IV 13-16?" In *Vetus Testamentum* 30 (1980), pp. 309-315.

–– "The Interpretation of דור in Ecclesiastes 1.4." In *Journal for the Study of the Old Testament* 34 (1986), pp. 91-92.

–– "The Mathematics of Wisdom: Qoheleth IV 1-12." In *Vetus Testamentum* 34 (1984), pp. 446-453.

–– *Qoheleth.* Sheffield: JSOT Press, 1987.

–– "Qoheleth IX 1-16." In *Vetus Testamentum* 32 (1982), pp. 158-169.

–– "Qoheleth ix 17–x 20: Variations on the Theme of Wisdom's Strength and Vulnerability." In *Vetus Testamentum* 30 (1980), pp. 27-37.

–– "Qoheleth XI 1-6." In *Vetus Testamentum* 33 (1983), pp. 222-230.

–– "Qoheleth xi 7–xii 8: Qoheleth's Summons to Enjoyment and Reflection." In *Vetus Testamentum* 34 (1984), pp. 27-38.

–– "Qoheleth's Use of the 'Nothing is Better'-Form." In *Journal of Biblical Literature* 98 (1979), pp. 339-350.

Ottley, Richard R. *A Handbook to the Septuagint.* London: Methuen, 1920.

Pleins, J. David. "Poverty in the Social World of the Wise." In *Journal for the Study of the Old Testament* 37 (1987), pp. 61-78.

Plumptre, E.H. *Ecclesiastes.* Cambridge University Press, 1881.

Podechard, Emmanuel. *L'Ecclésiaste* (Études Bibliques 11). Paris: Librairie Victor Lecoffre, 1912.

Quasten, Johannes. *Patrology.* Westminster: Newman Press, 1964.

Rankin, O.S. "Ecclesiastes." In *The Interpreter's Bible.* Ed. George Arthur Buttrick. Nashville: Abingdon Press, 1956. Vol. 5, pp. 1-88.

Reichert, Victor E., and A. Cohen. "Ecclesiastes." In *The Five Megilloth.* Ed.

A. Cohen. London: Soncino Press, 1946. Pp. 104-191.

Reines, Ch.W. "Koheleth VIII,10." In *Journal of Jewish Studies* 5 (1954), pp. 86-87.

— — "Koheleth on Wisdom and Wealth." In *Journal of Jewish Studies* 5 (1954), pp. 80-84.

Ryle, Herbert Edward. *The Canon of the Old Testament: an essay on the gradual growth and formation of the Hebrew Canon of Scripture.* London: Macmillan & Co., 1895.

Salmond, S.D.F., tr. *The Works of Gregory Thaumaturgus, Dionysius of Alexandria, and Archelaus* (Ante-Nicene Christian Library, vol. 20). Edinburgh: T. & T. Clark, 1882.

Salters, Robert B. "The Book of Ecclesiastes: Studies in the Versions and the History of Exegesis." Ph.D. dissertation, University of St. Andrews, 1973.

— — "Exegetical Problems in Qoheleth." In *Irish Biblical Studies* 10 (1988), pp. 44-59.

— — "A Note on the Exegesis of Ecclesiastes 3:15b." In *Zeitschrift für die alttestamentliche Wissenschaft* 88 (1976), pp. 419-422.

— — "Notes on the History of Interpretation of Koh 5.5." In *Zeitschrift für die alttestamentliche Wissenschaft* 90 (1978), pp. 95-101.

— — "Notes on the Interpretation of Qoh 6.2." In *Zeitschrift für die alttestamentliche Wissenschaft* 91 (1979), pp. 282-289.

— — "Text and Exegesis in Koh 10.19." In *Zeitschrift für die alttestamentliche Wissenschaft* 89 (1977), pp. 423-426.

— — "The Word for 'God' in the Peshitta of Koheleth." In *Vetus Testamentum* 21 (1971), pp. 251-254.

Sawyer, John F.A. "Hebrew Words for the Resurrection of the Dead." In *Vetus Testamentum* 23 (1973), pp. 218-234.

— — "The Ruined House in Ecclesiastes 12: A Reconstruction of the Original Parable." In *Journal of Biblical Literature* 94 (1975), pp. 519-531.

Schoors, Antoon. "The Peshitta of Kohelet and its Relation to the Septuagint." In *After Chalcedon: Studies in Theology and Church History offered to Professor Albert van Roey for his 70th birthday* (Orientalia Louvaniensia Analecta 18). Ed. C. Laga, J.A. Munitz, and L. van Rompay. Leuven: Departement Oriëntalistiek and Uitgeverij Peeters, 1985. Pp. 347-357.

Schürer, Emil. *The History of the Jewish People in the Age of Jesus Christ.* Rev. & ed. Geza Vermes and Fergus Millar. Edinburgh: T. & T. Clark, 1973-1987.

Scott, R.B.Y. *Proverbs, Ecclesiastes* (The Anchor Bible 18). New York: Doubleday & Company, 1965.

Serrano, J.J. "I Saw the Wicked Buried (Eccl 8,10)." In *Catholic Biblical Quarterly* 16 (1954), pp. 168-170.

Sheppard, Gerald T. "The Epilogue to Qoheleth as Theological Commentary." In *Catholic Biblical Quarterly* 39 (1977), pp. 182-189.

Slotki, Israel W., tr. *'Erubin.* London: Soncino Press, 1938.

Stumpff, Albrecht. "Ζῆλος." In *Theological Dictionary of the New Testament.* Ed. Gerhard Kittel. Tr. & ed. Geoffrey W. Bromiley. Grand Rapids: William B. Eerdmans Publishing Company, 1964. Vol. 2, pp. 877-882.

Swete, Henry Barclay. *An Introduction to the Old Testament in Greek.* Cambridge University Press, 1914.

Telfer, William. "The Cultus of St. Gregory Thaumaturgus." In *Harvard Theological Review* 29 (1936), pp. 225-344.

── "The Latin *Life* of St. Gregory Thaumaturgus." In *Journal of Theological Studies* 31 (1930), pp. 142-155, 354-362.

Telford, William R. *The Barren Temple and the Withered Tree.* Sheffield: JSOT Press, 1980.

Thurston, Herbert, and Donald Attwater, eds. *Butler's Lives of the Saints.* Westminster: Christian Classics, 1956.

Torrey, Charles C. "The Problem of Ecclesiastes iv 13-16." In *Vetus Testamentum* 2 (1952), pp. 175-177.

Trigg, Joseph Wilson. *Origen: The Bible and Philosophy in the Third-century Church.* London: SCM Press, 1985.

Vinel, Françoise. "La *Metaphrasis in Ecclesiasten* de Grégoire le Thaumaturge: entre traduction et interprétation, une explicatiuon de texte." In *Cahiers de Biblia Patristica* 1 (1987), pp. 191-215.

Von Rad, Gerhard. *Wisdom in Israel.* Tr. James D. Martin. London: SCM Press, 1972.

Whitley, Charles F. *Koheleth: His Language and Thought* (Beihefte zur Zeitschrift für die alttestamentliche Wissenschaft 148). Berlin: Walter de Gruyter, 1979.

Whybray, R.N. "Qoheleth, Preacher of Joy." In *Journal for the Study of the Old Testament* 23 (1982), pp. 87-98.

── "Qoheleth the Immoralist? (Qoh. 7:16-17)." In *Israelite Wisdom: Theological and Literary Essays in honor of Samuel Terrien.* Ed. John G. Gammie et al. Missoula: Scholars Press, 1978. Pp. 191-204.

Wilson, Gerald H. "'The Words of the Wise': The Intent and Significance of Qohelet 12:9-14." In *Journal of Biblical Literature* 103 (1984), pp. 175-192.

Zahrnt, Heinz. *What Kind of God?* Minneapolis: Augsburg Publishing House, 1972.

Zeitlin, Solomon. *An Historical Study of the Canonization of the Hebrew Scriptures.* Philadelphia: Jewish Publication Society of America, 1933.

Ziegler, Joseph. "Die Wiedergabe der nota accusativi *'et, 'aet-* mit σύν." In *Zeitschrift für die alttestamentliche Wissenschaft* 100 (1988), Supplement, pp. 222-233.

Zimmerli, Walther. "Das Buch des Predigers Salomo." In *Sprüche/Prediger* (Das Alte Testament Deutsch 16/1). Helmer Ringgren and Walther Zimmerli. Göttingen: Vandenhoeck und Ruprecht, 1962. Pp. 123-253.

── *Old Testament Theology in Outline.* Tr. David E. Green. Atlanta: John Knox Press, 1978.

Zimmermann, Frank. *The Inner World of Qohelet.* New York: KTAV Publishing House, 1973.

Zlotowitz, Meir. *Koheles/Ecclesiastes: A New Translation with a Commentary anthologized from Talmudic, Midrashic and Rabbinic sources.* New York: Mesorah Publications, ²1977.

INDEX

Scripture

Genesis 1:29 – p. 30.
 1:31 – 14, 67.
 2:7 – 298.
 2:8,9 – 30, 337.
 2:17 – 337.
 2:21ff. – 352.
 3:5 – 337.
 3:19 – 12, 78, 129, 294, 298.
 9:6 – 61.
 15:3 – 324.
 31:11-13 – 114.
 44:16 – 352.
Exodus 1:10 – 174, 340.
 1:16 – 328.
 3:2-6 – 114.
 22:26 – 332.
Leviticus 14:40-42 – 327.
 23:10 – 317.
Numbers 16:13 – 339
 17:8 (23) – 353.
Deuteronomy 23:21-23 – 112.
Judges 5:30 – 33.
2 Samuel 2:13 – 324.
 4:12 – 324.
 12:18 – 68.
 13:5 – 340.
1 Kings 3:4-15 – 24.
 3:13 – 33.
 4:21 (5:1) – 33, 325.
 4:29 (5:9) – 35.
 8:14,15 – 8.
 8:46 – 181.
 9:10,17 – 30.
 10:7 – 35.
 10:24,25 – 33, 325.
 11:4 – 184.
 19:10,14 – 327.
 22:38 – 324.
2 Kings 3:19,25 – 59.
 18:17 – 324.
 20:20 – 324.
Nehemiah 2:14 – 324.
 3:15,16 – 324.

Job 1:21 – 129.
 3:13-16 – 85.
 8:9 – 152.
 9:12 – 200, 343.
 28:28 – 108.
 35:9 – 330.
Psalm 7:14-16 (15-17) – 258.
 19:5,6 (6,7) – 11.
 34:14 (15) – 71.
 104:4 – 208.
 104:15 – 351.
 111:10 – 70.
 115:17 – 230.
 119:134 – 330.
Proverbs 1:1 – 350.
 6:10 – 88.
 10:17 – 43.
 10:27ff. – 44, 172.
 13:15 – 347.
 15:8 – 107.
 17:24 – 41.
 19:21 – 43.
 22:1 – 155.
 22:9 – 278.
 22:16 – 330.
 25:1 – 317.
Ecclesiastes – *passim*.
Song of Songs 1:1 – 341.
 7:5 – 324.
 8:6 – 341.
Isaiah 1:3 – 350.
 5:2 – 59.
 5:11 – 270.
 5:14,15 – 324, 337.
 7:3 – 324.
 13:9,10 – 352.
 22:9,11 – 324.
 32:2 – 168.
 36:2 – 324.
 49:26 – 89.
 66:23,24 – 308.
Jeremiah 1:11 – 353.
 2:27 – 328.
 6:6 – 330.

Jeremiah 8:17 – 264.
    20:18 – 85.
    31:31 – 323.
    36:22,30 – 332.
Lamentations 5:21,22 – 308.
Ezekiel 22:29 – 330.
    26:12 – 59.
    34:1-10 – 83.
Joel 2:10 – 352.
    2:31 (3:4) – 289f., 352.
    3:15 (4:15) – 352.
Amos 3:9 – 330.
    5:18,19 – 291.
Nahum 2:9 – 324.
Habakkuk 2:5 – 337.
Zephaniah 2:4 – 327.
Haggai 1:8 – 59.
Zechariah 14:12 – 269.
Malachi 4:5 (3:23) – 289, 352.
    4:5,6 (3:23,24) – 308.

Matthew 3:9 – 328.
    7:6 – 61.
    7:12 – 279.
    10:28 – 239.
    13:24-50 – 295.
    24:29 – 290f.
    24:32,33 – 295.
    24:41 – 292.
    25:31-46 – 73, 278, 296.
Mark 13:19 – 84.
    13:24,25 – 290f.
Luke 6:31 – 279.
    12:19 – 186.
    12:47-49 – 175.

Luke 18:9-14 – 334.
    21:22 – 84.
John 8:44 – 255f., 349.
    10:3 – 319.
Acts 2:15 – 351.
Romans 6:11 – 178.
    8:20 – 2, 22.
1 Corinthians 11:23 – 304.
    13:13 – 100.
    15:3 – 304.
    15:55 – 285.
2 Corinthians 4:4 – 65f.
    5:17 – 323.
Galatians 6:15 – 323.
1 Thessalonians 5:2 – 43.
1 Timothy 6:9 – 35.
    6:10 – 121, 273.
Hebrews 8:8 – 323.
    12:22 – 268.
James 5:20 – 254.
1 Peter 2:2,5 – 351.
    3:20,21 – 298.
    4:8 – 180, 254.
    5:8 – 66.
2 Peter 3:9 – 214, 344.
1 John 1:8 – 181.
Revelation 6:12-17 – 291.
    9:1-11 – 295.
    12:7-12 – 66, 259.
    14:9-11 – 73.
    16:1-21 – 84.
    20:1-15 – 73, 259.
    21:1-4 – 73f.
    21:11,23 – 284.

Scholars

Ackroyd – 337.
Allenbach – 318.
Balzer – 341.
Barthélemy – 320.
Barton – 323, 327-335, 337ff., 343-349,
    351ff., 355.

Bauer – 323, 351.
Beckwith – 317, 320.
Beyenka – 359.
Brown – 325.
Bruns – 353.
Buhl – 317f.

Cox – 329.
Crenshaw – 329.
Crombie – 319.
Danielou – 320, 356.
Delitzsch – 327ff., 331, 335, 341, 344.
De Waard – 326f.
Eaton – 323, 325, 328, 331f., 334f., 338f., 341, 343f.
Elliger & Rudolph – 321, 342, 345f., 348.
Feltoe – 318.
Field – 321, 324, 331, 338, 340, 342, 348.
Fox – 352, 354.
Frendo – 350.
Fuerst – 325, 329, 345.
Ginsburg – 325, 330, 333, 337f., 343f., 346, 348-353.
Good – 322.
Gordis – 323-340, 343f., 346-354, 356.
Hannick – 353.
Hengel – 329.
Holmes & Parsons – 321, 330, 338, 342.
Holm-Nielsen – 318, 320, 322f., 352.
Hyvärinen – 320.
Isaksson – 324, 329.
Jastrow, Marcus – 349f.
Jastrow, Morris – 331.
Jellicoe – 320f., 344.
Jones – 348f.
Kelly – 333.
Kidner – 329, 331.
Kittel – 321, 346.
Lagarde – 321, 336, 341-345, 350f., 353.
Lampe – 322, 324, 334, 345, 350f., 354f.
Lane – 321, 349.
Lane Fox – 319.
Leanza – 354.
Leiman, Harold – 346.
Leiman, Sid – 317f.
Levine – 350, 356, 359.
Levy – 328f., 345.
Liddell & Scott – 322, 328, 344f., 353.
Lloyd – 323.
Loader – 328, 338, 343.
Lohfink – 341.
Loretz – 328.
Maclaren – 327.

Martin – 327ff.
Metcalfe – 319f., 356.
Migne – 6, 318-327, 329-339, 341f., 344, 346-350, 353-356, 359.
Muraoka – 324.
Murphy – 318, 341.
Noakes – 319.
Ogden – 322, 328f., 351f., 354, 356.
Ottley – 320.
Pleins – 347.
Plumptre – 327f., 331f., 337, 341.
Quasten – 321.
Rahlfs – 321, 323-326, 329f., 333, 338, 340-343, 346, 349, 351, 355f.
Rankin – 325, 327ff.
Reichert & Cohen – 325, 329, 331, 334f., 337f., 341, 343f., 351, 355f.
Reines – 344, 347.
Ryle – 317f.
Salmond – 319, 330f., 333, 335, 337ff., 341f., 345, 348, 352-356.
Salters – 320, 322-326, 329, 334, 336, 340, 343f., 351f.
Sawyer – 352f., 356.
Schürer – 344.
Scott – 345, 347f.
Serrano – 344.
Sheppard – 354.
Sperber – 321, 336, 341-345, 350f., 353.
Stumpff – 331.
Swete – 320f., 323, 338, 342.
Telfer – 319.
Telford – 353.
Thurston & Attwater – 319, 330, 335.
Torrey – 333.
Trigg – 318.
Vinel – 319.
Von Rad – 327.
Weber – 321.
Whitley – 333, 348, 350.
Whybray – 339f.
Wilson – 354, 356.
Zahrnt – 327.
Zeitlin – 317.
Ziegler – 335.
Zimmerli – 329.
Zimmermann – 331.
Zlotowitz – 334f., 337f., 341, 344.

Subjects

Aboth of Rabbi Nathan – 97, 317, 332.
Allegorisation – 2, 259, 264, 275, 289-299, 315f., 359.
Ambrose – 316, 359f.
Amenemhet – 355.
Apocalypse of Baruch – 299, 354.
Aquila – 5, 9, 22, 26, 31, 39, 62, 114, 215, 293, 301, 310, 320, 325, 340, 344, 354f., 358.
Athenodore – 318.
Bonaventure – 354.
Canonicity – 1f., 306, 317f.
Christ – 52, 65f., 304, 316, 356, 360.
Didymus – 354.
Dionysius of Alexandria – 3, 323, 327.
Dittography/haplography – 49, 168, 177, 185, 197, 339, 355.
Eleazar ben Azariah – 1.
Eschatology – 18, 43, 66, 73f., 84, 153, 208, 259f., 269, 289-299, 314f., 354.
Ethics – 103, 122f., 133f., 145, 311, 358.
Eusebius – 318.
Gregory of Nazianzus – 6, 342.
Gregory of Nyssa – 319.
Gregory Thaumaturgos:
— life – 4, 61, 82, 116, 295, 318f.
— *Panegyric to Origen* – 4ff., 190, 306, 318f., 322, 342, 356.
Hexapla – 6, 310, 320f., 356.
Hillel and Shammai – 1, 85.
Hippolytus of Rome – 3.
Hiyya ben Nehemiah – 354.
Hugh of St.-Cher – 354.
Ibn Ezra – 33, 68, 333, 336, 340.
Jerome – 2, 6, 101f., 104ff., 316, 318, 340, 348, 354, 359f.
Jerusalem – 2, 8, 19, 24, 30, 32, 34, 212, 218, 226f., 269, 295, 323ff., 344, 350, 357.
Josephus – 340.
Judan – 184.
Kethib/Qere – 228, 331, 334, 337f., 345.
Koheleth Rabbah – 113, 118, 149, 184, 208, 235, 253, 317, 328f., 332, 335, 345, 353f.

Masoretic text – see under Septuagint.
Nicholas of Lyra – 354.
Olympiodorus – 354.
Oniah – 184.
Origen – 3ff., 102, 188, 268, 305, 310, 315f., 318ff., 322, 327, 333, 342.
Pamphilus – 318.
Peshitta – 22, 39, 51, 72, 76, 99, 114, 124, 156, 162, 166, 179, 181, 185, 196, 210, 213, 215, 225f., 249f., 253, 261f., 264, 267, 272, 287, 289f., 293, 297, 321, 323-326, 330f., 334, 339, 341ff., 345f., 348-353, 355f.
Philo – 87.
Rashbam – 340.
Rashi – 210, 322, 336, 338f.
Richard of St.-Victor – 354.
Rufinus – 6.
Rupert of Deutz – 354.
Septuagint:
— Codex Alexandrinus – 268f., 273, 325, 340f., 351, 358.
— Codex Sinaiticus – 268f., 272, 323, 325, 335, 337, 340f., 344, 351, 358.
— Codex Vaticanus – 163, 263, 268f., 272, 286, 325, 335, 337, 340f., 351, 358.
— Codex Venetus – 326, 333, 355f., 358.
— divergences from MT – 20, 24ff., 29, 39, 42, 51, 73, 75, 102, 114, 121, 131, 152, 168, 177, 179, 181ff., 185, 187ff., 195f., 198, 203, 205, 209-212, 215f., 225f., 247, 249f., 256, 261ff., 267ff., 271ff., 292f., 295f., 297, 301, 323f., 330, 334ff., 339, 343, 345, 352, 355.
Shepherd of Hermas – 3.
Shir Hashirim Rabbah – 341.
Simeon ben Menasia – 2.
Socrates – 318.
Solomonic authorship – 2, 6ff., 19, 24, 34, 93, 171, 184, 220, 289f., 302, 304, 314f., 317f., 321, 323, 333, 355.
Stylistic features:
— balanced formulation – 31, 33, 47, 68, 78, 97, 185, 210, 292, 309, 357.

— repetitiveness – 9, 13, 25, 45, 83, 128, 141, 158, 185, 208, 215ff., 221, 235, 255, 300, 309f., 357.
— semitisms – 8, 23, 29f., 76, 95, 102, 113f., 143, 156, 236, 283, 309, 340, 356.
Symmachus – 6, 9, 16, 22, 26, 31, 36, 39, 57, 77, 82, 90, 99, 102, 114, 125, 165, 171, 175, 205, 211, 213, 215, 264, 266, 270, 279, 281, 310, 320f., 326, 330, 334, 336, 339, 343, 345, 348, 352, 354f., 358.
Talmud – 317, 331.

Targum – 22, 26, 39, 72, 75, 82, 86f., 92, 97, 99, 114, 118, 145, 156, 172, 179, 181, 186, 196f., 205f., 210, 213, 215, 226, 240, 250, 253, 255, 267, 270f., 275, 277, 281, 287, 289-299, 306f., 315f., 321-353, 355f., 359.
Theodotion – 9, 22, 39, 50, 114, 205, 215, 264, 310, 324, 358.
Trinity – 100, 316, 360.
Vulgate – 22, 72, 92, 253, 261f., 264, 308, 321, 324, 329, 340, 351, 355f.
Wisdom tradition – 7, 39, 40f., 55, 88, 152, 172, 203f., 221, 244, 247, 253, 263, 265, 301ff., 305, 346f., 355.

Greek

ἀγαθός – 51, 57-61, 68f., 151, 190, 214, 221, 232, 263, 265, 268, 270f., 296, 307; οὐκ ἔστιν ἀγαθόν – 49, 67f., 80, 218f.; ἀγαθὸς ὑπέρ – 89f., 95, 100f., 148, 155, 164, 166, 228f., 245, 247.
ἀγαθωσύνη – 92f., 122, 132, 142, 145.
ἀγάπη – 62, 224.
ἄγγελος – 114, 207f., 275, 291.
ἅγιος – 6, 211f.
ᾅδης – 237, 323.
αἴρομαι – 83, 256f., 259.
αἰών – 65ff., 69, 231, 296ff., 354.
ἁμαρτάνω– 51f., 69, 166, 175, 178, 190, 247.
ἄνεμος – 22, 130f., 280f., 310.
ἀνήρ – 91, 192f.
ἄνθρωπος – 12, 16, 29, 38, 43, 86, 149, 193, 205, 218, 221, 241, 296.
ἀρχή – 66, 164, 266f.
ἀσεβής – 73, 172, 181, 187, 211.
ἀτμός – 9, 310, 322.
ἄφρων – 46, 88, 101, 112, 146, 159, 227, 247, 256, 265, 267f.
βάπτισμα – 298.
βασιλεύς – 7, 19, 33, 39, 101-105, 118f., 197-202, 243, 271, 274f.
βίος – 27, 44, 131, 141, 157, 187, 229f., 234f., 284.
βλασφημία – 199f., 202.
γέεννα – 237.

γῆ – 10, 12, 20, 45, 77f., 129, 189, 218, 270, 278, 293f., 298.
γιγνώσκω – 67, 144, 149, 184, 186f., 204f., 215, 240f., 268.
γυνή – 188-193, 234f., 291-294.
δεσπότης – 52, 199f., 307.
διδάσκαλος – 304, 356.
δίκαιος – 69, 172ff., 204.
ἐγώ – 23f., 41, 44, 74, 80, 186, 196, 215.
ἐκκλησία – 7f., , 18, 106f., 268, 314.
ἐκκλησιάζω – 18f., 106f., 301, 357.
ἐκκλησιαστής – 6ff., 18, 107, 301, 342.
ἔμφρων – 104, 158, 165.
ἐντολή – 3, 203.
ἐπιθυμία – 29, 35, 124, 131f., 145, 148, 286.
ἐπιστρέφω – 39, 46, 81, 91, 238, 299.
ἐπόπτης – 190, 307.
ἐσθίω – 50, 68, 89, 123, 125, 133, 138, 218, 232, 270f.
εὑρίσκω – 185, 192, 221, 302.
εὐσεβής – 73, 329, 358.
εὐφραίνω – 36, 68, 80, 106, 272, 285.
εὐφροσύνη – 27f., 36, 132, 159, 232, 272.
ζάω – 141, 157, 228.
ζῆλος– 87, 230, 331, 345.
ζωή – 44, 147, 234f.
ἢ εἰ – 189f., 342.
ἡδονή – 27f., 36, 286.

ἥλιος – 13, 167, 284, 290; ὑπὸ τὸν ἥλιον – 10, 16, 20, 22, 29, 38, 41, 45, 56, 73, 86, 91, 137, 153, 210, 218, 231, 236, 255, 357.

θάνατος – 77, 142, 145, 152, 155, 176, 188, 208, 231, 236, 284.

θαυματουργός – 4, 6.

θεός – 11, 20, 52, 64f., 107, 110f., 114ff., 133, 135, 138, 178, 190, 197f., 216, 219, 223f., 254, 268, 281f., 289, 302, 307.

θυμός – 26, 48f., 131, 158, 165, 186, 287.

καί γε – 320.

καιρός – 66, 69, 71, 175f., 203f., 240, 242.

καιροσκόπος – 64, 66, 69, 87, 260.

κακία – 48, 126, 170, 172, 289.

κακός – 38, 57f., 61, 66, 108, 144, 170, 226, 242, 268ff.

καλός – 14, 67, 252.

καρδία – 23, 28, 48f., 74, 157f., 181f., 186, 203, 210, 232, 251f., 286.

κρίσις – 73, 203f., 307.

κύριος – 3, 70, 208, 289.

λογίζομαι – 23, 74ff., 252, 284f.

λόγος – 15, 109, 150, 164, 197-203, 265f., 302f., 305.

λουτροφόρος – 298f.

ματαιότης – 2, 8ff., 12, 15, 22, 27, 37f., 42, 45ff., 49, 51f., 77, 87, 91, 94, 106, 115, 121, 123, 140, 143, 148f., 151f., 161, 171, 173, 211f., 217, 219, 225, 235, 237, 264, 285, 288, 300, 310, 322.

μερίς – 36, 80, 231, 236.

μετάφρασις – 6.

μόχθος – 36, 44, 46, 63, 87, 90, 133, 145, 268, 349.

οἴομαι – 16, 24, 26, 80, 223, 240, 252, 284.

ὁράω – 27, 68, 74, 80, 82, 85, 123, 132, 137, 143, 145, 209, 234, 238, 255, 258, 295.

ὀρθῶς – 95, 107, 171.

ὁρμή – 36, 106, 130, 132.

οὐρανός – 20, 56, 74, 110, 237, 275, 281f.

ὄφελος – 10, 151, 297, 305.

ὄφις – 259, 264.

παραβολή – 25, 324.

πατήρ – 6, 255, 349.

πένης – 124, 147, 244, 246.

πένθος – 131, 156, 158.

περισπασμός – 20, 48f., 52, 64, 94, 111, 127, 220.

περισσεία – 10, 38, 40, 63, 110, 118, 130, 151, 167, 169, 263f.

περιφέρεια – 25, 227, 266.

περιφορά – 25, 28, 38, 187.

πίνω – 50, 68, 133, 218, 232.

πίπτω – 83, 95f., 129, 257, 259, 293.

πιστεύομαι – 19, 304.

πλάνη – 41, 217, 227, 231.

πλοῦτος – 92, 124ff., 138, 239.

πνεῦμα – 13f., 77ff., 164, 207f., 253f., 260, 280ff., 298; προαίρεσις πνεύματος – 21f., 26, 36, 38, 45, 53, 87, 90, 106, 130f., 148f.

ποίημα – 22, 38, 86, 114, 169, 217, 236, 282, 307.

ποιμήν – 304, 356.

πόλις – 180, 212, 243, 268ff., 295.

πονηρία – 47, 86, 119, 137, 140, 144, 255, 287.

πονηρός – 47, 52, 64, 66f., 86f., 108, 126, 129, 134, 140, 144, 199, 201, 203, 206, 227, 242, 257, 260, 278f., 287, 307.

πρᾶγμα – 9, 15, 25, 43, 123, 150, 205, 252, 300.

πρᾶξις – 69, 108, 134, 183.

προγιγνώσκω – 71, 204, 281.

πρόνοια – 51, 169, 205, 213.

πρόσκαιρος – 10, 69f.

προφήτης – 7.

ῥῆμα – 15, 113, 115, 195, 203, 274.

σάρξ – 28, 89, 287.

σοφία – 20, 25f., 29, 37f., 40, 42, 47, 52, 166, 168, 186, 196, 220, 237, 239, 245ff., 250, 263.

σοφίζομαι – 42, 174.

σόφισμα – 42.

σοφιστής – 301.

σοφός – 7, 40, 44, 46, 101, 146, 159, 195, 203, 221, 224, 244, 265, 301, 303.

συκοφαντία – 82, 117, 161ff., 213, 330.

σύν – 5, 90, 196, 210, 273, 309, 335, 344.

συνάντημα – 41f., 77, 226f.

σῶμα – 15, 28, 49, 89, 155, 260, 287, 303.

σωτηρία – 50, 299.

σωτήριος – 116.

σώφρων – 101, 104, 192.
τέλος – 41, 43, 66, 112, 130, 145, 157, 208, 226, 230, 306.
τρυφή – 27f., 33, 36, 80, 220, 232.
τύραννος – 247, 255.
υἱός – 7, 29, 75f., 92, 128, 271, 305, 356.
φαῦλος – 159, 296, 307f.
φιλανθρωπία – 277.
φίλος – 253, 305.

φλυαρία – 42, 111, 113, 151, 181f., 265f.
φοβέω – 3, 70, 115f., 178, 215f., 239, 289, 306.
φυλάσσω – 3, 107, 117, 126, 197, 199, 304, 306.
χρόνος – 56, 67, 141, 215f., 297.
ψυχή – 10, 15, 28, 49, 53, 78f., 89, 125, 138, 143, 145, 148, 155, 158, 163, 207f., 252, 260, 286, 298f., 303.

Other Titles in the Septuagint and Cognate Studies Series

ROBERT A. KRAFT (editor)
Septuagintal Lexicography (1975)
Code: 06 04 01
Not Available

ROBERT A KRAFT (editor)
1972 Proceedings: Septuagint and Pseudepigrapha Seminars (1973)
Code: 06 04 02
Not Available

RAYMOND A. MARTIN
Syntactical Evidence of Semitic Studies in Greek Documents (1974)
Code: 06 04 03
Not Available

GEORGE W. E. NICKELSBURG, JR. (editor)
Studies on the *Testament of Moses* (1973)
Code: 06 04 04
Not Available

GEORGE W.E. NICKELSBURG, JR. (editor)
Studies on the *Testament of Joseph* (1975)
Code: 06 04 05
Not Available

GEORGE W.E. NICKELSBURG, JR. (editor)
Studies on the *Testament of Abraham* (1976)
Code: 06 04 06

JAMES H. CHARLESWORTH
Pseudepigrapha and Modern Research (1976)
Code: 06 04 07
Not Available

JAMES H. CHARLESWORTH
Pseudepigrapha and Modern Research with a Supplement (1981)
Code: 06 04 07 S

JOHN W. OLLEY
"Righteousness" in the Septuagint of Isaiah: A Contextual Study (1979)
Code: 06 04 08

MELVIN K. H. PETERS
An Analysis of the Textual Character of the Bohairic of Deuteronomy (1980)
Code: 06 04 09
Not Available

DAVID G. BURKE
The Poetry of Baruch (1982)
Code: 06 04 10

JOSEPH L. TRAFTON
Syriac Version of the Psalms of Solomon (1985)
Code: 06 04 11

JOHN COLLINS, GEORGE NICKELSBURG
Ideal Figures in Ancient Judaism: Profiles and Paradigms (1980)
Code: 06 04 12

ROBERT HANN
The Manuscript History of the Psalms of Solomon (1982)
Code: 06 04 13

J.A.L. LEE
A Lexical Study of the Septuagint Version of the Pentateuch (1983)
Code: 06 04 14

MELVIN K. H. PETERS
A Critical Edition of the Coptic (Bohairic) Pentateuch
Vol. 5: Deuteronomy (1983)
Code: 06 04 15

T. MURAOKA
A Greek-Hebrew/Aramaic Index to I Esdras (1984)
Code: 06 04 16

JOHN RUSSIANO MILES
Retroversion and Text Criticism:
The Predictability of Syntax in An Ancient Translation
from Greek to Ethiopic (1985)
Code: 06 04 17

LESLIE J. MCGREGOR
The Greek Text of Ezekiel (1985)
Code: 06 04 18

MELVIN K.H. PETERS
A Critical Edition of the Coptic (Bohairic) Pentateuch,
Vol. 1: Genesis (1985)
Code: 06 04 19

ROBERT A. KRAFT AND EMANUEL TOV (project directors)
Computer Assisted Tools for Septuagint Studies
Vol 1: Ruth (1986)
Code: 06 04 20

CLAUDE E. COX
Hexaplaric Materials Preserved in the Armenian Version (1986)
Code: 06 04 21

MELVIN K.H. PETERS
A Critical Edition of the Coptic (Bohairic) Pentateuch
Vol. 2: Exodus (1986)
Code: 06 04 22

CLAUDE E. COX (editor)
VI Congress of the International Organization for Septuagint
and Cognate Studies: Jerusalem 1986
Code: 06 04 23

JOHN KAMPEN
The Hasideans and the Origin of Pharisaism:
A Study of 1 and 2 Maccabees
Code: 06 04 24

THEODORE BERGREN
Fifth Ezra:
The Text, Origin, and Early History
Code: 06 04 25

BENJAMIN WRIGHT
No Small Difference:
Sirach's Relationship to Its Hebrew Parent Text
Code: 06 04 26

TAKAMITSU MURAOKA (editor)
Melbourne Symposium on Septuagint Lexicography
Code: 06 04 28

JOHN JARICK
Gregory Thaumaturgos' Paraphrase of Ecclesiastes
Code: 06 04 29

JOHN WILLIAM WEVERS
Notes on the Greek Text of Exodus
Code: 06 04 30

J.J.S. WEITENBERG and A. DE LEEUW VAN WEENEN
Lemmatized Index of the Armenian Version of Deuteronomy
Code: 06 04 32

MICHAEL E. STONE
A Textual Commentary on the Armenian Version of IV Ezra
Code: 06 04 34

Order from:

Scholars Press Customer Services
P.O. Box 6525
Ithaca, NY 14851
1-800-666-2211